The Story of **Burlesque**
in America

Leslie Zemeckis
Foreword by **Blaze Starr**

SKYHORSE PUBLISHING

I'd rather be a mistress

For the beautiful men and women of burlesque who shared their lives with me. I am a better, richer person for it. You have changed my life. This book is dedicated to you.

A rare photo of Lili St. Cyr

TABLE OF CONTENTS

Foreword

I started in burlesque in the 1940s. For more than thirty years I lived and breathed it. I wrote my biography years ago, but Leslie Zemeckis's *Behind the Burly Q* is the only flat-out absolute history of burlesque that is told by the performers themselves: from the straight men and comics, singers, musicians, and, of course, us strippers. I was never ashamed to say I took my clothes off, but not all the girls felt that way. Leslie persuaded many who had been embarrassed and ashamed to talk about their life in burlesque. *Behind the Burly Q* finally sets the record straight.

First in the film and now in print, *Behind the Burly Q* captures life in the theatres and clubs and offers an over-the-footlights perspective of not only what a burlesque show was, but also what life was like backstage. The book is filled with funny, sad, and downright tragic stories. With a passion and fearlessness to dig deep, Leslie uncovers the truth. It seems that until Leslie came along, no one cared to ask many of us what it had been like. No one ever asked us what *we* thought about burlesque. *Behind the Burly Q* is about our accomplishments, our love lives, and our heartaches. It is truthful, accurate, and fascinating.

From the moment we exchanged photos and I sold Leslie a couple of my handmade dresses, she has been a friend. It is obvious from the intimate details she writes that she has become a friend to many past performers who trusted her with the stories of their lives. Yet she never lets that friendship interfere with the truth. She has done her homework and brings insight and an encyclopedic knowledge to her storytelling. I was proud to share my story with Leslie.

Once I started talking to her, I couldn't stop. I told her about traveling on the road for years and performing in clubs across the country. I loved it and wouldn't trade my experiences for anything. *Behind the Burly Q* brought back those memories for me and the dozens of others whom she interviewed; those recollections are presented in this book with compassion and an eye for detail.

How was I viewed as a stripper? Some thought I was no good. But I knew better. Many of us were just using the assets God gave us. And I don't mean just body—brains and creativity, too. And the audiences loved us. I always used humor in my act. What else would you call making my boob look like it was blowing out a candle? Burlesque had its place. Like I said in my book, "The men need strippers. . . . They need to fantasize." I had them packed into my club, the Two O'Clock Club in Baltimore.

Leslie has a true understanding of the subject and has painstakingly researched burlesque, from its beginnings through its Golden Age in the '30s to its demise. I stopped in the '70s because it got too rough. Leslie sets right many misconceptions about burlesque and all the performers. We were not hookers or second-rate artists. I had a well-thought-out act in which my couch burst into flames. Where but in a burlesque show could I do something like that? A burlesque show was all that and more, not just a simple strip tease.

Burlesque provided an opportunity to many girls, like me, to escape poverty. I come from the rural hills of West Virginia. My daddy had black lung. We were lucky to get a new pair of shoes once a year. But burlesque got me out of the hills and I saw things most girls will never see. I met presidents and governors. I made a lot of money and I loved it. I made real good friends with the other performers, like Val Valentine. She's been my friend for decades. Leslie captures all the friendships and intrigues, the petty jealousies (yes, there were fights), and also the love we had for what we did and each other. There was plenty of romance and danger, too, and Leslie tells it like it was. Relationships were nearly impossible to keep when we were working most weeks of the year.

I have never seen this world so lovingly and authentically recreated as Leslie has made it in *Behind the Burly Q*. For someone born long after burlesque died, Leslie has brought together history and personal storytelling that covers all aspects of burlesque. This isn't my story alone; it belongs to many performers with very different stories. As one critic said of Leslie's film, it is "a veritable who's who of the grande dames of the burlesque stage." And what dames we were.

In *Behind the Burly Q*, Leslie has meticulously and interestingly separated facts from rumor and myth. By choosing to tell our stories, in our own words, Leslie has captured a lost American art that I was proud to be a part of.

Blaze Starr

West Virginia, 2013

Note from the Author

The idea for my documentary *Behind the Burly Q* came in 2006, as these things are wont to do, by sheer happenstance. For several years I had been performing a one-woman burlesque-inspired show. My research began with curiosity: Just what exactly was a burlesque show? Was it just women getting up and taking off their clothes?

This first question led me to several former strippers, eager to relate their varied experiences "taking it off" in theatres and clubs across America during the 1930s through 1960s. Not only did they relate what it was like on stage, but they also shared what their lives were like backstage—the gossip, the camaraderie, the temptations, and the hardships.

I became fascinated by these tales of traveling the "wheel" (performers traveled from town to town, playing a set of theatres in rotation, thus the term "wheel"). I dove into books, magazines, and newspaper archives, and I watched numerous documentaries. Some of the films focused on the more famous strippers' acts, but revealed nothing about how they got into the business and what happened to them when burlesque died. Some documentaries highlighted the rise of many comedians we honor today—Phil Silvers, Red Skelton, Jackie Gleason—but I could find nothing that broke the façade of baggy pants and tassel twirlers.

There were plenty of articles and some old footage of star Lili St. Cyr's bathtub act. But nothing about who she was, or what happened to her, until author Kelly DiNardo wrote *Gilded Lili*. I didn't read anything that provided me with details regarding the struggles these women may have incurred raising kids while on the road for much of the year, leaving younger ones with neighbors or relatives, at best. How did that impact the children? I interviewed sons and daughters; the stories were often heartbreaking.

Where did the men and women in these "naughty"—for surely that's what they were—shows come from? What did their families think of their chosen profession? Was it even entertainment? Surely the "nice" girls weren't strippers. Or were they?

The more I spoke with these former burlesquers, the more I felt compelled to chronicle their pasts, and in turn honor a piece of the American entertainment history that, until now, has been severely overlooked and misunderstood.

The performers were surprisingly forthright, generous, and open-hearted. They took me into their homes and presented me with photographs, scrapbooks, and ephemera of a bygone era, much of which has made its way into my collection. Their stories were enthralling, personal, poignant, hilarious, and most importantly, for many of them, never before told.

I became so fervent about preserving this little-documented bit of history that I decided to shoot a film. To begin, I sponsored a "reunion" of more than fifty former burlesque performers in Las Vegas at the Stardust, shortly before it was blown up. Along with my dear friend, co-producer and camera person Sheri Hellard, I spent a long weekend interviewing former performers one-on-one, watching a handful sing and strip. That weekend grew into two years crisscrossing the country interviewing everyone I could find that had worked in a burly show. With more than one hundred hours of interviews, I gathered so many great stories and I knew they wouldn't all fit into a ninety-minute film.

This book is the history and evolution of burlesque as told through the performers' voices. *Their* stories are what is important to capture before it is all gone; how they felt and how they behaved and how they lived.

Here, then, are *their* memories with all the lapses that result from recalling details from decades ago. Most discrepancies were minor and not worth pointing out. (One performer referred to Lilly Christine as the "Cat Woman," when she was actually billed as "Cat Girl.") Through four years of filmmaking, I double and tripled checked facts where I could. But these are personal recollections and opinions, and some facts were elusive.

I searched books, articles, and old girlie magazines gathering names of those who had worked in burlesque, matching stories, dates, and places. I was privy to many unpublished writings and spent hours in libraries big and small from New York to Los Angeles and Texas to San Diego.

It took a bit of detective work to track down former performers. A few I pursued for close to half a year, writing letters, emailing, calling, and sending cards. *Please talk to me.* I wrote about myself, told them about my kids. I used names of other performers I had already interviewed. After the first few interviews, things got easier. One performer would let someone else know I was OK, the *real thing.* They would then introduce me to a dozen more performers. I assured them I didn't want to exploit their past; I simply wanted to let them voice their stories.

Calls started pouring in from across the country. Sheri and I traveled from Florida to New York, to a decimated post-Katrina Mississippi, up to the San Francisco area, to the projects in New Jersey, and all points in between—for much of it, I was heavily pregnant.

I was warmly embraced by this community of forgotten performers and I was showered with memorabilia, trust, and ultimately their love. I was privileged to interview musicians, comedians, costumers, historians, authors, strippers, and families of those that had passed on. Old trunks were opened, glossy photos handed over. (All photographs included in the book are from my collection, unless otherwise noted.)

But strippers were only one element of the show I was seeking. I wanted to know about the straight men, the novelty acts, the emcees, and, of course, the comedians.

Listening to their recollections, I could smell the cigarette smoke and stale food backstage. I could feel the women's nerves and anxieties as they relived what it was like to strip for the first time. They told me about the fights and the feuds, the Stage Door Johnnies and the Mafia, and the ups and downs of working show after show with never a day off.

The resulting documentary, *Behind the Burly Q*, focused mainly on the women, as very few of the men were still alive. Their struggles touched me deeply. They had seen amazing things in the span of their lives. Some were barely hanging on, like Kitty West in Bay St. Louis, who had been completely wiped out in Katrina and living in a FEMA trailer when we filmed her.

As I continued my interviews, the "revival" of burlesque through neo-burlesque troupes was expanding in cities like New York, Los Angeles, and Boston. Some troupes had been in place for years, only now a wider audience had taken hold. Housewives were flocking to pole-dancing classes. Suddenly people wanted to know who these legendary strippers were.

"They knew me. They really knew me," explained ninety-seven-year-old Mimi Reed about her fame. She sat in her garden, grieving after the death of her partner of sixty years. I fell in love with Mimi. She had been a stunningly beautiful acrobatic dancer. I was fortunate to spend time with her throughout the last few months of her life. Ultimately I attended her memorial and the memorials of several others.

Sadly, many of the performers have since passed away, making mine their last and oftentimes only recorded history of their life in burlesque. I became pen pals with many, like Lee Stuart—straight man, singer, devoted family man. We exchanged emails up until his death. In one of his last emails, he wrote me: "I am getting in poor health with a new pacemaker and all the ailments that go along with a person my age. I find myself living in the past and missing old friends who have passed on to the big Burlesque stage wherever it may be. I am sure they are getting lots of laughs." I am sure Mr. Stuart is, too.

Eventually I amassed a large and varied collection of memorabilia. The collection includes dresses from Betty Rowland, Sherry Britton, and Blaze Starr (all three huge stars of burlesque in three different eras; the '30s, '40s, and '50s, respectively). I have been given boxes of photos, old comedy scripts, pasties, gloves, tiaras, and a purse. I have a cigarette holder of Blaze Starr's, a trunk Gypsy used to travel with, a lace parasol Rose La Rose used. I am in possession of props, personal affects, magazines, G-strings, and furs. Some of my collection, along with clips from the documentary, was part of a successful burlesque exhibit at The Museum of Sex in New York City in 2011.

At times, this project threatened to overwhelm me—so many details, so much information, dates and names and facts. But I kept returning to what the men and women had to say themselves. I kept returning to their voices. What they had to say about their experience in burlesque was history that hadn't yet been exposed. I wanted their voices to narrate the book.

Behind the Burly Q received rave reviews and was critics' pick, with a dazzling premiere at MoMA in New York hosted by Sharon Stone, Robert Zemeckis, and Alan Alda. But accolades from the press weren't the most important thing to me—it was the performers themselves who saw the film and who thanked me for telling their stories.

Burlesque thrived in its day and even though its time has passed, its influence is everywhere—in television, film, and music today. We owe much to the art form.

I hope in some small way to change the many misconceptions of burlesque and of the performers themselves—men and women who spent their careers marginalized, dismissed, and stigmatized.

The spirit of these performers is best summed up by Kitty West, who told me, "I'm seventy-seven, and . . . I can still kick ass." Yes, you can, Kitty. This is for you and those who were courageous enough to share their extraordinary lives with me. You all are an inspiration. I love you all.

Cast of Characters

The following is a list of performers mentioned in the book. Those names in bold I personally interviewed. Some dates are approximate, as records were often inaccurate or missing and the performers themselves often lied about their ages.

Bud Abbott (1895–1974)—Arguably the most famous straight man in burlesque.

Robert Alda (1914–1986)—A handsome "tit singer" and a straight man.

Alexandra the Great "48"—Gerri Weise, named for her breast size by her mentor Rose La Rose.

Joan Arline (1932–2011)—Joanie Connery, a stripper who worked the Schuster circuit. She performed with two white Russian wolfhounds and was an elder in her church.

Beverly Anderson Traube (1930–2007)—Born with rheumatoid arthritis, as a struggling actress she couldn't be a "waitress or be a typist," so she covered her crippled hands with long gloves and became a stripper.

Faith Bacon (1910–1956)—Born Faith Yvonne Bacon, she was the self-proclaimed originator of the fan dance. Hers was not a happy ending.

Al Baker Livingston, Jr. (1934–2012)—Best known as Al Baker Jr. a convicted mob money launderer. A former burlesque theatre owner and son of comedian Al Baker Sr.

Candy Barr (1935–2005)—Juanita Slusher, a Texas native, served prison time for possession of a minor amount of marijuana, basically ending her career as a stripper.

Helen Bingler—A showgirl who worked with Abbott and Costello, who named her "Bingo."

Nat Bodian (1930–2010)—A journalist who wrote and saw burlesque at the Empire in Newark in the 1930s.

Maria Bradley—A chorus girl and stripper who affirms working in burlesque was the best time of her life.

Sherry Britton (1918?–2008)—Homeless at fourteen and married at fifteen, this gorgeous stripper became one of the hottest acts in Burlesque. Wooed by everyone from Sinatra to Rex Harrison, Gig Young and David Susskind.

Earl Carroll (1893–1948) A theatrical producer most famous for his Broadway shows *Earl Carroll's Vanities*.

Ann Corio (d. 1999)—A stripper famous with the ladies who loved to see her perform at her favorite theatre in Boston, The Old Howard.

Lou Costello (1906–1959)—Funny man to Bud Abbott.

Candy Cotton—Carol Fox, a stripper who chose her name because of her hair style.

Ricki Covette—Irena Jewell, who topped out at six feet eight inches tall.

Sunny Dare (d. 2008)—Roberta Bauman, known as "Sunny Dare of the Blue Hair," got stiffed by Sally Rand on the road and had to strip to make enough money to get home.

Dixie Evans (b. 1926)—née Mary Lee Evans. She was the Marilyn Monroe of Burlesque.

Carrie Finnell (d. 1963)—Famous for her breasts, which she could make pop in and out of her gown. She often stripped even though she was an impressive three hundred pounds.

White Fury—Painted herself with buckets of paint and lit her tassels on fire.

Mara Gaye (1920–2005)—A former Rockette, she stripped from the '40s to the '60s and was an avowed nudist.

Rita Grable—Stripper who married singer and Sinatra contemporary Jerry Vale.

Nils T. Granlund (1890–1957)—Producer who discovered Lili St. Cyr among many others.

Leroy Griffith—Owner of burlesque theatres who employed Tempest Storm and paid her thousands.

Margie Hart (1913–2000)—Supposedly she is the stripper that caused Mayor LaGuardia to close burlesque in New York because she "flashed."

Daisy and Violet Hilton—Siamese twins who found themselves in burlesque when vaudeville died.

Mike Iannucci (d. 2007)—Star stripper Ann Corio's husband, the producer of *This Was Burlesque*, which ran for decades.

CAST OF CHARACTERS

Christine Jorgensen (1926–1989)—Born as George, Christine underwent one of the first sex change operations. She stripped after getting out of military service.

Sally Keith—She is thought to be the first tassel twirler who performed at Boston's Old Howard in the 1940s and '50s.

Tiny Kline (1891?–1964)—This Hungarian-born performer started in the circus. She became Disneyland's first Tinkerbell.

Fiorella LaGuardia—Three-time mayor of New York, he kicked burlesque and the name "Minsky" out of New York.

Daphne Lake—Got her start in the carnival.

La Savona—Svelta Goode, a Hungarian-born stripper.

Gypsy Rose Lee (1911?–1970)—Born Ellen June Hovick, her name is synonymous with burlesque.

Jennie Lee (d. 1990)—The "Bazoom Girl" who started collecting stripper memorabilia.

Lorraine Lee—Lorraine Gluck used to dance for Bonnie and Clyde and Pretty Boy Floyd and "earned a quarter." She was married to comedian Dick Richards.

Pinky Lee (1907–1933)—The "original" Pee-wee Herman, before the comedian with his own children's television show in the 1950s.

Joe E. Lewis—Singer turned burlesque funny man after the mob sliced his throat and cut out part of his tongue. He was a frequent headliner on the bill with Lili St. Cyr in Las Vegas at the El Rancho.

Eddie Lloyd—A top second banana who performed from the 1920s to the '50s.

April March (b. 1935)—Stripper born Velma Fern Worden. She was known as the First Lady of Burlesque because of her resemblance to Jacqueline Kennedy.

Lady Midnight—Born Benita Kirkland, her father was famed comic Monkey Kirkland. She got her first job stripping at her father's club.

Tony Midnight—Drag performer and costumer.

Dardy Minsky (b. 1926)—Performed as Dardy Orlando, Lili St. Cyr's sister, once married to famed burlesque impresario Harold Minsky.

Harold Minsky (1915–1977)—The youngest and most famous of the famous burlesque family, Harold produced burlesque shows in all the major burlesque cities in America.

Terry Mixon (d. 2008)—Born Gaby Olah, she had a problem with drinking that she blamed on lonely nights in the theatre.

Renny von Muchow—An acrobatic performer, he was part of Renald and Rudy, a novelty act that played for twenty-five years.

Vicki O'Day—born Westlin, she was lucky to live after a run in with the mob.

Taffy O'Neil—Born Idella Holmes, she performed at night and took her young son, stricken with polio, for treatment every day.

John Perilli—Drummer in the mid-1950s who worked with Irving Benson, Joe Dorita, Lili St. Cyr, and Rose La Rose at the Empire and the Adams theatre.

Sheila Rae (d. 2010)—Stripper.

Rags Ragland (1905–1946)—John Lee Morgan Beauregard, a loveable alcoholic, former boxer, and comedian.

Sally Rand (1904–1979)—Known for her fan dance and her "bubble" dance. Sally worked into her seventies.

Tee Tee Red—Protégé of Zorita.

Mimi Reed (d. 2007)—A straight woman who was ninety-seven years old when I interviewed her. She told me her biggest regret was "not being a stripper. I would have made a fortune."

Carmela Rickman (d. 2008)—The Sophia Loren of Burlesque.

Billy Rose (1896–1966)—Producer, married burlesque performer Fanny Brice.

Lily Ann Rose (b. 1933)—She started stripping when she was fourteen in Boston. Her mother and aunt both worked burlesque.

Rose La Rose (1919–1972)—Considered the "bad girl" of burlesque, Rose was a stripper who ended up owning her own theatres in Ohio, where she mentored many young girls.

Betty Rowland (b. 1916)—She was one of three sisters, who all went into burlesque in the 1930s. Dian Rowland died of a heart condition when she was in her twenties. Her other sister, Roz Elle, married a Belgian millionaire, the Baron d'Empain. Betty has never talked in-depth about Roz Elle, whose home was overtaken by the Nazis, who shot and ate her beloved pet dogs during WWII.

Jack Ruby (1911–1967)—Jacob Rubenstein owned the Carousel Club in Dallas. Strippers in his club were rumored to be prostitutes. He is best remembered for shooting Lee Harvey Oswald, the man believed to be John F. Kennedy's assassin.

Sequin—Donaelle Tamburello was a stripper who married a pianist and was the vocal coach to Tony Bennett and Judy Garland.

Georgia Sothern—Born as Hazel Anderson, she started stripping at fourteen. Known as a "fast strip," she would fling her body around the stage.

Blaze Starr (b. 1932)—née Fannie Belle Fleming, she was raised dirt poor but became one of the biggest acts in burlesque.

Lee Stuart (d. 2007)—Straight man from Kentucky.

Lili St. Cyr (1917–1999)—The highest-grossing stripper of the 1950s.

Tempest Storm (b. 1928)—Still stripping into her late seventies, Annie Blanche Banks achieved star stripper status in the 1950s. Gang raped as a teenager, she speaks about her affairs with Kennedy and Elvis, among others.

Joni Taylor—Joni DiRando, talking woman and chorus girl. By the time she was sixteen, she was supporting three children.

Lydia Thompson—In 1868, she brought a bevy of beauties to America and scandalized New Yorkers with her female cast all dressed in tights.

Mike Todd (1909–1958)—Theatre impresario and boyfriend of Gypsy Rose Lee. He produced *Star and Garter*, starring many burlesque talents.

Noel Toy (1909–1958) née Ngun Yee. The female performer Sally Rand and one of the only ethnic "exotics" to make it big in burlesque.

Val Valentine—Carole Licata, often billed as "Cupid's Cutie."

Abe Weinstein (1907–2000)—Owned the famous Colony Club in Dallas. He was punched by Jack Ruby the night Kennedy was shot.

Kitty West (1930)—Born Abbie Jewel Slawson, a New Orleans favorite in the 1950s, she was known as Evangeline the Oyster Girl. Her home and most of her possessions were wiped out in Hurricane Katrina.

Zorita (1915–2001)—Began working stag shows before she came up with the gimmick of dancing with snakes.

Introduction

Although its origins derive from France, Britain, and Greece, burlesque became a wildly popular American art form that thrived in the early to middle part of the twentieth century. When exactly it died, if ever, is a hotly contested point among connoisseurs. Burlesque has been a stigmatized, much maligned piece of theatrical history that has largely and deliberately been left out of the history books.

Aristophanes is widely credited as being the first burlesque writer, scribbling out parodies in 5 BC. However, this is clearly not burlesque as we think of it today, with strippers, pasties, drum rolls, and baggy-pant comedians with putty noses.

A "burlesque" of the 1800s was a play that made fun of popular "legitimate" plays of the time. There were no chorus lines, comedians, or exotic dancers. In 1931, author Bernard Sobel wrote that a particularly poor 1811 performance of *Hamlet* "originated what was to be called legitimate burlesque." From 1840 on, the term burlesque was applied to a wide range of comic plays that entertained the lower and middle classes in Great Britain.

In America, burlesque evolved from the European tradition into grand productions performed by scantily clad women—burlesque was still poking fun at the upper classes, at sex, and at what people were willing to do in the pursuit of obtaining it. It appealed to the masses of working-class people who packed theatres every week to see troops like The British Blondes, a bevy of beauties dressed in tights that shocked New Yorkers with the sight of their exposed limbs.

In 1869, former minstrel-show performer M. B. Leavitt took Lydia's Blondes and fused their show with the style of the minstrel shows popular at the time, consisting of gags, song, and dance performed mainly by white performers in black face. This new show followed a three-act formula that was to become the signature burlesque show we know today—an opening with a lavish song-and-dance number, a second act of variety performers, a third-act skit or send-up of a popular play, and, finally, a grand finale by the entire company. (Leavitt's Rentz-Santly Burlesque Company was composed of women only, quite a deviation from the predominantly male minstrel casts.)

By the 1920s, the striptease was introduced to offer audiences something that vaudeville, radio, and film did not. The striptease let burlesque escape the same fate as vaudeville.

During the Great Depression, a man could pay a single dime and fall into a big, raucous, sexy show and forget he had no work and was unlikely to find any. Former stripper Dixie Evans, known as the Marilyn Monroe of Burlesque, said that "people in that era were so depressed and there was no hope. The masses were just out of work and out of money, but for those few small pennies, it was worth it to see one of these great shows. [They were] mostly for the American public that had nothing."

The shows grew increasingly daring until 1937 when, fueled by public outrage, New York City Mayor Fiorello LaGuardia banned burlesque in his city. Burlesque's response was to slip across the river to New Jersey.

Eventually, comedians and musicians were expunged from shows as the strippers took over. By the 1960s, however, hardcore porn was widely available and burlesque was done. The best of the comedians went into radio, film, and television.

But what happened to the strippers and the thousands of performers who had worked in burlesque their entire lives?

On stage at the burlesque show

"There's a burlesque theatre where the gang loves to go
To see Queenie the cutie of the burlesque show ..."
"Strip Polka" by Johnny Mercer

On stage

CHAPTER ONE

Welcome to the Burly Show

"Audiences—it was always full. Always."

—Mimi Reed

"They were there to have fun."

—Maria Bradley on burlesque audiences

Chorus girls on the burlesque stage

1

It's been called a variety of names: a girlie show, burly show, tab show, vaudeville, medicine show, strip show, etc. But what was *it*? Its performers, numbering in the thousands, are now forgotten, anonymous men and women who lived, breathed, and died for it. At its height in the 1930s, there were fourteen shows running on Broadway simultaneously. Some considered it an art form—to others it was second-rate entertainment. It was a burlesque show.

Merriam-Webster gives us this definition: "theatrical entertainment of a broadly humorous often earthy character consisting of short turns, comic skits, and *sometimes* [emphasis added] striptease acts." Burlesque has been around at least as far back as the Byzantine era. The Greek-born Theodora, who later became Empress of the Roman Empire, began on the stage as a dancer and comedienne "who delights the audience by letting herself be cuffed and slapped on the cheeks, and makes them guffaw by raising her skirts." She was known for disrobing on stage before her audience and reclining naked but for a girdle encircling her nether regions. She was quite controversial in her time. It was rumored she worked in a brothel or two. (The same charges are often made against our modern exotic dancers. Like the "skirt raising" actresses of bygone days, strippers have long been equated with prostitutes.)

Stripper Val Valentine

2

Theodora was, perhaps predictably, also the victim of rumors about her voracious appetite for sexual intercourse. In my interviews I found that burlesquers were also frequently accused by the public of being sexually deviant. Was it the nature of the women's costumes—or lack thereof—or the erotic nature of the tease itself?

Former stripper Val Valentine told me, "Everyone thought we were preoccupied with sex. Most of the time when you were on stage, you were thinking, 'Oh, I hope there's a good restaurant in town.'"

Burlesque, as we remember it, was truly an American art form, even though it borrowed much from France's dance halls and Italy's *Commedia dell'arte* in the sixteenth century. In Paris, beautiful women danced the can-can—flinging their ruffled skirts over their heads, causing a sensation at the Moulin Rouge and other cabarets of the 1830s. The rumor was the girls didn't wear underwear, but there is no evidence of this.

On the London stage, popular shows and operas were "burlesqued," meaning they were mocked or made fun of. This form of entertainment was brought to America in 1866 with *The Black Crook*, a musical variety show consisting of skits, funny songs, and risqué situations with the women wearing skin-colored tights. It was a huge hit and had a record-breaking run on Broadway. It was a five-and-a-half-hour show and was purported to have brought in around $750,000 during its run. Audiences, both men and women, middle and upper class, loved the one hundred dancers, scantily dressed, parading across the stage. Burlesque had arrived.

Next, in 1868, came actress Lydia Thompson from England with her *British Blondes*, who introduced New Yorkers to tights and stockings as they sang, danced, exposed themselves, and cross-dressed. The show included parodies of current events, risqué jokes, song and dance, and variety acts. They featured beautiful performers galore and many shows sold out. New York was hooked.

Lydia's planned six-month tour of America turned into a six-year run. Before Lydia Thompson, there "were no big American stars" in burlesque, according to Rachel Shteir, author of *Striptease*.

Founded in 1870, Madame Rentz's *Female Minstrels* performed in pink tights to sold out crowds. M. B. Leavitt wrote "decency" into all his ads to get around the stigma swirling around burlesque. The shows became must-see events.

Twenty years later, in 1893, a Syrian dancer Farida Mazar Spyropoulos with the stage name of Fatima (who would later claim to be the original Little Egypt), introduced the hoochee-coochee dance at the Chicago World's Fair. The hoochee-coochee was something like a belly dance, only America hadn't yet coined that specific term. Fatima performed again in Chicago at the Century of Progress International Exposition in 1933, at the age of sixty-two. (This reminds me of the burlesquers I'd interviewed. Most didn't want to give up performing,

3

no matter their age. In fact, one seventy-something who did a strip at the reunion asked me for the tape because she wanted to shop it around for a job.)

The first Little Egypt might have been Fatima, but because several dancers used the moniker, there has been great confusion as to who danced where and when. Fatima would eventually file suit against MGM for using "her" name in the film *The Great Ziegfeld*. (Ashea Wabe, another "original" Little Egypt, died by gas asphyxiation in 1908.) In any event, Little Egypt's dance became synonymous with exotic dancing, prestriptease. Clothes weren't removed during the performance at this point.

Another early star was Broadway impresario Flo Ziegfeld's future common-law wife, Anna Held, who in 1905 molted to a number entitled "I'd Like to See a Little More of You." Because of her association with Ziegfeld, she would become "legitimized" despite her scandalous displays of leg.

As the more popular female sensations appeared on the stage, showing a little here and a little more there, louder became the protests from church groups and other do-gooders, which had the effect of making the burlesque shows—and the women stars—even more popular.

The element of taking off one's clothes on the stage was added, accidentally some claim, by a performer who removed a pair of cuffs because they were dirty. Mary Dawson went by the moniker Mademoiselle Fifi (no doubt hoping the French name not only made her appear "regal," but also disguised her true identity). This was sometime in 1925. The audience went wild; from then on, strip teasing was in demand. Burlesque had changed—many would say for the better, some would argue otherwise—again.

Another woman rumored to be the first "accidental" striptease was a Boston dancer whose strap broke during a show—and when her panties (or culottes or what have you), fell around her ankles, the audience howled their approval.

However stripping was introduced, and by whomever, once the striptease shimmied across the stage, it quickly became the lure that packed the houses. Burlesque had changed once again, evolving into what we now think of as a burly show.

Renny von Muchow, who performed with his partner Rudy for twenty-five years in burlesque as a novelty act, called the shows a "variety act with a little more spice." Former journalist, historian of burlesque theatres, and longtime resident of Newark, New Jersey, Nat Bodian said: "Burlesque was essentially a vaudeville show with strippers. They added the strippers to keep the men from going to the movies."

As a society, we like to judge others by what they do and often where they come from. As Dixie Evans articulated about her fellow dancers, "It's actually *who* you are. It's not *what* you do. It's how you conduct your life and yourself and your values." That's how the strippers, in particular, and all those that worked burlesque *should* be judged.

The women I interviewed were survivors. They escaped many things—poverty, abuse, and limited opportunities, including the limitations that prejudice against their own good looks brought on. In response to these, they turned stripping into an opportunity.

Some stumbled into burlesque after a friend or boyfriend suggested it. Some, like Lady Midnight, said, "I just knew I was gonna be a famous movie star." And when that didn't work out, burlesque offered the closest thing to celebrity.

"It was a job," Lorraine Lee said, in reference to stripping as a career. As a young girl whose father had abandoned the family, Lorraine had danced "for a dime or a quarter" with her sister at her mother's boarding house in Texas. Her mother sold beer and Lorraine danced for Bonnie and Clyde and Pretty Boy Floyd. "You can be a lady where you want to be a lady," her mother once told her.

"We didn't have books," Blaze Starr said of growing up poor. "We lived in the wilderness. No neighbors that read had any books." Education, let alone material comforts, was not an option for many of these young girls.

Chorus girl Helen "Bingo" Bingler was raised by a "wicked" stepmother. She had four teeth knocked out by a broom handle," explained her daughter Helen Imbrugia. "She was a showgirl. And she had an act herself where she bent over backwards on a chair and would drink water. When she worked with Abbott and Costello, they nicknamed her Bingo. I think what she wanted to do was marry and have children. But it was mainly to get out of the poor situation she was in."

Many of the strippers made something of their lives, earning more than they could have as a secretary or waitress. They traveled, met new people, learned to take care of themselves, and provided for their families. From the beginning, even though they knew they may eventually benefit from being in burlesque shows, the first time they stripped on stage was seldom easy.

"But you get used to it," Lady Midnight told me. She had had an abusive husband she needed to get away from. Her grandfather had been a black-face comedian, her mom was a singer and dancer, and her father a top banana of note. Her father offered her a job working in his club to escape her situation.

"Because I worked in black light," Candy Cotton laughed, "I really truly believed they couldn't see me." She said she "clothed" herself in darkness.

Lorraine Lee added, "I really didn't show anything."

It didn't matter.

For the audience, a burlesque show was a place to forget one's troubles during the Depression and an escape for the troops that packed houses during World War II.

Lady Midnight started stripping at her father's club

Like any industry, though, burlesque was economically driven. "It was a time where people couldn't get work anywhere else," Alan Alda explained. His father was Robert Alda, a popular straight man and singer.

Most performers worked hard, but seldom grew rich. Some headliners (the star strippers) like Lili St. Cyr commanded as much as $5,000 a week in 1950 (before dying broke and in obscurity). But the majority never earned anywhere near that.

Still stripping in her seventies, Tempest Storm boasted that burlesque brought her the ability to travel and a lifetime of "minks, sables, big homes, big cars, Rolls Royces. I have no complaints." She was still able to earn thousands of dollars performing when I interviewed her in 2006.

"It was called the poor man's musical comedy," producer of *This Was Burlesque* Mike Iannucci told me, fresh off dialysis. I interviewed Mike in the New Jersey apartment that he had shared with his late wife and legendary burly queen Ann Corio.

Mike was my toughest interview. He was very ill in 2006, but had graciously agreed to speak with me. I later discovered Mike was a controversial producer—some vehemently despised him, claiming he took advantage of the performers in his show. There was no denying, however, that he was an expert on burlesque and that he loved and missed his "Annie." During our conversation, he would sometimes stare longingly toward a portrait of his wife by Alberto Vargas, the Peruvian "pinup painter." Mike died two years after our interview.

Two comedians backstage

"During the '20s, '30s, and '40s burlesque was king," said Mike. "At its height, burlesque was *the* most popular form of entertainment offered across the country. Men *and* women went to the shows. During the Depression, there was no other affordable entertainment for working-class people."

"It was a clean show," Mike emphasized. Burlesque employed thousands, entertained more, and brought in enough money to keep Broadway alive. When I asked Betty Rowland, the "Ball of Fire," former stripper, and one of the last surviving "Queens," if there had been a stigma when she worked, she said "No. Because everyone was working in it."

"It was fabulous, . . . gaudy," said Dixie Evans. When the average man went to a burly show, "he could laugh. And let me tell you, there was nothing to laugh about in the '30s. But to fall into one of those shows . . ."

Alexandra the Great "48," a stripper, said, "There was a time when you could fill an opera house with two thousand people, beautifully dressed." Couples and women alone went to the burly houses. Dixie recalled Wednesday afternoons when the strippers had to serve tea to the ladies in the audience.

"Early burlesque was a family entertainment. That's hard to believe, but it was," recalled Alan Alda.

In the 1930s, burlesque branched out into nightclubs and cafés "because of the shutdown [by LaGuardia]," said Rachel Shteir.

Shows were filled with an extravaganza of beauties, fresh-faced showgirls in barely-there costumes. They featured excellent singers, talented comedians, specialty acts, an emcee, and musicians. The large casts sometimes performed as many as four shows a day, seven days a week. "I don't remember a day off," said Alexandra the Great.

"If we have a day off, we're washing our costumes," Betty Rowland added.

They were a group of entertainers who spent the majority of the year traveling together by train. "They were a bunch of people who loved trooping around with each other and making people laugh, making one another laugh," said Alda.

What did a burlesque show consist of? Everyone told me a little bit different version, but the main elements were as follows:

There was an opening act. Usually around fifteen chorus girls of all different shapes and sizes. And there was a "tit singer."

"And that was an official title," Robert Alda's son told me. "I don't know if you had to get a special degree for that or what. But he would sing while the chorus girls would come out, usually with not too many clothes on."

After that, a comic and a straight man would come on.

Then the first stripteaser came on. And mixed in would be novelty acts.

Then another skit by the comedian and straight man, possibly with a talking woman (usually one of the chorus girls making a couple extra bucks).

Then a song or a dance number.

Then there was the middle production, which they called the Picture Act. This was another huge number that lasted ten minutes.

And then the co-feature (another stripper) came on.

And "if there was a chorus line, they usually did a nice build up for the feature," former stripper and talking woman Joni Taylor told me.

Then the headliner or star stripper came out. These were the Betty Rowlands, the Tempest Storms, and the Sherry Brittons—the names that had men and women alike lined up outside the theatre before the doors even opened.

And then there was the finale with most of the cast.

The entire show lasted about an hour and a half.

"It was essentially a dressed-up vaudeville show with bare bosoms and a cho-rus," said Nat Bodian. "It was a pleasant afternoon." He smiled.

As America changed, so did the format of the shows. Hollywood films showed more and women's hemlines rose. To compete, the burlesque houses kept adding more strippers and the stars demanded bigger salaries. To save costs, owners cut back on musicians and comedians until eventually they canned music and featured one tired, old, baggy-pants comedian barely making it through his routine, with shouts of "bring on the girls" hurled at him. What had started out as a family show had degenerated into a show for mostly working-class men who came for the nudity, as much of it as could be gotten away with. The women "danced erotically to arouse the men. And the men got aroused, right there in the front row," said Alda.

Beautiful dancer Sherry Britton, who started as a stripper in her teens and rose to the top of the marquee, spoke of looking out at the audience as the men mastur-bated behind their newspapers. "I was a part of that," she said with shame and disdain.

Did things get out of hand in the audience? Rarely. "Guys would be jerking off in the balcony and girls would say 'watch out for the guy with the hat and the over coat.' You expected some seediness," explained Dixie Evans.

By the time musician John Perilli got a call from a conductor friend begging him to fill in for a recently fired drummer, burlesque was not well thought of. The musicians were looked down upon. "It wasn't considered a great art form," said Perilli.

As Alda mentioned, he suspected the men weren't there "to see the comedi-ans" or hear the band. It was girls, and legs, and bosoms. The audience wanted to see how far and how much the girls dared to show. And some dared a lot.

Once known as a burlesque performer, it was not so easy to get out, move on, or move up to a more "respected" role in show business. A lot of the comedians could move from burlesque into radio, film, and television. There were no young comedians coming up from the ranks to replace them. The old baggy-pants were getting older and began to die out, or were pushed out as the audience demanded more girls.

Expectations placed on the dancers changed, also. In the clubs, they were required to sit with the clients and drink. They had champagne quotas to make. Many developed problems with alcohol.

The quality of the dances changed, as well. There were fewer "acts." The women simply came on stage, stripped as much as they could get away with, and then left. The tease vanished. Stripping no longer poked fun at sex; it was now *about* sex. Women in bikinis were showing up on beaches. *Playboy Magazine* launched. A burly show was no longer the only place to see naked women.

When burlesque died, it cast out thousands of performers with no place to go. Most of them drifted away, abandoning stage names, covering up their past. Many of the men and women couldn't cross over into "legitimate" entertainment. They got into whatever work they could find—factory work, real estate, sales.

Performers down on their luck packed up their G-strings and their sequins, or their worn, tired sketches and props, and went back to "real" names and found whatever kind of jobs they could. For many, nothing would be as fulfilling as being on the stage. Others tried to forget burlesque; many denied it. Some buried their pasts so well that husbands and children never knew their mothers had stripped or danced in the chorus. Some had a hard time and never found "anything else to get interested in," recalled Renny von Muchow.

Why is burlesque still misunderstood? Is it because we don't have the original shows on tape to analyze, enjoy, and dissect? Is it because the performers themselves didn't continue talk about it?

"I don't usually tell people I was in the business," said Alexandra the Great.

"I was more embarrassed—I have a son—I didn't brag about it," recalled former stripper Maria Bradley.

Burlesque saw a huge number of talented performers come and go through its ranks. There was Fanny Brice, Jimmy Durante, Milton Berle, Jackie Gleason, Bert Lahr (the Cowardly Lion), and hundreds more.

Our comedy today came out of burlesque. Early radio shows consisted of performers such as Abbott and Costello, Red Skelton, Jack Benny, and Fred Allen, all recreating the same skits they had performed and refined hundreds of times on the burlesque circuit. Remember Bob Hope and all the beautiful women and comedians that flew across the world to entertain the troops? Pure burlesque. Variety shows followed the burlesque format with singing, beautiful women, sketches, and parodies of current topics and politics.

As the men and women of the burly show shared with me their memories, the stories were often contradictory. It was clean; it was naughty. There were kids backstage; there was never any family around. It was fun; it was degrading. You never really showed anything; women were flashing their "lower regions" all the time. The comedians were the worst and couldn't get jobs anywhere else; the comedians were brilliant. It was a hard living; it was the best time of their lives.

Sherry Britton said, "I was the only one who ever admitted they hated burlesque."

Some have argued that the burlesque strippers were early feminists. We perceive them as such and call them pioneers. We say they were women who used their sexuality as empowerment. It's a false viewing. Generally, they got into burlesque because it was sometimes the only thing they could do. Not one woman I interviewed spoke of trying to prove a point or of being empowered by their sexuality.

Author Kelly DiNardo comments: "I don't think people know where to put strippers in their own mind. Are these women that we should respect and admire for what they can do? Or are these women the dregs of society, or are they something in between? And I think when you don't know the answers to those questions, it's really easy to misunderstand their motivations [for] what they're doing. And the only [one] who can speak to their motivations are the women themselves."

These, then, are their stories.

CHAPTER TWO
The Reunion

"My mother found out I was working the burlesque theatre, told them I was fourteen. They let me go."

—Joni Taylor

"I'm not gonna do too long, because I know everyone wants to go out and get a drink."

—Sunny Dare

(from left to right) April March, unidentified woman, Alexandra the Great "48", Leslie Zemeckis, Val Valentine (seated) and Sunny Dare at the Stardust in Las Vegas for a burlesque reunion in 2006

THE REUNION

May 2006, Las Vegas, Nevada. The Stardust Resort and Casino.

What we thought would be a long weekend interviewing former burlesque performers turned into a four-year journey. Grabbing our video camera, Sheri and I headed to Vegas.

I wasn't sure what to expect. I had financed the reunion, but another woman had coordinated the event, inviting the former performers, securing the rooms, etc. The individuals that showed up were by and large former strippers, but there was also a straight man, chorus girls, several talking women, a costumer—about seventy-five performers in all. Many brought along their children and spouses.

For the sake of simplicity for the reader, I will refer to the performers by their stage names. On the second day of the Reunion, back in the convention room, we were treated to our own burlesque show with a rousing burlesque-styled band, various singers—including Sequin, singing from her wheelchair, and Sunny Dare, in the early stages of Alzheimer's—and a handful of the women stripped.

There was much camaraderie between the performers, most of whom had never met but knew of each other. The feature performers did not work together— they followed each other on the circuit. However, some of the performers, like April March and Alexandra the Great "48," had been friends for decades. Burlesque had been an insular world. The performers stuck together, traveling on trains, piling into hotel rooms near the theatres, drinking at the local bars—year after year.

"Most of us were not too catty. And supportive," former stripper Vicki O'Day explained about the past. "We don't all look great, but there's a common bond and a friendship."

True, most did not look like their former glossy photos; many looked like they were probably grandmothers.

One afternoon, former stripper and talking woman Joni Taylor led an enthusiastic "pass the mic" in which the ladies and men introduced themselves and gave short summaries of their time in burlesque. As performer after performer spoke into the microphone, I became increasingly more intrigued.

Stripper Lorraine Lee "broke into show business in 1937." She was sixteen. Her mom worked with legendary performers such as Sophie Tucker and Al Jolson. Her father was an organist. "I went to a theatre and asked people there . . . if I could go to work. They said sure. I worked first week for nothing, second made fifty cents. I was making ten dollars a week after a while. I couldn't go home for lunch or dinner. I'd take tickets, sold popcorn, and helped paint the set," she said. She finally quit school. "I was falling asleep in class" with the schedule of four shows a week in addition to all the behind-the-scenes work, she said. She would earn her GED thirty years later.

Lady Midnight told the group, "My stepmother said, 'Go to the Follies and introduce yourself and he'll put you to work.' I went there with my daughter under one arm and my sewing machine under the other arm."

"I started in a chorus line in [the] carnival. I was on All American Carnival for two years. Started at 18," related Candy Cotton. "[The chorus girls] thought they were going to the fair to be on a big stage." Needless to say, when they got a look at it, it wasn't what they expected—small and cramped. "A couple broke down and cried, but they put their feathers on and danced."

Sunny Dare told the group, "I was born on the carnival. My mother took care of snakes and my father broke horses so I sorta fell into this business very easily. I worked all over the world."

"I started in the carnival. I ran away from home and joined the circus. I did that when I was sixteen. Worked for a sideshow for four years, started out as a knife thrower's target, quit after a week when I got nicked and I realized the knife thrower had a bit of a drinking problem," said former stripper Daphne Lake.

"We rehearsed between shows Saturday and all day Sunday. We hated it." Joni Taylor said, while discussing work with the chorus.

After three days of interviews, Sheri and I realized we had much more to cover. The stories were so rich, these oral histories so untapped—we couldn't stop after a weekend. And so began our mission to recover every living memory of burlesque that we could.

CHAPTER THREE

Six Feet of Spice

"I was embarrassed and humiliated about my past."
"If I had a daughter in burlesque, I'd be upset."
—Beverly Anderson

Stripper Beverly Arlynne

Beverly Anderson was in her mid-seventies when I met her in May of 2006—a beautiful, statuesque redhead with long legs, a forthright manner, and gorgeous alabaster skin. She was running a theatrical talent agency, booking actors gigs out of a small office in Midtown Manhattan. It had taken some time to set up the interview through her son Fred, as he told me that her health was precarious.

The interview was set for a Saturday, so the phones were quiet, the hallways deserted. On her wall was a huge, poster-sized photo of her younger self—looking not much different from the woman seated before me, tastefully dressed in pants and a simple green turtleneck, her green eyes bright, her laugh quick and easy. Beverly was impeccably made up. If she was ill, she didn't look it.

In the photo above us, she wore elbow-length gloves, a modest bikini top, and a skimpy G-string with a sheer panel flowing from it. Later she told me she had the bikini top painted in because she had been self-conscious about her clients seeing her covering her breasts with only her gloved hands. Not many of her actors ever made the connection between the stripper in the photo and their agent sitting behind the desk.

She quit stripping when she was thirty years old and decided she needed the poster, which was originally pasted to the wall of a theatre in Canada, as a memento. "I saw what happened to the girls. Rough life. I wanted a poster as a reminder it would be fun later in life." She asked someone to soak it off the wall of the theatre. She rolled it up. At customs they "demanded I unroll it." Her semi-nude picture was "embarrassing" and seemed to amuse the customs officers.

And here, in her office, hung the same poster, a copy of which now hangs on my wall at home.

Beverly Anderson had been born in the "waspy, upper-middle-class town of Burlingame, California," outside of San Francisco. She came from a "careful," conservative household. From an early age, Beverly was determined to get into show business; her eye was on the stage. Like so many others before her, she wanted to be a star.

Since childhood, Beverly had suffered from rheumatoid arthritis. Her fingers were bent and twisted. "Most struggling actresses," she said, "worked as waitresses, or typists, while they were trying to get [an acting] job. I could do neither. But I could wear gloves and shoes and work as a stripper." This was a very interesting conclusion for a well-to-do small town girl who had never seen a strip show or traveled outside of California.

Beverly started as a showgirl working in the chorus line, dancing for Harold Minsky in Chicago. Harold was the adopted son of famed theatre owner Abe Minsky, who, along with his three brothers, essentially monopolized the burlesque world, owning and running various theatres. It didn't take long for Beverly to decide she wanted out of the chorus line—she wanted to be a headliner. She knew she had the looks and the determination to succeed.

While learning her trade in the chorus line and to earn an extra fifteen dollars, Beverly used to "catch the wardrobe" of famous stripper Georgia Sothern. She'd stand behind the curtains at the theatre and, as Georgia stripped, Beverly caught her clothes as they were flung through the curtains and hung them up. Georgia had been stripping since she was thirteen (for another Minsky brother named Billy). Her act was fast paced as she flung her body forward and back to the popular ragtime tune "Hold that Tiger." The act was electric. Georgia was a big star when Beverly worked with her, and to deter other strippers from seeing her act and stealing it, Georgia had the curtains pinned together, allowing only enough room for the gown to slip through.

"I peeked," Beverly said about watching Georgia. And "eventually I stole her act." By watching Georgia night after night, along with the other headliners, the young girl from Burlingame learned how to disrobe elegantly. Beverly would sing during her strip act. She admitted she "wasn't a very good dancer." And she had "a terrible voice," but "if they wanted to see my body, they had to listen to me," she laughed.

On the road, Beverly went out as the first or second strip, not the feature (the star given the final strip of the show). Her first night in a small Ohio town, Beverly read the local newspaper advertising her act alongside "Barbara with her boa constrictor." The two would be expected to share a dressing room, "and I thought, my God, I'm petrified of snakes," she said.

But then something happened to Barbara. She was bitten by her snake and was in the hospital. The little old lady who was the theatre owner told Beverly, "You have to be the star." Beverly readily accepted the role. "I was glad because I didn't want to dress with a snake," she said.

As the "star," the little old lady informed Beverly that she would be expected to "flash." To flash was a burlesque term for showing a woman's "bottom region," Beverly explained. "The farmers in Ohio would come at six, seven, eight in the morning [to the theatre] and stand in line because the star would flash."

Beverly was upset when the theatre owner gave her the assignment. "I'd never done that," she said. Being told to flash was devastating to her. "I thought that's just terrible. My mother would have a stroke. She didn't know what I was doing anyway." But it was Ohio and her mother was in California, so what choice did she have?

Beverly went back to her hotel. Next to the hotel was a fur shop. Hanging in the window were second-hand fur jackets and coats. A red fox-fur jacket caught her eye. She went into the little fur shop and explained she couldn't afford much.

"I said, 'Do you have any little pieces of fur that I could buy?' They sold me a little fur piece." Red fox fur.

Back in her room, she sewed it into a triangle and put it on invisible elastic. "All the while I was thinking, 'Well, it's gonna get a big laugh, and everyone's gonna think it's funny.'" She was certain she would be fired, but at least she'd go out with a laugh.

She did her number. And there was a blackout. And a drum roll. The lights came on. A pin spot hit the fur piece. "There was deathly silence for about two minutes. And then there were screams and howls and yells," Beverly recalled. From offstage, she could see the comics backstage laughing. From their vantage point, they could see her "flash" was nothing but a fake. But to the audience, the fur piece looked completely real. There were resounding cheers bouncing around the theatre. "Bravo!" the men yelled. Beverly left the stage and climbed the stairs, crying, waiting to be fired.

Pretty soon the little old lady came running up to Beverly and said, "Honey, that's the best flash I've ever seen, but can you trim yourself down a little?"

Once she'd become a headliner, Beverly gave herself the stage name Beverly Arlynne—spelled variously as Arlene, Arline and Arlenne. (Combing through numerous scrapbooks, archives, and newspapers, it's astonishing how the spelling of the strippers' monikers varied from publication to publication—either club owners were lazy or newspapers were careless.) Beverly chose the name Arlynne because she loved 1950s film star Arlene Dahl. Later, Dahl actually became a client of Beverly's at her agency. Beverly never told her she'd been the inspiration for her stripper name.

Beverly was also variously billed as "Six Feet of Spice," "Towering Spice," and "Spicy Towers." She eventually worked with other burlesque greats, including Blaze Starr and Lili St. Cyr, and was good friends with Dixie Evans. Making friends with the other girls was a rarity for Beverly. The women, she admitted, were women she wouldn't have befriended back home in California. Most of them were into drugs and alcohol. "It was depressing," she said. She added that, to her, those habits were not a good way to make a living. "I saw too many of the women going down the hill." Beverly looked off, sad. She admitted it was a less than desirable existence.

"It was a seedy life," she said, admitting that there were many times when she was on stage and was able to see "guys jerkin' off in the balcony." In addition to the men from town, Beverly also recalled various male celebrities stopping in to see the show as there were "dark little hideaways" where it was easy for the men to come and drink with the girls.

"After a while it eats you up. I wasn't meant to be eaten up by burlesque," she said. She knew she had to quit.

Sitting in her office, I marveled at Beverly Anderson, the innocent girl from an upper-class family. She had come a long way and had performed in many venues, as a showgirl in "legit" shows and vaudeville-type shows with comedians Smith and Dale. Her name was even listed on the same bill as Judy Garland at the Palace Theatre. Out of burlesque, she became the youngest female theatrical agent in New York, representing two Tony winners and an Academy Award nominee. "I bet I'm the only stripper who became an agent," she said proudly.

Was there a stigma attached? It was a question I asked everyone. "Definitely," she said. "I knew I'd come to no good end if I continued in it." And so she got out. She didn't want to be a stripper at thirty.

Later on, I asked her about this resurgence with neo-burlesque troops all over, especially in New York. She said it was "tacky" and she was "shocked people would be interested. If I had a daughter in burlesque I'd be upset." Her family never knew she was a stripper. Her mother died, never suspecting. "My husband only found out the week before we were married."

Her then-fiancé, Leonard Traube, was a press agent for Broadway shows and films and went to the papers to have them write a story on Beverly, who by then was a theatrical agent. The angle of the story would be how a former Latin Quarter showgirl became the youngest female agent in New York. Leonard approached the *Daily News*.

The reporter at the *Daily News* told her unsuspecting fiancé that he knew who Beverly was. She was "the one who used to be a stripper," the reporter said.

Her shocked fiancé could only say, "What?" She said he was surprised because she was so "straight-laced." Apparently it didn't deter Leonard from marrying her and having two sons with her.

She didn't tell her sons until they were 41 and 38, the year before I interviewed her. "I was ashamed of my background. . . . It was a tawdry way to earn a living," she said. However, she admitted that the industry and the experiences taught her a lot. Coming from a cloistered, sheltered existence, she saw parts of the world she wouldn't otherwise have seen. What she had known about New York back then, she had only read about in books.

Not all memories were painful. She had fond memories of the comedian and Johnny Carson regular Don Rickles who worked the burlesque houses. "They used to throw pennies at him," Beverly recalled. He was afraid the audience was going to blind him.

One night, the two were sharing the bill in Louisville, Kentucky, during the Kentucky Derby. "It was a hot, hot time." The nightclub was small and the tables were crammed tightly together, practically on top of one another, very close to the stage. She was doing a jungle act. She was backstage, running late, and heard the overture warning her she was about to go on. Because of the deformity of her hands caused by the arthritis, she "always wore gloves. I was the only stripper who never took off her gloves."

It was difficult to get the gloves on because the heat made her sweat, which made her bent fingers uncooperative. That night, she ran on stage, gloveless, and did her act. A man from the audience later went up to the owner and complained. "How dare you hire a crippled stripper," he said. She was immediately fired without pay.

With no money and clearly "desperate" for any help she could get, Don Rickles lent her enough money for airfare back to New York. Later, she went to The American Guild of Variety Artists (AGVA), the union for nightclub and variety performers, and got her money.

But that night, she was devastated. "I remember standing in the airport waiting for the plane to take me away and looking up at the sky and thinking, 'Gee, is there anyone for me? Is anyone on my side?' I was crushed. What's gonna become of me? I've got crippled hands. What the hell am I gonna do?" she said.

Ironically, Beverly Anderson's first job after she quit stripping was playing a stripper on the 1950s sitcom *The Phil Silvers Show*. Eventually, Beverly came to peace with her past. She no longer regretted her early career choice; it no longer hurt her to think about or discuss. She was no longer a scared and lonely girl, self-conscious about her crippled hands. She'd married a man she loved and had two children. I think she got a kick out of knowing she'd had a "scandalous" start.

As Beverly looked back at her time in burlesque, there was a light in her eyes that I'll remember always. "I think it was a great adventure," she said. "Thank God I survived. I don't remember the pain as much as I remember the good times."

CHAPTER FOUR

Don't Tell Mama (or the Kids)

"Even my husband . . . when I said one time to someone
I was a stripper, he said, 'You weren't a stripper, you were in burlesque.'
I said, 'Well, honey, what do you think I did in burlesque? I mean,
I didn't play the piano.'"

—Joan Arline

"My mother always wished that I had taken up some other form of work."

—Candy Cotton

For many strippers, there was reluctance, if not an outright avoidance, to tell their parents what they had gotten into. The stigma associated with burlesque was hard to overcome.

Kitty West, the stripper who'd lost almost everything due to Hurricane Katrina, told me her mother and baby brother had seen her perform. "Mother thought it was beautiful and saw that I wasn't doing anything wrong, and she came to grips with herself," she said.

Though April March's daughter knew how her mother made a living, she was proud of her mother. April would not allow her daughter to watch her performances, as April did "strip all the way, most places."

For many who had a relative already in burlesque, life was admittedly easier. Former stripper Val Valentine grew up backstage. She, like a few others, slid easily into burlesque with nothing to hide. Her mother's best friend had been a stripper and eventually would teach Val the ropes.

Lily Ann Rose, who got into stripping when she was fourteen, said she had forgotten all about her burlesque career and never talked about it with her children until one day, fifty years after quitting, she opened an old trunk and all the memories came flooding back.

Rita Grable, a buxom blonde from Brooklyn, invited her father to her show. She thought, "How am I gonna tell him what I'm doing?" She had been working in New Jersey, there were ads in the papers, and she was on the cover of many magazines. One day, she decided to just tell him. "'I'm working in New Jersey and would you like to see me?' He came. I didn't think I was gonna get through it. He said, 'You know you were the best one there.' I was so thrilled that he didn't reprimand me," she said. She was one of the lucky few.

Sequin, the former stripper, said her family never mentioned anything to her about her stripping. They knew, "but they never saw it either." She would send them cast off costumes and jewelry. "They'd brag about me," she said.

The performers weren't immune to the judgment of others. "You knew about the stigma," Dixie Evans said, shrugging, "but we're in a group all by ourselves. We were considered celebrities." Local places were thrilled to have the traveling headliners, even if they did stay in "third-rate places." And, because the women had money and spent it on minks and Cadillacs, "people would look at you and know you were in burlesque," she said.

When they stepped out of their circle, it was a different story. The women would get dirty looks, especially if they still wore their stage makeup and false eyelashes, as Dixie Evans often did. "At Saks we'd get humiliated. They meant to put you down," she said.

Though a lot of the women got into burlesque wanting to be "stars" and hoping it was a stepping stone to legitimate careers, it was not.

Lili St. Cyr, (lovingly and ironically pronounced *sincere*) one of the highest-grossing strippers ever, spent years trying to legitimize herself and her career, but when she was cast in movies, it was only ever as a variation of herself. She stripped in *Naked and the Dead* and performed her Dance of the Seven Veils in *Sinbad*. In *Runaway Girl*, her last film, she played a runaway stripper. She was in her forties.

A vast majority of the women got into burlesque as a means to feed themselves. Only a handful that I interviewed said they had dreamed of being in the business. But as Val Valentine wanted to make clear, "[they] didn't all come from bad backgrounds."

When she was eleven or twelve, Dixie Evans' father was killed on an oil rig. "My mother crawled into a shell and just sat with an old blue chenille bathrobe with cold cream," she said. Her mother practiced Christian Science. "Naïve," Dixie called her. She was tired of her mother not working. "Signs then said, 'Don't apply for a job if over 25.' And I was working. No money. My mother couldn't cope."

Dixie, born Mary Lee, began nude modeling in Los Angeles. She told her mom she was modeling for the *Sears, Roebuck and Company* catalogue. She didn't tell her about burlesque career for a long time. Dixie eventually became annoyed with her mother's pious attitude. "I finally ran away. I said, 'Mom, when that clock ticks midnight, I'm eighteen and I'm outta here and I'm away from you.' And I left." She went to Reno, Nevada. It was two years before she reconciled with her mother.

Others popped into burlesque briefly, later denying it. "But they were there. Ginger Rogers was the head soubrette at the Haymarket," Dixie informed me. Actress "Sheree North worked Larry Potter's Supper Club in Los Angeles *and* Earl Carroll's. Vaudeville and burlesque were very similar. If the vaudeville didn't have an act and there was an opening in a burlesque show, believe me, they'd take it. They wouldn't say 'Oh, I don't play burlesque.' Yes, they did."

CHAPTER FIVE
One Glove at a Time

"I threw up."
—Terry Mixon, on her first time stripping
"'You want to try a strip this week?' 'I'll try it.'"
—Betty Rowland on how she started

Stripper Sherry Britton

Just who performed the *very first* strip in history is a thing of speculation and myth in burlesque lore.

In *Burleycue: An Underground History of Burlesque Days*, author Bernard Sobel speculated that the "willful removing of one's clothes" (as opposed to

24

straps "accidentally" breaking) began in 1906, when a Millie DeLeon threw a garter to the audience—and thus began America's popular new attraction. Author Frank Cullen (*Vaudeville Encyclopedia*) claims the date was 1904 and that "Mlle. DeLeon" was publicity hungry. She was often arrested for "forgetting to don her body stocking." Her endeavors in the scandal-causing department earned her a promotion: a solo spot at the end of the show—when all the star strippers performed—plus she was excused from group dances and scenes with the comedians. (As a side note, a unique aspect of burlesque was the audience participation, and by 1915, Mlle. was having the men in the audience remove her garter for her.)

Morton Minsky, one of four brothers who dominated the New York burlesque scene, claims the strip started in 1917 when Mae Dix absentmindedly began removing her costume before she reached the wings. When the crowd cheered, Dix continued removing her clothing to enthusiastic applause. Morton's brother Billy ordered the "accident" repeated every night.

Others claim it wasn't until 1923. According to Rachel Shteir, "Mademoiselle Fifi was the one who the Minsky brothers say started striptease. She goes onstage and her cuffs were dirty. So she starts taking off her cuffs, and so the crowd goes wild." Shteir added that in those days, the dancers would come on stage with layered costumes and begin peeling down—not very far, mind you.

Before 1928, Shteir said that stripping consisted of two separate acts. The strip act was where one went onstage and shed her clothes as quickly as possible. And the other was the tease act, which was "more teasy, and it came out of this Jazz Age word 'teasing,' which meant to flirt."

A platinum-haired beauty, Hinda Wassua was unique for being one of the few exotics that never changed her name to sound less ethnic. The Minsky's brothers promoting their brand of Americana wanted their strippers to sound American. Thinner than the British Blondes, Wassua was a Midwestern Glamazon mythologized as being another "first" when her bra strap broke one night in Chicago at the State and Congress Theatre. It was 1928. Sobel wrote that Hinda was performing not at the State and Congress, but at the Haymarket, and the Lithuanian lovely (by way of Connecticut birth) was tap dancing and her clothing came undone and the audience cheered. The manager demanded she repeat it the next night. She eagerly did and went on to much acclaim.

"In the '20s, you could be funny because you could be ethnic—like The Polish Stripper," Shteir said. Even Gypsy Rose Lee wasn't immune to change. "Billy Minsky asked her to change her name and straighten her hair so she wouldn't appear so ethnic."

Author H. M. Alexander claimed in his 1938 book *Strip Tease* that after the broken strap, the idea spread like wildfire to the rest of the competing theatres and soon owners were demanding their girls "accidently" break a strap or two. Since it made them instant sensations, the girls were only too happy to oblige.

At the time, nudity was rampant on Broadway in legit theatres. According to Alexander, there were the Shuberts in the early 1920s, with girls who posed nude until "little by little they showed more."

An article in *Uncensored Magazine* claimed that Flo Ziegfeld copied the Folies Bergère extravaganzas, even with the price of a ticket being "four times" the cost of a burlesque show. Hollywood movies at the time showed more nudity and were more daring than the burly cue. It wasn't until 1934 that the Motion Picture Code clamped down and consequently brought nudity back to the burlesque theatre.

At the same time, Earl Carroll, the "Prince of Nudies," had his glorious revue parading across Broadway with bare breasts on display. This forced burlesque to step up and give the men what they wanted: boobs.

In the 1920s, the comedians went from heavily made up, putty-nosed caricatures to clean faces. They became one with their audience. The men in the audience identified with them. This decade also brought short flapper skirts and the baring of knees. To keep up, burlesque was forced to show more.

October 24, 1929, saw millionaires leaping out of their high rises and the Great Depression descended on the country, making a boon for cheap, common-denominator entertainment. Burlesque thrived.

And though France had its Moulin Rouge with plenty of nudity, the performers did not strip. Only in America did women peel off their clothes, teasing the audience with the promise of more. It was a naughty, flirtatious show, neither raunchy nor nasty. It was good-spirited fun and tongue in cheek. A flash, a hint, a glimpse—it was more the suggestion or hope of what one might see rather than the reality.

What was it like the first time you stripped? I asked this of all the women I interviewed.

For Beverly Anderson, it was a "disaster." She was booked to perform at a Long Island High School. It was supposed to be a "joke strip." Beverly was to come out in various bathing suits throughout the eras and dance to "By the Sea by the Sea, by the Beautiful Sea." She was wearing an elastic bathing suit over a two-piece for her final number. She had never rehearsed the number with "perspiration." The night of the show, as she peeled off the outer bathing suit, along came the two-piece beneath, leaving her stark naked in front of 250 shocked teenagers. She didn't know what to cover first, her top or bottom.

Rita Grable went to a high school for performing arts in New York. She was in a dance line at the Copa in Baltimore. When the show closed, an agent approached her. "Would you like to go into burlesque?" he asked. She thought, *Are you serious? I'm a dancer.* She was nineteen and making $66 a week in the dance line [in the 1950s]. The agent told her, "'I can get you $125 a week.'" She thought, *My god, what do I have to do?* "He said 'sorta take off this.' And I thought, 'How bad can it be?'" Grable said.

The agent then took her to a club. She watched other girls and thought, *It's not that hard, and I do have to pay the rent,* she said. "And it looked like fun. When you're nineteen, everything looks like fun. I did it and it was."

Lady Midnight's maiden strip was quite different, without agents or contract negotiations. "The first time I stripped was . . . at my father's nightclub. I never wanted to be a stripper." Born Benita Kirkland, her father was the well-known baggy-pants comedian Monkey Kirkland.

She recalled, "I started in chorus. A week later, there was a dancer who couldn't dance. I went in her place. Before you knew it I was the co-feature."

Candy Cotton also became a stripper by accident. "From being a chorus girl I went to being a stripper because the dancer didn't show up," she said. This was an excuse used to explain many of the girls' maiden voyages.

In Terry Mixon's case, the feature dancer was sick and the choreographer of the Old Howard, Bunny Weldon, told her, "You're going on. Get out there." Mixon put on the feature's gown and danced to her music. "It went over very well," she recalled.

For Alexandra the Great, fear consumed her during her first strip. "I was afraid I'd fall off the stage. I wasn't scared [of the stripping]. It's an adrenaline high—if you get through it. And that's the last time I felt it."

Dixie Evans was working as a page in a vaudeville show in San Francisco. The show closed and she couldn't get back to Los Angeles. She was sitting at the bottom of the stairs of a burlesque club while a girl was bumping on stage. Dixie was "terrified." Someone said to her, "You want to work? You'll make a lot of money. See Bernie at the Chinese Noodle Shop. Here's twenty dollars; get a costume." She bought a sheer pink nightgown, grabbed a pillow, and danced to "Mr. Sandman." She took off her nightgown. "That's all I had," she said.

Sunny Dare of the blue hair, born Roberta Bauman, "joined the Sally Rand brigade. And we ended up in Dallas, Texas. And we got stiffed for all our work. So, I had to do a strip to get enough money to get back home on."

Some first nights could be harrowing. "My first act, the women in the audience threw their fruit out of their drinks at me," Vicki O'Day said. "So I had to give them a little talk that I didn't want their husbands and everything. And then I was OK."

Vicki O'Day, formerly Westlin, started stripping relatively late, at age twenty-nine. She said in general the women in the audience liked her because "I wasn't particularly busty. I wasn't a threat to women. I put humor in my act."

One of the first things a stripper did was change her name. Candy Cotton chose her moniker because she liked "candy cotton and my hair was like it. It was a big fluff of hair."

Dardy Orlando took her last name at her famous sister Lili St. Cyr's suggestion. Lili's lover at the time was Jimmy Orlando, a wildly popular former hockey player who had dominated the Canadian rink. His was an easily recognizable name in Montreal, where both sisters performed.

Sometimes their monikers backfired. When Gypsy Rose Lee tried acting in movies, she was billed by her real name Louise Hovick because producers were worried about the stigma associated with "Gypsy," though they had hired her because of it.

Kitty West, aka Evangeline the Oyster Girl, said, "In those days we didn't have to show ... as they would say ... our private parts. Or strip down naked to be appealing."

A rare few of the women crossed over into "legitimate" entertainment in a small way. Ann Corio performed in B movies for Monogram Studios.

According to Shteir, most strippers "weren't really actresses; they knew how to do their act, sometimes sing, dance, and that was it. It didn't transform into a career in Hollywood."

Shteir continued, "It was the lowest form of entertainment in popular entertainment.... People looked down on it both in the entertainment world and just generally—like a lot of things that people look down on, they also coveted. Like the way people do with rap today. It's a double-edged sword."

Stripteasing in itself was a transient occupation. Some stripped for a relatively short time before moving on. Others became managers, like Lillian Hunt, and stayed in the world. Leroy Griffith segued from a teenage candy butcher to owner of burlesque clubs, to an owner of a strip club. It was a small community that provided protection for the performers. According to Shteir, the performers "sought out family" because of their difficult personal family situations and because the "women couldn't get out of the business so easily."

Lady Midnight recalled that "sometimes you'd get a judgmental look. In those days [people] thought you must be promiscuous.... We worked hard for our living, three shows a day, five on Saturday, four on Sunday. We never had a day off in the theatre. Ever."

CHAPTER SIX

Circus Life

"I didn't bump and grind much. Carneys put a damper on burlesque.
They were rough on the midway."
—Joni Taylor

"It was an amazing invasion into a community."
—Professor Janet Davis

The World's Columbia Exhibition of 1893 in Chicago was the start of carnivals in America. The word "midway" came from the Columbia Exhibition. "The circus created the midway—because from that big top to the marquee, the front door, that's the midway."

The midway would morph into rides, exhibits, and attractions, and eventually become crammed with sideshows. The midway was also where the "cooch" shows played. A barker would stand out front on what was called a bally platform with a bevy of scantily clad beauties and lure the "rubes" (local customers) into the tent for a scandalous, often all-nude show.

Carnivals and circuses were the premiere form of entertainment for most of America in the late nineteenth century and early twentieth centuries. For many, it was the only type of show available to rural America—and what a glorious extravaganza it was. Before most people had ever been to a zoo and before movie theatres appeared in every town, the circus brought exotic animals and fantastic spectacles—including nudity—to the masses. On opening day, there were long lines of chorus girls. Shows under the tent involved several hundred cast members. A circus often sat ten thousand people or more. Burlesque-style dancing and costumes were a part of the circus and carnival shows, of course. In fact, circus burlesquers had more freedom and they got away with a lot more nudity because the circus was smart enough to "market itself as 'education' for the entire family.... There wasn't a lot of censor," explained Dr. Janet Davis, a professor of American Studies at the University of Texas at Austin.

Circuses and carnivals were places where "people on the margins of society found a home and felt safe, where they couldn't elsewhere." Entertainment under the tents was a "freewheeling cheap amusement." It was "democratic," accessible to anyone because of the price and also the type of entertainment. It wasn't highbrow. This type of entertainment had much in common with burlesque in the theatres. It was a crucial forum "for telling stories about the rest of world, recreating spectacles and peace treaties."

The circus attracted lesbians, gays, and others who felt safe among the other "outcasts" of their day. Strippers, homosexuals, female impersonators. Freaks among freaks.

And though many considered performing in the canvas shows to be "low rent," it was a lucrative gig. Both Gypsy Rose Lee and Sally Rand worked Royal American Circuses and made a fortune. In 1949, at the age of thirty-eight, Gypsy performed eight to fifteen shows a day, and earned ten thousand dollars a week while touring with her four-year-old son and third husband. The huge sum of money wasn't the only reason Gypsy, at the height of her fame, was working so hard: It was in her blood—the love of travel, living out of a trailer, the rapport between the circus folks. The circus's GYPSY AND HER ROYAL AMERICAN BEAUTIES sign stretched high into the night sky—proof of the size of the crowds she could attract.

Gypsy's act consisted of scantily dressed girls who she would then slowly dress in her clothes, leaving herself in only a corset. According to *Billboard Magazine*, Royal American did a brisk business and Gypsy's tent was consistently packed. She was the first name attraction hired by Royal American. Sally Rand would follow.

Many dipped into the carny life, from Georgia Sothern (once billed as the Human Bombshell) in the late 1940s to Lili St. Cyr, who worked her last fair in 1970. Others I interviewed—Candy Cotton, Dixie Evans, Ricki Covette, and Mimi Reed—all worked under the canvas.

Dixie Evans claimed that she loved working for the circus. "I really did. I went with a bareback rider for a while. Up in North Dakota, Wyoming, and way up there, they don't have shows like we have in the big cities. So the [circus] trains would go up there with a big show at the end of the season when everybody's through with husking the corn and whatever they do way up there and everything. Oh, they look forward to these shows! And Sally Rand was a headliner. I mean the people adored her. They loved her," Dixie recalled.

The girl show revues, as they were called in the carnivals, were large burlesque shows, with chorus lines, variety acts, and strippers. These were not "cooch shows." The cooch shows had only a couple girls and they took off *all* their clothes. That was certainly not burlesque.

Daphne Lake had been a snake charmer on a circus for four years. But when the show closed, she was stranded in the South with little money. "I went to the girls show," she said. "They needed bally girls. Talker comes out on stage and talks about the show inside and 'look at the pretty girls!' A lot of times those people aren't in the show. I was pretty much a shill. I'd be there in my little evening gown—I had one gown—and make big smiles at the audience. In those days, as a car hop, I was lucky to see twenty-five dollars a week." Daphne made seventy-five dollars for three shows a day, seven days a week.

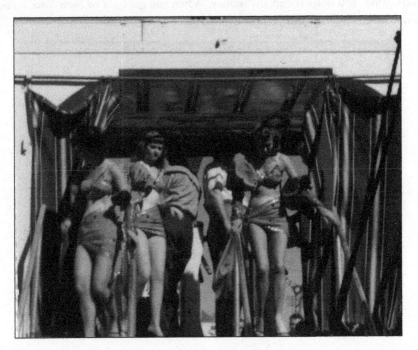

Bally Girls on the circus/carnival route

"Carnival life . . . that was hard. No matter if you were eighteen or twelve, that was hard," Candy Cotton said. "We did ballying between shows, out in front with the barker."

"They have a talker," Dixie explained. "He goes out, 'bally, girls, bally!' And most of the chorus girls all have to go out and bally like this, ya know." The girls would nod, bow, and smile to the circus attendees as their prospective audiences walked by the girls in their provocative attire.

"And we would get up onstage and we would pretend to be these exotic danc-ers that were going to thrill the customers," recalled former stripper Daphne Lake.

"You were on your feet a lot, swollen feet and all. We used to soak them in tubs of ice," said Candy Cotton. "One season was enough."

Dixie Evans agreed. "Circus life and carnival life was lucrative, but grueling. You do maybe ten to thirty shows a day. Whenever that weather is shining and the sun is out there, you do those shows," she says. "And always there's a little boy nine years old with a water pistol. Woo-whoop! Ha! Ha! Ha! Ha!"

"When you're through . . . you ride home, you just stop and get some Chinese and you soak in the bathtub, ya know. You don't go out. You don't smoke. You don't drink. You don't spend any money. When you get back to New York . . . boy you're mean and lean and you got a bankroll!"

CHAPTER SEVEN

Tiny Kline

"She was nude."
—Professor Janet Davis on Tiny Kline's appearance
in the cooch shows

"Tiny had always wanted to be a big-time circus star, but she
never rose to that stature."
— Professor Janet Davis

Disneyland is billed as the "happiest place on earth." Designed by Walt himself, the theme park opened in 1955. But it wasn't until 1961 that Tinker Bell would make her dramatic live debut at the park—flying from Sleeping Beauty's castle while fireworks exploded above her in the night sky. What the crowd below didn't know was that Tinker Bell was, in fact, a seventy-year-old former acrobat and burlesque dancer. Her name was Tiny Kline.

Tiny Kline was born Helen Deutsch in Hungary around 1891. She emigrated to America in 1905, when she was just fourteen. The ship's manifest from Ellis Island has her traveling with a dance company, but makes no mention of any family members.

Tiny lived and studied for a time in the Clara de Hirsch Home for Immigrant Girls. When she died in 1964, she left the bulk of her estate to the school in gratitude for "being my guardian when no one else in my family helped." The school was founded by German Baroness Clara de Hirsch with the promise to "improve the mental, moral, and physical condition" of the mostly Jewish immigrant girls and women, who had no other home or families.

Despite the school's positive influence on her, Tiny Kline was soon dancing burlesque in Altoona, Pennsylvania. It most certainly was not what the stern-looking Baroness de Hirsch was teaching her charges, though they did stress they geared their program to "train them for self-support."

Tiny decided to change her name from Helen Deutsch to the more elegant and French-sounding Helen Duchee. Like many immigrants at the time, Tiny wanted her name to "sound American." (She wouldn't get much more American than becoming Tinker Bell). Tiny kept the new name until she was teased and called a "douche bag."

By 1906, her sister Fanny had arrived in America and the two lived together. Fanny and the man she eventually married (a possible communist and the likely cause of a rift between the sisters) didn't approve of Tiny's career choices. "This was the relative who did the naughty things," noted Davis, who edited Tiny's memoir *Circus Queen and Tinker Bell*. In her will, Tiny leaves little to her sister.

Tiny was dancing in cooch shows that were paired alongside Wild West shows in the circus in 1911. She wore a heavily fringed outfit and opened with a series of slow, languid dances that would accelerate in pace throughout the show. Then there were the high kicks. "Tiny found it was very crowded, a very frightening space in some respect. She'd be behind the curtain and hear the barker. . . . You could hear the crowd, you could feel the crowd. Sometimes hands would be poking behind that curtain and that would freak her out," said Davis. Though Tiny would make it clear in her unpublished memoirs that she was not nude, Professor Davis, through her research, was assured she must have been.

Kline means "small" in Yiddish and in German. Tiny Kline stood only four feet eleven inches tall. She thought of herself as unattractive. Her body was compact and muscular. Tiny was told she looked too "ethnic" and too "Jewish." Although in her daily life she felt ugly, the cooch show gave her a sense of being desirable. Like others in burlesque, she found the whistles and howls of the men addicting. Hearing them, she could believe someone desired her. Audiences were vocal in their appreciation for her and her body.

Tiny refused to change much about her natural appearance when she was on stage, though she did agree to wear a platinum wig and pancake makeup to lighten her skin, which was "ruddy" like a farmer's completion. What she lacked in height, she made up for in determination and grit.

In 1913, she met the love of her life, rodeo trick horse rider Otto Kline. They met in the dining car. Otto Kline was a big shot with the Barnum and Bailey Circus, whose show involved vaulting from side to side over the back of his horse as it galloped at full speed. Tiny was still small time with the Cracker Jack Burlesque in Pittsburgh. They married two years later.

According to *Haunted Naperville* by Diane A. Ladley, they both claimed on their marriage documents they were American-born because Otto was German and at the time America was at war with Germany.

Just five weeks after the wedding, Tiny was back on the road with the Cracker Jack Burlesquers. The other women teased Tiny, telling her she should be knitting baby booties. During her last performance, the manager handed her an unexpected telegram: HUSBAND DIED IN RIDING ACCIDENT PLEASE ADVISE ON REMAINS.

In front of five thousand spectators at Madison Square Garden, the handsome, twenty-eight-year-old Otto had been riding his horse Kitty. The pair circled twice around the arena with the horse progressively running faster. Otto grabbed the front of his saddle. He began, like he always did, to swing over his horse, his feet tapping the ground on either side of Kitty. Otto's body didn't touch the saddle with each successive leap. Then, Otto lost his grip and flew head first, slamming his skull against the wooden sides of the arena. The sickening sound as his head struck the boards was heard "all over the Garden," according to the *New York Times'* coverage of the incident.

Otto's faithful horse Kitty stopped and stood by her motionless rider. He lived for only a few hours after the accident and died at Bellevue Hospital.

Tiny was grief stricken. On the train to New York, she was comforted by a minister's wife. At the morgue, she slipped off her young husband's wedding band and a handkerchief and kept them with her forever.

Several days after Otto's death, Tiny received a letter from him. He had posted it from Baltimore the day of his accident. Otto explained he had cut his hand while cleaning his saddle—a pick had jabbed into his hand. He said, "it shouldn't matter when I'm riding this afternoon. See you tonight." Tiny knew then that she had solved the mystery of why one of the best trick riders in the world had perished so violently, but it was of little comfort to her.

Months after her husband's death, Tiny decided to visit the show ground of Barnum's circus and saw another cowboy rider with her husband's horse, Kitty. Impulsively, Tiny threw her arms around the horse. By the end of the trip, Barnum managers hired her to ride in the parade, which didn't involve much. She worked a statue act, where women and some men performers wore grease paint and little else. They assumed a pose of classical statuary, usually wearing white or silver reflective paint. It was legal as long as they didn't move. Tiny performed in this way during her first year at Barnum's.

The circus was a very hierarchical group. The statues were on the lowest end of the scale. Their dressing room, such as it was, was in an isolated part of a crowded dressing tent, near the flaps. Occasionally stray men from the local town would try and peek their heads in for a free preview.

When the circus wintered, Tiny returned to burlesque. She found burlesque to be good, reliable work and obviously had no hang-ups about appearing in the "all together," though she denied she was. It was a steady source of income for her for thirty years.

Next, fearless Tiny did Roman riding—her feet straddling a pair of horses as they circled the arena at high speeds. She seemed to find her passion when she tried her hand at aerialist work. She worked with rings until Lillian Litzel told her, "You have a square neck and strong body; you should do the iron jaw." Lillian was the leading aerialist of the circus; she had a temper and the star power to have all her demands met (including her own private Pullman car). Tiny took Lillian's advice.

Working a few minutes at a time over several weeks, Tiny would hold in her mouth a thick leather strap and hang by her teeth. She noted in her unpublished autobiography that "once the neck gets use to taking the weight of the body, it's a difficult breaking-in process. It's great once the first couple months pass."

Tiny excelled at what was known as the Slide for Life. Many died attempting to perform the same feat she did daily. She would climb a rope to a tiny platform high above the crowd, and then put the strap in her mouth and slide, held only by her mouth, on a steel cable down to the bottom of the arena in mere seconds. She loved it.

The diminutive widow would continue both with burlesque and her aerial thrill act. Over the Steel Pier in Atlantic City, New Jersey, she would hang from a blimp ten feet in the air.

The year 1938 would be her last with the circus. Ringling Brothers was disrupted by a union strike and later joined forces with another circus. Many of the personnel were downgraded or displaced. Tiny wasn't allowed to do her iron jaw act and she retired, deciding she would rather not work at all if she couldn't do the thing she loved. She was in her forties.

Tiny had lived frugally and saved her money. She bought a house in Inglewood, California (Tiny would be buried at Inglewood Park, where coincidentally Lillian Litzel and Gypsy Rose Lee are buried). The neighborhood children were alternatively "terrified and fascinated by this incredibly fit woman who wore shorts and blouses tied at her waist and was always gardening." The woman who had performed hanging by her mouth without a net at great heights was terrified of cars and wouldn't drive. She bicycled everywhere.

In 1958, at the Los Angeles Coliseum, Tiny was doing her Slide for Life when Walt Disney saw the show. He thought Tiny would make the perfect Tinker Bell for his new theme park. He had wanted to incorporate the magical fairy into the park for some time and now saw the perfect opportunity.

Three years later, Tiny Kline began her nightly climb up the interior steps of the Matterhorn. Once at the top, she would get into a leather harness and attach herself to a cable. Davis relates that "when signaled she would let go and slide 168 feet above the ground to Sleeping Beauty's Castle. She would tap her wand in the air and a grand firework display would begin. She was seventy years old." Tiny Kline became Tinker Bell every night for the next three years until she quit mere months before succumbing to stomach cancer.

By this time, Tiny's hair was completely white. Perhaps this is what gave rise to the urban legend that Marilyn Monroe was the model for the petite fairy.

CHAPTER EIGHT
Those Marvelous Minskys

"The Minskys at best were crafty, ingenious producers;
at worst 'flesh peddlers.'"

—Rachel Shteir

"... The climate of that community has gone lower and lower
ever since the night they closed Minsky's and tried to
take our name away from us."

—Morton Minsky, *Minsky's Burlesque*

Ann Corio at the Winter Garden Theatre

The name is legendary in burlesque circles.

April 20, 1925, was immortalized first in book form and then in the 1968 film *The Night They Raided Minsky's*. The film was a mostly fictionalized version, based on a true incident involving stripper Mary Dawson (who danced as Mademoiselle Fifi) and the raid of a Minsky theatre that resulted in it later being shut down.

Interviewed about the film in the *Charleston Gazette* in 1975, Dawson claimed her character in the film differed from her in that she was never a stripper (she was an "exotic dancing Venus") and that her real-life father, who was depicted shutting down the club in the film, was actually a Quaker who had nothing to do with why Minsky's was shut down. Her father did make Mary quit the business several times, but finally gave up when he realized burlesque was in her blood.

In Morton Minsky's book about the family business, *Minsky's Burlesque*, Morton claims Mademoiselle Fifi stripped to her waist before entering the stage. She was a tableau artist (which was legal) and could *pose* nude as long as she didn't so much as wiggle an eyelash. If she moved something, she'd be promptly arrested.

At eighty-five, Mary Dawson was proudly teaching her twelve-year-old granddaughter her routine and boasting "I can still move every part of my body" as she twirled a green snake around her neck and shoulders.

The Minsky family came into the business in the early 1900s. Louis Minsky had four ambitious sons: Billy, Herbert, Morton, and Abe. The eldest son Abe started showing racy films in a Nickelodeon theatre on the Lower East Side. When Louis found out, he quickly shut him down, buying New York's National Winter Garden, where he allowed his precocious youngster to take over the sixth floor. If his son was going into the "naughty" business, he might have thought, he should at least go bigger and make some money.

The National Winter Garden was in an ethnic neighborhood. Abe began to produce burlesque shows after failing at showing films. Burlesque seemed to do the trick with the neighborhood's large immigrant population, and soon the Winter Garden was a hit. Brothers Billy and Herbert joined in the fun and profit.

Borrowing from what he saw at the Folies Bergère in Paris, Abe introduced the runway. The girls shook and shimmied among the sweating masses, invitingly an arms-length away.

The Winter Garden drew a large working-class crowd. (Ann Corio would later become the queen of the working class—perhaps she learned how to relate to the masses after her stint at the Winter Garden.)

At the time, there was nowhere else for immigrants to go for cheap entertainment that didn't require language skills they hadn't yet acquired. Barely clad girls were easily understood. The comedians with their broad physical humor were perfect for the menagerie of languages in the neighborhood. Legendary funny man Red Buttons (his straight man was Robert Alda) claimed that, for a comedian, graduating from Minsky's was like graduating from Harvard. It was a fertile training ground for the top rate—and not so top rate—comedians. Morton figures the reason audiences loved the comedians was that the material was already familiar (and this was in the 1930s). The audience didn't want new material. They were comfortable with the tried and true.

Burlesque, and Minsky burlesque, was made for the masses, the blue-collar crowd, the average Joe—and Jane, at least for a time—who wanted to be amused. Broadway was too expensive and didn't cater to their needs or tastes. Nowhere else did, except for burlesque.

To please Father Minsky, the brothers tried to keep their burlesque "clean;" however, they had to sell tickets and give their audience what they wanted.

"Theatres at that time were going broke," said stripper Betty Rowland. One-reeler movies were shown between the live show. "That's how they found out the stage show; Girls shows were a big hit."

It was brother Billy who introduced nudity into burlesque in 1925. Billy Minsky didn't invent strip. He just brought it out from the back room.

The youngest brother Morton soon joined the expanding enterprise. Between the four, they independently owned and operated dozens of theatres in New York, down to Florida, up to Chicago, over to Boston and Newark, and in many cities in between.

Because of the competition among the brothers, they kept pushing the nudity. "It was a competition to who could take off the most," recalled Betty Rowland.

The brothers Minsky were known for producing "stock" shows instead of being a part of the wheels operating at the time (Columbia Wheel, the American Wheel, and the Mutual Wheel) that traveled from theatre to theatre. The brothers created their own wheel: They figured how to turn out highly entertaining shows while drawing large audiences.

By the 1930s, Bernard Sobel was complaining Billy's girls were "grinding" on the floor along with the now "requisite bumps" expected in such a show. In the "old days," Sobel explained, the "hootch number" played right before the curtain came down. Now every other act was "filler-in for the strip numbers."

The Minskys transitioned burlesque from "an immigrant thing to being something of a must-see event. They drew in the literati. They advertised in New York. They were relentless promoters and self-promoters. They were responsible for making it an American form of entertainment."

In 1937, the Minskys appealed to Congress before the House Immigration Committee, with Herbert Minsky arguing that stripping should be "kept entirely American." There was a bill at the time to restrict foreign talent from invading American shores. Herbert told the committee that there were "100 to 150 burlesque theatres in this country doing their part employing vaudeville performers. We pledge ourselves not to employ foreign strip-tease artists in our cradle of American burlesque."

There had been nude women in Paris and throughout Europe, and American burlesque certainly borrowed from that. But what American burlesque had that nowhere else had was the actual removal of clothes. (Morton Minsky claims Josephine Baker copied Mae Dix's banana costume. Dix would peel the bananas off her skirt while she sang "Take a Look at This." Baker's act would make her a certifiable star when she exported her bananas to Paris.) Disrobing in front of the audience was an intimate act not seen before and done in a way obviously meant to titillate, which is what made the concept so shocking to some.

"The Minskys emphasized that a good strip-tease dancer must know exactly the right psychological moment to remove each garment. 'It is not just a matter of going on the stage and taking off clothes—it needs finesse.'"

Stripping implies getting ready for sex. The nude posing on Broadway stages was completely different. The "statutes" were removed. They were art, cold, lifeless, meant for only gazing upon. With stripping, there was an implied invitation, a more immediate intimacy, which is why it was frowned upon. These women appeared to be preparing for sex. They were making the gesture. And it was a palpable one in the theatre.

"It wasn't what you took off, it was the way . . . the sultry, the sauciness. The French were nude for years before us. Americans came up with the striptease," Dixie Evans said. "When Americans came up with the striptease, the French girls ran out and put on clothes. They were already nude."

The last showman of the line of impresarios was Harold Minsky, who, according to his former wife Dardy Orlando Minsky, used to carry a "bar" of little bottles of alcohol in his suitcase.

Harold was Abe's adopted son. He was born in 1915. At nineteen, Harold took over the business from his father. Every summer his parents went to Europe for vacation and the theatres would close due to the heat in New York City. Theatres weren't air-conditioned. The performers begged Harold to keep his doors open; the girls were broke and they desperately needed the money from the performances. So Harold stayed open, and though a ticket cost a dime, "he made over a million dollars." (This was possibly something of an exaggeration, but surely a sum large enough for Abe to hand over the reins.) "No one kept theatres open in

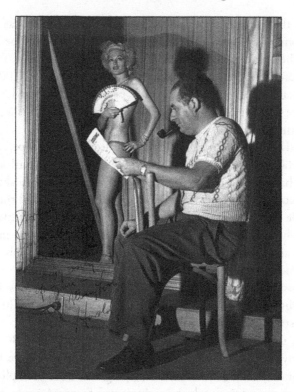

Stripper Dardy Orlando and her husband producer Harold Minsky

the summer. Legitimate theatres didn't have shows. The father retired. He said 'It's all yours,'" said Dardy Minsky.

"Harold was the first one to do nudity in a nice way," said Dardy. "When the father started it, there was no nudity. He hired girls and did a review. For two years it didn't make any money. One night a girl's strap broke, costume fell down, breast exposed. The next night there was a line around the building."

Harold would become responsible for discovering and grooming dozens of the most famous names throughout the 1930s into the '50s. Many owed their careers to his guidance. Harold claimed to have targeted future headliner fourteen-year-old Sherry Britton from an audition. By the mid-1940s the other Minskys were out of the business, and it was solely Harold running shows known for their large casts and elaborate productions.

Not only did Harold "find these sweet little girls and turn them into strippers," but he also employed and nurtured first-rate comic talents such as Phil Silvers, who credited Harold as being responsible for his success.

Dardy Minsky, Lili St. Cyr's youngest sister, was working as a showgirl, doing bits with the comics and stripping. She was working at Earl Carroll's when she met Harold at a party in New York. He was smoking a pipe, looking utterly conservative in a button-down Brooks Brothers and tweed suit. "I thought, 'Can't go wrong there,'" said Dardy. After a complicated romance due to Harold's controlling, busy-body mother who didn't like Dardy, the two finally married. Dardy soon gave up her career to raise two children and help Harold with the shows.

"Harold did hiring and firing. I would come up with ideas for shows and things," said Dardy.

"Mr. Minsky made every girl work and cooperate to make every girl's act look big," said Dixie Evans.

Once you worked for Harold, you knew you were in the big time. Harold was a prolific workaholic. "He had clubs all over the country, and would produce a show and take it to Havana." Some of the showgirls were so scared of traveling and of landing in an unfamiliar country that they got drunk on the plane before takeoff.

In 1956, Harold brought his brand of extravagant burlesque shows to Las Vegas, then still a desert town that Lili St. Cyr called "quaint." Harold, Dardy, and their two children moved there while he put on a show at the Dunes. He kept a chorus line, top-rate comedians, a snazzy band, and, of course, the star strippers. He did smashing business, for the first time making burlesque accessible to an upper-middle-class crowd. Originally presented with a six-week contract, Harold and Dardy stayed nine years. She dabbled in painting, holding some exhibitions, but hated bringing up children there. Except for the desert and horses, "everyone in Vegas in the '50s was either pit bosses or owners. You couldn't have a social life," she recalled.

Harold took a hands-on interest in the show and the strippers. Rita Grable remembered working for Harold in the 1950s and called him a "wonderful man." He told her he would make her the headliner of the show.

"He had the first show at Dunes that played burlesque. Harold brought a writer in and wrote a parody." Rita did a song, some spoof on a current hit. "It was like a Broadway show because he had comics and me and Carrie Finnell with tassels. She was wonderful. Older. Harold had them build a long runway."

Harold's sister-in-law and frequent Minsky headliner was Lili St. Cyr, who loved and admired Harold. She nicknamed him "Solid," because she considered him to be a solid citizen. She would do anything for Harold and vice versa. He painted her dressing room and installed a bed so she could sleep there at nights instead of returning to her hotel, garnering extra hours of much-needed sleep.

For Lili, men "would be lined up around the block," said Dardy. Harold would have to keep going back to Lili, asking her to add another show. Lili would pretend to think about it, then name all the pieces of a sterling silver set she wanted.

Harold would get her the sterling set along with baskets of cash. "She loved cash," Dardy recalled. And apparently Reed & Barton's Silver Baroque Sterling.

April March was the only act that ever starred for Minsky who didn't have to audition first. Harold later cut her act back, though, which she found offensive. "Sir," she said. "I do thirteen minutes." In response, Harold said, "Ms. March, seven will be sufficient. Always leave the audience wanting more.'" April would join Minsky at the bar after shows for cokes and talk every night. It became a ritual. He started buying her stockings, with a seam up the back of them. "Buying three boxes of 'em," she boasted.

Working in a Minsky show was "a lot of work," said Betty Rowland. There were four shows a day, seven days a week. "You get to practice a lot."

Once when stripper Lilly Christine—nicknamed the Cat Girl because of her feline moves; green, slanted, catlike eyes; and long, thick mane of platinum hair—was on stage, "a man in the audience fell out of the balcony. After the show Harold went up to him and, instead of asking him how he was, he says, 'How much do you want to do that for every show?' Always the showman!" Dardy laughed.

Harold "would have Dardy, believe it or not, check out the women's breasts, to see what kind of breasts they had," said Beverly Anderson. Harold was "too classy to do it himself," she explained.

Running a show wasn't easy. "Censors would come in," Dardy explained, "and see the first show and they they'd ask you to change stuff. We never had a problem." Unions were a whole other matter, but there was no getting around them and their hold in the theatre.

"Harold would stand out in front of theatres with money and the politicians would come by—unions were terrible. He'd pay them off. Unions [are the] biggest crooks." Harold was running two theatres in Chicago. Someone from the union called him at 8 a.m. and told him to hire two more men in the lighting booth, and their salary would have to be retroactive. Harold argued, truthfully, that there was no room. The union said "they can sit in the balcony in case of an emergency." Then the musicians' union called. "We want three more musicians in the pit." Harold argued that three more musicians wouldn't fit in the pit. The union told Harold, "They can sit outside in case you need them." Harold hung up and closed the theatre, and moved it all to New Jersey. "All you could do was give them money."

Harold wouldn't fly, so one time leaving New York, they stopped in Chicago on the way to Las Vegas and Dardy took the children to Marshall Fields. "We ran into three people who worked at our theatre. They were out of work. Selling shoes in Marshall Fields. I said, 'That's your union.'"

According to Dixie Evans, Harold once precipitated reconciliation between Dardy and her more famous sister, Lili. "Dardy looked just like Lili. Minsky would do anything Dardy asked." According to Dixie, Dardy "stole" Lili's bubble bath act and Lili, flying into Chicago, found out. The two didn't speak for months.

Dixie was working for Harold in Newark. After the show, Harold "made the sisters kiss and make up." He told Lili and Dardy, "'Now girls, you end this feud.'" Dixie remembered sitting around the bar afterward, doing an imitation of Marilyn Monroe's signature walk to the delight of Lili and Dardy. "Lili said, 'This is the way Marilyn walks.' And got up and did her version."

Dedicating his life to his business and running a first-rate show and a tight ship came with a price. Harold would divorce twice and have a serious drinking problem, according to Dardy. However, during his time in the wings, everyone who was anyone in burlesque worked for Harold Minsky.

In 1937, New York's Mayor LaGuardia banned burlesque and the name "Minsky" because it was synonymous with the filthy shows he wanted out of New York. With the expulsion of burlesque, Harold picked up his New York clubs and moved them to New Jersey, where burlesque thrived at the Empire and the Adams Theatres.

In 1970, Lili St. Cyr (by then Harold's ex-sister-in-law and once the reigning burlesque queen of Las Vegas) performed her last Nevada show for Harold at the Aladdin Hotel.

Dardy eventually divorced Harold, tired of his ever-present entourage of buddies that followed him and the relentless drinking at her Vegas home. Harold toured his shows in various dinner theatres around the country. He remained in Vegas, producing burlesque shows. He died in 1977, looking far older than his sixty-two years.

Harold changed the scope of a burlesque show like no one else. His productions had elaborate costumes and scenery and big lines of girls. When he died, there were no authentic burlesque shows left. Nor was there anyone around who knew how to produce a Minsky-type burly show. Lili once said, "If we had a few more Harold Minskys, burlesque would last forever."

CHAPTER NINE

The Peelers

"They didn't think highly of us; they thought we were a different breed.
Same attitude we have about hookers that hang on the corner."
—Maria Bradley

"Women would strip and the finale would be she would display
her breasts, which were usually beautiful."
—Renny von Muchow

"Vaudeville became burlesque with strippers," tells Nat Bodian. "They added the strippers to keep the men from going to the movies. The idea was: What reason was there, if you could go to a movie, to go to a live show? . . . And one of the answers was because it had naked women."

They were called strippers, peelers, bump and grinders, ecdysiasts (meaning "one who molts or sheds"), exotic dancers, stripteasers, and burlesque queens. During the Depression, work was plentiful for the burlesque performers. As Broadway shows closed, girls pounced on peeling for a living and comics crossed the avenue to work. It was steady employment, but "theatres could be the grungiest. Sometimes in bad neighborhoods. A lot of shows with little, if any, time off."

"Performers were always asking, 'Were strippers prostitutes?'" said Rachel Shteir, "and whenever strippers themselves were asked, they would always say, 'We don't really have time to be prostitutes—we're in rehearsals.'"

"A lot of people were of the opinion that you were a hooker," said Carmela, the Sophia Loren of Burlesque.

Many, like Georgia Sothern and Sherry Britton, started as young teens. It wasn't uncommon for mature-looking thirteen, fourteen, and fifteen year olds to lie about their age and get a job. Minsky, who hired Georgia, complained to her once, "'Georgia, you're acting like a child.' And she said, 'I am. I'm thirteen,'" laughed Dixie Evans.

Not all the girls who got into burlesque became as wildly famous as Sally Rand, who would perform in front of the Queen of England or, as her son said, dance for 17 million people in her lifetime.

There were hundreds of girls who joined burlesque for mere weeks, or as long as it took to buy "a Frigidaire or a car or something," Betty Rowland explained. A smaller percentage worked twenty to thirty years in the business.

They would not all would become "queens" of the stage, either. Some would have a few pictures in the girlie magazines, while others were regularly plastered on covers of *Cavalcade of Burlesque* or *People Today* and *Modern Man*. For some, it was a blip, a mere breeze across the stage, then marriage and normal life. For others, it was the highlight of their lives. They were defined by their time as strippers. For some, all that remains are photographs without a name or a story.

Once the ladies dropped their rhinestone G-strings for the last time, the burly fans quickly forgot their names and faces and they faded into obscurity.

"It's completely vanished; we have our striptease culture in the alternative lifestyle, but that's quite different. That isn't an industry. Burlesque was an industry, part of the entertainment machine," said Rachel Shteir. Most modern-day historians refer to the 1930s as being the "Golden Age" of burlesque, though in 1938, Sobel was bemoaning the fact that the current burlesque was a far cry from the "Golden Age" of the 1880s. The burlesque show was continually morphing and transforming itself. A burlesque show of the 1880s looked nothing like one in 1934, and the same would be said for shows twenty years later. The 1930s Golden Age was a dazzling, provocative, hilarious show. It was the burlesque we think of today, with star strippers and talented star comedians. It was a big show.

Most of what we know and celebrate about burlesque has all too much to do with the strippers. Shows would very quickly become tailored around the disrobing damsels. Everything was a prelude until the next bare-legged babe bumped across the stage. Even the co-feature's act was geared toward the much anticipated star stripper and the crescendo of the show, climaxing with the last few minutes of the feature's routine before the curtain closed.

During the 1930s, some of the legendary glamorous goddesses of stripping, as beautiful, if not more so, than any Hollywood movie star, were Ann Corio, the curvaceous and auburn-haired woman who ruled Boston's Old Howard theatre, and Gypsy Rose Lee, who raised the art of the stripper into a symbol of sassy intellect. That was part of her tease: *See I'm taking off my clothes, but I'm quoting Homer while I do it.*

Usually strippers were something to gaze upon and fantasize about. They were mere feet from the audience, accessible, tantalizing, fiery, forbidden, sexual. They were moving *objets d'art*. One could and did shout at them in the theatre, holler and stamp and masturbate over their lusciousness, but the stripper wasn't expected (and most didn't even want) to speak, though a few did. Georgia Sothern, Sherry Britton, and Lili St. Cyr and dozens more performed in everything from run-down theatres to glorious former vaudeville houses, ornate and gilded. They also took it off in chic cafes and nightclubs. The clubs were often a more posh setting amongst a mixed crowd that dressed elegantly and ordered cocktails. There was no booze in the theatres. In nightclubs, the stigma (for both the performer and the audience) was less pronounced, if it existed at all. Well, she's taking off her clothes, but it isn't *burlesque*. No one said they "snuck into" a nightclub and saw a stripper, as they did about going to the theatres.

In the nightclubs, men weren't masturbating under newspapers or in popcorn containers, but the experience wasn't without its seedy bits. Sherry Britton would be propositioned by men and women to join in on threesomes, and one couple wanted to take her out to watch pornos.

Sherry Britton at far right. The girls were expected to mingle with the audience.

Strippers in the Golden Age brought an element of glamour to the business. They were professionals and acted as such. They arrived with costumes and sheet music ready to go. Many brought a flourish of art to their performance, turning their relatively short time on the stage, anywhere from eight to fifteen minutes, into a memorable turn.

In the theatre in general—and it all varied—the exotics danced to three "trailers," or songs. Sequin, like most, danced "slow, medium and ending fast" to rouse her fans. The women relied on their fans. They needed men to return to the theatre. A full house was crucial to raising one's profile and salary.

About Tempest Storm, who danced wild, Dardy Minsky said, "She liked the audience to go crazy, so she'd ask for more money when she came back."

Some ecdysiasts were earning a living while others thought of their participation in burlesque as an investment; Tempest, Ann Corio, and Carrie Finnell were some of the better-known strippers who worked for decades. That took endurance, training, and professionalism, in addition to the obvious looks and charisma. Few had reputations for being divas or difficult.

**

Glamour was very important to Joan Arline (real name Connery). Like most young girls, she took dance classes. At the age of twenty, she was working as a private secretary when she decided to quit and try her chances as a chorus girl. Joan was "pulled out of chorus and made a soubrette." She did solo dance numbers and a specialty parade. "I stopped dead for someone taking a camera and I held a pose."

After thirteen months on the stage, she told her husband Don she wanted to do her own act. He was older and asked, "'Do you want to work your derriere off or be a star?' I wanted to be a star and make money. He said 'Go into burlesque.' I about died."

She was a tall blonde with long legs that would carry her from burlesque to performing in every Follies Show from Palm Springs to Branson, Missouri, well into her seventies. She did a strip at the Las Vegas Reunion that earned admiration from the other women I was seated with. "She's the real deal," they said.

Joan also began doing bits with the comedians Scurvy Miller, Harry Clexx, and Harry Conley. After she learned that a "star" stripper didn't do bits with the comedians, she stopped. Her agent at the Schuster Agency got her a job at the Palace Theatre in New York as the "extra added attraction," which was a step up from a talking woman (one who did bits with the comedians). "I did the crawl. Nothing's sexier than a woman crawling if she knows how."

She worried she would forget to take her clothes off. "I never forgot to take 'em off," she said with a great deal of pride. During our interview in her lovely, spacious home in Palm Desert, Joan was surrounded by her old luggage trunks, her costumes and photos of days past. She had carefully preserved her life in burlesque.

One night while working a club, her husband Don sneaked in to watch her strip. He was sitting at the bar between two guys that appeared to know each other. One of the gentlemen poked Don while Joan was on stage doing her thing. The man said, "Boy I'd like to get into *that* tonight." Joan's husband turned to him and said, "Maybe you'd like to, but *I'm* going to."

Joan was a disciplined dancer and would practice in front of a mirror to see all her angles. Fifty years after her opening, she could still fit into a lace black corselet that showed her lean figure. A corselet was a bra-girdle undergarment popular in the 1940s.

She would have her share of adventures. On another night in a club, she got cold and "something popped out." Her pastie shot off into the audience. "I was so embarrassed. I had to go retrieve it."

This was not an uncommon occurrence, but that didn't make it less embarrassing for any of the girls. "One time one of my pasties flew off and hit a guy in the eye," laughed Candy Cotton. Tee Tee Red added: "They got tape on the inside. You always made sure they were on good."

**

Chorus girl Joni Taylor was petite, dark haired, and down to earth. At fourteen, she snuck into to the Casino Theatre in Pittsburgh. She applied as an usher. "I wanted to be on the stage. I had danced since I was three years old." She did a timestep and they hired her and put her in the chorus. "I didn't tell my mother."

After three months, however, her mother found out, stormed down to the burlesque theatre, and told the owners her age. They let Joni go. But two years later, she was back, again lying about her age, saying she was eighteen. She was hired. There were twenty-two girls in a line. Ten show girls did nothing but pose on pedestals; they were taller than Joni, who was five feet six inches tall. When the captain of the line retired, they replaced her with Joni.

Eventually Joni stripped. Usually the stage manager named the strippers. The house singer decided she would be known as the "Tantalizing Joni Taylor."

"I worked with them all," Joni said, naming strippers Rose La Rose and Blaze Starr. "You're usually with a set show for five or six weeks. Sometimes you don't see people for many years." Joni herself would never be a star stripper, but she was an excellent talking woman.

Joni also did a lot of tassel work. She would lie on the floor and twirl up. "Play around and hope you learned you could do it. You watched other strippers. I loved to work fast. If I stood still they could really see me," she said.

**

Kitty West, aka Evangeline the Oyster Girl, had them lining up on Bourbon Street in New Orleans to see her emerge from a giant oyster. The tourists "weren't gonna leave until they saw Kitty come out of that oyster shell," said Dixie Evans.

Kitty West was born June 8, 1930, in Sugarloaf, Mississippi. Her name was Abbie Jewel Slawson and her mother was a distant cousin of Vernon Presley, Elvis's father (Elvis would indeed catch her strip act). At three years old, she was working in the cotton fields. Her beloved mama would put stockings on her arms to protect her. She saw her mama give birth in the cotton fields. "And it's because of her I wanted to change everything," she said.

Kitty's parents were sharecroppers; they were poor and she had half a dozen brothers and sisters. "I always dreamed of being famous when I was small. I'd go behind trees and dance while we picked cotton. My little colored friend taught me movements and steps that you can't be taught," Kitty said in her smooth-as-honey voice.

As a young girl, she got a job in an ice cream parlor, making a dollar a day to pay for her dancing lessons. She was molested by a man there. Then she went to school to become a nurse. Her father abandoned the family and his responsibilities, so it fell to Kitty to help her mother financially. She started dancing at clubs, earning twenty dollars a night, which was "great money." She would eventually earn $1,500 a week.

In 1947, sixteen-year-old Kitty moved to New Orleans to become a nurse. She was walking in the French Quarter when a man stopped her. "I looked innocent and country," she said. He said to her, "I've never seen anyone like you. Where are you from?" He was the emcee at the Casino Royale and he hired her, designing a headline act for her.

It took six months before she worked in front of an audience. She learned to walk and to ballet. To Kitty it felt like "being reborn again."

"Someone got sick and couldn't go on. 'Do me a favor Kitty and go on in her place.' I was scared to death. It was packed. Standing room only. So I did. I went on, and the house, it was nothin' but roarin'. I was scared because I could see my grandfather staring at me. He was a minister and I thought the devil was gonna get me because I had sinned ...

"I went and I had to talk to a priest and a Lutheran minister and a Pentecostal minister. And they said, 'It's all within you, in your soul and your heart. You're not sinning. You're doing an act. You know the difference between right and wrong.' I said, 'But I'm showing my body.' He said, 'Well that's you. That's your conscience. That's what you have to deal with. You can find peace within yourself. I had to come to terms with a lot of things."

Kitty is a woman of enormous pride and dignity. There were things she would not do. "I did not take off the bottom. I didn't have to. . . . In my day, we were called exotic dancers. I was respected highly from all walks of life, but I do know that some of the girls and a lot of the places were not. . . . Garrison would raid the places all the time because they wouldn't wear pasties, and he would close them down. They didn't have to raid me." She wore a net bra and wide panties to avoid breaking any laws she said. "Garrison was the DA in New Orleans. The night life, he was against it. And he thought naturally exotic dancers were the ruination of Bourbon Street."

Kitty would work through the 1940s and '50s, becoming a tourist attraction in New Orleans. At the time, "Bourbon Street wasn't seedy. I wouldn't even go now. Back then, you saw so much glamour, so much beauty. Movie stars would come to town and go to the back of the Casino, the bar. Casino Royale was one of the nicest places. It was high class."

Kitty despaired over what had happened to burlesque and the strippers. "Like monkeys swinging from a pole. They come out naked and they got off naked. What are you gonna applaud for? It's a disgrace the way it's turned and changed. They're not sophisticated anymore. . . . You didn't have to strip; it all goes back to poise. We didn't have to show our private parts or strip down naked to be appealing or sexy. The tip of a finger was important. How you rub your shoulder."

Kitty described her own act, which broke records throughout the industry:

"It was a story. 'We take you on a mythical trip to the bayous of Louisiana. Where deep in the mist lies the Lady in Waiting who will come out every one hundred years during mating season. Is it that time?' Then the shell would open slowly. With one leg coming up, then I would lift myself up and I would stand up. Then I would step out of the shell into the audience looking for my mate. And I would search in vain, dancing all around the stage. I kept looking and finally I'd spot my man, but I couldn't have him and I knew that because he was taken, and I was still waiting, and if I didn't find him I'd have to go back to the shell and be doomed for another hundred years. In the end is where I didn't find my mate and I had to go back to the shell without being mated."

Her act was eight minutes.

"You have to incorporate your whole body into the act—that's the difference between a monkey on a pole. I worked and rehearsed most of the time. You had to drive in those days to tour." It was harder in those days, traveling with her entourage of manager, booking agent, maid, trunks of wardrobe, and the shell, which opened "about as big as a sofa," but she could manage it with one arm. It had a mechanism where you could touch it and it'd open slowly.

When her oyster act premiered, she thought something was missing. She had a formula made up and dyed her waist-length hair green. She did this for one or two years, but then learned that she'd gotten skin poisoning from the dye. She then went blonde. "[I'm] naturally dirty dishwater brown. I always wore white gowns, with boas with silver in it." She always dressed in a white evening gown when she went out to dinner. Kitty patterned herself after Gypsy, who was a friend. "I thought she was fantastic," she said.

She had her first child, then quit dancing for two years, and then went back. She had a new shell made. She worked the Sho Bar in New Orleans along with flamboyant stripper Blaze Starr. Kitty's husband was good friends with Governor Earl Long.

"I don't care for Blaze. . . . Blaze Starr," she narrowed her eyes. "In her film [Blaze] wanted to copy my oyster shell and that's why she had the clam, because I would have sued her. My act was copyrighted—even today. I had my lawyers send her a letter."

In 1949, Kitty had her picture in *Life Magazine* chronicling an onstage cat fight with Divena, a stripper who peeled in a glass box filled with water. A plethora of "Divenas" had been on the carnival circuit, and they appear to be somewhat mythical, like Little Egypt. According to *Girl Show* by Al Stencil, the Divenas performed underwater strips, advertised as "the world's loveliest feminine form." There was an abundance of them.

Kitty explained that "Divena was from California. She came in and it was a publicity stunt, but I was the last one to know and so was she. Mr. Lyle says, 'Kitty, we have somebody coming in.' He planned this. He says, 'She's gonna take top billing.' I said. 'Mr. Lyle, that's not what my contract says.' He put her on and really ran a big ad in the paper telling everybody about Divena from California, underwater strip. All this time wanting to get me stirred up."

And on Divena's second or third night, Kitty became infuriated. "[Lyle] says, 'I'm gonna have to let you go and she's taking over.' I got the fire ax and went out there and busted that [Divena's tank] into a jillion pieces. . . .

"*Life Magazine* and everybody was there shooting. That's when he told me it was all a joke. I even lent her a suit to wear to court. [Divena] was gonna sue me. I had to straighten that out. She continued her act for a few more weeks. I went back to being the star. She went back to California. And I think she got married."

Divena's real name was Clarice Murphy. *Life Magazine* captured an action-packed picture of Kitty as she broke Murphy's tank and the water spilled across the stage. It was phenomenal publicity.

Unfortunately, Kitty's oyster has been lost. It, along with all her memorabilia, was destroyed in Hurricane Katrina. She showed me her scrapbooks covered in toxic filth. Pictures were torn, faded, and now irreparable.

**

When a girl chose to get into burlesque, it was because she sought to see her name in lights. April March was one type of girl, a raven-haired beauty, short and lush, born with the very unstripperlike name of Idella in Oklahoma City. She took ballet lessons as a child, "as all young girls did. I wanted to be an actress when I grew up. I wound up in burlesque," she said.

Alexandra the Great spoke highly of April March. "April was Class with a capital C. . . . She suggested more with her eyes than she did with her body."

Lying about her age, April got a job selling flowers and cigarettes in a club in Oklahoma City. The club had exotic dancers. She wondered how the women could live with themselves after taking their clothes off in such a fashion in public. One night, a man literally bumped into her and said, "Excuse me, are you in the show here?"

She told him no.

"You ought to be in show business," he told her.

She asked him if he owned a nightclub. "Yes, in Dallas. If you ever decide to get into show business, here's my card," he said.

"You can put me in the movies?"

"Oh, that might come later."

"So off to Dallas I went," she told me.

The man, Barney Weinstein, was Abe Weinstein's brother. Abe owned the Colony Club, a classy joint in the Dallas downtown area. Barney owned the Theatre Lounge.

The ravishing April knew she was going to Dallas to strip. She wanted to be in the movies and figured this was the first stop.

Barney had a girl make her a costume. One day, as she was rehearsing with the band, Barney proclaimed, "We've gotta come up with another name. . . . I've got it. April March is your new name."

"But March comes before April," she protested.

"Not in your case," was his response.

April was a nervous wreck the first time she stripped. She made eighty-five dollars a week. Her parents didn't know. "They thought I was tap dancing," she said.

April March

In 1953, Taffy O'Neil had a dry cleaning route. She met a dancer and saw her show. "I thought the money sounded good." She was then introduced to an agent, with whom she would stay for the next nineteen years. Her first job was in a club run by a married couple. The man was a drummer by trade and he practiced with her two days a week for six weeks. He asked her to gain ten to twenty pounds. She drank banana shakes, but couldn't gain the weight.

Her first strip was at a club in Santa Monica. The bartender introduced her. The club was for "people going in or out of the business, to get them on stage." She danced behind the bar and then took her makeup case and went home. This was something her agent advised her to do so she'd avoid being after hours in the clubs. From there, she moved on to better venues.

She found the work "physically rewarding. The endorphins light you up like you're in love. A good, invigorating feeling."

A newspaper took her picture and ran a story on her titled "Mother by Day, Stripper by Night." They took pictures of her son and had her pose as though she was ironing—an activity she never performed.

**

La Savona is a bewigged, heavily accented, tiny woman. She was born in Czechoslovakia. She was young when the Germans took over during World War II. At the end of the war, she met a fellow dancer who then asked her to partner with him. At fifteen, she was in the chorus of a ballet in the opera. The duo danced ballet all over Europe. When she arrived in America, she tried to do ballet work, but "there was no such thing," she said. She didn't think anything was wrong with stripping; the only problem was "they wanted bosom, big bosom. I don't have big bosom."

**

By most accounts, Zorita was not considered "glamorous." In many pictures, she looks as if she could, and would, kick the daylight out of anyone staring at her so much as cross-eyed. Zorita could be aggressive and raunchy. She was a savvy, tough talking bisexual who charged men stock in General Motors to sleep with her.

"Her real name was Ada," said her protégé Tee Tee Red. "Tough with a good heart."

Zorita died in 2001. Those I talked to remembered her mostly for working with snakes. She ended up in Florida, wearing muumuus. Zorita was a friend and admirer of Sherry Britton. Among Sherry's things is a note from Zorita ("Memories, Love Zorita," her "Z" drawn like a snake with tongue and eye) and a pile of pictures, including a newspaper article with Zorita in her later years, swathed in fur, a shrunken white-haired old lady with a belligerent look in her eye.

If press articles are to be believed, Zorita was working in the carnival at seventeen. "I'm not the intellectual type," she had said. She was married at least three times and had a daughter. Articles claimed she was only five feet three inches tall and weighed 135 pounds. She appears taller and heavier in photos, though.

"I had some fun times with Zorita," said April March. "I worked several clubs in Miami. She bought a club from Martha Raye. Zorita was a great party gal. She had an old vintage Rolls Royce. When any celebs came to town, naturally they went to Zorita's. Judy Garland, Desi Arnaz . . . One night we went to a restaurant for breakfast after the show. Judy Garland was there—quite inebriated. Zorita was flamboyant, fun-loving. I never got close to her snakes."

Terry Mixon was working the Old Howard in Boston when Zorita appeared on the bill. "Zorita came through. I was scared, I didn't work that week. I have a phobia of snakes." At first, Zorita did, too.

Zorita claimed she was terrified of snakes. They "drive me up the wall," she had said. A snake charmer helped rid her of her phobia by giving her two snakes. Although she beat her fear, she claimed to never grow fond of her snakes. "To me, they were like part of my costume," she said.

**

The peelers came from all over America, an inordinate amount from the rural, poor south. According to Dixie Evans, "Most all came from hard back-

Chorus girls rehearsing downstairs at a burlesque theatre

grounds. Yes. I think about all of us, like me raised with no father, no money. Most girls came from that."

Stripping, working in burlesque, was a way for these young girls to make something of their lives. And, though now what little we know of so many of them comes from yellowing pictures in old magazines, they were *someone* in their time.

CHAPTER TEN
It's a Mad, Mad World

"The comics were the main thing in burlesque. Not the woman."
—Joan Arline

"You could see the sweat flying off them."
—Alan Alda on standing backstage

Comedians on stage

Straight: Too bad about Molly losing her youth.
Comic: Why, has she found another one?

Straight woman: I wonder if Jack still loves me.
    Next straight woman: Of course, sweetie, why should he make you an exception? (*Uncensored Magazine*)

A burlesque show was the "best school for the comedians," touted author Sobel.

According to Chris Costello, "Burlesque people are different; you show them, you talk about the old skits, you talk about the circuit and they come alive. It was the training ground. There is no training ground today. The circuit honed their craft."

Early burlesque would have two or three top bananas. "Top banana meant you were *the* comic that carried the whole show," explained Mike Iannucci. Every comic would have a straight man. "Between strips, the comics would come out. There would be a second banana (or a feature comedian) on the bill with his partner, or he would do bits with the talking women."

If any of the comedians didn't go over well, the audience would scream "bring on the girls," remembers Harry Lloyd. "That was part of the fun of a show."

Dixie Evans said many of the comics started in little Jewish vaudeville houses and then joined burlesque shows. Although this was the way many comics made their living, the majority of comics denied being involved in burlesque.

"[There was] always competition on the stage. You always want the best spot, etc." said Alan Alda. There was as much rivalry between the comedians as between the strippers. In H.M. Alexander's *Strip Tease*, the author noted how "comics would rehearse new bits in a corner so rivals in the same show won't copy it."

Harry Lloyd, who grew up on the circuit watching his father, Eddie, perform his comedy, said that this was a very frequent occurrence. "They all claimed they wrote every scene. A young comic, long time ago, he'd have ten scenes. Others would steal it and adapt to that scene and claim it was theirs. They would bitch about it. 'I did that scene fifty years ago.'"

Straight man Lee Stuart agreed with Harry. "They all had a different style, [but there were] a lot of copycats. Everyone's doing everyone's material."

Milton Berle was one man who was so notorious for stealing material, he made it a part of his act.

"They took old comedy skits and found a way to present it in a fresh manner that kept them and the audience alive," remembered Alan Alda.

This list of names that staggered through burlesque is impressive. Will Rogers, W. C. Fields, Ed Wynn, Phil Silvers, and Red Skelton (son of a circus clown) were just a few. Bobby Clark was known for his round "glasses," which were thick black rings of paint drawn around his eyes. Danny Kaye toured with Sally Rand and Joey Yule (Mickey Rooney's pop) worked the circuit for years. There was Jimmy Durante and Fatty Arbuckle, who performed with the Merry Maidens Burlesque. Joe DeRita, who took the original Curly's place in the Three Stooges, trained in burlesque. Jerry Lewis's dad started as a burlesque comedian. Jackie

Gleason was the feature comic at the Empire Theatre in Newark at an impressive 260 pounds.

In the 1890s, a young W. C. Fields joined a traveling burlesque company as a juggler. As so many of the comedians would, he met his future wife on the job.

In 1903, Al Jolson got his start at the age of fifteen with the Dainty Duchess Burlesquers. Unfortunately not all names are remembered today. Joey Faye, though he worked for more than sixty years with Gypsy Rose Lee and Abbott and Costello and counted Phil Silvers and Rags Ragland among his contemporaries, is largely forgotten. So, too, is Irving Benson. Names like Stinky Fields and Boob McManus mean little today.

Harry Lloyd recalled one man who many no longer connect with the world of burlesque. "Jess Mack was a straight man who became an agent, he booked you." Jess Mack was also a publisher for *Cavalcade of Burlesque Magazine,* which promoted stories about his clients, most of which were a bunch of fake stories simply written to promote the performers.

The pace on the circuit was demanding and the lifestyle was often unhealthy. Many comedians, though already old, looked decades older after working in burlesque. Author Martin Collyer recalls comedian Joe E. Lewis doing twenty shows a day. There was "a lot of drinking, smoking, gambling, cursing," Alda recalled.

Rags Ragland was a notorious boozer. He joked that "burlesque was just a way to pay for his drinks."

The routines were old, tired, and familiar almost from the beginning. When Red Buttons started in television, the skits he used had the audience in stitches. But they had been playing in burlesque theatres for over fifty years. The bits were familiar enough that the audience expected and enjoyed them. Johnny Carson reintroduced another generation to standards such as "crazy house" and the "school room" scene on *The Tonight Show.*

Rita Grable said that "Johnny Carson did it several times in his show, people running in and out, doors opening and closing, girls coming in."

The Crazy House was classic and known for its crossovers. A comic would be in bed, a girl would walk by. Another comic would come out from somewhere. Comics would be going crazy trying to figure what was going on. In the school room scene, Ann Corio played the teacher and the comics were the students. Ann was good friends with Johnny Carson. "He loved the burlesque comedy and did some of the crossovers and sketches with us. Johnny loved Ann," said Mike Iannucci.

"People would laugh their sides out at these silly skits," recalled Dixie Evans.

"They created illusion to be seen from the front," Alda said, recalling how he would watch them work from the sides and from his vantage, he could see them work and he could see them thinking. But from the front, all appeared flawless.

Morton Minsky wrote that by 1919, the bits were stale. But "ritual was ingrained" in the humor. Frequent targets of the gags were homosexuals and the mentally ill, as well as various ethnic groups.

Red Buttons bookended a certain era of burlesque, starting as a sixteen year old with Robert Alda as his straight man on the circuit. He ended his long run in 1942 when he was raided on the stage of Minsky's *Wine, Women, and Song.* It was the last burlesque show in New York. Mayor LaGuardia had finally succeeded in booting bare burlesque bosoms off Broadway.

Buttons found his first wife in burlesque, a stripper named Roxanne.

He had his own show in 1952, *The Red Buttons Show,* which would boast among its writers Neil Simon. Three years later when the show was canceled he was considered a has-been, though only thirty-six and rich. He continued in nightclubs and films, later winning an Academy Award for the 1957 film *Sayonara,* in which he played opposite Marlon Brando.

The comics' bits were slightly naughty and absurd. It's hard to imagine laughing at many of them today. For example, this is a sketch Harry Lloyd recited to me:

Straight: Hello there, bud.
Comic: 'Bud?' Do I know you?
Straight: No, sir.
Comic: Do you know me?
Straight: No, sir.
Comic: Well, let's keep it that way.
Straight: Alright, fella.
Comic: 'Fella?'

Not that the audiences always laughed. Sometimes the baggy-pants were simply a painful prelude while waiting for the exotics to transform the stage with their tantalizing flesh. The men in the audience would holler "bring on the girls." (And in turn, the girls heard their fair share of, "take it off.")

Judge Oliver Wendell Holmes used to come weekly to the Gaiety theatre with an armload of newspapers. He read them when the comics were on, waiting patiently for the strippers.

"You know why, why would people come to see a burlesque show at noon? Are they really coming to see the comics at noon? My guess is some of those matinee performances were deadly and then the comics would really be entertaining one another rather than the audience. No wonder they drank. They were skilled artists, and imagine getting up doing this amazing thing, and there's someone saying, 'Where are the girls?' It wasn't always wonderful for the performers," said Alan Alda.

Joan Arline added, "It was the satire of life. That was what every bit was."

Renny von Muchow, however, said "the humor was great and simple."

Largely based on broad physical humor, one didn't need to have a PhD to understand what it meant when a pretty girl walked by and the comedian's tie would rise up. All manner of props could elevate in the room of a pair of baggy britches that were the uniform of the top bananas. It was humor with a common denominator for the working class crowd. It wasn't elitist. It wasn't pretending to be witty and sophisticated. It was raw, basic laugh-out-loud gags.

"Scurvy [Miller] would get a little silly. He'd pour from a bottle down by his penis. You learned timing," said Joan Arline. "And to hold pose as [the liquid] peaks and comes down then you could say your next line. You couldn't cut his laugh, he'd kill you."

She added that "Scurvy Miller . . . was an elegant guy, really a very sweet nice man, and then he'd take his teeth out."

Stripper Joan Arline doing a bit with comedian Scurvy Miller

"Billy 'Boob' Reed would come out and have this beautiful girl at the table and 'Sure, have a little drink honey.' And he'd be getting her drunk. Then he'd hold a bottle and that was a burlesque trick, you hold a bottle up and you spit it out about five feet while you're doing it." Or he'd be "getting sloppy drunk, she'd have to carry him off," stated Renny von Muchow.

He added, "Peanuts Bohn had a funny long coat and a funny hat and someone would poke fun at him and he'd go, 'What the hey.' Never say 'hell.' But they got around that. And Billy "Boob" Reed would say 'You god daaa' and he'd never say the word 'goddamn' or something like that."

"You go past the comics' room and they'd always have a big piece of wax paper on their trunk, a big raw onion and a big piece of limburger cheese. Oh boy. And a picture of Red Skelton," said Dixie Evans.

Betty Rowland recalled, "They had fun teasing the girls. 'Cuz they had to follow the girls."

According to Joan Arline, "Harry Clexx was one of the funny ones. [He'd turn to you with] his eyes crossed and he's saying, 'Oh my God, my little pecker's hanging out,' to you quietly, and you're supposed to not smile. He'd do everything he could to break you up. But God help you if you broke up."

"Comedians would blackout their teeth to break you up. They were always trying to take you out, you know, a comedian's a comedian. What they are on stage, they are off stage," said Maria Bradley.

Betty Rowland said, "People loved the comics. A lot made it. Some went into Broadway then into burlesque, then TV, then legit shows."

Through the years, burlesque would continue to poke fun at ethnic stereotypes, with the humor becoming broader. Because burlesque humor was obvious and universally appealing, the movies began to borrow from it, including the Keystone Cops who stole their slapstick style directly from burlesque.

Actor Alan Alda, son of straight man Robert Alda, recalled how often he would be thrust into a scene. Red Buttons and others "would take me on stage when I was six months old and I would pee on them and they'd have stories to tell for the rest of their lives."

He was also part of the schoolroom sketch, sitting in a high chair with a bell that he rang. The comics played students. "They did private jokes. Because the audience hadn't come to see them, they'd come to see the strippers. They told me, Phil Silvers and Rags Ragland, I was ringing the bell on all their punch lines. They thought that was hilarious. It didn't matter about the audience."

Another time a couple comics decided to play a trick on Robert Alda's partner, Hank Henry, while he was performing a solo sketch. He was a drunk in a bar that was going to rob a safe, but he was so drunk he could barely make it over to the safe. "They put me inside the safe," Alda recalled. "I'm watching through a crack. I can remember. I can still see the light coming through the crack. It's a three- or four-minute silent pantomime of the skit. My heart is racing. I'm three! The comics said to me, *Step out and say 'father'*—another joke I don't get. He

[Henry] gets over, he opens it, I step out in this little squeaky voice and say 'father.' He breaks up, everyone else breaks up. The audience is completely confused. . . .

"Afterwards, here comes the company manager." Egged on by the same comedians, they told little Alan to ask for ten cents for being in the scene. "I go up and say, 'Can I have ten cents for today's show?' 'No, you can't kid.'"

Rags Ragland, born in 1905, was a legendary burlesque comedian, known both for his formidable talent and his antics off stage. He was only forty years old when he died after years of abusing alcohol. At the time of his death, he looked at least a decade older. Well respected and admired, he counted among his friends Frank Sinatra, Phil Silvers, and Orson Welles. Rags was a former boxer who became a house comedian with Harold Minsky, who cannily signed him to a contract for several years. He towered at six feet five inches and was a notorious ladies' man. Rags was good pals with Georgia Sothern (whom he pursued romantically, but she wasn't interested) and discouraged her from dating Errol Flynn, though she didn't listen.

The highlight of his life, he claimed, was dining with President Theodore Roosevelt at the White House with his buddies, restaurateur Toots Shore and Frank Sinatra.

His act was playing a "professional dumb guy." However, he was noted for his intelligence and he was, in real life, a gentleman.

According to New York journalist Jack O'Brian, Rags knew he was going to die and did so bravely (in 1946) after lying in a coma for days due to kidney failure. Sinatra would sing at his service in Hollywood.

"Dick Richards was a comic Romeo," Maria Bradley remembered. Richards was married to stripper and talking woman Lorraine Lee. "Funny guy, and friendly. He wanted to go out with everybody. A sweetheart though. He was married to a talking woman, always taking the girls out," Bradley said. Richards was described as gnome-like in a black derby and oversized overcoat.

Dick was born Richard Gluck. He, like so many who didn't have a "big name," worked more than thirty years, starting in 1939 in burlesque, never moving on like some of his contemporaries. He started at the Eltinge Theatre in New York on 42nd Street. He considered burlesque a stepping stone to greater things, though nothing more ever happened. His wife Lorraine said they had never retired; they just moved into dinner theatre and kept on performing. His income in burlesque never kept him flush—between gigs he would play the piano in nightclubs—but he loved it.

Gus Schilling was a rubbery faced comedian—think Jim Carrey. Schilling was a hard drinker and smoker, a protégé of Orson Welles who cast him in *Citizen Kane*. In the burlesque houses, he played nervous and confused characters. Gus and stripper Betty Rowland lived together and claimed to be married, although they weren't. Betty says he was married to someone else. His drinking would cause her to eventually leave him. Schilling died of a heart attack just short of his forty-ninth birthday, his face marred by years of hard living.

Bert Lahr was quoted in *Uncensored Magazine* as saying, "I still credit everything to my training in burlesque." Ironically, he was performing in a Broadway musical titled *Burlesque* when Hollywood came calling. His co-star was P. S. Ruby, whom the same talent scouts said lacked ability. P. S. Ruby would change her name and go on to an enormously long and successful career as Barbara Stanwyck. Stanwyck, even more ironically, would go on to star in Samuel Goldwyn's *Ball of Fire*, stealing Betty Rowland's act, costumes, and name. Betty sued, unsuccessfully, though it made for good publicity.

Former boxer Billy Hagan was known as "Cheese 'n' Crackers" because that is the line he would shout when a beautiful dame sashayed onstage. His father, said to be a religious man, used the expression instead of cursing. It made Hagan a star. He would play with his vocal pitch, squeaking his lines out in a high voice, then suddenly dropping it to somewhere below his solar plexus when a girl entered the scene. He worked in burlesque until he was an old man, dying at age ninety-seven.

Happy Hyatt (Herman Hyatt) was a fat guy—over 300 pounds—who wore a derby, rolled his eyes and spoke with a gravelly voice. He sang loudly backstage. He retired after an infection in his foot required his leg to be amputated.

Lady Midnight's father was a well-respected comedian by the name of Monkey Kirkland. "He started as a dramatic actor. He was a very handsome man and a ladies' man. He started out as a chorus girl—nobody knew he wasn't a girl." Lady Midnight sometimes was his talking woman.

"I did straights for Monkey," Lee Stuart said. "Monkey was one of the funniest I ever worked with. Monkey had a saying that everybody stole. The straight man would be chasing him around and Monkey would stop all of a sudden [and say,] 'just be careful; I'm gonna flick a booger on you.'" The humor, though juvenile, never failed to garner laughs. Monkey would drop a pinto bean on the stage then step on it making a fart sound. He "was a good singer; he did moan and low," Stuart said.

Monkey worked up until his death in a car accident. He ran a stop sign and was hit by an oncoming car. "People had to pull him out," said his daughter, Lady Midnight. (Lady Midnight would suffer her own devastating car accident in 1969, where she broke most of her bones including a savage break of her left hip.)

Eddie Lloyd was a typical lifer. He performed his entire professional life as a second banana. The "best second banana," bragged his son, Harry.

Monkey Kirkland

Born in 1892 in New York of immigrant parents, Eddie Lloyd would meet his future wife on a show. She was in the chorus. He worked with everyone who came up through the ranks: Alda, Silvers, Ragland, Gus Schilling, Abbott and Costello, Harry White, Irving Benson, and Monkey.

Harry used to go with his father Eddie to Milt Schuster's office. Schuster was the leading burlesque booker at the time. Eddie Lloyd was a "Booster for Schuster." In the 1940s and '50s, "you had to bring a cigar. You weren't welcome without it. All the comedians brought it," Harry said.

Harry was literally raised backstage "on the wheel." He was on trains all the time. It was "exciting. I grew up on Chinese food," Harry said. He would knock on the doors of the chorus girls and call out "Are you decent?" They called him "Sonny."

He remembers his parents tried to keep him away from strippers at a young age. But he claims his proximity to them was harmless and had no lasting effects.

And though it was a "rough life," Harry said that Eddie had loved it. When not hauling his family with him, Eddie traveled the wheel. He would be gone for six weeks at a time, a different town every week.

Lloyd was noted for an eccentric dance. His costume consisted of baggy pants, a large tie, an untucked shirt and oversize plaid coat topped with a derby hat. Lloyd would come out, dance around, and for the finale he would squat down doing small steps across the stage. "So all you saw was a coat, like a cone moving across the stage. It got a tremendous hand."

Eddie and his straight man on stage: A pretty girl walks by, Eddie would purr.

Comic: She's got TB.

Straight: What?

Comic: Two beauts.

"They would be so entertained by that and it was harmless. A different era. That was the nature of the humor," Harry explained. "Most scenes involved a young lady walking across the scene and double entendre."

Eddie worked until his seventies, dying with a trunk-load of "bits." A lot of the bits by then had been transferred to film and television by burlesque comedians like Phil Silvers. "The humor and whole burlesque was fun, not porn, nothing of that nature. It wasn't dirty."

In 1939 or 1940, Eddie went to Hollywood to "break into movies. . . . It didn't happen. He never wanted to call a comedian, like friend Phil Silvers, or anyone for a favor. That was not his nature. He wanted to do everything on his own."

He also worked in Montreal, which had a thriving burlesque business during the 1950s when the wheel was "kinda over."

"A man who became successful in film stole his routines." All Harry would say was the comic later appeared in *Guys and Dolls*. "He will be nameless."

In the beginning, the shows had humungous casts: fifteen chorus girls, an emcee, two comedians, four talking women, two straight men. As time passed, they got cut down to maybe ten total burlesquers.

"Audiences were appreciative," Harry said. But if the pace lagged, "they'd scream 'girls, girls.' They'd want to see more." Harry admitted in general the audience went for the girls, but appreciated the comedians. Harry said the audiences were "very vocal."

And though Eddie loved the work, he talked Harry out of following in his footsteps.

Comedian Steve Mills was a former candy butcher who started at Billy Minsky's Winter Garden in 1928. "Steve, the man was genius," said Mike Iannucci. "The nicest man, no larceny in him; he would do anything to help anyone. He was the top banana."

Iannucci continued, "Steve Mills . . . he lived to be ninety-three or something. He enjoyed every minute of his life because he *entertained*. He got more laughs than anyone—Red Buttons, etc. He was the classic burlesque comic.

Dardy Orlando and Pinky Lee

The Hollywood Theatre in San Diego had "stock comedians for a long time," said Dee Ann Johnston, daughter of the owner. "Eddie Ware—'hello there Eddie Ware'—stock comedian and stock straight men. They used to sing."

Pinky Lee was also a "wonderful talent," recalled Dardy Minsky, who did bits with him at Earl Carroll's. He would play the xylophone while she walked behind him out of his sight, slowly peeling off her clothes. The audience would applause and Pinky would say "You want more?" And on and on the number went, as Dardy stripped down.

After one opening, "Mr. Carroll would give notes. He said to Pinky, 'You were so good, but it's the dinner show. Please don't sweat.' How am I gonna stop sweating?' 'I don't know Pinky, it's your act.'" According to Dardy, who worked with him for years, Pinky "had a wonderful talent for getting contracts with the movie studios. They would fire him, but they would have to pay him over the years."

The beloved comedian was born Pincus Leff in 1907. An early day Pee-wee Herman, he would have his own children's television show in the 1950s. He wore oversized bows, checkered pants, and a checkered coat and spoke with a trademark lisp.

Mike Sachs was a blind comedian who played the Old Howard in Boston regularly. He got his start in vaudeville when he was just a kid. His wife Alice Kennedy was a "classy woman. She was the prototype talking woman, older woman. She'd lead her blind guy out and he'd talk about seeing the girls," said Eddie Lloyd. The audience didn't know he was blind, which had happened suddenly. Sachs said the last thing he saw before he went blind was the eggs on his plate.

Harry Conley was born around 1892. Like many, he ran away from home as a teenager and joined a vaudeville show. He would become a top banana for Billy Minsky. A staple of his act was browbeating his wife on stage.

Conley would say, "What the hell's going on? I put you out in the cornfield as a scarecrow, and look what happens. The crows brought back every kernel of corn they stole." His stage wife stood silent through the abuse. He would continue to perform despite a stroke that paralyzed half his body.

Phil Silvers worked for Harold Minsky for years. In the mid-to-late 1950s, he was the star of the television show *Sergeant Bilko*. The show garnered multiple Emmy nominations and wins.

Silvers, on a break, was in Florida and bored. He called Harold, who told him to meet him in Chicago and they'd go out. "Lili's [St. Cyr] working," Harold said. Silvers said he had always wanted to meet Lili so he went to Harold's theatre in Chicago.

"He was a sweet charming gentleman. Full of beans." And full of himself, recalled Dardy. Lili was becoming more reclusive, so Dardy told Phil, "'I can't do this ahead of time; she'll never meet you. Come after the show; we'll go backstage and knock on the door. That way she couldn't say 'no.'"

Dardy took Phil backstage and knocked on her sister's dressing room. Phil entered and was stunned by Lili's appearance, as she was sitting semi-nude in a sheer black negligee. Dardy introduced the two. "Oh hello, Mr. Silvers," Lili said, "and what do you do for a living?" That simple question took the wind out of his sails; he couldn't believe Lili didn't know who he was. "You know actors, they have such egos," recalled Dardy.

Many women in burlesque began their careers by working with the shows' comedians. "Dancers or lesser strippers come out with the top banana, they would bounce humor off her," explained Renny von Muchow.

"No matter what you were doing—the chorus or stripping—you were always required to do the scenes. You know, work with the comics. And that was a big deal because you got paid $2.50 extra." Maria Bradley recalled.

"Comics set their own scenes. Before eleven on Sunday, a comic would post programs for the next week and you'd know if you were in the scene. You rehearsed between shows," said Dee Ann Johnston, daughter of theatre owner Bob Johnston.

Joan Arline learned a lot by working with the comics. The talking women and comics would parade back and forth in front of the curtain while the scene changed for the next act on the bill.

Joni Taylor worked as a talking woman with comedian Charlie Robinson. "Sometimes I blacked out teeth, had fat rollers in my hair, sometimes I dressed as a man. You had to be very versatile do scenes. Usually comics were picking on bald men in the front row. [The] audience loved them. Jack Rosen and Al Anger—they got as big applause as any strip."

Others refused to be a talking woman or quickly moved out of it. It wasn't until burlesque changed and was near death that the inimitable Lili St. Cyr was forced to do bits with her comedian in Las Vegas in the late 1950s. This was something she had avoided for nearly twenty years in the business.

When burlesque shows cut down on personnel, comedians scrambled to stay in the game. Eddie Ware at the Hollywood Theatre continued to stick it out. On weekends, he played the theatre, but the other four days of the week he drove a cab, said Dee Ann Johnston.

Like the strippers, there was a mixed view of the burlesque comedians. Dardy didn't think the rest of the cast "looked at comedians as being intelligent or interesting." Their skits were bawdy and low down. "They weren't big hits with the casts."

Beverly Anderson said, "The comics in burlesque were mean, vicious, angry and frustrated. They had tried to make it in show business, probably on Broadway or vaudeville, and couldn't do it so they were regulated to burlesque."

The funny men went into nightclubs when burlesque was over.

"Comedians . . . they were mostly old men. The good ones were in their eighties; the younger ones were too young to be funny," said Maria Bradley. "The comics didn't care about becoming a Red Skelton. They just enjoyed what they were doing; they never thought about going into legitimate theatre."

"They were happy with what they were doing," said Renny von Muchow.

In 1965, Ann Corio presented *This Was Burlesque*, a revival of what a burlesque show had been. At the time Ann and Mike started their show, it had been "eight to ten years between the good burlesque comics and then the strippers took over. Then eight years later we came back. They [the comedians] were gone. They hadn't done a job. They did nothing . . . for those years when burlesque died." Maybe they would do the odd date at a club. But according to Mike Iannucci, "they had almost no work. They loved it when we came along. We gave them steady work doing what they loved to do."

The comics knew that Ann would not allow any raunchiness at all. "Ann wouldn't let comics say 'hell' or 'damn' on the show. And they didn't have to say those words," said Iannucci. She knew all the comics. She brought back Steve Mills, Dexter Maitland, Ma Bateman, Charlie Robinson, and Maxie Furman.

Mike recalled a special New Year's skit where Steve Mills "would come out as Father Time with a beard. He'd walk across stage. We timed it so that it would be exactly midnight when he got to stage right. Then all hell would break loose, the confetti, girls would push out Baby New Year," which was comedian Billy Ainsley dressed in a diaper, in a carriage. The cast would sing *Auld Lang Syne*.

The production was filling "1,200- to 1,300-seat theatres. Packed. Our show was a new life for the comics after being out of work."

Maria Bradley said, "Ann used to stand in the wings and she'd be hysterical; then she'd holler at [Steve Mills] because he said something off color. Laughing, she'd say, 'You know you're not supposed to say that.' Mills was the one most guilty of doing double entendre. He was so funny, you were kinda glad he said it because it made the audience howl. Yet at the same time, you were hoping it wasn't going to close down the theatre."

Despite the misconception, the comedians were the stars of burlesque. For a time, they were the kings of burlesque and the reason people came to the theatres . . . until the strippers took over. Though some were bemoaning the takeover in the 1950s, writer and burlesque expert Bernard Sobel claimed in his book that as early as the 1930s, the "fun [had] trickled out. . . ." He complained "it was nothing but a strip show."

Val Valentine said, "Most of the comedians were very old and some of them *real* old. There were never any newcomers. There was never anyone new coming into the business."

Maria Bradley added, "The comedians . . . you know, I think they just died on the vine with all their wonderful memories."

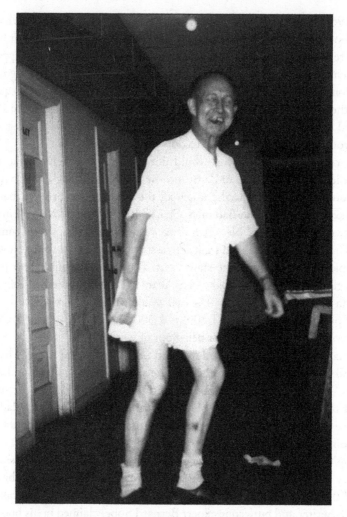

Comedian backstage

CHAPTER ELEVEN

The Straights

"They usually sang in the wings, safe from tomatoes
and other thrown objects."
—Ann Corio (*This Was Burlesque*)

"It was my kind of trash."
—Lee Stuart

Straight man Lee Stuart

The straight man on the show was also the show's tenor. Ann Corio claimed they couldn't sing. Unlike the comedian, the straight dressed elegantly.

"The role of the straight man is very interesting," Alan Alda explained. The straight man's job was not to be funny, but to help support the comic. It was

73

a "subtle" role. One played extraordinarily well by such straight men as Bud Abbott, Dexter Maitland, and Robert Alda.

"He never got the credit he deserves, as a straight man in burlesque," Chris Costello said about her father's partner Bud Abbott. One time in Las Vegas, the duo performed their "Who's on First?" routine. "Dad had done ad-libbing and threw Bud totally off and didn't know where to get back into routine. They couldn't figure out how to get back into that one point. . . . Bud would have a way of bringing him back in."

Bud Abbott "was one of the most sensitive human beings. He wasn't the character people knew him on screen," said Chris Costello.

When Abbott and Costello broke up, "it was difficult for Bud. That's all he knew. . . . [He] tried to resurrect the humor with another comedian, doing fairs." But it didn't work. He couldn't capture the chemistry he had had with Lou Costello. "You couldn't recreate that era and that style of comedy."

Dexter Maitland was another classic straight man. He sang, usually when the chorus girls did some numbers. He sang while Ann Corio was on stage. He "had a whiskey tenor—slightly off-key singing."

Lee Stuart was a dignified and handsome man I was introduced to at the reunion. "I was nineteen years old and I wanted to get into show business. The straight man is six feet tall, wears a hat, dresses very nattily, and speaks very distinctly where you can understand every word. I was not a good straight man. I heard one of these comics talk to the boss. And he says, 'I thought you had a straight man for this show.' He says, 'Well I got three men.' He says, 'Yeah, you got three. You got a gay guy that sings opera. You got a dancer that can't talk, and you got a hillbilly from Arkansas that don't know the difference between the proscenium arch and a condom.' And so, I said, 'Well, I better learn something.'"

Lee would go on the road as a blackface doing straights for a minstrel show. "Burlesque was like going to school for me. We could do a scene once and I could not miss a word. I trained myself to pay attention."

He continued, "One straight man, Jack Coyle, I watched him. He was smart, six feet two inches, well-dressed, spoke good English. I admired him. I patterned myself after him. You watch someone, if he's got a good line, you find yourself using it in a week or two. . . .

"Freddy Frampton—he's akin to Rags [Ragland]. Freddy spoke with a W. C. Fields accent, nasal—to me he was funny. I found myself unconsciously copying him. While I'm doing straights, I'm doing W. C. Finally, they had to tell me, 'Kid, you're not supposed to be funny. You're supposed to give the straight line.'"

THE STRAIGHTS

When Lee Stuart started in burlesque in 1947, "there was only one straight man on the show. The juvenile would do the bit parts." There was a line of six or eight chorus girls when he started. When he left in 1957, the chorus line was down to four or five girls.

CHAPTER TWELVE
The Tit Singer

"I lived in a cocoon of weirdness."
—Alan Alda on life on the road with his father

"This pig was stealing my parents from me."
—Alan Alda

Sherry Britton (center) and "tit singer" Robert Alda (right)

Straight man Robert Alda was born in 1917. "I think," his son, actor Alan Alda, admitted. According to newspaper reports, he was actually born in 1914 in New York. His father had emigrated from Italy.

Robert was born Robert Alphonso D'Abruzzo. Taking the first two initials of his names, he became Alda. "In those days," Alan explained, "you either denied your Italian heritage or played to the stereotype."

He studied architecture and was a junior draftsman "on some buildings still standing in New York today." He was handsome, with dark eyes and hair and a beautiful voice. "When the Depression hit, he needed to make some money and began singing at various movie theatres during amateur nights. Somehow that got him into burlesque as a straight man."

Alda would become one of the best straight men in the business. As the straight, he had to understand timing: how to set up the comic so the comic wouldn't have to do all the work himself.

Robert was also what was known as a "tit singer." He would sing to the opening number while the chorus girls danced, "usually without their shirts on," but no doubt with pasties. "That job was known officially as the tit singer," Alan explained.

He was a young husband and father, married to Joan Browne, who gave birth to Alan, their only son, when he was twenty-one. Robert was intelligent and sensitive. "You can't step into the funny. He was very good at it."

Robert's partner was comedian Hank Henry. The two wrote their own sketches, or modified others' work. The sketches were basic, Alan explained. "It's hard to imagine people laughing" at them. But of course, it was a more "innocent time," he said.

Hank and Robert created an act with a pig. Hank Henry said to Robert, "Get outta here, and don't come back until you can bring home the bacon."

At the end of the sketch, Robert walked in with a pig under his arm. And he said, "Well, I brought home the bacon!"

Alan continued, "In order to do that sketch, they lugged this pig around with them everywhere they went, from town to town. All over the Eastern Wheel, I think it was called. And they put the damn pig in the back of the car, and there wasn't any room for me. So they left me with two crazy aunts in Wilmington, Delaware. This pig was my sibling, you know. This pig was stealing my parents from me. . . . Now the damn pig was going up to the dressing room instead of me."

Six-year-old Alan was sent to a boarding school while his parents traveled the circuit. "I hated that pig," he admitted. When they ditched the pig act, Alan rejoined his traveling parents.

Alda's mother had won a beauty contest that led to a tour in a vaudeville show. "The whole act was a bunch of young women in bathing suits. That was the act. That was unusual in those days. She didn't have any talent of any kind. She was very loving in spite of the fact that she was schizophrenic and paranoid," Alan said. And though her symptoms didn't manifest until he was eight or nine, he still remembers it as being a difficult childhood.

It was hard on her husband. "He didn't complain or talk about it. Both suffered from it, but didn't say anything. No one talked about mental illness; it was a real shame. In the same way you didn't talk about cancer or calamities. It seemed to bring discredit to the family."

Soon Hollywood called and Robert was offered a contract. His first movie would be a biography of Gershwin, *Rhapsody in Blue*. It was a huge hit.

"Because of my mother's growing mental illness," Alan said, "it was difficult for him to climb up the Hollywood ladder, socially—that's how they did business then. They never went to parties where he would meet people to advance his career." Instead, every Sunday night Robert's old burlesque buddies would come by the house. Some of the comedians had gone into writing or acting for the movies, some were still in burlesque, and they would do sketches for one another.

There was a small area in the house the old friends used as a stage, two steps up from the living room. As Alan explained, the old corny sketches that had been repeated for decades in burlesque were trotted out. And even though everyone had seen them over and over, the "audience" would laugh.

That was Alan's "education of show business." The professionals were so skilled at what they did. "There was an appreciation of the improvisational moment when you take something that everyone knows and make it fresh." He grew up watching his father's friends, who had that skill of doing the "same old thing the way it's never been done before."

Robert would go on to star on Broadway's *Guys and Dolls*, originating the role Marlon Brando would perform in the film.

When Alan was eighteen, his mother was finally institutionalized. They were in Amsterdam when it happened. Robert was working. "No one took her to a doctor. She drank, to medicate herself."

Alan watched his dad on stage from the wings. "He'd make a banana curve" to the microphone at center of the stage. Alan dismissed it as his father playing at a "movie star, and it [seemed] phony." He realized much later it was the kind of movie star entrance "the audience wanted. They don't use a fourth wall. It's direct communion with an audience. It's impossible to do on film."

In later years, Robert suffered strokes and still "wanted to perform up to the end . . . but couldn't say much." Alan's father died the same year as his mother. They had been divorced for twenty-five years. "Neither one knew the other was dying across town in different hospitals. I would shuttle back and forth," Alan remembered.

Robert was "proud of his background," Alan said. "I think it was a badge of having lived through a training ground and tough work. It was hard work. And you learned a lot. You could stick him out on a stage and he'd take over. He could emcee any kind of show."

Years before his father's death, Alan cast his father on *M*A*S*H**. "Here we were, father and son playing this scene, and we actually have to figure out how to do this sewing maneuver. And so now father and son, just like the two characters, actually have to learn how to cooperate. And if it weren't for this background that he had in burlesque of writing corny sketches, I wouldn't have to have been put into this corny situation, where I actually had to cooperate physically, mentally, emotionally, intellectually with my father. It was a wonderful moment in our lives."

CHAPTER THIRTEEN

From A to C

"By chance he happened to meet Bud Abbott, who was the most
sought-after straight man."
—Chris Costello

"What the guy didn't know is that those pies were being thrown into
people's faces through the course of the shooting day."
—Chris Costello

Abbott and Costello were the most famous comedian team to emerge from burlesque. Everyone had a story about the pair, each proud to have shared the stage
with the talented and legendary duo.

Lou Costello was introduced to burlesque through the Ann Corio show,
explained his daughter Chris Costello. He was a "dancing juvenile," who came
out before the top banana and warmed up the audience—only he would get the
laughs. Ann Corio took an interest in Lou and started to groom him. "Ann loved
my dad," Chris remembered.

Lou Costello with Ann Corio

Ann Corio introduced him to his future wife, one of the ponies (the short chorus girl on the end) on her show.

The story goes that Lou was so struck by stripper Anne Battler that he clumsily knocked over a prop on stage, which in turn hit her—and knocked her out.

Lou pursued Anne despite the accident. Anne complained to her friend Ann Corio, "Why do I want to date a burlesque comic? If I want to starve I can starve on my own."

"Cut to five years later," Chris laughed, "and Anne and Lou are living in a twenty-two-room home south of Ventura with a swimming pool, maids, butlers—the whole nine yards."

One day at the house, Corio turned to her friend. "Well, Anne, what's it like to starve? This is amazing for starving."

From the Corio show, Lou Costello soon got a partner and started on the circuit, "which wasn't the blue circuit," said Chris. This was a term I never heard anyone else mention in all the interviews I conducted. Chris claimed whatever circuit her father was playing wasn't as "dirty" as some of the others. He only believed in doing the "clean circuit."

Soon thereafter he shared the bill with the older-by-ten-years straight man Bud Abbott, whom "everyone wanted to work with."

Born William Abbott, "Bud" was born into the burlesque circuit; his father was an advance man. Bud had been working for at least a decade prior to meeting Lou Costello. Lou's straight man was sick and Bud filled in. The rest, as they say, is history. They worked all the burlesque theatres for a few years: New York, New Jersey, Chicago, Philadelphia, and so on.

They would know phenomenal success, their routines etched in American history. As the burlesque houses were closing, Lou wanted to get to Hollywood and get into movies. "Bud would have been happy to stay in burlesque," said Chris.

The two appeared on the Kate Smith radio show, which was burlesque-oriented, as were all early radio and television shows. Lou wanted to do their "Who's on First?" routine, knowing it was their ticket. But the manager of the Kate Smith program wouldn't allow it. He told them to do anything but that "silly baseball thing."

Lou threatened to leave, saying, "We have no material," which forced the manager to let them do the routine, catapulting the two into stardom.

"His roots were burlesque," Chris explained. He loved it. Most of their routines are still familiar—and funny—today. They came out of what they perfected on the burlesque stages.

In radio, Bud raised his voice and created the "whine" so their voices wouldn't be identical. His high-pitched voice differentiated the two on the air.

"There was a 60/40 cut. The straight man usually got 60 percent. Then when they came out to Hollywood, Dad said to Bud, 'I think let's change it. Now let's do 50/50.'"

While making movies, "they would bring their stooges on the set. Pie throwing. Matchsticks, you know, in the shoes. There was a little Italian baker that baked all these fresh pies every morning. And Dad would go in on his way to work. And he would buy up twenty, thirty pies. And this baker was so thrilled to think that Lou Costello loved all of his pies. What the guy didn't know is that those pies were being thrown into people's faces, you know, through the course of the shooting day."

Chris continued, "They were always in competition. If Bud Abbott put a pool in and it was so many feet, my dad would have to put his pool in and extend it a few more feet longer. They were like brothers. . . . But God help someone if they said anything derogatory about the other."

Chris admitted that they loved each other, but they fought sometimes, too. "One of our maids left to work for the Abbott family. That was it. There was no talking to Bud Abbott for like six months."

Bud and Lou split up in 1957—"amicably," Chris confirmed. Comedy was changing. "It was slowing down. They were slowing down. [Lou] wanted to get into dramatic acting. That's all he wanted to do. Bud wanted to stay part of Abbott and Costello."

Lou had developed rheumatic fever during the War Bond tour. "Every five to seven years, fluid would build up around his heart." Chris believes had he lived even six more months, there would have been viable medical treatment for his heart condition.

Lou died in March of 1959. Like his deceased son Lou Jr. who was buried on his first birthday, Lou was buried on *his* birthday. He would have been fifty-three.

"It stunned Bud. Bud never got over that. He kept saying, 'I lost my best friend.'"

Abbott and Costello onstage

CHAPTER FOURTEEN

Backstage

"Chorus girls would go home and do laundry between shows."
—Taffy O'Neil

"Backstage was always very lonely."
—Alexandra the Great "48"

Backstage at the Follies with stripper Betty Rowland, the Ball of Fire

The chorus girls were already on stage for the opening number. Twenty-two pairs of feet slapped across the stage. The musicians in the pit were wailing loud and fast and hard. The house singer with his slicked-back hair and dark suit was singing a song to the full audience. From the wings, the comedian and his straight man checked props in their pockets. Backstage, the air was thick with the smell of tobacco, and clouds of smoke billowed over the heads of the comics and chorus girls. The place smelled like a combination of deli food—sour and meaty from the town's Chinese restaurant where the cast dined between shows.

There was a quick blackout, applause, and a scramble as girls poured off the stage, feathered hair-dresses bouncing, and a novelty act moved in front of the curtain to juggle.

BACKSTAGE

It was continuous motion backstage as a couple hefty stagehands lugged props. Strippers and novelty acts rushed up and down the stairs to the green room and the communal dressing room at the top of the stairs. Three older comedians sat around a table smoking cigars and playing cards. They stole sips of contraband whiskey and kept half an ear out for how the first team was doing on stage. So far, no cries of "bring on the girls!" The routine must be going over well.

In her dressing room, neither big nor lavish, but private with a tiny sink screwed to the wall, the feature stripper sat melting dark makeup in a flattened spoon over a lit candle. With a steady and practiced hand, she began to bead her eyelashes. She applied a tiny drop of molten black makeup to the end of a couple lashes. Beading made the eyes pop. The stripper already had on her opera hose, G-string, net panties, pasties, and net bra and was about to shimmy into her aqua silk gown that fell to her feet. A rhinestone necklace adorned her neck. The room smelled heavily of powder and perfume. There were scattered vases of flowers from admirers. A silk robe and a couple other dresses were tossed over a chair. On a red velvet chaise were a variety of gloves, hats, and shoes. Her suit, prim and proper, that she would wear back to her hotel was hanging on a wardrobe rack. Makeup bottles and jars were neatly assembled in front of the mirror along with cards from boyfriends taped to the mirror.

A rap on the door by the stage manager, an old man named Charlie who had been with theatre for nearly forty years, let her know her cue was coming up. Applause wafted down from the audience. They sounded well-behaved. She hoped to change that with her bumps and her forward thrusts. Her dance was on fire.

The click of shoe taps thundered past her closed door, disappearing at the green room down the hall where an acrobatic duo warmed up their muscular bodies with lunges and a few contortions. Propped against some furniture, a tired chorus girl caught a nap. She was hung over.

One of the older talking women, married to the comic, was ironing her dress, worn and well starched.

The club owner's teenage son was running the spotlight. He dropped in a lavender gel and switched to a blue light for the co-feature.

Upstairs, the chorus girls were jammed into a crowded room, vying for space in front of the mirrors. It was hot and humid with no way to breathe anything but perspiration, thick makeup, and cheap perfume. G-strings, washed and drying, hung from light bulbs around mirrors. Girls stole makeup from one another, tried hiding valuables, and had petty arguments, always with a cigarette in hand. Bottles of Stage White, a makeup that made the girls' skin look like satin, were in use.

While the comics were on stage, the house singer gargled, adjusting his bow tie, a cigarette dangling from his mouth.

The choreographer and the backstage manager were arguing. The manager checked his watch; the co-feature was taking too long. If she stayed any longer on the stage, she would drive the union musicians into overtime. "Wrap it up," he yelled from backstage. The G-string seller slunk by with a box of sparkly panties, hoping to lure more sales than his competition, who had come the week before.

While the performers sweated it out under hot lights in a stifling theatre with rows and rows of men applauding, yawning, and hollering, a candy butcher and bouncer kept their eye on things. Backstage was its own chaotic caldron to get the show on and get it on timely and right.

Come behind the curtain to witness the whirl of nonstop activity that made a burly show.

**

"Shows had to go fast. A lot of mothers came to make sure their daughters were dressed well in the show. It was survival, actually," said Betty Rowland.

In 1947, Lily Ann Rose was fourteen and working at the Casino Burlesque Theatre in Boston. Backstage, other girls stood around talking and smoking heavily. And it wasn't always cigarettes the girls were smoking. "I remember once [in Chicago], standing in line to use the bathroom and the girls in front of me were passing a lighted butt around. I did not know what it was, but when it came

Backstage preparing

Betty Rowland backstage

to me I smelled it and it smelled horrible. One of the girls said, 'go ahead, puff on it.' I smelled it again, made an awful face and said, 'no thanks,' and passed it to the girl behind me."

The theatre was not only permeated with the smell of cigars, cigarettes, and pot, but also some food. Joan Arline recalled, "Sammy Price, every Saturday, would come into the theatre with rye bread, limburger cheese, and onion. And every Sunday it smelled like someone had left a pile of you know what. . . . Oh, how we looked forward to the limburger. We'd have it for supper between shows. We were asphyxiating each other on the stage because we stunk. God, it was good."

"There was a smell in the theatre, mold or something," Alan Alda also recalled.

Joni Taylor said, "Backstage had a life of its own. Always a green room for waiting and listening for cues and once in a while, the stage hands ran in and out to get something."

Dardy Minsky remembered being so tired, she'd frequently fall asleep on the props backstage and wake just in time to hear her overture.

One time, as the chorus girls were dressing, "we all decided something was wrong," said Joni Taylor. "A lot of our net panties were missing and a lot had been fumbled with and were wet, if you get what I mean. We had high rafters in that theatre.... Our stage manager was Maddy Mixon [stripper Terry Mixon's mother, also a stripper] and she had her own dressing room near the chorus room and we all heard her say, 'What are you doing up there?' and then she started yelling for the stage hands for help and here was this guy in the rafters." The offender would use the rafters to go from room to room. "He jumped from the rafters and ran to the entrance door and jumped out over about twenty steps. The stagehands got him and called the police and they found he had broken both of his legs on that jump. We all decided the crotch of our chorus pants must have been worth it."

Another time in New York, Blaze Starr was the feature strip. She often performed with dangerous cats, including a baby black panther. Blaze and Joni were upstairs in their dressing rooms when all of a sudden they heard screaming downstairs. "Blaze went running down and her panther had chased Solly [a stagehand] up the entire curtain. The audience was already in the theatre and waiting for the first show to start," Taylor said. They thought it was part of the show "and we all got a great laugh from that."

The chorus girls shared a crowded, smoky, hot dressing room. The feature stripper had her own room. Dardy Minsky recalled the chorus girls hanging their G-strings around the lights of their mirrors to dry after hand-washing them.

Joan Arline declared, "Some dressing rooms [were] terrible." Crowded, smelly, dirty. But they made do. In Detroit, when she worked the Gaiety, the theatre "had a leaning board [a board where performers could lean on their back at an angle so as to be able to rest while wearing tight and elaborate costumes]. They were passé then, but it had one. It was wonderful," she said.

Sherry Britton backstage

The competition and the pressure to excel led to fights. Sherry Britton claimed to have been beaten up nineteen times by other strippers.

"They will fight backstage, yes. And they have to call the front of the house. The stage hands don't know where to grab. They're trying to stop the girls, separate them, pull 'em apart," said Dixie Evans.

"I've heard stories of anti-Semitism and people getting beat up and that sort of thing." Alan Alda recalled numerous fights among the comics, especially after a few drinks at the bar that was inevitably next to every burlesque theatre, no matter the town. Tempest Storm remembered how "they'd put itchin' powder in people's costumes if some girl got a bigger hand onstage."

Lili St. Cyr hired two stagehands to guard her tub after some girls put ice cubes in it prior to her slipping into it during her performance.

"Better not use someone's music. Whatever they tell you, do the opposite. It's cutthroat back East," said Dixie Evans.

Mickey Jones was a stripper known as the Jungle Girl. Joni once asked her, "Could I have your sheet music?" Unlike so many, Mickey said sure. That kind of generosity was not common among the competitive world backstage. Everyone tried to hold on to their gimmick.

There were other petty resentments from other cast members.

"Sometimes an emcee resented the fact that some dumb broad thought she had a body and was the star of the show. That he was. And maybe he should have been. They'd screw up your intro or make you wait a long time backstage. One made me wait a long time. He wouldn't tell me what his last joke was. I'm in a gown and fur. I'm starting to sweat. And I had those poor dogs waiting," said Joan Arline, who performed with two Russian wolfhounds.

But as much rivalry as there could be among the strippers and comedians, there was a feeling of us-against-them. The burlesque performers looked out for one another; they stuck together.

"You knew about the stigma, but we're in a group all by ourselves," Dixie said. "There was some protection and comfort in that."

"They made the best of it. They were pretty good to one another. They stuck by one another," said Alda.

Backstage friendships formed an intractable bond between the performers. Blaze Starr would always remember and be grateful to Val Valentine for the time Val brought her soup when she had the flu.

"You met wonderful people, you were like a family," Sequin explained. "I had a party at my apartment, a luau ... fruit and coconuts, poi, [but] no liquor. One musician got angry: 'What do you mean you don't have any liquor?' 'Well, I don't drink.'"

Val Valentine

Blaze Starr and Val Valentine. Friendships were close backstage.

Sometimes the closeness was taken advantage of. As a chorus girl, Dardy was sharing the cramped room with others. She became furious and appalled when another girl used her mascara cake. "You had to spit in it to work it."

Dardy plotted her revenge, and a couple weeks later, the chorus girl showed up for work with a red swollen face. She said she didn't know what had happened. Dardy told her *she* did. Dardy had a stagehand find her a dead mouse—rampant backstage—and then she stuck it in the girl's cold cream. "She never borrowed my mascara again."

There were feuds, real and imagined, printed in the girlie magazines. Most were simple publicity stunts. In 1942, according to *Billboard*, Sol Goodman, Blaze's employer at the Two O' Clock Club, was charged with striking a dancer after he broke up a three-way fight among dancers backstage.

A very real altercation between Lili St. Cyr and Tempest Storm did occur, however. Tempest was just starting out and Lili was the headliner at the El Rey in San Francisco. "I admired Lili St. Cyr," Tempest said of the older (by almost a dozen years) headliner. "But when she came in as the star at the theatre, she resented me."

As the star, Lili would go on last, after the other girls.

Dixie said, "[Lili] claims that Tempest had a couple of her outfits held with straight pins and Lili got one stuck in her toe."

"I was just starting out and here's a big star bitching about me," Tempest remembered.

Dixie said, "Every time she gets with a group she'll bring that up. 'I didn't. I didn't. It's not my straight pin.'"

"Well, I got so mad . . . I took my wardrobe out of my dressing room. I said, 'I'm getting the hell out of here. I don't have to take that crap,'" Tempest said.

In later years, when asked about Tempest, Lili always said she was alright—if you were a plumber.

Morton Minsky wrote that one of the "greatest feuds" was between Margie Hart and Rose La Rose. Margie had her nose surgically altered. Rose claimed to like it so much she went to the same doctor and purchased the same nose. Margie was so furious, she punched Rose in her new nose, giving her two black eyes.

Performers felt very proprietary about their acts and names, looks, dances, and even the music they chose to play while onstage. Some of the papers played up a feud with Rose La Rose when she tried to sue a black stripper who was dancing as Rosa La Rosa.

"A lot of the girls back then, when they were headliners, you couldn't wear the same color gown. You couldn't use any music that was even similar to theirs," Carmela said.

When the girls weren't onstage—depending on who they worked for at the time—some would socialize, others would go home to do laundry or see their children, and some weren't allowed a choice.

Producer Lillian Hunt of the Follies in Los Angeles had "all girls between shows on army cots in the basement. Girls couldn't go out between shows. Every time it rained, the cops would be in the green room or the basement. Rats running on pipes, cops shooting rats off water pipes in the basement. Vice, etc. would hang out, look at the girls. And become friendly. You mutually understand one another. You met policemen and gangsters."

"Between shows we'd go to the bar," Lady Midnight said.

"One time after too many drinks after the show," Maria Bradley remembered, "after drinking martinis for first time, I stood against a wall and slid down. I had a hangover for a week. I didn't drink martinis after that."

Like the circus, there was a hierarchy in burlesque shows. Some headliners would have nothing to do with the chorus girls, or other acts backstage, preferring to stay in their rooms.

There were also unwritten rules among the performers themselves. "Strippers didn't allow talking women or chorus girls looking at them. Nobody in the wings," explained Sequin. They wanted to protect their special something at all costs.

Maria Bradley said, "Strippers didn't talk to chorus girls; they were the stars."

Dixie recalled Red Skelton, after he had become a big star, showing up at the theatre to take Charlie Pritchard—an old comic in his eighties with a big putty nose—out on the town. "Big-time stars a lot didn't really reach down. But some did. Lou Costello and Bud helped out their fella old comedians." Lou made sure his friend George "Beetlepuss" Lewis was taken care of in a sanitarium when the old comedian came down with cancer. Stars, like Lili St. Cyr, weren't seen backstage. "Lili became reclusive. She always was. She'd ride around in a limo, with curtains drawn. You didn't see her between shows," recalled Dixie Evans.

Candy Cotton said, "I'd stay in my dressing room doing beading and reading, so I stayed out of trouble."

April March lived a similar backstage life. "I stayed in the dressing room. . . . I had to watch my soap opera."

As a feature it meant "you're around a lot of people but it doesn't mean you spent a lot of time with them. I was pretty much on my own," admitted Alexandra the Great. "I had my own dressing room. . . . I was very shy anyway. I was there to work. I was always ready. I didn't do much between shows."

Dardy Minsky preparing to go on

Lillian Hunt counseled Taffy O'Neil not to "mix with the girls; they'll try and undermine you." Lillian promised to keep them out of the wings when Taffy was on. "I was friendly, but you can't be too friendly or they'd come in your dressing room and bother you and make you nervous."

A few, a very few, brought their children backstage. Val Valentine was backstage as a young girl with an aunt.

"Many times backstage, I'd sleep in fan boxes, about a five-foot box she'd stored fans in, slid under dresses that would hang. That would become my bed," Sean Rand recalled, about his mother Sally Rand.

Typically the musicians would be playing cards. "They'd have a bookie come in to book horses," said Renny von Muchow.

Alan Alda recalled, the "chorus girls were up there and they'd change in front of me." They called him 'Allie.' He could "smell sweat and clothes. Here's what it meant to me: the chorus girls would take me up to the dressing room, then they'd say, 'We're going to change our clothes; turn your back.' I could smell the costume and perfume. I remember thinking, *They don't know this means anything to me. Boy, do they have it wrong.*"

Backstage had both its dangers and its solace; it was truly a home away from home.

CHAPTER FIFTEEN
The Censors

"Use of a bed in skits must not be abused by raw dialogue or action."

—Boston License and Censor Bureau

"Never let your nipple show."

—Maria Bradley

What one saw in burlesque very often depended upon *where* one saw it. There were a variety of different rules for each burlesque house.

"Some towns were a little bit more strict than others. Most of the towns you could not show your breasts unless you had pasties," Beverly recalled. There had to be a certain amount of coverage while dancing and most towns were thorough. "They didn't want the cops coming in arresting the girls and stopping the show," said Beverly Anderson.

Since the beginning of burlesque, censors would come to the theatres and inspect the shows. Theatre operators made it clear to performers what they could and could not do in their theatres, could and could not wear, and could and could not say.

Below is a partial list of rules that were posted backstage at the Old Howard in Boston, Massachusetts.

ATTENTION: BURLESQUE THEATRE PERFORMERS

ATTENTION ALL FEMALE PERFORMERS MUST NOT AT ANY TIME HAVE ON LESS THAN PASTIES (GLUED DIRECTLY ON BODY) LARGE ENOUGH TO COVER ENTIRE NIPPLE PLUS A FULL NET BRASSIERE OF SUFFICIENT SIZE WHICH IS NOT TO BE REMOVED AT ANY TIME.

NO BUMPS OR GRINDS IN A FLAT-FOOTED POSITION.

NO FONDLING OF PRIVATE PARTS OR BREASTS AT ANY TIME.

BADGERING AUDIENCE FOR REPLIES IS FORBIDDEN.

SKITS REFERRING TO PERVERTED PERSONALITIES ARE TO BE KEPT AT A MINIMUM.

MALE PERFORMERS ARE NOT TO TOUCH BUTTOCKS OR BREASTS OF ANY FEMALE.

BLASPHEMOUS LANGUAGE WILL NOT BE TOLERATED AT ANY TIME.

CONTINUED VIOLATION OF ANY OF THE ABOVE-MENTIONED REGULATIONS WILL RESULT IN THE REVOCATION OF BURLESQUE THEATRE LICENSE.

—LICENSE AND CENSOR BUREAU

Lily Ann Rose said, "In Boston, the Watch and Ward Society censored everything. And they would come in on Monday morning and watch the show and if there was anything in there like 'damn' or 'hell,' it had to come out. After the censors came in, then the next show went on and they did everything the way they always do it."

"Boston was the strictest. You had to be careful not to do anything suggestive," said Sequin.

Every city felt the pressure from politicians and local church groups trying to clamp down on what was assumed to go on in the burlesque theatres.

Maria Bradley pointed out that "those who were against burlesque usually hadn't gone to one. The same men and women would easily pay bigger dollars to see a Broadway show featuring the same amount—if not more—of nudity."

Chorus girls with the required pasties

AGVA (American Guild of Variety Artists) union was founded in 1939 to govern live performances in the variety field, including circus, cabaret, and touring shows. In Philadelphia they screened the strippers' performances before they went on.

"The vice squad was at every opening," said Dixie Evans. "'We're going to check your show.' After the show they would tip their hat. 'Everything is fine, just keep it that way.' City Ordinance came and told you just what to do. We did, [but] girls wanted extra applause.

"On New Year's Eve, the City Ordinance was a bit more lenient. They would come in and tell the house, 'We're gonna be out of town on New Year's Eve; do what you want.' At the finale the girls would all line up and holler out to the audience, 'What's your name?' Then with a rotation of their pelvises, they would spell out the name. The vice squad knew that it was a traditional thing and the audience would shout longer and longer names. And New Year's Eve there wasn't a big audience," said Dixie Evans.

The censors were on the look out not only for lewd behavior, but also for profanity. The comics were not allowed to curse.

In 1932, Ann Corio would testify in front of the Watch and Ward that her act was "art." Her testimony didn't convince anyone and the Old Howard in Boston was shut for thirty days, despite Mayor Curley and his wife's repeat attendance at Ann's shows. "The Mayor's entourage would come into the theatre after the show had started and set up his folding chair, then the Mayor would come down and enjoy the show."

The laws varied from state to state and county to county. "Blue law" stated you couldn't work on Sundays. To get around that, shows went on at five minutes past "midnight on Sunday—really Monday," said Joni Taylor. In Chicago, the police censors would come in for the first show on Friday and afterward tell the comics which jokes to delete, and they would tell the dancers which "wiggle to unwiggle."

"Buffalo, New York—they weren't allowed to make any hoops or hollers," or else security guards in the aisles would pound their billy clubs, said Taffy O'Neil.

April March said, "In Dallas you had to wear a net bra, net pants, big front on 'em and a big, big wide strip up the back."

White Fury added, "We had a lot of laws. Three or four inches of cloth on either side. Full bra a lot of places." So she sewed tassels onto a flesh-colored bra.

"Detroit was known as the Vatican," Joan Arline rolled her eyes. "You had rules for how you could bump. You couldn't do two. You couldn't do a series of bumps. You had to have two-inch piece on [the] front panel. I didn't use fringe. It had to show that you had like a bikini bathing suit fuller than what they wear now. If you were a blonde, you had to wear [a] brunette [G-string], you couldn't wear black; blonde you couldn't wear a nude one. Every blonde was not bleaching there. You carried two sets of nets, flesh or black with ruffle to show you had it on."

"If you touched a curtain on stage, if you grabbed it and it hit near your stomach or legs, the stage manager gave you a talkin' to when you went off," recalled Lorraine Lee.

Because of the laws in Green Bay, Wisconsin, April March couldn't even strip onstage. "I had to get off the stage and go to the dressing room to remove even a glove, and then go back and dance and then go back again. I said, 'Why do they need a stripper here?'"

"It was to get around laws that said you couldn't leave the stage with anything less than what you arrived with," explained Betty Rowland. "You couldn't take off anything in front of the people. So we used to go in back of the curtain and come right around, and take it off. You 'changed costumes,' that's what they said."

"Indianapolis was known as Tit Town," said Joan Arline. "'Where you working next?' 'Tit Town.' Everybody knew that was Indianapolis. The minute you touched up here . . . they were crazy over your boobs."

In most houses, red lights were installed in the footlights and if a cop or censor was coming in, the girl at the front would hit a button and a red light would flash that warned the strippers to tone it down.

"They had a little box on the side where they had pasties and if there was a light on the stage and if they thought cops were coming, the light would go on and you had to run over and grab the pasties and put 'em on real fast. It also meant no flashing," said Lady Midnight.

Alexandra the Great went out on the "flashing circuit" with the encouragement of her mentor Rose La Rose. It didn't seem to bother her. Men would sit with newspapers on their laps and popcorn buckets covering their privates. But the dancers never felt threatened. Not that the strippers had much recourse if customers acted up—Sherry Britton encountered an obscene customer during a close dance and the theatre owner defended him, not her, when she complained.

Besides a shooting or two (more on that later), nothing much dangerous happened in the theatres.

"The audience was there to have fun," said Maria Bradley.

CHAPTER SIXTEEN

A Bump . . .

"A sharp hip movement where the lower section of the body is thrust
forward or bumped provocatively."
—*Uncensored Magazine*

"A bump is when the muscles of the buttocks are contracted
and lower part of the spine bends forward sudden-like, throwing
the front portion of the private parts forward."
—Testimony from the 1951 trial of Lili St. Cyr

Some women like Georgia Sothern and Tempest Storm worked the curtains, pulling the fabric between their legs in a suggestive manner. "Bumps into the curtain are not very subtle," said Alan Alda. "But at the same time, it's innocent. It's like, 'Here's that gesture.' There was something open about it. It wasn't dirty. It was just erotic."

To bump is to jolt, to hit against, to collide with. Some of the more "wild" dancers did exactly that to their legions of fans. They thrust themselves right into large paychecks and onto the covers of magazines. People paid attention when they burst onto the stage.

"I'd come booming out of the curtain and let them have it," recalled Vicki O'Day.

One of the most popular bumps came from stripper Evelyn West and her Million Dollar Chest. She was born Amy Coomer in Kentucky. She claimed to have insured her magnificent bosom for $50,000 in 1947. Hugely popular, she remained in the gossip columns for years, including being featured in *Life Magazine*. Alfred Kinsey, founder of the Institute for Sex Research, attended numerous burlesque shows as research for his famous report "Sexual Behavior in the Human Female," but for some reason refused to interview Evelyn. She put humor in her strip, telling the audience "I know you're looking at my shoes." Retiring, she moved to Florida, shedding "Evelyn" and reverting to Amy, leaving the stripper behind. She died at the age of eighty-two.

The Cat Girl, Lilly Christine, was a star in the '50s—a more voluptuous, wilder-looking Lili St. Cyr. In fact, oftentimes pictures of the two are mistaken for the other. Born Martha Pompender, she was a blonde, curly-haired stripper in the era of Tempest and Blaze Starr. She looked athletic, healthy and buxom. She was named the best exotic dancer in New Orleans in 1951–52. She crouched low; she spread her legs apart.

She claimed to have years of dancing, both modern and ballet, under her G-string belt. "Pillow of Love" was something she performed at Prima's 500 Club in New Orleans, a little scenario about a girl singing for her lover in a faraway land as she lay her head on a pillow. She claimed to "make love to her audience." Lilly would ask the men near her if they wanted to put their head on her pillow (Ann Corio did a similar bit). As she wore only a G-string and a mink-edged negligee, the censors complained her act was indecent. They also complained she didn't even dance. She, along with a dozen other exotics, was arrested in New Orleans in 1958.

She died in January 1965 of peritonitis at age forty-two, though there would be more sinister rumors regarding her demise. "She didn't believe in operations or cutting on her body," said Kitty West.

(There was a real fear among the dancers of having their appendix out. Lili St. Cyr would have hers frozen instead, so greatly did she dread her perfect body being marred by a scar. Morton Minsky relates that Margie Hart also had a phobia about having her appendix removed. Margie said "a wrinkle on your face isn't as bad as one on your stomach." And Sherry Britton was horrified by the chorus girls, with their "multiple scars from surgeries for VD.")

Where did these girls learn to bump? Some were taught by former stripper Lillian Hunt, who mentored dozens of strippers including Tempest Storm, Taffy O'Neil, and Blaze Starr. She ran the Follies theatre in Los Angeles.

"'Lillian Hunt?' We used to call her something else. Bossy thing ruled the roost," recalled Dixie Evans. There was one performer she couldn't control, though.

Lili St. Cyr was the star at the Follies. The president and vice president of RKO Studios showed up to catch Lili's act. According to Dixie, Lillian was "racing around backstage, telling Lili, 'Hurry up. They want to see you.' Lili is sitting with her hands in two big bowls of hand lotion. 'Tell them to make an appointment.' 'You get up and go out there. We've never had the president of a major motion picture studio in this burlesque theatre before.' 'Tell them to make an appointment.' So they made an appointment. Lili never showed up. Lillian was screaming. 'Lili, you didn't make the appointment.' 'Yes, I did drive to the studio. And the guard would not let me on the lot. I would have had to park ten blocks and walk the street through rubble and mud, so I just drove home.' Lillian called the studio and made another appointment. They were there at the gate with roses. There she is with her beautiful suede suit, ascot, and mink coat."

Lili St. Cyr was one of the last "elegant" strippers. Times were changing and audiences wanted to see jungle acts and floor work and the squatting and spreading of legs.

Bumps were not so much forbidden, but they were expected—which led to trouble for the dancers and heralded a change in the burlesque scene.

CHAPTER SEVENTEEN

The Paddy Wagon

"I was put in a paddy wagon and taken down to the Tombs.
I spent the night in jail."

—April March

"I was met at the bus station by the town's sherriff and
invited out to dinner."

—Vicki O'Day

"When it's time for a shakedown or a shakeup, the police grow suddenly moral, and the burlesque show suffers proportionately," said Bernard Sobel.

"Harold used to stand out in front of the theatre on a Friday night with envelopes," said Dardy Minsky. "And the politicians would come by and he'd pay off everybody."

In the early days, instead of a red light serving as a warning, the end girl in the chorus would signal when the police came in and the show would instantly clean up. Usually raids on clubs and theatres coincided with a political election. The strippers and the owners were arrested—a prize for the politico's constituents.

Some clubs in particular, such as Miami's Jungle Club and Red Barn, were targets whenever an official ran for office. Both club owners and the strippers would be hauled off to jail—repeatedly.

Club owner Leroy Griffith was used to raids, but one night it was relentless. He and the dancers were arrested for "an hour or two. We'd go right back and open up the same night." In Miami, some politicians had revoked his license. It didn't stop Leroy from having the show go on. "I would go into the box office by myself for a minute. They would come in and arrest me for operating a theatre. I would get in the police car. We were arrested twenty-four times, I think, in one night."

The headline in the paper the next day joked "when they advertise 'they never close,' they mean it." Leroy said it was "politicians wanting their name in the papers. You have those problems in this business."

"I was routinely arrested," confirmed Dixie Evans. Once in Miami, the club was packed. The police came backstage and said "follow us." Dixie and the others were getting in the back of the prowl car when she noticed her landlady going into the club. Dixie made a fuss and the obliging officer told the landlady, "'She'll be back in ten minutes; it's only routine.'" They went down to the station. The girls were booked and released in time for the next show.

Kitty West said, "I went to the jail and I just stood in front and they took pictures is all. Isn't that cute?"

In 1951, Zorita was arrested for holding her snake suggestively at the Two O'Clock club. She paid a fine of $42.90 and returned in time for the next show.

Alexandra the Great was arrested twice. Once "at Walgreens. I had a pistol in my coat, and somebody saw it and I was arrested. That was taken care of," she said. Club owners and managers bailed out their stars.

Betty Rowland was arrested several times. She blamed it on both politics and shows competing with one another. "Clubs would call the vice squad to get the competition in trouble."

In 1952 where Betty danced, the club's manager was "involved with police." The cops came into the Burbank Theatre in Los Angeles. The regular girl at the front was in the bathroom and whoever was selling tickets insisted they buy a ticket. There was an argument and the officers threatened to close the club and arrest everyone inside. "They did arrest me," Betty said. She was sentenced to three months. The fine was steep. "Five thousand dollars to get out. I could tell stories about the judge." Her boyfriend at the time paid the fine. "We didn't make that kind of money. Money went for costumes and press agents."

Another time Betty was sentenced to three weeks in jail in Lincoln Heights. She has vivid memories of her time there. "When it was mop time again, a couple of guards walked up and presented me with a smaller broom adorned with a big red bow. 'For the Ball of Fire,' they said. . . . The day started at 5 a.m. in order to get in line for the toilet. Each morning was a bed inspection—it had to be neatly made—then it was breakfast, when we'd line up for coffee and bread rolls. . . . At night playing dominoes helped to pass the time until lights out at 8 p.m."

Betty was in absolute misery. "I cried every day, but quietly, because on the first day as I was weeping one girl said, 'Oh come on, stop the bawling.'"

Betty was involved in many lawsuits. She sued a radio station in Los Angeles because they "refused to give her time on the radio for the accomplishment" of advertising her "artistic abilities," claiming her acts were immoral and indecent. In response, Betty offered to give the judge a free show so he could decide himself if her act was truly immoral and indecent.

In 1943, she sued Samuel Goldwyn Inc. Betty alleged she and the company had entered into an agreement whereby she would be "technical adviser to Barbara Stanwyck" for the motion picture *Ball of Fire*. Betty alleged in her complaint that Stanwyck was to "enact certain dances done and performed by plaintiff [Rowland]." Betty was promised $250.00 a week for work commencing four weeks prior to the start of filming, through the nine weeks of shooting. Betty lost her case.

Sherry Britton was arrested in 1936, along with nine others, after appearing in "Scanties on Parade." The ten pleaded guilty and threw themselves at the mercy of the court, who sentenced Sherry. According to court records, the judge stated, "Believing you will profit by the leniency of the court, you are placed on probation for the period of two years. . . . If you behave properly, you will be released."

In Philadelphia, Blaze Starr also had herself a problem. "Politicians were trying to close [Philadelphia]—not allowed to bump and grind, solid bra, not see-through, a real bathing suit as far as you can strip. I was dating a captain on the police force. Then he comes in one night with his boys like he never knew me and arrested me. And I thought, 'You son of a bitch—I'll fix your ass, because one day I'm gonna be famous and I'm gonna tell your wife.' And she did, including his story in her autobiography. The captain was thought to be Frank Rizzo, who went on to become mayor. "They came in, put me in a wagon with three or four other strippers. They're crying, 'What am I gonna tell my babies?'"

The boss got Blaze and the others released. But she was in there two hours. "It was awful. I've been claustrophobic ever since." Years passed, and Blaze never forgot the humiliation. "I put him in my book. He died a few years ago. Climbed the ladder, then he died. Men do things to you. I'm not bitter."

That wasn't Blaze's only run-in with the law. She was also arrested in New Orleans at the Sho Bar and weeks later at the Black Cat Café. Both times the charges would be thrown out.

La Savona was arrested in New York. "They arrest the whole place. The boss had a problem with one of the cops. I got a lot of nice publicity."

"Sometimes they just liked to arrest ya," said former stripper Ricki Covette, "for kicks."

Sally Rand was arrested too many times to count, once four times in one day. Her son had all the newspaper clippings to prove it, starting in 1933. In fact, Sally

Stripper La Savona on stage

had always kept meticulous books on her press and they came in handy. She was brought to court, but she proved she was somewhere else because she had the ink to prove it.

It was demeaning and frightening for the girls as they were hauled off to jail. Sometimes forced to pay an exorbitant fine, many had to spend the night behind bars. It was just another hazard of a job that riled the pious and gave a platform to the hungry politicians. The strippers were caught in the middle.

After Lily Ann Rose was busted and banned in Boston, she swore she'd never break another law. "And I kept that. . . . I didn't get a traffic ticket until I was fifty-seven years old," she said.

Not all the arrests or shutdowns of the shows was without justification.

In 1953, Boston's venerable Old Howard was shut down because of flashing. By this time, there were no longer large choruses; it was mostly strippers. The acts became "downright naughty." Both Rose La Rose and Irma the Body admitted to "going too far" at a performance, causing the banning of burlesque in Boston. The police snuck in a camera in the theatre and caught Irma the Body apparently doing something she shouldn't have.

The bumps and the grinds were killing burlesque.

CHAPTER EIGHTEEN
The Little Flower

"It makes no difference if I burn my bridges behind me—I never retreat."
—Fiorello LaGuardia

"There is no Democratic or Republican way of cleaning the streets."
— Fiorello LaGuardia

A big picture number

The Great Depression was on. Soup lines barely kept the long lines of unemployed fed. Hooverville shacks were a mainstay in Central Park and elsewhere across a frightened and starving nation.

"People in that era were so depressed and there was no hope," said Dixie Evans. "The masses were just out of work and out of money." But the burlesque shows drew in the desperate who sought shelter, the possibility of laughs and the glorious site of beauty. It was a refuge.

On 42nd Street in New York, the burlesque theatres pasted large posters of the voluptuous strippers in all their glory for anyone to see. There was a growing resentment among "legit" theatre owners, who were watching their missing profits flow into the burlesque houses. Church congregations griped repeatedly to the police and politicians; they didn't like all that flesh on display. Burlesque houses were—incorrectly—thought to be dens of sexual activity and prostitution. Trouble was brewing for the burly q.

New York's Mayor Fiorello LaGuardia had entered office in the mid-1930s, at the time burlesque was prospering. Much to the consternation of Broadway theatre owners, the girl shows were taking a substantial bite from their box office. Legit had become too expensive to produce and too costly for the average unemployed Joe to afford. Broadway shows were tanking. But for a dime or a quarter, a man could spend a few hours in a dark theatre forgetting his troubles. In the privacy of a dark theatre, a man could slip into another world, of fantasy and hope and escape.

A man could believe—for a few hours, anyway—that the flesh on display was available, as were all the riches America had to offer. A man could identify with the comics who looked just like him. They were generally scruffy, wore ill-fitting clothes, talked and walked like an "everyman." The men in the audiences felt comfortable and among their own. They belonged. The burly q and all its layers of fantasy and cheap gags was perhaps the only thing keeping a man's spirits up in an otherwise dismal time.

Fiorello ("little flower" in Italian) LaGuardia was a fat-faced, greasy-haired, five-foot-tall, three-term mayor who had it in for burlesque, among other immoral, corrupt goings-on in his town. Vowing to reform most everything in the Big Apple, LaGuardia took aim at burlesque, considering what went on there to be filth. He believed it when he was told burlesque incited sex crimes. Burlesque was a den for prostitution, he thought. He would remove it from his city.

Burlesque wasn't without its part in its own downfall. Mike Iannucci said, "The fact that the strippers took over, the comics lost their power and it became a strip show—that's when it got raunchy. When you give someone an inch, they take your arm, that's how some of the strippers were. People were offended. LaGuardia started getting complaints and he said, 'Either clean up your act or you're gone.' And they wouldn't clean up their act and he banned them. He had the power at the time and that was it."

LaGuardia's cohort in sweeping the streets of New York clean was Paul Moss, the Commissioner of Licenses (a former blackface performer in vaudeville as a child in the 1890s, according to *Nightclub City* author Burton Peretti). As a 1937 *Time Magazine* article stated, "the power to license is the power to reform."

Moss, under pressure from LaGuardia, refused to renew the license of fourteen burlesque theatres in New York. LaGuardia upheld the ban. And bye, bye burlesque. "May 8, 1937, he banished it from New York," said Mike Iannucci.

"Everyone ran to their agents," remembered Betty Rowland. Suddenly a dwindling field for the performers was crowded with actors and girls willing to cross over to burlesque.

According to Peretti, one vindictive denouncer of burlesque wished any woman who worked in burlesque to be "out of employment for a long, long time and to go hungry." Ouch. The women were vilified and targeted.

The repercussions of banning burlesque shows in New York were widely felt. Thousands were out of work. "But in six months it was all back," with new rules and new names for the shows, Betty Rowland said.

Negotiating with the politicians, some theatres reopened with the word "follies," or "reviews." "Burlesque" and "Minsky" were forbidden. The ban didn't touch nightclubs in LaGuardia's city that continued to thrive with the same sort of acts from the strippers, with the same amount of nudity. For whatever reason, the mayor chose not to go after these institutions.

Booking more exotic dancers than jazz musicians, 52nd Street would flourish with just as much nudity as the theatres. Instead of Swing Street, it would be thereafter known as Stripty Street, and in the late '40s would begin the reign of Lili St. Cyr and dozens of other burlesquers considered glamorous and appropriate for the upper-middle class.

New Jersey "became the base for burlesque in that era," said New Jersey resident and historian Nat Bodian, and brother of Al, who wrote the screenplay for the 1953 film *Striporama* starring Betty Paige and Lili St. Cyr.

One appreciative reporter bemoaned, "If Burly goes, who will train the Red Buttons and the Jan Murrays [a slapstick comedian] of tomorrow?"

Eventually the politicians would find their way to New Jersey by the late '50s attempting to ban nudity and dancers on the stage, ramping up arrests of strippers. The Empire built in 1912 was a one-thousand-seat theatre. In 1957, amid another anti-burlesque climate, dozens of strippers were arrested; the Empire lost its license and closed. The beautiful, historic old theatre was leveled and made into a parking lot.

CHAPTER NINETEEN

The High Cost of Stripping

"You make big money but it does cost money to stay in the game."
—Dixie Evans

"The biggest majority think 'no talent,' 'prostitutes.' 'Low lifes.'"
—April March on what people thought of burlesque dancers

While the average stripper could make a living, often a very good living, saving for the day when the net bra began to sag proved far more challenging.

Beverly Anderson said she made good money "but always owed money." There were travel expenses, wardrobe, press agents and agents' commissions that came out of every salary.

"I learned a lot how to survive off my salary," Sequin said. In the beginning she made $150 a week. "Every time you went around the circuit, you got another gown and another $100 dollars." Eventually her salary would rise to $750 a week. Considering the cost of gas in 1950 was 18 cents, the cost of a car roughly $1,500, and the average income $3,200, Sequin was doing very well.

Terry Mixon made $50 a week in the '40s, which she said was "a good salary."

Twenty years earlier, Betty Rowland was paid $16 a week when she started out as a chorus girl performing four shows a day. Eventually, when AGVA was formed, conditions improved. "The chorus girls would have a couple days off."

"AGVA didn't stick up for us," said Maria Bradley. "It was a nightclub union. They didn't do a darn thing for us. We'd still have to rehearse without pay and if you didn't want to rehearse, you were out of a job."

Starting as a chorus girl in 1953, Joni Taylor would volunteer "for anything" to earn extra money. "If you can dance, they encouraged you to do a strip here and there when someone did not show up or someone became sick coming in off the road. And they also gave you bit parts like walk-ons and you got paid extra for that, and if you had to do lines, you made more for talking. . . . I really loved the extra money," she said.

However, to some, it was a trap doing scenes and bits with the comics. To open one's mouth on the stage cost the girl's star status and a star's salary. "If you were a good talking woman, you would never get any more money and you would never become a feature," explained Val Valentine.

Many strippers refused to work with the comedians, striving to become the headliner and get the salary that came with it.

Al Baker Jr. said, "Comics in them days were earning maybe $175, $200 and some of the real, real good comics might have gotten $250."

Renny von Muchow added, "The burlesque houses paid us $300 a week for the act and we did four shows a day for that."

"Every six weeks you had to do a strip and you got the magnificent sum of $1.50," said Lorraine Lee, sarcastically.

"I never was stood up for my pay either, and I know some people were and a show would close and the bosses would flee," said Sequin.

When Lee Stuart started doing straights, he said, "I signed on for thirty-five dollars a week. Which in those days, you could get a room at the Earl Hotel for two dollars, and you could eat for a dollar a day. So I thought I was in the big time."

"I think what kept a lot of girls in burlesque at the time was the money. Because what they were paying for scale was nothing. It was chump change. We were making money," said Val Valentine.

"At sixteen, I had three children, and I was supporting those children," Joni Taylor recalled. As a chorus girl she made forty dollars a week, which was enough to feed her family and then some.

Many sashayed in and out of burlesque, retiring once they married and had children, going back in when they needed the money. Tee Tee Red said, "We got in trouble financially, my husband and I. I said 'Well, let me go back on stage and I'll get us out of trouble.' I booked myself for one tour and made $1,500 a week and I was out of trouble in no time."

Like celebrities today, the women relentlessly pursued publicity by hiring press agents to keep their names in the papers. Keeping up appearances as a feature was expensive. Many spent thousands on their wardrobe and lifestyle to impress fans, agents, and club owners.

"God, [if] you don't have a mink coat and a Cadillac, the agent's not gonna give you any money," Dixie Evans said. "You don't dare go in the agent's office with a cloth coat." One had to dazzle the agent, who got you the work. One had to make a lasting impression, both on and off the stage.

Mimi Reed

Carole Nelson recalled her Aunt Ann Corio "walking in late to Christmas Eve mass, with the big mink coat and the jewelry and smelling of all these colognes. Just grandeur. She was larger than life. She was Auntie Mame."

"We had the power. We had the money," said Dixie Evans.

Lili St. Cyr blew through the thousands she earned weekly. "I always have to make money to pay for things." Lili rarely ever took a vacation or time off. She needed to work—spiritually and financially. Many women like Lili were not supported by husbands or family. Indeed, they were doing the supporting. They made it on their own despite the turned-up noses outside the theatre.

Gypsy seemed to hang onto her money. In 1940 she purchased a townhome on East 63rd Street in Manhattan. The fairly stripped exterior belied the lush interior. There was a private courtyard, twenty-six bedrooms and seven baths. Gypsy had gold monograms applied to the doors.

Others, like Sally Rand, invested in property. Blaze saved and bought the Two O'Clock nightclub in Baltimore. Ann Corio made a living during her heyday, lost it in a divorce, and earned it again and then some with the success of her show *This Was Burlesque*, which ran almost thirty years.

Tassel twirler Sally Keith "had a half a million dollars here and thousands there her furs and her jewels," claimed her niece Susan Weiss.

By contrast, the everyday working comedian and straight just made a living. Alan Alda declared his father never made money to boast of—not in burlesque or in movies, where he had a studio contract, or in the nightclubs. Burlesque was steady income. And when it was over, one could take a job in a piano bar (Alda) or sell hot dogs (Al Baker Sr.)

Alexandra the Great had a deal with Rose La Rose, her mentor. "She coached me. I worked her theatre five months while she prepared me to go on the road. I always went back to Rose. That was my agreement with her. I worked for Rose three or four times a year at the Town Hall. I would always work there at a certain price. Elsewhere my price was different," she said.

"I knew that there would be a day I'd quit, but I really didn't prepare for it financially," remembered Vicki O'Day.

Many never organized for the day burlesque and the big salaries would vanish. It was a slow death, yet unexpected to those who were blind to its imminent demise. As their looks faded and their bodies were no longer desirable, the strippers couldn't compete with the women coming into the stripping profession—for surely it wasn't burlesque any more, no matter what the marquee outside called it. As early as 1930, Sobel was complaining: "Teens were flooding the market, knocking out the older burlesque women." It was nothing compared to the competition that arrived in the 1950s and beyond.

"All the girls were much younger. I was starting to hear about age. That would be the first question they'd ask me," said Tee Tee Red. "I didn't want to retire."

In the beginning, the strippers were "experienced. Towards [the] end [if you were] young, walking and breathing? Walk to time? You're in," remembered Dee Ann Johnston.

"You think, 'Oh this gravy train's gonna run forever.'" April March looked wistfully away, full of thoughts of the day when she was being courted by princes and getting paid for it.

The other cost was the continued discrimination and attitude towards the strippers, in addition to having to deal with arrests and fines. They were stuck with what they were doing. They couldn't move up the show business ladder.

"Few crossed over. Gypsy was the closest. Other women crossed over in small ways. Mostly, no," said Rachel Shteir.

The fact of rising costs both with unions and the greed of the theatre owners changed the landscape of the burlesque show. Eventually the size of the orchestra was reduced, one union musician at a time, until eventually live music vanished from the pits and the payroll. They were replaced by tape. Comedians were slashed, novelty acts dropped.

"Our careers in show business ended when flesh acts were not in demand anymore," said Renny von Muchow.

Val Valentine said, "The unions closed a lot of the theatres because they couldn't keep up with the salaries."

"Unions were terrible," Dardy Minsky agreed. "They would put you out of business. They told you what to do. It was all crooked."

When Lee Stuart started in 1947 there were six to eight girls in the line. When he quit ten years later, they were down to four or five. "They cheapened it by taking personnel out of it. They kept cutting down the personnel. And then the chorus girls started stripping."

"So it got down to comics and strips," said Val Valentine.

The entire chorus was soon abolished. The large opening number, middle picture number, and the grand finale dropped. All the while, the feature strippers asked for bigger and bigger salaries, which helped push out the smaller acts.

Uncensored Magazine compared the costs of producing a show: In 1935 the average salary of a chorus girl was $21 a week. Other salaries were: the straight man, $50; the house singer or the juvenile (Bud Abbott's starting career), $35; the feature stripper, $125; musicians, $60. A producer's salary was $125.

By 1954, the chorus had dropped from twenty-six girls to sixteen at $75 a dancer per week; straight men were up to $175; a feature stripper anywhere from $350 to $4,000—or more for the big marquee names.

Due to the rising cost, some theatres were down to less than a dozen performers for a two-and-a-half hour show. In 1954, the average price for a ticket was still only $1 or $1.50. *Uncensored Magazine* claimed Minsky's still prodigious show cost $12,000 a week to produce, but it was, of course, a more elaborate affair and drew the majority of the crowds lining up to see the Lili St. Cyrs and Tempest Storms. By then, dozens of burlesque houses were closing.

Since AGVA had been representing the strippers, and all acts in burlesque, minimum salaries were enforced, which wasn't without controversy within the union itself. In 1951, Gypsy Rose Lee was an AGVA official. In 1953, there was a move to throw out the strippers, as they were believed to be giving the entire profession a bad name.

Jack Ruby so detested the competition down the strip at Weinstein's Colony Club with its popular "amateur stripping nights" that he tried to break AGVA of its policy to allow "amateur" strippers to perform in the union houses for less pay. Ruby (mirroring the growing resentment across America) was jealous of the continued success of burlesque in such class places as Weinstein's. He despised their success. Ruby, like the mayors and councilmen and church groups, was a pot about to boil over.

CHAPTER TWENTY

Family Life

"I married a piano player—and that was the thing to do."

—Joan Arline

"My family was very proud . . . not like some . . .
'Oh, you cannot go there.' What striptease?
I just show my bum, nobody touches me."

—La Savona

Some girls were introduced to stripping through boyfriends and husbands. When Joan Arline's husband suggested she join a burlesque show, she was deeply offended and wouldn't speak to him for weeks. "We didn't have burlesque in Connecticut. If you knew what it was, you didn't admit it." Joan, who died in 2011 at age seventy-eight, didn't stay offended for long. She loved her chosen profession. Her husband Don might have gotten her into peeling for a living, but she would strip herself of that marriage and go on to another three.

Stripper Kay Hanna said her husband had taken her to a burlesque show. She thought "Gee, anyone can do that." When her husband got hurt and was unable to work, she "had to make money." She found an agent and started making club dates in Philadelphia.

The first time she stripped, she couldn't believe she was actually doing it. "Wow," she said. "I was horrified to think I had to do this. But you get through things." Her husband then started promoting her. They didn't stay married much longer. She divorced him and left. "It was too difficult. We were in these clubs, both of us drinking too much."

Her ex-husband called the authorities several times and had her arrested at work. "He was mad at me so he was going to make it difficult for me, so he complained about me," she said. Eventually she quit the business because it was "getting a little too rough." She retired and did clerical work.

Sequin used to ride with her father, a bootlegger running liquor up Highway 1 in California. They would stop in honky-tonk places "and I'd get up and I'd sing. He'd be behind the bar doing whatever he was doing with bootleg whisky."

As a young woman, there were few singing jobs available, so when her boyfriend Ted suggested she become a stripper she didn't so much as flinch. Her boyfriend took her to a few clubs in Los Angeles to see how they did it and ended up booking her into Strip City in 1954.

Lillian Hunt would eventually train her. Sequin was influenced by Lili St. Cyr, who worked with fancy props and sashayed ladylike across the stage. Sequin liked that concept: "the lady, but the tease." Sequin would meet her future husband and love of her life at Minsky's Adams Theatre in Newark. Tony Tamburello was Tony Bennett's coach and musical director of forty years. It was love at first sight. She was one of the lucky ones.

"Married life didn't work. You were there, he was there," said Val Valentine.

Blaze was a hopeless romantic with her affairs, always believing "my man's gonna come along," she said. "He never did. Oh God, I've been in love about five times."

Sally Rand told her son, "I married the man I shouldn't have and vice versa." Sean thought she had four husbands, but "Sally only talked about three." He read about a supposed husband named Gray when he was young. "She had lots of boyfriends," he remembered.

Sally's engagement to one of her husbands, Turk Greenough, garnered headlines. A Helen Greenough claimed she was still Turk's current wife. "How can he marry that fan dancer if he's married to me?" she had asked. According to Mrs. Greenough, Sally met Turk at a rodeo in Cheyenne, Wyoming, in 1935. When Turk took the prize, Sally ran up to him for his autograph. Mrs. Greenough claimed Sally was just the type of "society woman" that would turn her bronco buck's head.

Sally did turn his head so sufficiently that he untied himself from his wife and the two were married in 1942. However, Turk left for the army in '43 and the two never had the chance to live together. They eventually divorced.

In 1950, at age forty-six, she married her manager Harry Finkelstein. This was a more manageable, and common, relationship.

"Usually you had maybe three talking women and they were married to the comics or the straight man or something like that," said Al Baker Jr. "It was a family thing."

Lorraine Lee met her future husband Dick Richards backstage in St. Louis. "I saw a pair of white sneakers, no socks, seersucker shirt, Irish face, no hair. He throws his arms around the singer, says, 'Benny, have you been true to me since I've been gone?' Now Benny's a big guy and he says, 'Oh, Dickie bird.' I found out later, he had asked everyone who could best do the scenes. I got elected. I worked with him upteen years." They were together thirty-five years: "I told my mother when I met him, 'He's Jewish.' 'Well, does he treat you nice?' 'Yes.' 'If he treats you good, that's it.'"

Comedian Dick Richards was married three times, twice to strippers. Lorraine Lee, a former stripper (who looked anything but in our interview with her grey bob, glasses, plaid shirt, and silver horse earrings) was his last wife.

"Dick was a comic Romeo. Funny guy and friendly," said Sequin. "He wanted to go out with everybody. A sweetheart, though. He was married to a talking woman, always taking the girls out."

Richards claimed he hated the early years of burlesque because the shows were so grueling, but the benefit was the girls.

Lady Midnight admitted that she had gotten married because she didn't want to go on the circuit alone. "Jimmy Matthews said, 'Oh well, let's go, we can share a room.' So we married in April on stage of the Follies Theatre." Lady Midnight knew that Jimmy was in love with her, but the feelings weren't mutual. She wasn't attracted to him: "He said he was 45. He could have been in his sixties . . . he barely made it to my shoulders."

"Once we were on the road for about two weeks, [and] he decided to try to get into bed with me and I pushed him away and got my own room. After about three weeks I decided I didn't want to do what was demanded of me [which meant getting completely nude at some of the clubs. 'Something we didn't do in LA.'] So I called it quits and went back to the Follies. We were divorced in May." She admitted the marriage "was also a plus in the publicity factor. . . I never got to see him again."

Vicki O'Day said, "I was married to four different men, but husband number three I married three times, so he was three, four, and five. And then number six lasted about five minutes."

"I got married in Hawaii when I was thirty and then I married four times after that, but I forget the times," said Alexandra the Great.

April March also shared her experiences with love on the road. "I never found a man that I didn't fall in love with. When I fell in love, I felt it was right to be married. I was terrible." She looked sheepishly at her daughter, who was sitting next to her while we talked. "I had too many of them. Liz Taylor and I have the same amount."

Kitty West was an exception to most of the strippers' marriages. "I was married fifty-two years. And he was my greatest fan."

Some husbands would be jealous of wives who made money popping pasties for other men. Lili St. Cyr complained of this often.

One of Tee Tee Red's husbands "couldn't handle it. The marriage didn't last long," she said. She had met him when he was bartending and he knew of her work. She earned more money than him. "I was the breadwinner," she said. That rubbed him the wrong way.

"My last husband said, 'You're in a degenerate business,'" Tempest recalled. "It shocked me. Yet, here he was living off my earnings." This was the African American singer Herb Jeffries. "It's the business I was in when you met me. You drive big cars and go on cruises. You're spending my money," she said she told him. Jeffries, a former actor, was known as the Bronze Buckaroo for his low-budget cowboy flicks. "He was a great singer, but he was lazy," Tempest said.

With rumors of their marriage pending, "a columnist called me. . . . He said, 'I'm gonna talk to you like a father: Don't do it. He's a has-been,'" she said. Tempest did not like being told what to do. "The more people told me not to do it—I did it. Which was stupid, detrimental to myself." Jeffries would direct Tempest in the film *Mundos Depravados*, billed as a "sex murder mystery." The fifteen-years-younger Tempest played Tango, the dancer. Jeffries and Tempest eventually divorced, to no one's surprise.

Like Tempest, too many of the women in burlesque supported husbands with their hard-earned salaries.

Straight man Robert Alda's wife understood he worked nightly with a bevy of half-clad strippers running to and fro backstage. Sometimes it was too much for the stay-at-home mother. "One night she accused him of having an affair. When he denied it, she tried to stab him with a paring knife," recalled Alan, who was six at the time and witnessed the struggle. She was "paranoid," he recalled. But "sometimes paranoid people are right," he said.

Photo courtesy of Alan Alda

Robert Alda, his wife Joan, and son Alan

Barry Siegfried, son of stripper Mara Gaye, attended a show with his father. "[He] took me to a show that my mother was doing. When we sat down and the show started, my mother came on stage and I said to my father in a not-so-quiet voice, 'What's mommy doing up there without her clothes?' . . . I had wonderful parents. They taught me values of being independent, using my brain and not following the masses. I grew up as an honest person. They didn't hide anything from me," he said. But it didn't mean they were as open with the neighbors. "The burlesque part of my mom's showbiz career was kept quiet," he said.

"When you start to have children and they're in school, you have to be careful who you tell," explained White Fury. "A lot of people didn't approve because they didn't know. They thought it was a bad thing. Or girls that were dancers were bad people."

April March said of her daughter, "I sent her to Catholic School and she took my 8x10 photo to school. And I had to go see the Mother Superior. She said 'I would appreciate it if you didn't give your daughter your 8x10s.'"

Most of the strippers did not take their children on the road, except sometimes during the summers when the kids were out of school. Most were left behind.

Once Tempest divorced Jeffries, he raised their daughter. "My daughter traveled with me when she was small. At seven, she went with her father. We thought it best because I was traveling so much." Tempest admitted the separation was hard. "And she kinda resented me and we were estranged for about ten years . . . until four years ago. We became very close." Tempest's daughter danced for a couple of years, too. She called Tempest once and asked, "Do you have any costumes?"

Lady Midnight had no choice but to have her daughter backstage at the Follies in Los Angeles. She was single and needed to work. "She loved going downstairs to the rehearsal room to watch us practice. She was also sometimes allowed in the wings when the show was running." The comics would watch her three-year-old daughter. "They got a big kick out of her and guarded her as if she were a precious diamond."

"As a child, I was standing in the wings. And no one thought that that was weird." Alan Alda shook his head.

Candy Cotton's daughter would visit her during the summer. Once when working in Toledo, "she walked across stage one day to get to me." Candy Cotton said her daughter stayed at her mother's in New York during the school year. Sometimes it was the housekeeper who was left to watch her son and daughter. She hesitated when I asked if she was close with her children. "Closer with my son than daughter," she responded. The separations seemed to be harder and more unforgiving for daughters. Candy Cotton's stint in burlesque didn't seem to faze her son, she said. For her daughter, it was another matter.

Carmela, the Sophia Loren of Burlesque, was living alone in Las Vegas when I met her. We had many conversations on the phone during the last months of her life. She said she started dancing young. At age five, she would run to her "mother's bookie and he'd say, 'Tap for me,' and give me a nickel and a bag of chips."

She was a cocktail waitress when a woman named Lola Beaver came in and taught dancing. And "this club owner thought I'd be a good stripper," she said. "They talked me into being a stripper. I can't learn from anyone else. I have to do my own thing. What a disaster. [The audience] made fun of me. The stage was tiny. I was trying to put my wardrobe down and a guy reached up and grabbed me. I lasted a week there. Went to another place. I had to learn to relax and that I was on the stage for a purpose. Took me two months. I started doing splits and yoga and back bends."

She told me she was the proud mother of two children. Her son was an ordained minister. Her daughter sold real estate. From our conversations, I had the distinct feeling that as proud of them as *she* might be, *they* were not an active part of her life.

"I had a wonderful Philipino neighbor and his wife. They were great with my two children, and they used to take care of them. And I used to call them every night and I laid the law down, and I said, 'I expect you to abide by my wishes and you will check in with Six Toe and his wife,' which was the Philipino man."

April March said she spoiled her daughter Cyrese, who was left with grandparents, as often as she could. "All my boyfriends used to come over to the house. They wanted to see my mom. They thought she was beautiful," explained April's daughter Cyrese. April had Cyrese when she was eighteen. Cyrese explained, her voice shaky and teary-eyed, that "sometimes it wasn't so pretty growing up. I didn't fit into the social groups. That was really hard. I was shunned. I remember going to a girlfriend's home. She was on the floor with her siblings. Her mother answered the door. This is really sad. I still remember this and it breaks my heart. Her mother said, 'Oh, my daughter's not home.' 'She's sitting right on the floor.' 'She's not home to you.'"

Vicki O'Day's daughter told her years later that it was difficult having a very pretty mother.

After one interview with a former stripper, whose name I will not print to protect her and her daughter, her daughter broke down and confessed she had been abused as a child one of the times her mother had left her behind. The daughter had spent years hating her mother.

Tee Tee Red didn't speak much about her three children at all.

Sean Rand said, "When I was first in school when I was younger, people would come over and say, 'Your mother does this dance, or whatever, and then she takes her clothes off.' And I was a little bit embarrassed. . . . She picked up on that and sitting down explained to me what the dance symbolized: two herons flying over a moonlit lake in the Ozarks of Missouri."

Some strippers that didn't have children traveled with *their* mothers. Rose La Rose traveled with her Italian mother. Dixie Evan's mother spent a majority of her time, once they reconciled backstage, on the road. Her mother would "babysit the star's poodle or baby." Her mom was "tickled to death." Dixie said her mother "loved those girls," and the old comedians would sit and talk to her all day.

Gypsy's son, Erik Preminger, was hauled around both in the carnival and theatres. He would never quite move out from under the dominating shadow of her astounding success. He writes books about her, gives interviews, and does much to keep her memory alive.

Gypsy would ban her own troublesome mother from backstage. And her memoirs would cause a rift with her sister, actress June Havoc, who thought the recollections of Mama Rose portrayed her too endearingly. June wrote two autobiographies that told a a different story. She believed her mother was mentally disturbed. June also wasn't happy with the way she was portrayed in her sister's memoirs, as she was the one supporting Gypsy and their mother. Wherein Dainty June in *Gypsy* elopes, and as she exits the curtain her story is over. In reality, June had a harder time. After she ran away from Mama Rose, she was oftentimes destitute as a teenage bride, living on bus stops, while Gypsy began to make her own, very good, living. June remembered her sister as "ruthless" and her mother as "lethal." She said they were really "the same person."

It was easier for the comedians to travel with family. Usually, if the mother wasn't working in the show, she took care of the kids, providing some semblance of routine and normalcy despite the hardships.

Harry Lloyd said, "I wanted a model train set. We had no place. We never lived in a place where I could have it."

Al Baker Jr. openly adored his parents. Raised on the circuit, he too would eventually get into burlesque, owning and operating theatres. In 1947 the whole family traveled to California when Al Jr. was thirteen to work the Burbank Theatre. They drove out in Al Sr.'s 1942 Buick and stayed at Lou Costello's house. "Bud and Lou were big at Universal. They were king," he said. Al Sr.'s friends, other comedians in burlesque, "begged" Al Sr. to come to California and try and break into films. But "he was conservative, he knew he was the best in the business and could work fifty-two weeks if he wanted. And that's what he liked. Never got into movies," said Al Jr.

Having a parent in burlesque often led to unconventional lifestyles. Barry Siegfried said, "I grew up as a nudist because they went to the nudist club in the late 1940s. I spent every summer of my life at this place. In the 1950s you didn't talk about things you did as a family that other families did not do. I was raised an *outdoor* nudist, but when it came to being in the apartment at home, my parents would say, 'Now you don't walk in front of the window without any clothes on.' But this was a time when you could lose jobs over this kind of information," he said. His parents were also into bondage and discipline, using restraints and ties. It was "lighter than S&M," though, he said.

Barry's mother was a dark-haired stripper named Mara Gaye. She and her husband, who managed her career, were free spirits. They were "into everything," he said. When Mara died, Barry went through closets and found tons of magazines, porn, and S&M material.

"I wouldn't change my childhood for anything, because that's the childhood I had and that's what I work from," said Alan Alda, "but it was a form of abuse to not protect the kid from some of the stuff that the kid would see."

Tee Tee Red

CHAPTER TWENTY-ONE
All You Need Is Love

"What kind of a person would work in burlesque?"
—Maria Bradley

"I couldn't sing or dance or do anything, but I was bound or determined to get into show business."
—Dixie Evans

Mimi Reed wasn't remotely interested in being interviewed by me or anyone else. However, I persisted and I'm grateful. At ninety-seven, Mimi claimed she couldn't remember anything about her time in burlesque starting from the 1930s, when she was a specialty dancer.

Six months earlier, her partner, friend, and lover of sixty years, Thareen Aurora, had died. Mimi was despondent.

I kept up a correspondence and phone calls for nearly six months. Finally Mimi agreed I could stop by her house and chat.

When I walked into her garden on a sunny Los Angeles day, there was a stiletto-thin red-headed sprite with close-cropped hair determinedly banging on a picture frame with a hammer.

Mimi had clear and brilliant blue eyes, a sharp nose, and she wore a colorful housecoat down to her ankles. She was trying to extract a picture of her and Thareen. She seemed no older than someone in her seventies.

When she had time to sit with me, everything poured out. She recalled with great detail everything about her years in burlesque working with Abbott and Costello, Robert Alda, Joey Yule, Georgia Sothern, Margie Hart, and Betty Rowland.

One of Mimi's specialty dances was performed with a giant rubber ball like Sally Rand. In 1944, at the Hollywood Casino, *Billboard* called her singing "warbling," but said her Afro dance was "lovely."

The dressing room in her house, next to her bedroom, was covered with 11x14 black-and-white photographs of her and Thareen. They had had

Specialty dancer Mimi Reed

side-by-side dressing tables with big light bulbs surrounding each mirror. They had performed together in theatres for years.

There was a picture of "Allie" Alda at three or four years old holding his dog, looking exactly like the seventy-one-year-old man I had interviewed.

Mimi, at the height of her beauty, looked like Rita Hayworth with big red lips and a svelte figure. She had been gorgeous. Thareen was shorter, almost stocky with dark eyes and hair. Mimi and Thareen billed themselves as Reed and Aurora, "Nutty but Nice."

Mimi brought out a stack of scrapbooks and photo albums and we spent a few hours flipping through them. She had toured in the carnivals, in nightclubs, even going to Cuba with Thareen, who was an opera singer. Mimi had been in burlesque, circuses, then legit theatres. The pair had been on the road a lot.

Born in Connecticut, Mimi started dancing when she was a child. She performed with her sister, another gorgeous dancer who looked just like her. They billed themselves as the Reed Twins. They danced in movies in the chorus line in Los Angeles. "Betty Grable was with us," she said.

Eventually Mimi's sister quit the business, married, and moved to Santa Barbara. Mimi moved back East and worked for Minsky. When I asked her if she had ever stripped, she stated, "I should have. I would have made a lot of money. That's my regret. I would have done a lovely job."

Besides dancing with her balloon, she did comedic dances. She went to the dance director and told him what she wanted. "He gave me the foundation, to which I added. I did a voodoo death ritual. I carried a real skull. And one night it slipped off the tray and crashed. Teeth all over. Oh, it was a mess. . . . [A friend] had skulls sitting around his office. He sent me another one."

Mimi had once been married to a straight man named Ray Parsons, who was a "big Crosby-type singer." Mimi was also a talking woman. "Sometimes I had to make a fast change." She would do her solo acrobatic dance then run upstairs and change. "I had a split second to change for my entrance. If I didn't make it, they would just ad lib 'til I got there. During intermission, we'd rehearse. I was valuable as a talking woman and dancer."

She also danced in the big production numbers. "The pay was low compared to what a stripper made. Sometimes it got very tiring."

Thareen's grandson, Stewart Edward Allen, told me "Mimi and Thareen were both playing at the Burbank and they met backstage and Thareen just knew, it just clicked—'I want to spend the rest of the life with this woman.' And I don't think Mimi's marriage was a great one and I certainly know that Thareen's was

Mimi Reed (on right) and partner Thareen Aurora

not a really satisfying relationship. . . . They were obviously a couple. They obviously adored each other." They ditched their spouses and moved in together.

When Mimi met Thareen, they started an act that featured a stray cat they had found. The cat was named Minette and they trained her to jump through hoops.

They bought their LA house together in 1948, where they enjoyed life after show business. When Mimi retired, she worked for an architectural firm. Thareen stayed at home taking care of their pets and the garden, and they would share afternoon cocktails around the bar in their living room with neighbors and friends.

Mimi was grief-stricken by the loss of her soul mate. I spent afternoons at her house, listening to her stories, sitting with her on her bed, trying to get her out of her funk. Her depression was much deeper than that. After several months, she grasped my hand and told me she didn't want to live. It broke my heart. She would lay in bed, half listening to the television. The spirit had slipped out of Mimi like air from the balloon she had once danced with.

Mimi died in 2007. Stewart said her cancer had gotten her, her days ending painfully. But she died in her own home, in the bed she had shared with the love of her life, Thareen.

**

A love story of another kind was the enduring friendship of Rudy and Renny. I interviewed a nearly blind former acrobat Renny von Muchow in his Yonkers home with his wife Dorothy von Muchow, who used to belly dance and worked Wild West shows.

Renny had met Rudy when he was fourteen and Rudy was thirteen. "They had a contest in school to see who the strongest boy in school was. And sure enough, Rudy and I came out to be on top. And we liked it so much, and we gained such a reputation for our strength in school. So we became hand balancers. Burlesque shows at that time showed novelty acts. And some of them were acrobatic and we said, 'Oh, we can do that. Why don't we do an act that no one else can do because they're not strong enough to do it?' And we developed the act called Renald and Rudy, which kept us together for twenty-five years."

Their act was seven to eight-and-a-half minutes. Occasionally they would do a single trick, like they did on the Phil Silvers show, such as a high handstand.

They balanced one above the other, gripping arms, or cantilevered side by side. Their strength was applause-inspiring. Renny suggested they keep their bodies looking as much alike as possible, and in photos it is difficult to tell the

123

two apart. Amazingly muscular and tan, they wore tight white shorts, or pants, and usually no shirts.

They also had a glass floor made. "It would come up with us posing on a gold rock. We'd break pose, go hand to hand, sitting around us were nude girls, quite a distraction for two guys with their hormones running."

Novelty act Renald and Rudy

No one seemed to love burlesque or his part in it as much as Renny. He lit up when he talked about it, reliving all the characters. "Georgia Sothern would set the place on fire when she'd come out," he remembered.

"It wasn't work, it was play—and we were paid for it, paid well and traveled."

From the strippers, they learned lavender light "made the skin glow. We carried our own special lavender gels."

Unfortunately, as the duo grew older, they went in different directions. When burlesque ended for the pair, Rudy had a hard time coping with the end of the partnership. He drifted.

"Rudy lives a solitary life in California in a trailer park," Renny said. "Unfortunately, he never got interested in anything else to get into, to make a living when he got out of show business. He did think he would like to become a hairdresser. He tried it, didn't care for it. Then decided he would become a dog groomer, took over a store on Hollywood Boulevard. And he was very, very busy—doing well—but he says, 'I kept looking out and seeing the sunshine and I'm in here working,' and he walked away from it. 'Gee, Rudy you don't do that.' A lot of show people can't bring themselves down to earth enough to take a job that's 9 to 5. I'm afraid Rudy's one of those. Eventually he had to take something. He became a school bus driver. He enjoyed it. He didn't have to apply himself too hard."

Renny and Rudy saw each other occasionally over the years. "We never liked to write letters. Years go by without writing, but when we get out to California, we meet and it's just like old times. Rudy's like a brother to me. He's more than a best friend. We know each other so well. One thing that held us together, we did this thing together so well, it was as if we were born to do it. We'd discover a new trick, a new movement, bingo. In minutes we'd have it going and play off each other."

CHAPTER TWENTY-TWO

Florida

"My whole thing was I wanted to bring burlesque back and give it the respect it had."
—Al Baker Jr.

"I faked it in the beginning. I wasn't much of a dancer."
—Sequin

Florida seemed to be a large repository for the retired burlesque community. Sheri and I had a trip planned that was to be loaded with interviews. There was Sequin, the husky-voiced singer and former stripper I had met at the Vegas Reunion; Leroy Griffith, a club owner, who still ran at least one club in the heart of Miami; and Lily Ann Rose, born Lillian Kiernan Brown. Author David Kruh had introduced me to a book Lily had written. A dancer at thirteen, Lily had been a protégé of the tassel twirler Sally Keith (whose relatives I had interviewed outside of Chicago). *Banned in Boston* recalled the adventures of Lily's mother, who was in burlesque in the '20s. Lily took a job in the industry in the '40s. Lily and I had been corresponding via email. She assured me she had a "trunk load of photographs waiting to be documented." Her scrapbooks and house were a treasure trove. She wanted them all documented. She offered us a room in her house to spend the night. We declined. One thing about all "my ladies": they were generous to a fault. Many asked if they could "adopt" me.

While in Florida, I was also planning on meeting Al Baker Jr., to whom April March and Val Valentine had introduced me. Al would be coming down from Boca Raton. His father had been a comic and his mother a dancer and talking woman. Al Jr. had grown up on the circuit, touring with his parents. Later he opened his own clubs and was friends with Leroy Griffith, Val and April's former employer.

**

South Beach Miami. Neon lights, a balmy night breeze and tanned bodies walking along the boulevard. Art deco hotels lined the streets next to our hotel. It must have been something elegant and new sixty years prior. . . .

Collins Avenue, just a salt splash from the beach, used to be crammed with burlesque clubs. From the Gaiety, where Zorita and her python often performed, to the Five O'Clock Club, to the Paper Doll Club, where "The Ding Dong Girl" peeled with bells attached to various body parts. There had been the Red Barn, an old farm building; Rainbow Inn; and Place Pigalle, where Siska and her birds sometimes pecked the peeler. At the Jungle Club, one ate food with fingers, not utensils. In 1956, Miami boasted at least thirty burlesque clubs on Biscayne Bay.

One of the top spots was Lou Walter's swanky Latin Quarter. Located at 159 Palm Island Drive, the Latin Quarter was smack in the center of Palm Island, accessible only via the narrow causeway. The grand marble entrance was impressive and bespoke of the club's elegant clientele, such as Joseph Kennedy, who had a regular table.

When Al Baker Jr. arrived, I liked him immediately. He was late, but apologized profusely. He was a short stack of energy. He was still handsome with dark hair, shirt unbuttoned down to his stomach, revealing a hairy abdomen with a nasty scar slicing through him, a result of a recent heart surgery. Around his neck he wore a big gold chain that spelled "A.B. Jr.," a chunky gold watch, and a big diamond pinky ring. He was still the charming ladies' man. He wore blue-tinted glasses and chewed a wad of gum throughout the interview. He worshipped his parents, his father especially.

His father, Al Baker Sr., had been a well-respected straight man. Like his son, Al Sr. had been a handsome and dark-haired man. He had worked the Hirst circuit and was beloved in the business. Al Jr.'s mother, born in 1912, had been a singer and toured with the "Irish Nightingale" Morton Downey, a popular singer in the 1920s and 1930s. When she was about twelve, she had gotten in a horrible car accident. One foot got mangled under some metal. Her toes were twisted "around where her heel should be." It was set wrong and never grew. But you would never know it, claimed Al Jr. She hid it well, buying two differently sized shoes. As she got older, the pain gave her a fair amount of trouble. Later she had to wear a brace, which was hard for her. She was "very vain," Al Jr. said.

While on tour with her sister, she met Al Sr. and they fell in love. He was a week ahead of her on the circuit. Arriving in various towns ahead of her, he would book her a hotel and leave a present in the room for her. After they married, she became his talking woman. When Al Jr. was born in 1934 ("the year of the big flood in West Virginia"), she basically retired. "She didn't want to raise a kid backstage." At three or four, he fell "real sick with rheumatic fever." An only child, he was pampered and doted on, and spoiled. He became a "rough kid," but was extremely close with his parents.

He appreciated their sacrifices. "My parents went without things to do for me."

For a time, they all traveled together while Al Sr. toured. Al Jr. loved being on the road. "Everyone had a good time . . . everybody was happy," he said. They ate together, traveled together. For the troupe of performers, it was one big, extended family. When he got older, Al Jr. was sent to military school in the winters while his parents continued on the road.

Al Sr. never earned a huge income. He made a decent living, but would supplement his income dancing in marathons. Sometimes he would dance for two days straight. "He never wanted for work," Al Jr. said. His agent had been Jess Mack, a former straight man himself, who booked Sr. on the circuit.

Talking about the strippers, Al said, "Girls then wore more clothes than the girls today. It was an innocent time. The performers were professional. A show was rehearsed in a half hour. You were always performing with someone different and everyone was familiar with the old routines. . . . [The comedians] went out and never missed a line for a two-and-a-half hour show." Al Jr. admired his father's pals.

"None of the comics are left." Al recalled how differently the comedians could go over depending on the audience. "A comic could be funny in New York, or Philadelphia, but come to Canton, Ohio, or another town and they might bomb."

In 1947, Al Sr. was booked into the Burbank Theatre. The Burbank was the project of dentist Davis Burbank, who had purchased 4,600 acres in the San Fernando Valley in 1867. The theatre was not located in Burbank but in downtown Los Angeles, and would change its name in the 1960s to the New Follies Theatre.

Al Sr. retired around 1956 after winning a sweepstakes. He had invested his money pretty well, but he couldn't "sit around," so he started working for a theatre. He was the general manager. He even appeared on TV in a couple episodes of *What's My Line?* He would do anything to stay busy after years of constant work.

Al Jr. had performing in his blood. He told his father he wanted to study acting. His father told him, "'You're NT.' 'What's NT?' 'No talent.'" Sr. told his son he'd better learn to work the front of the house where the money was.

At sixteen and hard to discipline, Al Jr. was thrown out of school. He got a job selling candy in the aisles of shows. There he met Leroy Griffith, eighteen, who was the assistant concessions man.

Eventually Jr. worked for Mike Todd and "blew through" his money. "I was a big shot," he shrugged, chewing his gum and smiling. He knew he'd been a punk. He didn't have regrets.

At thirty-five, with a wife and newborn daughter and seven dollars in his pocket, Al Jr. drove in his pink Buick to Canton, Ohio, and rented a theatre and started putting on shows. "I was collecting thirty-five dollars a week unemployment," he said. Eventually Jr. owned or managed many theatres, including the Troc in Philadelphia. He ran a theatre in New York that had "porns and strips." It was $2.50 to get into during the day and $12 at midnight. April March and Val Valentine both stripped for him. He paid Blaze Starr two thousand dollars a week. "She was nice with me. She demanded big money," he said.

Another of Al Jr.'s strippers was Zsa Zsa "Chesty Morgan" Gabor. She had a seventy-three-inch chest. "A Jewish girl. She was in the Jewish army in Israel. Married a butcher who got shot and killed. I found her in a scratch house on 10th Avenue," he said.

From the pits, he smelled pot coming up from the musicians. His father told him "'never do that or I'll disown you.' And I never did. I'm seventy-two and I never did drugs in my life," he said.

Though Al Sr. has been dead since 1997, Al Jr. admitted that he still missed him.

During the interview I received a phone call and excused myself.

It was TeeTee Red. Just days before leaving for Florida, I had sent her a letter with my cell number, letting her know I was going to be in Miami and asking whether I could interview her. She was calling to say she could do the interview that night if I came to her in Miami Shores.

I returned from my call in time to hear Al's story about producing pornos.

He told his crew, "Make this picture in three days but I'll pay you for five. We went in and did all the sex in one day. *Sessions of Love Therapy*. Sammy Davis Jr. was a porn freak. Whenever we made a picture, he had to get a copy of it." Sammy visited the set, which was apparently so quiet, he told Al, "You can even hear a pube hit the ground." Sammy invited the cast to a party at the Ambassador. This was in 1968 or '69 and Al Baker rented a theatre to show the completed film and ran it at two in the morning for Sammy Davis.

He had "found" *The Devil and Mrs. Jones* actress, Michelle Graham, living in a commune and made a "corporation for her." At the time, he owned the Trocadero in Philadelphia. He bought her a couple snakes, she did a Q&A, and she would do a number. "She seemed fine for a while. I was getting her five thousand dollars a week. I'd give her a certain salary and the rest in corporation. She went off the wagon."

** **

Next up was Mr. Leroy Griffith. Leroy's current club was a seedy "titty" bar in South Beach that smelled like stale booze and cigarettes. It boasted the attendance of minor celebrities such as Paris Hilton. To get to Leroy's office, we walked past "showers" that were designed into the walls of the clubs in front of cocktail tables. I was horrified. *This* certainly wasn't burlesque.

Leroy turned out to be a big teddy bear of a man. He was gentlemanly and soft-spoken with a huge diamond pinky ring. He was reluctant to appear on camera.

Leroy had started as a candy butcher, selling candy and trinkets before and during intermission of the burlesque shows. He eventually owned theatres in the North. In 1960, he opened the Mayfair with Tee Tee Red. A ticket for the show cost $4.50. That was a "big ticket" at the time. The Mayfair sat four hundred and put on three shows a day.

From a book on his shelf, he pulled out snapshots of Tempest Storm. His face softened. The two had had "a thing," though Leroy was many times married. They were still friends. Tempest held a special place in his heart. Al Baker said she still called Leroy if she needed money.

Tempest Storm

"In those days, I was paying Tempest $1,800 a week," Leroy said. She "broke all records at the Gaiety in New York. Standing room only. And that was 1,400 seats and for an afternoon show. For two weeks she packed the house." Leroy would continue to book her, up to and including five years prior to our arrival in Florida.

**

Dirty, tired, and hungry, we loaded our equipment in the car and drove towards Miami Shores and Tee Tee Red.

Pictures of Tee Tee in her youth showed a pretty, freckly faced, long-haired redhead with a killer body and perky smile. She was more girl next door than femme fatale. I had been told she had been Zorita's protégé and possible lover. Zorita had been a snake-dancing, bisexual, gold-digging stripper who had died recently. Zorita had lived in Florida and owned a club after retiring from stripping.

Tee Tee Red

Zorita had started in New York. She was originally from Philly. Born in 1915, she had been adopted by a strict Methodist couple. Zorita had been a beautiful woman with short, platinum hair and stocky thighs, who died in 2001. She was no lean and lithe flower, but a sturdy woman. She was nobody's fool. She boasted of making the men she slept with give her stock in GM. So she ended up better off than most. I wished more of "my ladies" had given more thought to their future financial security. I found many of them living in dire straits with no children or a pension to turn to. For many, it was a matter of what they could sell, or who could give them a few bucks, to pay rent and keep food in front of them.

The area of Miami Shores where Tee Tee was working for a dermatologist was run down. There was sunburnt grass for lawns, bars on the windows. It was dark by the time we pulled up next to her big, dented yellow Cadillac. It was the only other car in the small parking lot.

A petite, short-haired woman greeted us. Life's worries were scratched deeply into her face. Tee Tee had a husky voice. Nothing remained of her fiery good looks. Her formerly red hair was bleached, thinning, and dry. Her face was puffy. Times had been hard. She was guarded and she admitted later she didn't feel as free to talk because she had her six-year-old grandson Joseph with her. Her daughter, Joseph's mother, had a drug problem and ran with the wrong people. Tee Tee helped watch Joseph. She locked the door behind me. "We keep the door locked, so we don't have any surprises."

Tee Tee's cell phone rang immediately and through the evening. She looked concerned. "That's my daughter," she said and ignored it. Joseph sat quietly as Tee Tee answered my questions.

She had been born in Wiggum, Georgia, "around Moletree and Murphy." Murphy was her maiden name. She was the only child of a single mother. Her mother was her mother and father, and her "best fan." At some point in her childhood, she and her mother moved to Miami.

Tee Tee started in burlesque when she was seventeen after entering a striptease contest. The prize was one hundred bucks. It was at the Gaiety Theatre in Miami. There, Tee Tee met Zorita, who was a "star at the time. . . . [She] took a liking to me right away."

Tee Tee won the contest and "got drunk as a hoot owl on champagne." She stayed all night and both women were entranced by each other: the older, tougher, been-there-done-that Zorita and Tee Tee, wanting to be someone.

The Gaiety offered her a job. Zorita became her manager and told her how to present herself on stage. "Every first night, I always had butterflies in my stomach."

Zorita told her, "Every time you want to take something off, back up to me and I'll undo it." Tee Tee was good. She could dance to anything.

Zorita taught her about body makeup to cover up little flaws. "I used it in the beginning. I used a lotion, a cream that would hold the powder, then powder down all over to be the same color all over. It wouldn't come off and it evened out the skin tone." At the end of the night "[Zorita'd] give me a shower out in the back after every show. She'd turn the hose on me."

Zorita soon retired from stripping and did the announcing of the show at her own club in Miami. She always announced Tee Tee as having the "cutest little TT's in town." One night she looked at the younger woman and pointed to her pert breasts. "Tee tee," she said. She then pointed to her crotch. "Red." The name stuck.

Zorita was known for working with boas and pythons. She used them to terrify both the audience and the performers backstage. Zorita would come on stage with the boa draped across her broad shoulders. She was not a delicate little woman, by any means. She was a big-boned woman with big hips, solidly built. "She twirled around on the stage. . . . She'd twirl in such a way that the snake would fly out around over everybody's head and you could see everybody ducking. . . . They'd all start screaming. She did it on purpose." Tee Tee laughed. "She had total control of the snake."

Sequin also worked with Zorita. "I was doing a cocktail act and I came off to go backstage," she explained. "She opened the door and had her snake in her hand and went up in my face. It had cellophane around its mouth."

She would "shove it at you," said Rita Grable. And keep it in the dressing room, which frightened many strippers who weren't eager to share their space with a reptile.

"I used to help her tape up its mouth and tape up its a-hole so it wouldn't do anything on the stage," Tee Tee said. "Scotch tape." I asked if the snakes bothered her. "They can't hurt ya . . . all they want to do is squeeze you. Zorita never had problems with her serpents. She would change them periodically." Apparently Zorita didn't want to be bothered feeding her snakes the little animals, like bunnies and rats, that they required. Instead Zorita would simply give her snake away and get a new one. One snake in New York crawled out the window. They found it on the ground and joked that the snake had committed suicide. The snake was named Elmer and Zorita called the press and told them he had been jealous because she used her other snake, Oscar, more often.

Zorita "was tough with a good heart. She didn't take no nonsense." Was she misunderstood? "Yes." Was she making up for a tough, unloved childhood? "Yes."

Before Zorita retired for good, she and Tee Tee traveled together as a team. Zorita was the feature and Tee Tee the co-feature. "I would go on just before her. The star always goes on last," Tee Tee said. Tee Tee was announced as "Zorita's Extra Added Attraction."

Tee Tee came up with a gimmick of sorts. "I would take a bra and use it like a sling shot and aim it at people. Miss them right side their head, or hang it on pasties and twirl it around."

Suddenly Tee Tee's eyes darted to the side and in a sharp tone she reprimanded. "Joseph, I'm gonna get angry with you." Her grandson had been about to or had touched our lights. No problem except to himself. They were very hot and he could burn himself. "I'm very strict," Tee Tee explained. "Now get up there and sit down ... come on, be a gentleman ... don't make a fool of yourself." Joseph started to tear up and hide his face. Her voice softened. "He's embarrassed now." She assured him she loved him. There was pain in her eyes. She said she wanted him to do well in school. She was compensating for her absent daughter. I wondered how absent Tee Tee had been from her daughter's life when she had been on the road.

Tee Tee worked New Orleans the same time as Blaze Starr on Bourbon Street. They were both features in New Orleans at the same time, but worked opposite sides of the street. Blaze at the Sho Bar, Tee Tee at the 500 Club.

According to Tee Tee, Blaze had been Zorita's first protégé in Baltimore. Tee Tee said Blaze and herself were in "competition" for Governor Earl Long. Tee Tee called him a "dirty old man."

Tee Tee loved working the 500 Club. The owners would bus the audience in for the show. It was always a full house. The other entertainment around her was good. She remembered Allouette, who twirled tassels on her boobs and on her rear. There were famous singers. She couldn't remember all the names.

There was a "peep show" on top of the 500 Club. It was a small room where the girls would take turns dancing by themselves. There was a small window and the men would sit on stools and watch the dancers through the window as the girls gyrated to records in the middle of the room. They couldn't see the customers. The girls would dance for twenty minutes.

Our interview with Tee Tee kept returning to Zorita.

"Zorita was my manager and had me under contract," she said. In Baltimore some Vegas people "wanted me for their show. I didn't want to go. I was afraid to go. I didn't know what was on the other side. I was happy what I was doing," she said. Was the small-town girl afraid of the big leap? Many burlesquers had a hard time straying from what was familiar, the money they knew they could earn, and their fans. They might want to "be a star" in Hollywood, but very few made any steps in that direction, preferring to stay on the circuit year after year, til most opportunities had passed them by. Surprisingly, very few were bitter.

Tee Tee was proud she had been in the Jerry Lewis picture *The Bellboy*, but "never got the break that [she] needed."

She answered every question and laughed easily, if not exactly carefree. Her past seemed to be filtered through many troubles, whether current or old I couldn't tell. She didn't seem particularly eager to talk, but she didn't hesitate, and as she warmed up she began to float more freely from memory to memory. Her eyes began to sparkle a little.

Tee Tee always checked out the stage wherever she went prior to a show, so there would be no surprises. One night she didn't have time. During her act, the heel of her shoe caught in a tiny hole on stage and Tee Tee "landed in the whiskey bottles." It was a runway stage that went out into the audience. She just flew out over the audience and landed upside down.

Tee Tee "worked until go-go came in." Most of the nightclubs were gone by then and the stage was so tiny, "the strippers couldn't have costumes, not an elegant long gown or cape to strip out of. So the girls came on without any costumes. . . . Towards the end I started doing yoga on the stage."

She told me she mostly retired after she married and had her children, going back in if she needed the money. "I ended up being the breadwinner." I looked over at Joseph. Tee Tee was still the breadwinner.

She was a little vague whenever the subject of her children came up, saying she didn't work much when they were little, yet moments later saying she didn't retire until she was nearly fifty. It sounded like she was in and out of burlesque, working clubs at various times. Her mother came and went, helping Tee Tee with the kids between marriages.

Florida was always Tee Tee's home base. She always came back to Miami.

When she wasn't on stage, there was enough drama in her life to keep her busy. Once, she'd gotten in an auto accident and drove through a brick wall of a church. "They didn't appreciate that," she said. Her Lincoln Continental windshield dissolved into powder, she claimed. She banged up her knees pretty badly and couldn't work for a while. She went to Leroy Griffith and he gave her a job. Since starting this project, I have continually heard stories of burlesque people looking out for each other, sticking together in difficult times.

The car accident wasn't the only event that ever threatened her ability to work. "I got mugged. I was almost killed. The man beat me to a pulp," she said. Tee Tee had pulled into a local gas station about 10 o'clock at night. She filled her car up and, as she was getting back in, someone grabbed her by her neck, "slammed" her to the ground, and started beating her up. He broke her arm in three places. "Before that, I could work circles around anyone my age," she claimed.

Even though it was nighttime, the gas station had been "lit up like a Christmas tree." There were witnesses and, fortunately for Tee Tee, a cop drove up during the attack. The mugger had just gotten out of jail and wanted a car. "He mugged me December 12th. He'd gotten out December 1st." Tee Tee said she never really recovered from the incident.

Where did this happen? Tee Tee pointed across the street to where I had just come from buying batteries.

Tee Tee, the dynamite stripper with the all-American looks, had been pummeled, the zest taken from her figuratively and literally. She ended up in the hospital, her body broken, her dreams shattered. She had never really saved any money.

As the months passed, she became desperate. A doctor friend gave her a job, the same doctor she was working for now. What did this former glamour girl with the attention of governors and a wardrobe that included minks think about her life in this dismal doctor's office with the cheap paneling and her six-year-old grandson in her charge? I think it had become a daily struggle for Tee Tee to hang on. But she was doing it. She wasn't giving up, though there would be even more heartbreak in store for her.

A year later, I called Tee Tee. She was crying. Her daughter "had been dumped under a tree like garbage" in the neighborhood where I had interviewed her. She was dead. Tee Tee's long struggle with her daughter's addiction finally came to a desperate conclusion. Tee Tee said she would continue to raise her grandson Joseph.

**

Lillian Kiernan Brown is an erudite and energetic woman not afraid to tell it like it is. Charming and well-spoken, she wasn't earthy like some of the other women I interviewed who had stripped. She was refined, self-educated, and held herself in high esteem. She had a loving husband and children. I think the only thing missing for her was being back in the limelight. She very much missed being on the stage and the center of attention, adored by many admirers.

She was still tall and beautiful, with sharp blue eyes and short, cropped blonde-red hair. She lit up the screen. She told a story in an entertaining way. And she had many to tell.

Lillian had a great sense of humor and intelligence. She searched carefully for the right words. Besides her book *Banned in Boston* about her time in burlesque, she had been writing for various newspaper columns since 1966. While in Morocco, married to her first husband, who was a navy chief, she started working for the base newspaper and had her own show on the Armed Forces Radio.

Lillian's current husband, Jim, was tall, handsome, and gentlemanly, though slightly deaf and not in good health. He retired to the den while we conducted the interview with the TV on full blast, shuffling in every now and again to her annoyance and gentle reprimands. She would remind him this was her interview, *please be quiet.* She did not want anything taking away from her moment.

Lillian—also known as Lily Ann Rose, Lloma Rhodes, Shadow, and Statue—had an intriguing story. Born in Cambridge, Massachusetts, she had wanted to be in burlesque since she was three years old. Ann Corio (a big star at the Old Howard at the time) would come for dinner at Lillian's grandmother's house because she had worked with Lillian's mother and aunts. Corio, the burlesque queen, and Lillian's grandmother, Josephine, were both Italian. "I wanted to be just like her. I came out and started doing a strip." Her grandmother stopped her before she could remove her diaper.

Lillian's mother, Margie, and her Aunt Lillian worked in vaudeville as part of the Patent Leather Girls, traveling in vaudeville shows during the 1920s. When vaudeville died, her Aunt Lillian retired from the stage and raised young Lillian while Margie dove into burlesque, variously, as a talking woman, chorus girl, and stripper. Lillian's younger aunt Karin worked burlesque also, but didn't start until the 1930s.

Lillian's father was long gone. "I never did find my father. He was what they called an auctioneer in vaudeville and burlesque and a talking man on the circuit and in carnivals. His stage name was Joe Rose but his real name was Herman Mendelsohn," she said.

His parents escaped from Russia before Hitler got in to power, and came to the U.S. as immigrants to make a better life.

Grandma Josephine was an extraordinary woman for her time. She loved the "risqué" shows and was not ashamed her daughters were a part of them. She marched for women's rights, telling Lillian, "Don't ever let anybody tell you [that] you can't do something because you're a woman."

At the time, women were not allowed to go to the movies unescorted unless they were "ladies of the evening." So Lillian's determined grandmother dressed up like a prostitute so she could see her five-cent movies.

Margaret LaManna, stage name Margie LaMont, lived on and off with her dreamy-eyed daughter, Lillian, perhaps teaching her a dance step or two or a phrase from a popular song. Married four times, "always to the wrong person," Margie had "a lot of problems. Mental. She was not a drunk," Lillian said, possibly not fully comprehending the definition of alcoholism. "She wouldn't drink every day, but when she did drink, she'd disappear and she'd be gone three, four, five months." When the beautiful Margie resurfaced in her young daughter's life, she would always be remarried and pregnant. It was a "trend," and then she'd sober up and "give the baby away," leaving it with her newly estranged husband's family. Margie knew she "wasn't able to take care of it," Lillian said.

An old newspaper article Lillian had in her possession showed a wide-eyed blonde Margie with the caption begging, "Identify Amnesia Victim."

One of Lillian's half-sisters was kidnapped when she was just six months old by her father and hidden for years because Margie was so "unstable," Lillian said. Margie searched for her, but would die without ever finding her daughter. When Lillian was eighteen, the half-sisters found each other and have been close ever since.

Lillian believes her mother had multiple personalities, which would explain her strange behavior and long disappearances.

Margie worked mainly at Boston's famous Old Howard theatre, which had once been a church and a vaudeville house. It had seen the likes of Sarah Bernhardt, Fanny Brice, Fred Allen, and John Wilkes Booth tread the boards there.

Lillian herself got into burlesque proper when she was fourteen. It was 1947. "It was summer vacation and school was out," Lillian said. She went to The Casino in Boston to try out as a chorus girl. Naively, she didn't think her mother, who was performing down the street at the Old Howard, would find out.

"I wanted to be up there," Lillian said emphatically. "I had to show my legs." (Which I could see during our interview were still long and shapely.) Lillian explained she didn't look fourteen, as she had been wearing makeup since she was

Photo courtesy of Kathleen Fries

A teenage stripper Lily Ann Rose

three or four and was always "glammed" up. Photos of the buxom beauty confirm this. She was beautiful and mature-looking for her age.

Lillian, of course, was hired, at twenty-five dollars a week for three shows a day. It wasn't until five days later that her mother discovered her daughter's new profession. Between shows, the performers used to go eat at Joe & Nemo's, a restaurant in Scollay Square where burlesque thrived in downtown Boston. Lillian was there and so was her mother. Margie sat her daughter down and gave her a lecture, telling her if she worked the chorus line, that's where she'd remain for the rest of her life. Margie told Lillian she should finish school in the fall. Contradictorily, Margie also suggested Lillian go to Sally Keith's and try out for her new review. Sally was looking for girls.

Who was Sally Keith?

"Sally Keith," Lillian explained, "was the greatest tassel dancer that ever lived." The fabulously well-liked Sally dazzled crowds at the Crawford House. She was a Jean Harlow look-alike who was loaded with diamonds and furs.

This was a perfect opportunity for Lillian, who piled on the makeup and beat it down to the club. At the audition, waiting her turn, was Lillian's Aunt Eleanor, whose stage name was Karin. Karin occasionally worked the Casino and Old Howard and was jealous of her voluptuous teenage niece. Karin told the attention-getting teenager that if she auditioned, then Karin would have no chance and would go home.

"You know how much I need this job," her aunt told her. Karin could easily manipulate the teenager. "She did financially. I said, 'Okay I won't try out.' I sat in a corner and watched." After the auditions, Sally noticed the pretty teenager and asked her what she was doing there. Thinking quick, Lillian told her she was looking for a job. What could she do, Sally wanted to know.

"I'm a secretary." Sally thought about it and said "that's just what I need," and tossed Lillian her clipboard and pencil. Lillian spent the next year and a half following the vivacious blonde on tour and in her beloved Boston, where Sally packed them in.

"I learned how to produce a show," Lillian said. The Sally Keith Review was filled with dancers, comedians, and singers. Lillian had to learn about lights, costumes, and talent.

Sally was "good to me," Lillian said. Lillian wrote Sally's PR. By learning to write, Lillian learned something that took her beyond burlesque and through the rest of her life.

But Sally had her demons. "She reminded me of my mother," Lillian said. Sally drank too much. Lillian, though underage, was responsible for driving Sally's gold Cadillac when Sally couldn't, or didn't, drive. "I was a big help to her," especially when the hard-partying Sally got drunk and "couldn't function," Lillian said.

After a couple months playing "Secretary," as Sally addressed her, Sally enlisted Lillian to help her pick out new costumes for the showgirls. Lillian tried on four or five different outfits. Finally Sally finally turned to Secretary and asked, "With a body like that, why do you want to be a secretary?"

Lillian was honest. "Sally, I have to tell you the truth. I don't want to be a secretary. I want to be a stripper."

Quickly Sally had the dance captain put a number together for Lillian. She was the girl in gold for a statue act. "In those days, if you were scantily dressed you couldn't move." Barely clad beauties would pose on the stage as frozen statues in tableau. Lillian was covered head to toe in toxic gold paint. It was a popular "outfit" at the time and performers only had a short period of time to be covered in the paint, then they would have to get out of it. "You could die from it. In fact, a lot of performers did die."

Lillian also did a shadow act, dancing behind Sally to *Me and My Shadow.*

The first time she stripped, Sally dressed Lillian in a scarf covering her breasts. Lillian had a parasol and was supposed to swing it in front of her then remove the scarf behind the parasol, keeping the parasol in place.

Tassel twirler Sally Keith

"But I was so excited that I just threw the parasol. And I let it all hang out . . . and almost got the show closed." The censors and police threatened to immediately close the show if Lillian performed again. From then on, clever Sally disguised the young girl or had her perform under a strobe light so she wouldn't be recognized by the censors.

After so many months spent away from her grandmother, Lillian got homesick and went back to Boston and got herself an agent. She would go on to strip without the guidance and protection of Sally.

The glamorous Lily Ann Rose, as she was billed, made a lot of new friends, including the notorious bank robber Teddy Green, who was responsible for one of the largest robberies in Massachusetts's history. A frequent guest at grandma Josephine's house, Lillian's grandmother thought the nice gentleman was a Laterene Coffee salesman, as he always brought cans of the coffee as a gift when he visited. Caught and sentenced, he spent time on Alcatraz where he studied law. Eventually, Green would get his conviction overturned.

One night driving together on the way to the theatre, comedian Teddy English played a powerful joke on Lillian. He was teasing her relentlessly, saying she would be expected to show her "little fur cap" that night. He kept teasing her until finally she was a "nervous wreck. I didn't know what he was talking about," she said. However, at the theatre a chorus girl quickly told her what Teddy was referring to. "So, I said, 'well, I'm not gonna show my fur cap.' So I went in and I got my razor . . . and I shaved my little fur cap. Then I flashed it that night because I thought I had to."

What did her grandmother think of her stripping? "She thought I was the most beautiful and best dancer in the world. . . . She was proud of me."

Lillian worked in burlesque until she was twenty-two and suffered the humiliation of being arrested. She had been working outside of Boston and it "was a time when strippers were really being hunted down. I got arrested for lewd and lascivious conduct." Even today, fifty years later, I could see the shame in Lillian's face at the memory. The degradation and regret washed over her. *How lewd was she?* She was wearing panties and a bra, covered in ruffles. "Ridiculous."

She spent time in jail, but the judge let her go, because there was no case, no proof of lewd conduct. "I was really scared. . . . I promised I'd never break the law again . . . and I never did," she said.

Lillian continued, "My mistake was going into burlesque and wanting to take my clothes off. I should have followed my dreams . . . to be on the stage, . . . to be a star. . . . I didn't have to do it by taking my clothes off."

In 1953, Margie died when she was forty-two. "She OD'd on pain killers," according to Lillian, and was buried in Worcester, Massachusetts, alongside her last husband, Clicker Joe. "She said she was thirty-nine. . . . [Burlesquers] always lied about their age."

"Why was he called Clicker Joe?" I asked.

"He was in an industrial accident and lost an arm." He had a claw and, as an avid burlesque theatre-goer, instead of clapping, he had to "click" his approval. Lillian said he was crazy about Margie. They had a son together, but tragically, three months after Margie died, their baby boy, just thirty-six months old, was accidentally killed by a car.

When Lillian's mother died, Lillian was booked into a club in Boston on either the day of Margie's funeral or the day she died. At that point, "I never missed a show," she said. When Lillian entered the dressing room to prepare for the show, she looked up on the wall at the lineup of names from a previous show, an old show. "And my mother's name was on there—'featured attraction.' That was probably the best show that I ever did in my life . . . I wanted to do this for Margie. I think I stopped the show that night," she said.

Lillian tells me she has no regrets. When she left burlesque, she shuttered up her old pictures and costumes and press clippings and gave them to her Aunt Lillian, who kept them for her. She married Jim Brown, a "juke box man." She didn't tell her husband or kids about her past. "I forgot about it. For fifty years." Then in 1996, her aunt died and she "inherited her things and that trunk. When I opened that trunk it just popped out. I had forgotten it."

When asked if she would do it over: "I would do it in a minute and I wouldn't change a thing. If they said I could live my whole life . . . over again—I wouldn't change a thing."

**

Sequin had captured me with her voice at the Reunion. She sang a sultry song titled "Sugar" from her wheelchair. It was a rousing and sexy song. She was talented and I wanted to know more of her story. In her prime, she was amazingly beautiful, buxom, wide-hipped, with short dark hair à la Ava Gardner. She was now confined to a wheelchair, whether for health reasons or her incredible girth I didn't know.

During her first strip, she recalled, she was "very nervous. Getting out of clothes, I didn't know what to do. Everybody's looking at you. It was exciting. Once or twice, then I wasn't nervous after all. Afterwards, [I was] usually drained and thought of all the mistakes I'd made. I wasn't much of a dancer. Some were really trained. I just moved to the music."

Sequin became popular, posing for the cover of many pin up magazines. "I was a celebrity. I missed it from the get go."

She had a booking agent in New York who sent her on some strange trips, she recalled. Dick Richards helped her work the Ohio circuit. "You always wound up in Buffalo or Boston at the end, then Newark and start all over again. . . . I'd say I was on the road forty-eight weeks out of the year. I started when I was twenty-four, retired when I was twenty-eight."

She married Tony Tamburello, a pianist, vocal coach, and arranger who, besides a long and enduring relationship with Tony Bennett, counted Judy Garland and Jerry Vale (Rita Grable's husband) as clients. "It was love at first sight because he knew all my keys. He arranged the last music for my farewell to burlesque at the Empire. Then he wrote me arrangements for nightclub work. A year later I married. I retired again."

Sequin

CHAPTER TWENTY-THREE
On the Road Again

"New Orleans was a city of glamour."
—Kitty West

"In theatres it's a seven-day week, close Saturday, drive or fly to the next performance and you open again on Sunday."
—Alexandra the Great "48"

Train travel could be long and difficult. Ricki Covette (far right) and others.

"Burlesque life, like circus life, was largely based on travel," explained Professor Janet Davis. "It was a hard life, but an addictive one."

Every major city had at least one burlesque theatre. Working the circuit meant months on the road away from family and home. When performers pulled into a new city, they were rushed to prepare for the next show. More often than not, they had mere hours to even get to the next city and the next theatre, gather music and props, throw on wardrobe, rehearse and be ready for the 1 o'clock show.

"First time I worked St Louis," said Alexandra the Great, "when I got my schedule it said 'Buffalo, NY.' It didn't look that far on the map. But I drove *all night* in a snow storm."

Sequin had similar experiences. "Agent would book me from one end of the state to the other."

"I was booked two years in advance. And all the other girls, too." said Dixie.

If you were a feature attraction, you would "come in at noon, maybe on at 2, maybe no rehearsal," said Betty Rowland. Those were the traveling features. "Stock players stay at one theatre all the time. Chorus girls are stock. Principals travel. Sometimes a local stripper, a 'favorites of the neighborhoods' would come in and do a strip." That favorite might only be a hit in her hometown. It was a short, thrilling dip into burlesque for many local girls.

Sequin would frequently stay in "housekeeping rooms with kitchen privileges. One show person would tell another what would be the best place to stay. Everyone knew where to send you. Usually nice and clean," she said.

There was this thing called the wheel in burlesque. In the 1900s, there was the Columbia Wheel. There would be the American, the Empire, and the Mutual. Burlesque theatre owners formed circuits where a company of performers toured for forty weeks, going around like a wheel from one theatre to the next as a group. This went on for nearly thirty years, which was why many stayed so long in the business. It provided constant income for the players.

There were forty shows touring on the wheel in the early part of the 1900s, according to *Burlesque* by Sobel. By 1905, there were seventy shows playing and touring the circuit with huge casts of chorus girls, comedians, novelty acts, and strippers.

Competing wheels kept popping up, striving to outdo one another. According to Martin Collyer, however, "the cleanliness would rise and fall."

These traveling shows brought a bit of Broadway to middle America. Mike Iannucci explained, "Burlesque was the poor man's musical comedy. The Ziegfeld Follies was the major show on Broadway. Burlesque was like the step below them. It was always a good entertainment."

Shows had dialogue, comedy, dancing, strips, and singing. They played four or five times a day. To keep the audiences coming back, they needed to rotate the comedians and strippers weekly.

The wheels spun fast and furious. Betty Rowland said, "There would be a dress rehearsal the night before you opened. After show another dress rehearsal. Then 11 the next day, the show would go on. . . . The pace was crazy: 'Here's your costume, move it.'"

At the Hollywood, they rehearsed Thursday and Friday mornings, threw a dress rehearsal Friday afternoon, just before the 3:30 matinee, then they were off till the 8 show. It was an exhausting schedule.

Sally Rand claimed to have performed in all fifty states.

"It's an extremely disciplined business. You have to be there when the theatre curtain goes up or somebody else will be there next show," said Betty Rowland.

A burlesque show had "no stage waits. That show moved. It was wonderful. It was a theatrical show. Everything entertaining but had a flair, crazy and gaudy," said Dixie Evans.

"Scramble and stumble, backstage, quick changing," remembered White Fury.

Sequin traveled the Ohio circuit, which included Canton, Cincinnati, Cleveland, Buffalo up to Boston, ending at Newark to "start all over again." It was stressful making the next gig. "Sometimes, you'd have not a lot of time," she said. As her show was prop heavy, she drove with a trailer loaded with furniture, wardrobe, and her "kitchen stuff" so she didn't have to spend time and money eating in restaurants. She traversed the country this way for years. "I loved it. It was fun," she said. She often slept in her car.

The Wheels started petering out but the Hirst remained, regularly booking acts into the 1950s, though there were far fewer theatres to perform in. By then, most of the performers drove their own cars; train travel didn't make sense.

"I traveled to nightclubs and drove myself in a big white station wagon with the big white dogs. I made an entrance," said Joan Arline.

Alexandra the Great said, "I traveled all the time alone. I was always traveling from one city to the next by car and I was always worried about breaking down so I did have a pistol in my coat. I didn't have anything in it, but I had a gun."

"On tour was pretty hard," said Kitty West. "You'd meet strangers, rehearse with different bands, different owners and all. We had to drive in those days. I had to go with my whole entourage. I couldn't fly with an oyster shell and trunks of wardrobe."

Once the cast pulled into town and checked into the hotel, they would search out a place for cheap eats. There was always a bar next door to the theatre where they would meet for drinks, sometimes before the show, often between shows, and inevitably after the show.

One of Alan Alda's earliest memories was "walking down the aisle on the train while the company was playing cards and drinking, joking. They called a long train trip a two-bottle jump." As a young boy, Alan would sleep on top of some seats jammed together. The humor on the trains was "raw, mostly not mean-spirited. But there would be fights."

Al Baker Jr. said, "You traveled with like twenty-two chorus girls, you traveled with wardrobe. You had your own car on the train where it would go from place to place. Your trunks, one trunk would be in the hotel for you and the other trunk would be at the theatre . . . and it was, you know, it was 'show business.'"

"The burlesque theatres used to pay your freight from town to town and you could take trains," explained Carmela. "I didn't like that so much because sometimes you had cockroaches on those trains."

Beverly Anderson recalled one incident when she needed to move quickly between towns, going from one show to the next. "One time [a musician in the company] was going to drive to Canada. He said there was no room for me in the car. He could have squeezed me in." She was not going to be daunted. "I hired a cab driver to stand in the wings and catch my wardrobe for me as I threw it off in the wings. He threw it in a bag and then got me in the taxi and went to the train. But I had to ride all night long sitting in a G-string and net bra with a coat over me." She got there on time.

"I worked all the time," said Alexandra the Great. Jess Mack was her agent. He would call her and say, "'You need a vacation.' So he'd send me someplace to work and I always thought I was on vacation. [He] sent me to Hawaii." She was held over in Hawaii for three months and ended up living there six years. "I rarely took time off. I worked 90 percent of the time." So did most of the headliners.

Joni Taylor was on the road from 1953–56. During the summers, she came home when the burlesque theatres closed. Then she'd travel to Atlantic City and work the Globe on the Boardwalk.

Holidays didn't close the shows. "Every holiday was a big spectacular," said Dixie Evans.

Maria Bradley remembered, "Christmas we had to work." But she had no regrets about the missed holiday. "I wish I was young and right back there where I started."

They worked every holiday no matter what the season. "Fourth of July, Minsky put sparklers on you coming upstairs, blacked house, flag unrolls. Audience used to whistle and stomp and scream," said Dixie Evans.

In San Diego, the Hollywood Theatre was a family. "The performers came to Thanksgiving dinner," said Dee Ann Johnston. "We still do the same. For any out-of-work actor."

"They traveled around the country together pulling into Toronto in the middle of a snow storm and piling into the theatre, living in a crappy hotel with green wooden walls," remembered Alan Alda. They were gypsies in the long tradition of roving performers. The entertainers did the best they could making homes away from home.

"We used to travel with two shopping bags, right? What was in those shopping bags? A coffee pot, three dishes, three knives, three spoons," recalled Al Baker Jr. "You ate in the room. In every hotel when you checked in, it says, 'No cooking in the rooms.' But in the morning by nine-thirty or ten, you'd smell that coffee brewing."

Sequin had similar experiences. "I learned how to make spaghetti sauce in an electric percolator," she boasted.

Stripper Lorraine Lee and her husband Dick Richards had a system to make their life on the road comfortable. "We carried a big suitcase with a set of dishes bought in Las Vegas for five dollars. We carried pots and pans. He was a great cook. We just lived out of that," she said. They carried a bedspread with them and "Dick would tear pictures of Modigliani paintings" from books and they would tape them around their room. "He would put scarves over lamps." When they arrived at a town, usually as early as 7 a.m., they would rush to a hotel with their suitcases. Lorraine would carry on to the theatre and unload their wardrobe. They'd rehearse and "by 12, we were operating fine. He stayed in the apartment and grocery shopped." Closing night, the curtain would fall by 11 and by 11:30, "we'd be in the car on our way to the next town." They did that for years. "It was . . . you know, it was a home away from home. Wherever we were."

"It was an adventure for me," said Vicki O'Day. "Some hotels were awful. The funniest was in Denver called the Friendly Frontier. They had women wrestlers and dwarf wrestlers and strippers and truck drivers there. They had Sunday prayer meetings. We all went down to that, which was booze and music. A 250-pound waitress fell in love with a dwarf wrestler and he'd sit on her lap. It was a crazy thing."

Some girls traveled with their managers or manager/husbands, like Tempest Storm. Others traveled on their own.

"Working the road is very difficult," said Alexandra the Great. Even though she was only onstage an hour out of the whole day, she said, "You're ready and there all day. It gets lonely. You have a lot of time, but then again you don't. An hour between shows. You always have to be close. You can't get too far from the theatre."

Tee Tee traveled all over the country. To keep her from being lonely, Zorita gave her a little Pomeranian she named Stripper. In the winter, Tee Tee would wear her mink coat that "someone gave [her]," and she would put Stripper in her sleeve when it was snowing or if she traveled by plane to keep the puppy warm and safe.

In Phoenix, Sequin acquired a medium-sized puppy she took on the road with her. "It grew and grew and chewed up many pairs of shoes. They let you have a dog in most of these places. She gave birth to eight puppies in one of these little houses in Ohio. I'd come home between shows to see how many puppies had been born. She had them on the bed."

April March said raising a daughter long-distance was challenging. "I never went on the road more than six weeks at a time. I had her stay with some people.

I called every night. Of course I spoiled her to death . . . right?" She looked at her daughter during our interview when she said this. "Right? I always called her before she went to bed." Her daughter didn't see her mother perform until she was twenty-one. "Ann [Corio] brought her in the wings, once, and I was so mad. I danced to the side. Ann said, 'Catch your mother's gloves.' I said, 'Take her away. Take her away. I don't allow her to see me perform.' Ann said, 'There's nothing wrong.'"

April March

Betty Rowland would book a three-month contract. There wasn't "much of life outside of theatre. With four shows a day, five on Saturday, the social life was usually with people in the theatre." It was an insular group. They stayed together.

Local towns on the circuit considered the features "celebrities. Mom-and-pop places were tickled to death to have us," said Dixie Evans. She recalled one restaurant, Captain Joe's in Newark, a swanky place that sent her a note: "'Come eat on me, bring autographed photo.' We were looked up to in most places."

A stripper with her gimmick – a snake

The closeness of traveling and performing together week after week led to pranks and hijinks. Maria Bradley recalled one particular night: "Freddy, a big gal. She didn't like us, we didn't like her. You know those marshmallow cookies? We put eyelash adhesive between the two cookies, hoping . . . I don't remember what that outcome was. Or a long pony tail, we'd hang it on the back of a costume before a girl went on stage."

Alan Alda would hang out in the alleys of the theatres with cops and horses. That was his playground. It was, Alda related, a "sense of living a life in a world different from middle class at that time."

Comedian Eddie Lloyd's son Harry said, "The travel and hours and amount of shows they did was a rough life. I was raised backstage. I was on trains all the time and in hotels. It was exciting. Most of the theatres were named Gaiety or Roxy."

Each city left distinct impressions on the performers. "I loved Boston," Blaze Starr said. "That was a burlesque town. I loved the seafood in Boston."

In the '50s, strippers were packing them in clubs in Havana. Just an hour flight from Miami, the sunny glamorous spot was a source of work for strippers, comedians, and novelty acts. Surprisingly, rules were more stringent there and the strippers showed even less in Cuba than back in the United States.

Mimi Reed played Havana in a show with a large cast for four months. "They had big, beautiful casinos, beautiful grounds. Birdcages filled with macaws. We loved Cuba."

In Cuba, Betty Howard (the "Girl Who Has Everything!") bumped to the beat of bongos. The petite, big-breasted blonde packed the clubs.

Another stripper, Bubbles Darlene (Harold Minsky named her.), caused a stir when she emerged from a cab and walked down the streets of Havana covered in her outfit of a transparent raincoat and black undies. Billed "America's Most Exciting Body," Darlene proudly displayed her wares to the ire of the police. Her publicity stunt landed her picture on the front of the newspapers, securing many future gigs, making the arrest and subsequent fine worth it.

Dixie Evans found traveling to be a way for her and a lot of the performers to see parts of the country—and world—they would not have had an opportunity to visit with 9–5 day jobs. The discomfort and inconvenience of constant travel allowed many of the women, in particular, to broaden their horizons in ways unavailable to them otherwise. It made everything worth it.

CHAPTER TWENTY-FOUR
Sugar Sugar

"Out front the big sign says doors open at twelve o'clock, noon. That didn't mean the show started at 12 o'clock noon; that meant the doors opened."
—Dixie Evans

"Candy butchers were funnier than comics, most frustrated actors."
—Val Valentine

Candy butchers were an integral part of the burlesque show. They were men, sometimes teenagers, who sold boxes of candy up and down the aisles of the theatres before the show and during intermission.

"The candy butchers paid for everything," Dardy Minsky explained. "They had the concessions. They would put up the money for the shows, they put money up for the scenery, they would put money up for the security bonds for the unions, everything."

"The concession companies are the ones that really opened the burlesque theatres because they made so much money," added Val Valentine.

"The burlesque theatres did not own the candy concession; they leased it out to candy concessionaires," said Nat Bodian.

Candy butchers appeared at World's Fairs, carnivals, burlesque theatres, and even on trains. Before inventing the light bulb, Thomas Edison had a brief career hawking candy on trains. Besides candy, the pitch men also sold "naughty" pictures, books, and magazines, always with the lure of a far more risqué or valuable prize hidden in the next box of candy.

The August 1927 edition of *Popular Mechanics* ran an article detailing how the circus candy butchers "either bought the candy privileges outright or shared his profits with the . . . owner of the show."

Their rehearsed spiel swung from anticipated exaggeration to outrageous lies.

"In between the acts, they had this candy pitch man. He would stand up at the front of the theatre and he would hold up a box of candy," said Nat Bodian.

Candy Butcher:

Ladies and gentleman. In each and every candy box is ten pieces of Atlantic City's salt water taffy and in each and every box is a little pair of dice. You hold it to the light and you see little Fatima, she does her dance nude. A certain number of these boxes will have a ten dollar bill in them.

And in one box there's a gold watch and in one box is a gold pen—

"Of course the box was worth about a nickel or dime in 1930 money and they would get about a dollar for it," said Nat Bodian.

Dixie Evans recounted: "And one young man will jump up from the audience and yell, 'I got the gold pen.' Oh. And then they'll be selling more candy boxes. 'Oh, I got the gold watch.' And then the candy butcher backstage, 'Give me the watch, give me the pen. I'll see ya next show.'"

Rita Grable said, "There was an artistry of that to itself."

Candy butchers went out of business when theatres put concession stands in the lobby, eliminating one more unique aspect of a burlesque show.

On stage at the burlesque theatre

CHAPTER TWENTY-FIVE

Theatres

"Theatre work was hard. You were always in motion. Very hard work. I don't see how people got into trouble. There was no time."
—Alexandra the Great "48"

"You just keep rolling, if things are not going well."
—Taffy O'Neil

Working in the theatres was very different than working in the clubs. Every performer had a preference.

"I liked theatres because [the audience] can't get close to you. On the runway once in a while, they'd stand up and try and grab you. But you could back up easily," said Lady Midnight.

Taffy O'Neil preferred supper clubs where it was mostly couples. "I didn't care for the theatre. It was mostly men," she said.

Lillian Hunt was running the theatre where Taffy worked. Lillian's husband Leon was a singer who was tending bar. Taffy suffered from nerves before the show. "We went and had drinks. Finally I didn't hear my shoes on the stage. I relaxed, had a drink. I could dance without hearing a 'clump clump clump.' You are out there so alone in the theatres."

"You get stage fright when you play the big places," said Dixie Evans. "You're conscious of the spotlight. Be very careful not to trip backstage. Nightclubs it's slam bam. Theatre is different."

"I always had opening night/day jitters. Always a nervous wreck," said April March. "I always had a cigarette."

A performer played differently in different cities. Some might be hometown favorites, others returning stars.

Betty Rowland's favorite was the Follies theatre on South Main Street in Los Angeles, as well as the Gaiety in New York. In LA she became "famous," which boosted her box office when she returned to New York.

The Dalton brothers owned the Follies. The theatre was a beautiful building built in 1910. It would be demolished in 1974. Three brothers—Pete, Roy and Frank Dalton—were "the Minskys of LA. Pete Dalton, he'd make scenery himself." There was a rehearsal room and a scenery room backstage. Betty Rowland claims the Dalton brothers "paid to close the Burbank theatre," which was also on Main Street. (In 1983 the Burbank was turned into a parking lot, as so many other great theatres would be.)

The theatre wasn't only a refuge for drunks and out-of-work men, but also for girls who worked for the telephone company and had split shifts that needed to spend four hours somewhere before going back to work. Dixie Evans said they would "brown bag it and go to the burlesque shows." It could also be refuge of another kind. "When it rained, you had a place to stay for four hours, for twenty-five cents."

Taffy remembered, "We had women in there with their shopping bags to kill time before they went to catch their bus."

There was a saying in Boston: "You can't graduate from Harvard 'til you've seen Ann Corio" at the Old Howard, said Mike Iannucci. Doctors would come to the matinees. It was an "elite audience." Corio was so popular with women audiences that management had to install a ladies' room at the theatre. "She played to 60 to 80 percent women," Mike estimated.

"When they rung down the curtain for the last time at the Old Howard, all the stock brokers on Milk Street wore black arm bands for a week," remembers Dixie Evans. "It was an institution; anyone who had gone to Harvard, they would have gone to the Old Howard." Out in the California desert at a burlesque museum called Exotic World, Dixie Evans managed burlesque memorabilia. She said, "Old elderly guys would come and say, 'I remember the Old Howard.'"

Theatres ranged from the derelict to the truly magnificent. Many had previously been major vaudeville houses, which meant dressing rooms were usually nice, the lobbies and stage beautiful. "Back East, doormen wore gold epaulets," said Dixie Evans.

"Minsky theatres were especially nice. Wednesday afternoon was Ladies' Days. We had to serve tea and cakes to the women. The women are saying, 'Oh, *this* is what it's like.' They'd be laughing their sides out."

Blaze Starr ruled the Two O'Clock Club in Baltimore, eventually buying it. The Two O'Clock was located in a section of Baltimore known as The Block that would eventually become a dangerous, seedy part of the city.

In Cleveland, Ohio, there was The New Empire, where Danny Thomas got his start in burlesque selling candy in the 1920s. The theatre was renamed the Town Hall in 1945. The Queen of Toledo, however, was Rose La Rose, who purchased the Town Hall in 1958. In *Woodward Avenue* by author Robert Genat, he claimed the guy at the door taking tickets was "seedy" and the old theatre smelled "musty." In fairness, the theatre was already more than one hundred years old when Rose took it on and did a rousing business.

Rose ran a tight ship ("She was strict," remembers Dixie Evans.) and the theatre was well maintained and clean, with strippers such as Sally the Shape; Yum Yum the Bon Bon Girl; Lola "Whatever Lola Wants, Lola Has"; and Paper Doll. Rose would do many battles with the City Council, which was constantly trying to shut her down.

Strippers and friends Val Valentine and "naughty" Rose La Rose

"Rose's was the most fun of all. She always came down. When you work a theatre long enough, you start to know guys who come in. I got to know a lot of college kids," said Alexandra the Great. "Once off the Philadelphia turnpike, I picked up a hitchhiker and it was a guy that was in the front row. He's a doctor now."

The Empire Theatre was in downtown Newark. The Empire opened in 1912, boasting one thousand seats. Seats cost more in the downstairs orchestra.

In San Diego, the only burlesque house was the Hollywood, formerly the Liberty Theatre. Bob Johnston was the owner for about fifty years. He was a former candy butcher born in Ireland who immigrated to Canada, then down to San Diego. A former vaudeville performer himself, how he got the theatre is a little "sketchy," said his daughter, Dee Ann Johnston.

Johnston started as either a part or full owner of the theatre. Dee Ann's mother, Fanny, was also in vaudeville, and in 1928 she came to San Diego and was booked into the Hollywood. She overslept and showed up late to the theatre, where Bob told her, "You're late. I can't use you." The two were married in 1930 and remained married for sixty years. She was a choreographer and eventually "passed the torch" to Dee Ann. Fanny helped light the shows; "she knew everything," Dee Ann said.

The Hollywood had 425 seats, a balcony, and a fly loft. There were four live shows a day and on Friday, Saturday, and Sunday they showed movies in between shows. It took a while for the theatre to do well. Dee Ann's parents were "eating pork and beans out of cans."

Once the war started, "The Navy made [business] good.... You couldn't even get a seat in there," said Dee Ann. After Pearl Harbor, with the Navy in San Diego, "business became a real business. They worked hard." The audience was 90 percent men and Johnston also owned the bar next door. Her dad "never missed a show."

"He always had union orchestra and hands. Four guys in band. Big organ. Drummer on stage right, sax, clarinet, trumpet player, Seven days a week. A grind," Dee Ann described.

Dixie Evans commented, the "bigger the theatre, the better the band."

They did full productions that changed every month with sometimes thirty people on the stage—and it was a "small stage."

"Mom broke Lili [St. Cyr] in. Fired Dardy. She thought she was terrible," Dee Ann said. Years after her start in San Diego, Lili St. Cyr was a headliner and returned with her third husband, Paul Valentine. They did a number that included the head of John the Baptist.

"These girls were performers; they could dance." There was a stock group in San Diego of chorus girls, strippers, and comedians, although Johnston would bring in headliners such as Betty Rowland and Tempest Storm.

Bobby "Texas" Roberts was eighteen and started working there as a dancer after high school, and became one of the "stars of the Hollywood."

Jane Cafera was simply called "Irish." She came into the Hollywood as a feature and stayed in San Diego, marrying the company singer, Larry Kane. Irish was a popular local and worked for the Hollywood for years.

Jimmy Stein and "Say No More Jo" Claude Mathis worked comedy there. Mathis "was a San Diego guy. His wife was a stripper til she got too old, then she sold tickets," recalled Dee Ann.

I asked Dee Ann if she ever felt a stigma attached to being daughter of a burlesque theatre owner. "Never really bad," she said. She attended a private school when she was growing up.

Toward the end of the Hollywood, go-go bars were taking over downtown and pornography was taking over old theatres. "They didn't do 'completes'—total nudity. Once that happened elsewhere, guys went elsewhere. Business [became] iffy." Shows began to run only on weekends. The show dropped from a cast of thirty down to ten or twelve.

By the early '60s, the girls were "doing more than they should have done," but still always wore a G-string, Dee Ann said. And though the vice squad was in there a lot, they had no trouble. "He ran a clean ship," she said.

Dee Ann explained there were always bouncers in the theatre. There were two aisles. Her father would take the stage during the overture "Beyond the Blue Horizon." He would then announce, "Remove your hats, feet off chairs, this is a stage show, not a stag show." Then the two big bouncers would stand at the front of the theatre facing the audience. "There wasn't any trouble," Dee Ann confirmed.

The theatre closed in 1970 and is now a parking garage on the corner of 3rd and F Street in downtown San Diego.

Some of the strippers coming into the business in the late 1950s and '60s, when shows no longer resembled early burlesque and many theatres had closed, took the show off in some unusual places.

Vicki O'Day's first job was working in an old "brothel in Arizona at an old mining town." The building was built in the 1800s and lined with walled-off rooms on the second floor. Vicki danced in a back bar.

In Minneapolis, stripper Sheila Rae danced on a "stage" on the bar, which she complained was the size of a "cutting board. You could only make about two or three steps, bartenders serving drinks under you."

"New Orleans was fantastic," claimed Kitty West. "You'd run in between shows and get Chinese food.... Carrie Finnel and Kelley Smith and Sally Rand would visit between shows.... In those days, it was a town of glamour. You wore furs. You didn't go in tennis shoes like I do now. You dressed. Always gloves. Suits during the daytime—and furs."

"New Orleans had jazz bands and all the different nightclubs up Bourbon Street. New Orleans [was] all burlesque," remembered Tee Tee Red. "Theatres you could only stay two weeks at time. They had to keep rotating the shows because there was no alcohol. Cokes and popcorn [were] sold, and hot dogs. And you could hear the barkers selling it up and down the aisles." Outside the 500 Club where she was working, a man would yell her name all night. "Come see. Come one, come all."

Lili St. Cyr was purportedly the first stripper to play a big resort in Las Vegas in 1950 when the town was still "quaint," as she called it. It was a remote desert resort not yet filled with the high rises and Disney-like amusements that we know today.

Lili performed at the El Rancho, where a big neon windmill beckoned visitors from afar, promising a classy show along with gambling. As a wedding present (for one of her six marriages), owner Beldon Katleman gave her a six-year contract. She brought enormous attention to the club. First lady Eleanor Roosevelt attended one of her shows and posed for a picture with Lili, who looked elegant in a long black satin gown.

Dardy recalled the club owners in Vegas as being "all ex-hoodlums from Cleveland.... We'd call them 'pineapple growers from Cleveland.'"

On the road, Dixie learned respect for both her profession and those working behind the scenes. In Pittsburgh, she once bought some small props from a local dime store and went to the theatre and placed them on her set. The union stage hands didn't like it and at her next show, when she went on the stage, it was bare. Nothing was set up for her. She ran off crying. A stage hand told her there was "no union stamp on that." After that, she made sure her props had the union label otherwise they'd "throw your stuff off stage."

"Stage hands had a strong union," said Sequin. "They wouldn't let my boyfriend on stage. They set up the swing and it broke. Down I went."

With the gradual decline of the theatres, the burlesque industry turned to film to boost revenue—but nothing can approximate a show with the audience participating with whooping and hollering, and hot musicians pounding it out.

"Most of us who were performing," Lady Midnight wrote me, "at the theatre [Follies] were approached to be in [*This Was Burlesque*], doing a show just as we did every day. It was put together exactly like a regular burlesque show, with an opening production number which was choreographed by our resident theatre choreographer, Lillian Hunt, and with the same skits we did on stage.... We were given some special instructions we had to follow, one being that we had to keep our movements very mild. Try doing a bump without much motion! The corny music was dubbed in during the editing, and I have to say it was far different from the music we used at the theatre."

Lady Midnight said she was paid "a hundred dollars for a few hours' work, and in those days that was pretty good money! Plus, since we all worked together every day; we had a good time doing it."

"We didn't know at the time where [the films] would wind up," said Betty Rowland. Only later did they find out the films "were to be sold in magazines."

Taffy O'Neil shot *Kiss Me Baby* directed by Lillian Hunt. "You didn't have [an] audience to respond to. When things [are] going really well, it's like a marriage, and when it's not going well, [it's] like a divorce."

Lili St. Cyr received five thousand dollars for a day's work recreating her bathtub act (that got her arrested at Ciro's) for the film *Love Moods*. Many of the films were quickie movies that the strippers and comedians recreated on stages in front of empty seats. What has been preserved is in many instances the only record of some dances and skits. Without the cries of "take it off" and live musicians pounding to the strippers' beat, the films don't translate. These recreations probably contribute to our confusion about why this form of entertainment was so popular. All the performers said how *electric* it was to perform.

"Standing behind the curtain, waiting for it to play before the curtain opened, was always very exciting to me and I would silently pray each and every show, 'Please God, let them like me!' That particular moment was always especially emotional to me," said Lady Midnight.

These quickie films were also used as stag films.

As burly theatres closed, those were played in lieu of live performances and in tents in carnivals. As live burly was dying, the thought from producers was, "We'll get into film and film them and take those around."

The stag films were rites of passage for men—a private event where they could see women stripping. Sometimes the movies played at small country fairs, the ones that couldn't afford to hire live performers.

"Burlesque changed," said Lady Midnight. "We didn't have any more chorus line in theatre. It started getting different. Then clubs started in more and more. Theatre just wrapped up."

The Hollywood closed in 1970. Bob Johnston got up on the stage at the end of the opening and said, "You know I'd rather go out of here in a box than have this theatre close on me." According to daughter Dee Ann he never got over it. He lived to be ninety-three.

CHAPTER TWENTY-SIX

Legendary Ladies

"A woman's greatest asset is a man's imagination."
—Ann Corio

"I confess that I am a brazen hussy, if out-of-shape women want to call me that."
—Sally Rand

They are the faces that changed burlesque. Now yellowing images in defunct magazines, they once commanded huge salaries and scores of followers. Offstage they led exciting, tumultuous lives with their share of ups and downs and adventure that kept their name in the papers.

ANN CORIO

Ann Corio made burlesque accessible to the *ladies* with her class act. The female audience packed her favorite theatre in Boston. Her performance showed them a burlesque show was "art," as she claimed after she and the cast were hauled into court on trumped-up indency charges. She won the case.

Ann Corio came from a strict Italian-American, Catholic, New England family. She was one of a dozen siblings (more or less, no one had a real answer as to the amount). Ann was a classic beauty with auburn hair, green eyes, and a stunning figure.

At fifteen, Ann ran away from home. According to her third and last husband, Mike Iannucci, Ann and a girlfriend from Hartford, Connecticut, auditioned for a show opening in New York. The "two went down and all of a sudden she was in burlesque," said Mike.

Ann's father was always too "busy making a living." Ann was "always mama's girl," and when her mama found out she went "bananas." One night at the show, sitting in the front row, was Ann's Italian mama. Backstage Mama told Ann the show was all right. "As long as they looka, but no touch." In the 1930s and 1940s, it was "the looka, but no touch era."

Ann had a refinement about her. She was poised and dignified, with a strong sense of self-worth that would carry her through a career in burlesque lasting nearly seven decades.

After six months toiling in the chorus, she became a headliner and "she was competing with Gypsy. Gypsy appealed to the more sophisticated audience, society people. Ann appealed to the truck driver and the bus driver and the mechanic. They all came to the show, with their wives," Mike explained. "She was the darling of the burlesque aficionados."

Mike continued, "Gypsy was a sophisticate. . . . She talked her way. Ann didn't have to talk; all she had to do was walk on the stage and everyone went, 'Wow.'"

Ann ruled from the stage of The Old Howard in Boston, a former church and later a vaudeville theatre.

Ann's first husband was Emmet Callahan, who discovered her when she was young and helped guide her career. He was (variously and allegedly) an executive of a chain of burlesque theatres, manager of the Apollo Theatre, and a theatrical agent. He was older and became her mentor. They were secretly married (according to newspaper accounts) on Christmas Day 1934. In one column written by Walter Winchell, who often related the burly queen's comings and goings, he noted Ann and Emmet, though separated for two years, continued to dine out together, and he continued to manage her and buy her jewelry. When she did divorce him, she accused him of "deserting her and discoloring her eye and bruising her leg."

In 1942 Ann quit burlesque to star in B pictures in Hollywood. Her movies weren't "released," she would claim; they "escaped."

They cranked them out fast. "They didn't want them good; they wanted them Tuesday," Mike Iannucci recalled.

She never considered herself a good actress. She did it because she needed to work. It was a way to keep going and have a living because she didn't have children. She continued in burlesque between pictures for "special occasions."

Her next husband, Bob Williams, was a nightclub comedian with a dog act. He appeared frequently on *The Ed Sullivan Show*. "He was a real evil guy," Mike said.

She became pregnant with twins but miscarried. "He treated her just awful."

When trying to have her divorce decree set aside, one paper claimed Ann said Williams only wanted to get divorced to help his career. They lived in Malibu on a ranch Ann had bought. According to her niece, Carole Nelson, Ann had turned all her properties over to him so she lost everything in the divorce. Ann was devastated. Williams's attorney was so appalled, he even apologized to Ann after the hearing, saying, "This shouldn't be the way it ended up."

Ann moved in with a sister and was not involved in burlesque during the 1950s. It wasn't until Mike came along and convinced her to put together a burlesque show honoring the golden days of burlesque that Ann revitalized her fame and fortune.

Mike was a handsome, stocky, well-built football player of Irish-Mediterranean descent who had played ball for twenty-three years. He played for the Pittsburgh Steelers from 1945 to 1962. "I knew nothing about show business," Mike said. "A friend of mine on the team got involved in [a] stock [theatre] company and got me involved. And I hired Ann in Bristol, Pennsylvania." Despite their age differences—he was almost twenty years younger—it was love at first sight. "We were together since we met. We hit it off the first day we met and that was it."

Stripper Ann Corio and much younger husband Mike Iannucci

Mike had never seen a burlesque show. "I came up with the idea—why don't we do a show depicting the history of burlesque as it was in its finer days?" Mike had trouble convincing investors to put up the money. However, the investors eventually made "a ton of money back. They believed in the show," he said. Ann hired comics and strippers she had worked with and she was the director. Mike produced. *This Was Burlesque* debuted on Broadway in 1961.

How did Mike and Ann get burlesque back in New York and on Broadway after LaGuardia had banned it? Mike said, "It wasn't a law that was legislated. I researched it and did the show. I had no trouble. The censors came by and saw the show." LaGuardia was long gone by then. "No one else fought the law until I came along."

Burlesque had changed since Ann's reign. "It had generated to strictly stripping and the bad type." When they ran the show, Ann was tough.

"We emphasize comedy," Ann explained at the time. "We are not offensive."

Ann would stand backstage and listen. "She'd listen to comics from a speaker in her room and wouldn't stand for bad words and swearing. She was a flag-waving American," according to niece Carole Nelson. She was strict and she was known to have a temper that matched her fiery red hair.

Ann put a lot of the comedians back to work that had been unemployed when the strippers bumped them off the stage. "They had almost no work. They loved it when we came along. We gave them steady work doing what they loved to do." They employed Steve Mills, Dexter Maitland, and Claude Mathis (who was eighty-one in 1981 and still with the show). Most were old men.

This Was Burlesque had a couple strippers (though most shows by then had six or eight), four or five comedians, and two straight men (all but banished from burlesque in the 1960s) and a chorus line. "Later burlesque, they never had a chorus line again," Mike said.

They put "a little chubby girl out of step in the chorus, next to the tree-toppers. The little chubby girl, it was a comedy relief. We had all different sized girls. They opened show, did two or three numbers, then did a finale parade out with beautiful costumes."

Carole remembered her aunt cutting costumes on her dining room table and recalled Ann being very motherly towards her. Ann told her she "was the daughter [she] was meant to have." Carole in fact lives with the suspicion that she might be her "aunt's" daughter, as so often times happened in those days.

Ann's strippers were all "clean." At that time, strippers in New Jersey "could do almost anything. . . . Ann never took them." The strippers in Ann's show had to work according to how Ann wanted it.

Like so many of the strippers told me, Ann never exercised besides dancing in the show. Carole said she had a "great sense of humor and loved animals." Bozo the Cat was the mascot of *This Was Burlesque*. The cat would occasionally walk on the stage during the performance. There were numerous pictures of Bozo in Mike's apartment. The cat was born in a theatre in New York. "Bozo was the pet of all the comics."

On June 24, 1981, the *New York Times* reviewed a revival of *This Was Burlesque*: "Miss Corio, who looks radiant, does it all by the book and, whether you like the book or not, it is to her credit that she catches the flavor of the old burlesque with little attempt to ennoble or elevate it. This is close to the real thing."

Ann closed the show with her strip. Ann's act was only six or seven minutes. "She didn't have to do any more. That was her act throughout her entire burlesque career."

When *This Was Burlesque* was no longer running in theatres, Ann would take segments of the show on the road. Eventually Ann and Mike invested in dinner theatres and their pace of travel and work slowed down. One of Ann's last appearances on the stage was in Los Angeles in 1985.

Her health was poor the last three or four years of her life. There was a rumor, told to me, that Mike would tie her in her wheelchair and leave her while he went to gamble. He supposedly lost their beloved home in Connecticut to gambling debts.

She began "fading from us in life," her niece noted. Ann had dementia and had a difficult time speaking. "The last day I saw her, she just stared across the table at my mother [her sister] as if she did not know her."

Carole said, "Her last show that I saw, she was about eighty. And she was tired."

"Ann got sick in the early 1990s; she passed away in 1999. That was the end of the show. . . . Without her the show really lost most of its luster," said Mike.

Ann always closely guarded her age. The family celebrated her birthday on November 9. "We didn't do birthdays," Carole said. "It has been reported she died in her eighties, but she was ninety."

"We were together twenty-four hours a day, seven days a week, for like thirty years," Mike said.

Those who worked for Ann loved and respected and feared her. And though there was mixed reaction from the burlesquers to Mike himself, from downright "awful" to being a generally "bad guy," there was no doubt he loved her.

"I'm pushing seventy-six. I want to take it easy and hope that someday people say, 'He did a good job,'" Mike said.

**

SALLY RAND

After Gypsy Rose Lee, Helen Gould Beck—aka Sally Rand—is arguably the most recognizable name associated with burlesque.

Sally Rand

Sally's act consisted of dancing nude, or nearly so depending on the venue, concealed by two, five-foot long ostrich fans, and, later, shielded by an opaque rubber ball. She would play peek-a-boo with her body by manipulating her fans in front and behind her, like a winged bird as she swooped and twirled on the stage, usually to "Clair de Lune."

She was amazingly graceful given how heavy the fans were. She did not strip, but she did tease, flashing a hint of flesh as her fans swooshed and soared.

"She was a little different. She might have had a little bit of controversy here and there because she was totally nude," said Dixie Evans.

"One of the big things, she didn't like being referred to as a stripper," her son Sean explained. Sally would say, "I'm not up there stripping to tease anyone."

Born dirt poor in 1904, in Elkton, Missouri, in the Ozarks, her father was a rough rider with Teddy Roosevelt and she remembered sitting on the future president's lap.

She was blonde, beautiful, and at 105 lbs., stood no taller than five feet. Dixie once offered to help Sally pick up her things backstage. Sally told her, "No, that's how I get my exercise." She was respected and beloved by scores of fans for decades. "I thought a girl who went on the stage without stockings was a hussy," Sally once said. Boy, how she changed her tune.

Sally Rand started, as so many did, in the chorus when she was just fifteen or sixteen in New York City. At the time, she had a lisp. She had no money. To survive, she would go to restaurants or diners, wait until patrons finished, and steal the leftovers.

Sally would claim to be the inventor of the fan dance, performing it one year prior to the start of the Great Depression. She remembered seeing people jump out of windows. In 1927, she was a "deb star," her son said, and "a WAMPUS Baby Star." (WAMPUS was the Western Association of Motion Picture Advertisers in the United States, an organization that promoted young women as potential stars.)

Her lisp and her Ozarks accent, however, weren't what Hollywood was looking for, though the film director Cecil B. DeMille would later give her a new name. He chose "Rand" from the maps and she picked Sally because she figured the large S would look good in lights.

Sally's fame started in earnest in 1931 at the Chicago World's Fair. "She saved Chicago," Dixie declared. Sally got a job dancing in the Streets of Paris concessions, owned by the city fathers. (The Fair's various pavilions and exhibits were owned by a variety of corporations and organizations.)

The fair suffered from poor attendance, with not nearly enough paying customers to support the millions of dollars poured into it. That is, until Sally did a Lady Godiva down the midway.

Sally had heard Mrs. Hearst was going to have a Milk Fund Ball at one hundred dollars a plate. In Depression-era 1932, one hundred dollars a plate was beyond decadent. Much of the country was starving. As a child of poverty, Sally was "offended," Sean said.

So she got an idea. She thought, "I can get a horse, put him on a boat and bring him in through Soldier's Field." She wore no clothes except for a long blonde wig and sat astride a rubber-shoed horse named "Mike" and rode into the Milk Fund Ball. Sally claimed the stunt was a stab at society ladies who were spending thousands on their gowns while those around them went hungry. To top it off, the next day she rode Mike down the midway.

"And all of a sudden clippity clop . . . what is this coming down the promenade? Right in front of all the people is a big prancing horse with a nude Sally Rand," laughed Dixie Evans. Sally went home, went to bed, and the next day a "girlfriend called, 'Sally you're on the front page of every newspaper.'" Although there were later reports that she'd in fact been wearing a nude body stocking, Rand's fame was cemented from that day forward.

The Century of Progress World's Fair had cost $38 million and it "was going down the drain for lack of visitors." Sally pulled the fair out of the red. "It was the only concession that made a lot of money," said Dixie Evans.

A couple years later, Sally was still trying to break into Hollywood and starred in a movie with George Raft and Carole Lombard. She performed in nightclubs and returned to the 1934 World's Fair doing a bubble dance using a large weather balloon as a sort of encore to the previous year's fair. She was earning upwards of ten thousand dollars a week, Sean claimed, and acted as her own agent, publicist, and costumer.

"My mother adopted me in 1948. I grew up backstage," he said. Sally was forty-four and it was long before adoption was the popular thing to do. It would have been difficult for a single mother, especially one who worked naked, to adopt. But she did. Sean traveled with her, though eventually Sally's parents took care of Sean while she was on the road.

Sean was born in Florida. His birth mother had given him up after her husband in the Navy died. When his gun backfired, he wasn't wearing asbestos and he "disintegrated." The woman gave birth when Sally was in the room and she took custody of him shortly thereafter.

"I never had a birth certificate," Sean said. Sally's lawyer working on the adoption "went crazy and the paperwork fell through the cracks."

Sometime much later, the birth mother tried to take him back and Sally, being the famous Sally Rand, "it was easy to track her movements down."

When he was fifteen, Sally arranged for him to stay with a showgirl friend, Sunny Nivens. Sally came with "a wad of money," gave it to Sunny, and said "Take Sean. Go here. Don't open the door, even for police."

Sean was hid several times by different showgirls as his birth mother "relentlessly tried to find him." She also relied on chorus girls to hide and protect him.

Sally had tremendous "guts for her time. She had the women's lib thing. Ahead of her time," recalled Sean. She continued to perform at World's Fairs—in 1936 at the Texas Centennial and again in 1939 in San Francisco. She was in great demand. She considered her act to be tasteful, an art form that had a purpose and meaning.

During Texas Centennial, Sally introduced Texas to her *Sally Rand Nude Ranch*, a sideshow attraction featuring fifteen girls posed with six shooters and hats strategically placed. The beauties lounged around with the letters SR branded to each thigh. Some sat on horses or played with a beach ball. A ticket was fifty cents. Sally herself served as hostess.

When Ann Corio produced *This Was Burlesque*, Sally worked the show for two weeks filling in for Ann, who was having surgery. She did her fan and "bubble dance," working with a giant balloon or ball. Sally was a "hillbilly," according to Mike Iannucci. Sally loved her work, and many said her balloon dance was incredible. She performed the dance to "Clair de Lune" and other classic pieces of music. "You never saw anything—if not nude, almost—but you never saw anything the way she maneuvered the fans."

She lived a full life offstage, as well. She married four times. Jimmy Thatch was the love of her life, though she never married him. He became an admiral and retired to Coronado Island, near San Diego, California.

She married a guy named Frank when she was fifty. Frank was thirty-one and it lasted eight years. She was friends with Charles Lindberg and became an aviator herself.

Sally loved gardening and painting. Needlepoint was one of her favorite hobbies. Sean "hated yard work," but because of his exposure to it through his mom, he ironically ended up working in the nursery business.

Without an agent and publicist, Sally took care of herself, as so many did in that era. She was tough in a little package. "She could get the four-letter words going and get in their face if they deserved it. She had to take care of herself for a lot of years," Sean said. She worked at a time when she was paid in cash and was robbed several times.

Sally Rand onstage toward the end of her life

Towards the end of her long career she was still getting big money—$2,000 to $2,500 a week plus expenses. She saved and invested. At the end, she had money, and a house, and apartments she had for income. She didn't have "great wealth at the end. But she took care of herself," Sean said. Sean explained his mother was never unemployed, giving her last performance just months before she died at age seventy-five.

She spent the last eight days of her life in the Glendora hospital in August of 1979. She had checked herself in. Sean got a call that his mother was in the hospital. She was in intensive care. The heart specialist told Sean, "Your mother isn't doing well. She's had a heart attack [within] the last two years. It did damage to 75 percent of the heart muscle." Sean knew nothing about a heart attack. Sally was a tough old trooper and had never mentioned it. Her lungs were not in good shape, either.

She wanted Sean to take her out of Glendora Hospital and take her home. Sean asked the doctor if he could; he would do anything for his mother. Though her home was just miles away, "the doctors didn't think she'd last to the house."

She passed away and "everyone from the show business world called in, from Bob Hope to Frank Sinatra. . . . I went to pay the bill. In 1979, it was a ten thousand-dollar bill. The hospital said, 'It's paid.' An anonymous person had called in and said, 'Tell me the number and we're gonna pay it.'"

Years passed and at a "Sally Rand night" in Glendora, someone from the hospital, an ex-administrator, got up and said, "I have something to reveal. Sammy Davis called in and paid Sally's bill."

Sally knew Sammy Jr.'s father from vaudeville; he had danced with Bill Robinson, "Mr. Bo Jangles." She'd given a lot of money to Sammy's father, and Sammy Jr. remained forever grateful. This was just another example of the burly performers looking out for one another. I heard it time and again.

Throughout the years, several places and people have claimed to be in possession of Sally's original fans. Alexandra the Great claimed she "bought fans from Sally Rand when she was in Toledo."

In the 1960s at a dedication ceremony, Sally turned over a pair of fans to the Chicago Historical Society, the *very* ones she had used at the World's Fair of 1933, she declared.

After the ceremony in the cab, Sean asked his mother, "'Those were the *very* fans?'" He knew how her fans took a beating—after all, he had been on the road with her for two decades. "She looked at me and says, 'No, dummy, those aren't the fans, but that's what they wanted to hear today. Those fans were gone six months after the show.'"

Sally was the consummate showman. She spent her career giving the people what they wanted.

**

GEORGIA SOTHERN

Georgia Sothern was known as a "hot" performer. She was a vivacious, red-headed (and sometimes blonde) powerhouse who literally flung her body about the stage to the tune of "Hold that Tiger." She was an uneducated, unattractive woman who came from nothing but gained much notoriety on the burlesque stage. She was hugely admired by fellow performers and fans alike. She created an act that worked for her. It was fast paced, frantic, and orgasmic. She worked with stocky legs, a flat chest, and still created an illusion of glamour and beauty.

An ad for Georgia Sothern

What she lacked in appearance, Georgia made up for in energy. "Georgia had something. She wasn't an attractive woman," Maria Bradley recalled. Photos of her later in life reveal perhaps one or two nose jobs. "She electrified audiences," Bradley said.

Georgia did an athletic strip. As the orchestra blasted, she tossed her body, flipping it forward and back, cranking her neck high and low. She was fast.

She was born poor in Atlanta, Georgia. Her real name was Hazel. "She couldn't even spell 'southern.' She left out a couple letters," said Dixie. "She was only twelve, thirteen years old and she traveled with her uncle, who was in vaudeville. And he died of pneumonia. So all these others strippers and chorus girls were in the hotel and knew about the old man dying, so they said, 'What are you gonna do?' She said 'I don't know.' 'OK here, put some makeup on and do this and do that.' And they took her to Minsky's." They hired her. Georgia quickly became a star stripper.'

"She was little," said Maria Bradley, "but she did something on that stage, that it was like magical, you know. She . . . if I can use the word 'humped' . . . the scenery and the curtain . . . they howled because they loved it."

"She wasn't a dancer," said Rita Grable.

Because she was the feature and traveled from theatre to theatre, "you could steal her act and she wouldn't know the difference," Beverly Anderson explained. Beverly herself copied Georgia by spying on her offstage though the slit in the curtain while getting paid to catch her clothes. "I used another song; I watched her very carefully. I got from Georgia how to move as a stripper." In 1957, Georgia claimed the strip teasers that tried to steal her act were "still in the hospital."

Rita thought "she was dynamic" with her flaming hair, talking to the audience as she raced across the stage. "She was helpful to me. When I first started, she'd say, 'Put some rouge in your cleavage. Put two little white dots in the corners of your eyes to open your eyes.' She taught me a lot about makeup, and how to do certain things with your body, how to be a little more provocative. I would think, *I don't know what I'm doing.* She'd say, 'You're gonna be OK.' Sure enough, it was. I made a lot of money."

Georgia was a scrappy defender of burlesque who declared to reporters she would fight the ban on burlesque in New York. She noted that the regulars who had been attending burly shows for years didn't show any signs of their morales being hurt. If burlesque was banned it would make "bread-liners" out of all the thousands of burlesque performers instead of "breadwinners," as she told the *Salt Lake Tribune* in 1942. In a later interview, however, she scornfully remembered the men in the audience looking like they'd escaped from the "zoo."

Her life would be filled with danger and intrigue. As a teen, she accidentally witnessed a murder. She dated mobsters and one husband was a drunk who, in a rage, shot her with a prop gun. In 1949, she filed for bankruptcy, saying she had only seven dollars in cash. In 1957, she complained about a hundred-dollar hospital bill.

By the time she appeared on the David Susskind show in 1962 with a panel of strippers, including Zorita, Sherry Britton, and Hope Diamond, Georgia was much diminished in size and vibrancy. She worked until just a few years before her death of cancer in 1981 at the age of seventy-two.

SALLY KEITH

"Sally Keith was the greatest tassel twirler that ever lived. One would go one way, one would go the other. She could make those things sing."

—Lily Ann Rose, her protégé.

"She was just amazingly popular."

—David Kruh

Stella Katz was born in 1913, the fifth of ten children, eight of them boys. It was a "very observant Jewish family," recalled Susan Weiss, Sally's niece. Her father was Sally's brother, the second-youngest in the line. The family home for Sally and her siblings was a crowded two-bedroom apartment in Chicago. It was a "difficult life," Weiss said.

"As a kid, she'd take the tassels off the window shades and play with them," Weiss said. An auspicious beginning for a woman who would become hugely popular by swinging her tassels for sold-out crowds in Boston.

At fifteen or sixteen, Sally got her start by entering beauty contests. And how could she not win, with her platinum hair and big blue eyes? Sally was gorgeous. Soon someone discovered Sally and took her to the East Coast, where she developed an act, got an agent, and made a name for herself despite her lack of education. Susan thought she started to perform in 1930 or 1931.

Sally could twirl her four tassels in opposite directions, a tassel on each bra cup and one on each butt cheek. She'd start one, then a second, then a third. And they would all be going in different directions. She sang and danced. She always had an orchestra. She invested in custom-made costumes, changing often throughout the show. Sally would wear tap pants and little boots. Sometimes she sported big majorette-type hats with feathers in them.

Sally Keith

She toured London and Paris and New York. She lived in Boston in the Hotel Lennox while performing at the Crawford House Theatre. The Hotel Lennox was on infamous Scollay Square, home to the Old Howard and other burlesque theatres and clubs. She worked with Abbott and Costello, Jimmy Durante, and even shared the bill with conjoined twins Daisy and Violet Hilton. Sally partied with Jackie Gleason and was mentioned by Johnny Carson on his show when she died. Ed McMahon, who had performed at the Crawford House, had been a friend and fan. Sally was Boston's own local treasure.

"The act was unique. But there was something about her look, her genuineness" that David Kruh attributed to her success. "She was a generous woman. When Father Curly's son [Curly was a parish priest] had a fundraiser, Sally always did her part." She gave shows to local army camps. She even offered Father Curly her tassels to sell for charity. He kindly declined.

After a famous fire destroyed much of the Crawford House in 1948, Sally's supposed items that were lost were staggering and included mink, fox and ermine; a wardrobe worth thousands; tassels; and jewelry.

Sally knew how to capitalize on her larger-than-life stature. She was glamorous and colorful. When she was in the room, everyone stared at her. She was affected and eccentric. She wore big jewels and fox furs with claws dangling down her chest. She was extravagant, but a warm, sweet person. She made piles of money and enjoyed her expensive lifestyle. She had a Cadillac with leopard-print seats that she didn't know how to drive. Others would drive it, like a young Lily Ann Rose.

Her good nature was taken advantage of by many, including her first husband, agent Jack Parr. He tried to control her life. He took advantage of her financially. She divorced him when she was only twenty-two.

Publicity was a big thing for the girls. The more times your name was in the paper, the more popular you were—and the more money you could demand. Many girls "did" their own publicity, including numerous "stunts." Lili St. Cyr was an expert at it for years—her tricks included the staging of a fight between a husband and "lover" in view of a photographer who also happened to be a friend.

Susan Weiss claimed Sally's most notorious publicity stunt was being robbed at the Crawford House. The headline in the paper screamed in big, bold print Sally Keith ROBBED BEATEN.

"That I know was a publicity stunt, because I remember my parents talking . . . about how they had to get the makeup on her legs just right, the black and blue marks."

Many stories were created for publicity's sake. And indeed in the photograph of Sally showing her bruised legs, she does seem cheerful.

Sally Keith showing off her bruises after her alleged robbery

There were other harmless inventions, including the claim she sent money home to her father who was a Chicago policeman. In reality, he painted houses.

Lily Ann Rose, however, would beg to differ. "She was robbed. And she was paranoid." She deposited most of her jewels in the bank after the robbery except for two diamond necklaces. Sally and Lily each wore one to keep it safe. "She was paranoid about being robbed again. She had a drinking problem. She reminded me a lot of my mother. You know, she would drink and then she couldn't function," Lily said. Sally was "addicted, like my mother to Stingers," she said. Stingers was a syrupy-sounding drink of brandy and crème de menthe.

At fifty, Sally married her second and last husband Arthur Brandt. They moved from Florida to New York. In 1967, Sally died of cirrhosis of the liver. She was only fifty-four. "It was shocking," Susan said. "No one knew how bad her problem was." Shiva was at Susan's parents' house.

SHERRY BRITTON

The girl with the curtain of long black hair that hung down to her waist was born in New Jersey as Edith (Edie) Zack. She told me she had taken her stage name from a liquor store on a bottle of Harvey's Bristol Cream. Sherry was "well respected and established in New York," remembers Dixie Evans.

Star stripper Sherry Britton died an honorary brigadier. The title was given to her for her work entertaining the boys during WWII. She stood a mere five-feet three inches, but was a giant among strippers in the 1930s and '40s. She was tough, sweet, smart, enthusiastic, cherished, wild, fierce, sexy, tasteful. And a fighter. She would proclaim herself "the queen of the small claims court," as she was always taking someone to court. Perhaps that is why her last husband encouraged her to get her law degree from Fordham University. She would graduate magna cum laude, at the age of sixty-three—an accomplishment she was very proud of.

When I first spoke with her, her voice over the phone was shaky and weak. She had recently been released from months in the hospital after a terrible fall, wherein she tangled with her dog's leash. She had been on "death's door," she related. She was frail and had a nurse living with her.

She begged off meeting me. She had been burned recently in another documentary she "despised" and was wary of being involved in another. I promised her this experience would be different. Sherry had been one of the biggest stars of burlesque. I had to have her story. She was one of maybe four "greats" still alive when I began my interviews. She was eighty-seven in 2006.

"Whatever beauty I had is gone," the frail voice deferred. "I was gorgeous. I had an eighteen-inch waist." She didn't want to be photographed.

"I won't put you on camera then," I promised. *Can I at least come and record your stories?* Without her, my efforts would be meaningless. Over the next several months, as she slowly recovered, whenever I flew to New York, I would call and try and see her. She usually wasn't feeling well enough, but we started a phone friendship and slowly she began to trust me. *I'm not feeling well enough to put on my makeup,* she told me, and *I never am seen without it.* Then I won't wear any, I told her. She laughed.

I spent months talking to Sherry, hoping she would grow strong enough and would change her mind about being interviewed. Finally, she agreed I could audio record her.

She had a lovely apartment overlooking Gramercy Park. Knocking on the door, I wasn't sure what to expect. The pictures I had seen of Sherry showed a raven-haired beauty. Her figure was a ravishing hour-glass. She had dark eyebrows and eyes. In photos of her from the 1940s, she was at the peak of her beauty and fame.

I was shocked when she opened the door. She was still gorgeous, but unexpectedly short, barely reaching to my shoulders. In pictures, she was not only regal, but statuesque. I never imagined her so tiny. She had dark, curly hair. She wore red lipstick and her brows and liner were in place. She wore red elastic pants and a flowered top. She was stunning.

"You're beautiful," I gasped. And she was. She wasn't the twenty-year-old beauty I'd seen pictures of. I knew her story of being oft-engaged, a femme fatale. And she was eighty-seven years old, but she seemed decades younger. She had a wit and vibrancy about her even in her declining health. She acted and talked like a contemporary. She invited me into her immaculately kept apartment, bright and yellow. Paintings of her hung over her dining table. A table was covered with the handwritten chapters of her unpublished biography *From Stripper to Brigadier General*. Unfinished, it remains unpublished and a whopper of a good story. I even tried to have my literary agent (at the time) take it on.

As she spoke, I fell in love, as so, so many before me had.

Sherry became a dear friend. At the end of the interview, we drove to her doctor's appointment with the nurse who shared an apartment with her. I would call and write Sherry. She had an enthusiasm in her voice that I always found to be uplifting.

Young Edie had a crushingly hard childhood. She was born in England to a mother who first tried to abort her with a twelve-inch hat pin, then later abandoned her when she was two. Sherry's father started "cavorting with different people." She would live in fifteen foster homes and a couple orphan asylums.

At ten, when she was back with her mother and her mother's new husband, the husband "performed oral sex" on her, she said.

At fourteen, she moved in with her aunt. However, Sherry was becoming a voluptuous young beauty and her aunt had a "young, handsome husband" with a wandering eye. Another uncle raped Sherry. "And so [my aunt] felt that I might now be attractive to her husband, so she threw me out. I was homeless, sleeping in people's cars, parks, the subway," she said. But not before her aunt beat up the young teenager. After a year on the streets, she met a guy who asked her to marry him. Unbeknownst to the naïve girl, he was already married, but pretended to go through a ceremony. "It was a phony marriage. . . . He put a ring on my finger. And I thought I was married," she said. She had no idea what getting married even was. She believed him and assumed she was. "And I was pregnant four times that year. And he beat the shit out of me. It was terrible. Horrible," she said. Her pregnancies ended in abortions. She always wanted a baby and likely would have been a lovely mother. She was nurturing, as testified by her cousin, Melaine, whom she helped raise when she was born.

Sherry was trapped in the relationship. "My aunt helped me get away from him. He found me, got on his knees, and begged me to come back. I didn't. His wife found us and I found out we weren't married. He was twenty-eight."

The same aunt introduced Sherry to a life of dancing and stripping. "Bobbie got me into burlesque and so I was in burlesque, which I despised for six years. It was so weird for me." Through all my hours of discussion with Sherry that would grow more intimate and broad over the months, she was blunt and fearless. Despite her tough exterior, she was full of love and wonder for everything.

"It was disgusting to me. I could see the men masturbating and knew that I was part of that. And realized that that was probably all over the theatre—each theatre. And the only thing that I enjoyed was making my costumes and the beautiful music." She stripped to classical music. "All kinds of music that had nothing to do with burlesque—I enjoyed those two things." She couldn't understand that those around her had no self-respect or respect for one another. She survived beatings at the hands of jealous strippers backstage. "I was so young and became a star immediately. And so they were very resentful."

Sherry stood apart from the other strippers for many reasons. "I was the only one who didn't take off my G-string. Everyone else took off their G-string. Yuck. I got fired a couple times until they realized people came back hoping to see the forbidden fruit, so they stopped firing me," she said. Bizarrely, she would balance a glass of water on her "fifteen-year-old breasts" and walk across the stage.

"My father showed up and he said, 'My daughter is in burlesque?' I said, 'Where were you? Where were you? What was I supposed to do?'" she said. She faced him square, knowing he hadn't been there for her, hadn't protected her from abandonment, hunger, rape, humiliation, and sadness.

Even though she "hated burlesque," it didn't mean she did not like working in the nightclubs stripping. She did. But the clubs were very different than the theatres.

Sherry moved into nightclubs, appearing at Leon & Eddies on 52nd Street for six or seven years straight, starting at the age of sixteen and breaking all attendance records. Nightclubs had "vaudeville acts and I sang and danced and did not have to strip down as much as I did in burlesque."

She enjoyed singing. "I felt that [stripping] had its place at that time in burlesque with the scenes with men, the girls, and production numbers, so that I felt that it was a legitimate showing, but what I've seen the last few years . . . there is no comedy and production numbers."

Sherry knew she was beautiful and desirable to many men. She had her nose shaved and made slimmer on three separate occasions. She loved to dance and sing. She was innately classy. She knew her worth as a person and a performer, though she would repeatedly run into trouble due to her stubbornness. She held off men that loved her; she was suspicious and could be cold.

"I wouldn't get married. I just wouldn't. I was alright being engaged, but when it came to being pushed into marriage, I couldn't do it. When it's something the other person doesn't want, *they* want it. These men all wanted to get married. They had a woman they could take to grandma and not be ashamed of and still have a garden full of all kinds of lovely things men would treasure. I lived with several men," she said.

She began a stint cruising the streets of New York, picking up men and bringing them back to her apartment for sex. She wouldn't allow them to spend what remained of the night.

"I had a lot of one-nighters. And I didn't realize it was hurting their egos not to be invited back again. One of them was [Academy Award–winner] José Ferrer. Ferrer never admitted we were together."

She continued, "I was engaged fifteen times, but rejected each fiancé before he could reject me. I liked being engaged."

She had great, tumultuous romances with men, both married and not. Her beaus included Harry Belafonte and composer Richard Rodgers, and she had an affair with at least one woman. David Susskind was a fiancé. She dated "exhilarating" actor Rex Harrison. "The most romantic man of all was Jackie Gleason," she said. She's mentioned in a biography (a copy of which she kept, with the page marked, in her apartment) of "sweet" actor Gig Young, with whom she had a love affair and who killed himself, though thankfully not because of her.

She said she had a horrible, "demeaning, and disgusting experience" with the "oversized" Frank Sinatra. Sinatra courted Sherry, and they spent one "disastrous night in bed." "How could he resist touching this body?" she said. She was astounded. "It amazed me. No kisses, nothing."

It started in Miami Beach when she was invited to a party the crooner was giving in his suite at the Fontainebleau Hotel. The party lasted into the night and every time she tried to leave, she was persuaded to stay by "Mr. Crew Cut, Joe Fischer" (really one of the Fischetti brothers, as in FBI's Ten Most Wanted).

Eventually Sinatra got Sherry into his bedroom and immediately unzipped his pants. She contemplated what to do and decided to get into bed.

"A story I'm not proud to repeat, but it happened." To her it was a "mystery how Sinatra managed to snare such lovely women . . . outsized Frank Sinatra." With no foreplay whatsoever, he "mounted" the shocked Sherry Britton. She said she "felt like a pound of hamburger."

She left before anything happened.

Afterwards, she felt guilty, knowing Sinatra could not sleep alone and she called to apologize. He wouldn't speak with her. "You're on his shit list," his people said. Sherry didn't much care. "Spectacular bust as a suitor. No sweet talk. No career, just zip."

She got married at age thirty-seven to Buddy Boylan, stage name "Mark Reddy," a singer and half of a comedy team. "I tricked my way into it," she said. "By that, I mean everybody was saying to me, 'You ought to be married,' and there were two of us at the time, well known that weren't married. Laverne Andrews, one of the Andrews Sisters, and me. Laverne was sweet and nice but so completely dull. I got married to Buddy, big gorgeous hunk, and we were walking along Fifth Avenue," where they ran into Laverne, who was with her new husband.

To Sherry, Laverne asked, "'How come you got married?'

Sherry responded, "I married the first man who didn't try and drag me to bed."

Laverne replied, "I married the first one who did."

Sherry and Buddy's marriage lasted two years. She said he was "impossible. Really emotionally a mess. And people said, 'If you knew that before, why did you

Sherry Britton backstage

180

marry him?' Because I was nuttier than he was. And I was," she explained. "He didn't pursue me and everybody else did. So I went after him."

During WWII, she toured hospitals and sang and met the wounded soldiers. In Valley Forge, Pennsylvania, there was a cosmetic reconstruction hospital. She sang to boys with "empty eye sockets." There were so many "boys without faces. . . . And I looked across and I said to the boy who was guiding me—he had two dimples and no teeth, a bullet had gone through him—'If that boy comes over to me, I'll die.' He did. This poor boy's face was inside out. He had a sense of humor, and he had a delightful personality, started telling me where the different places on his face came from—like twenty-seven operations—and finally he said, 'They just made me an eyelid and the only comparable flesh is on a man's penis. So forever more I'll be cockeyed.'"

For her work in the hospitals, she was told she was to be honored with the rank of Brigadier General. But she didn't go to Washington for the ceremony where she would have met the president. "I was an idiot! I didn't go." They sent three military men to New York who presented it to her on stage at her beloved Leon & Eddies.

Despite love affairs, adoring fans, and nonstop work, Sherry "fell apart and wound up in the psychiatric [ward] of NYU. It was horrible. They put me on Librium and I was on Librium for thirty years."

In 1969, she was out of burlesque due to an injury in a dimly lit club. She approached legitimate theatres. "I starred in fifty-three Broadway shows. And at fifty-three, I married Bob. I stopped working. And he wanted me to become a lawyer, so at sixty-three, I graduated from Fordham University Magna Cum Laude. I'd never had high school. It was really a miracle." She also claimed to speak five languages.

Bob Gross, three years younger, was the love of her life, and her last husband was by her own account an "ugly man." But he made Sherry laugh. He was the wealthy owner of Astra Aircraft. The two married in 1971 after many hard years (for Sherry) seeing each other on and off.

"I married late. Too late given, too soon taken." They discovered that Bob had lung cancer. Because of a surgeon's negligence, she nursed Bob for seven years. When he was ensconced at Mt. Sinai Hospital, she spent her nights on a cot by his side for months on end.

She did her last strip at sixty-three at the Players Club. "I did my whole show. I had written it and that was the last time."

She adored her family, kept in touch with a wide circle of friends, played cards, and rarely drank. She had wanted children, but settled for being a good aunt and family woman. She had been blessed with amazing genes. "I looked twenty years younger than I was without cosmetic surgery," she said. Though she

Sherry Britton backstage

did admit to having a peel around her lips, and when it got rid of the wrinkles, Bob's family was disgusted with her.

Bob was a "voluptuary. He liked *doing* things, not seeing things." They went to see a stripper on 42nd Street. Bob wanted to leave. When the girl finally came on that they had come to see, she was "beautiful but she stripped down to nothing and she was shaven," she said. The couple behind Sherry and Bob said, "She looks like Kojak." According to Sherry, Bob said it was worth going to the show just for that line.

Witty and self-assured, when she was once asked what she thought of when she stripped, she replied, "Men."

Another time, on meeting someone, the woman Sherry was introduced to said, "Honey, you should change your name, there is a stripper with the same name." Sherry was amused.

Sherry had her share of heartbreaks and heartaches. But she also had an indefatigable spirit and a sense of wonder about the world and people.

"In burlesque, I felt that there were two of me. One on the stage, and one watching me undress for all the morons in the audience. . . . It's incredible to me that anyone could have lived that life and survived with any sense of self-respect or any compassion or any love for humanity at all. It amazes me. But thank goodness I remained a decent, loving person."

Sally Rand advertisement for her "Nude Ranch"

Route Sheet featuring Lotus Dubois

Stripper Sherry Britton

Novelty dancers Jon and Inge

Backstage

Candy Barr

Dixie Evans, the Marilyn Monroe of burlesque, performing her tribute to MM's "'The Prince and the Showgirl"

Chorus girls dressing

Prepping the trunk for travel

The entire cast out for the grand finale

The inimitable Harold Minsky and his girls

Burlesque performer
from the 1920s or earlier

Stripper just off stage

April March showing some leg on stage

Comedians center stage

A fan dancer center stage

With all my love to the dearest sweetheart in the world Shirly

Dancer Shirley Corbins

Stripper Tee Tee Red

Dardy Minsky with a soldier on stage in Los Angeles

The lovely Ann Corio

CHAPTER TWENTY-SEVEN

Birds of a Feather

"I said, 'You might be a baroness, but I'm the queen of burlesque.'"
—Betty Rowland

"Rose Zell went to work at the Paradise in New York, and Dian was working one burlesque show called the Eltinge, so she was a star there. And I was working for Minsky. We had it all tied up."
—Betty Rowland

They were three beautiful sisters: the oldest Roz Elle (variously Rose-Elle and Roselle), a middle sister Dian, and the youngest Betty Jane born in 1916, in Columbus, Ohio. The three sisters started dancing together in vaudeville. An older sister, Lorraine, would remain in Columbus, out of show business. Their mother was Ida. Their father, Alvah, was a probation officer.

The three sisters toured in a five-girl dance act. When the act broke up, the sisters decided to remain on the road. They were soon in burlesque (without their parents' knowledge) and in New York, where they were being chaperoned by another girl's mother. The sisters would say "we'll go home next week. We never did." Soon the parents came to New York and found them. The father got a job working in a hotel and the family was together again.

By 1935, they were squarely in burlesque. Nils Granlund, in his book *Blondes, Brunettes, and Redheads,* says the sisters and mother were living at "a drab theatrical hotel." He had discovered Rose-Zelle (his spelling) working at the Irving Palace Theatre on 14th Street and said her "beauty was startling." She was sixteen. Betty Jane was thirteen.

In no time, the three separately made names for themselves. Roz Elle was working the Paradise, Dian was the star at the Eltinge, and Betty was with Minsky. The sisters were close and continued to live together.

Betty often describes her work as "The Three D's," for dancing, dollars, and dishes. Because of the sagging economy during the Depression, she sometimes earned "dishes" instead of cash.

Money wasn't the only problem. The worries about being shut down by the authorities were real. Rowland said she was fined $250 in 1939 after a trial in which a police officer described and imitated her burlesque act on the witness stand.

Betty, a contemporary of Sherry Britton's and also one of the last "queens," would soon be the only surviving sister, and when I interviewed her, she was in her nineties. Betty knew everything about burlesque, a form of entertainment she had enjoyed and in which she found much success, if not financial reward. She was a star during its Golden Age, billed as "The Ball of Fire," both for her red hair and fiery strip. She was petite and buxom, fresh-faced and wholesome looking.

"They enjoyed talent at that time, and then Roz Elle left me by myself and I started stripping because I didn't have her anymore," she said.

Betty worked when there "was no stigma," she explained. There was a lot of talent in the burlesque theatres.

Betty Rowland

The first time she stripped, she forgot to take her clothes off. She "didn't do too well the first time."

She began to work her way up in a show by experimenting. When a stage manager suggested she start stripping, she piled on hat, gloves, and much more.

Betty admitted the "costume was a bit much. Not enough music to get it all off." She eliminated some clothes and did more dancing.

Though she enjoyed steady work, it wasn't until she went to California that audiences appreciated her, (Vicki O'Day explained the rivalry between the coasts: "We on the West Coast were snobbish. We were a tad cleaner than the East Coast.") When Betty returned to New York, they appreciated her more, she said. She soon went to work for Minsky.

"The dance directors helped you, would look for special music," she said. She was smart enough to get help. "I tried to help one girl with doing floor work." The girl's feet were dirty and Betty said, "Let's start with your feet." The stripper became insulted and "never spoke to [Betty] again." Betty still shakes her head. "It didn't look good with dirty feet. Distracting."

Betty explained, "A typical show had a chorus line, and the dancers were usually short girls, tap dancing. Burlesque was coming out of its cocoon, because vaudeville was going into it. Burlesque was adding comics and others who couldn't work in Broadway shows. . . .

"We had the advantage of beautiful theatres, musicians, and talent," she said. She worked with Abbott and Costello, Red Skelton, and Red Buttons. They were "topping the other with talent."

"Stripping wasn't the big thing, but got to be that way because of competition," she said. But there was a difference in the talent. "A lot just took off their clothes and said, 'Look at me.'" Betty's act "was nonstop. No one could ever copy it." At the time, there wasn't too much copying of acts. "It's *you* when you strip. When you try someone else's act, the audience is thinking of them."

Betty would carry on a long-term affair with burlesque comedian, actor, and Orson Welles protégé Gus Schilling, who she lived with (although some publications stated erroneously that they were married). Gus had a drinking problem and was married to someone else. "It was just easier to tell people we were married," Betty explained.

She did an act with Gus, a recognizable one in burlesque where Gus was downstage singing. Betty was behind him, stripping to wild applause.

Betty married again after "show business got tired of [her]" to the man who owned Dalton Lumber. A newspaper article in her scrapbooks says an "Owen S. Dalton" was in fact a restaurant man and holder of real estate interests. They were married in 1956.

Whomever Owen Dalton was, the marriage didn't last, despite (according to Betty) his naming the development "Rowland Heights" in Los Angeles after her. She believes, though, John Rowland was given a land grant in that area in the 1800s. He also named one of the streets "Ball Road." The two were separated by March of 1962.

Betty Rowland and "husband" Gus Schilling (second from right, and far right).

Betty would go on stripping until she became a part owner and hostess at a bar in Santa Monica, California, called Mr. B's in the late '60s. She sold her interest in the business, but remained working as a hostess for the renamed 217 Lounge. She was saddened over the death of actor Chris Penn, a frequent client at the bar, whose photo she kept in her apartment.

"I get to keep my clothes on," she said of her hostess work. She eventually would claim the owners had cheated her out of her ownership of the club, and the club ultimately closed. Betty was forced to quit working in her early nineties. As Betty was growing increasingly frail and unable to take care of herself, though still mentally sharp, a friend of Betty's moved her into an assisted living facility run by nuns. At the time of this writing, she is taken care of comfortably and kindly by the sisters, who know all about her past. And though Betty would prefer not to be there, she is making the most of it, as she always has.

DIAN

Not much is known today about the beautiful, blonde middle sister. She was advertised as "Society's Favorite." She looks a lot like her sister Betty, though her hair was platinum. Dian Rowland had had scarlet fever as a child, which left

Dian Rowland on stage

her with a leakage of the heart. The doctors informed the family she probably wouldn't make it to thirty years old. One night, Dian didn't come into the theatre where she was working. They found her dead in her apartment. She was just twenty-nine.

ROZ ELLE

Born in 1917, Roz Elle was the oldest sister. She married a wealthy prince—well, actually a Baron, and went to live in a French chateau.

Also petite like her sisters, Roz Elle was quite literally the "Golden Girl." She worked with her nude body spray-painted gold, a sometimes dangerous occupation. Many people died from the toxic paints, Lily Ann Rose said.

187

She was making $3.50 a day at the Irving Palace in New York. Theatre impresario Nils Thor ("Granny") Granlund hired her for three times that amount. Granny had her nude body painted gold and stood her on a pedestal, and in slow motion she performed an acrobatic dance. It took three pails of hot water at the end of the night to remove the paint. She became known as "Goldie."

Golden Girl Roz Elle Rowland, who performed in gold paint

In 1934, she went with the show to the Dorchester House in London, the current Dorchester Hotel. She was earning two hundred dollars a week. Roz Elle was about to meet her Baron.

Baron Jean Empain, of the Paris subway family, was a millionaire and play-boy—part of the "black satin and pearls" crowd in Egypt. He and Roz Elle started going together.

When Roz Elle became pregnant with his child, he promised Roz Elle that if she had a girl, he would support the baby and her. But if she had a son, he would marry her. In 1937, Roz Elle had a boy, Edouard-Jean, nicknamed "Wado." She was nineteen; three days later (according to one report), they were married.

For a honeymoon, the Baron took Roz Elle on a safari on the Belgian Congo. They lived for a time in a castle in Alexandria, Egypt.

She had traded her $3-a-day job posing in gold paint for her husband's annual income of $10 million. Baron Jean Empain was the cheif stockholder of the Paris subway system, along with numerous other companies. He owned houses in Brussels, London, and Egypt; a stable of ninety race horses; ten automobiles; yachts; and even his own airplane.

They lived in a sumptuous mansion outside of Paris, and she became "quite elegant," stripper Margie Hart's sister Kathleen explained. "You would believe she was born into it." Dian and Betty visited frequently, staying at their Chateau de Bouffemont. The mansion, built in the nineteenth century, was and is colossal,

Baroness Roz Elle and her stripper sister Dian with Roz Elle's beloved dogs—eaten by the Nazis, she claimed.

189

with gilt rooms and wide grand staircases. Today it sits over the prestigious Paris International Golf Course. Betty had scrapbooks full of photos of her in Egypt and France, living the good life with Roz Elle and the baron.

Roz Elle's happiness was short-lived, however.

During WWII, the baron fought but was captured in German-occupied Belgium. Wounded on the battlefield, he was taken into prison by the Nazis while Roz Elle was living in the south of France. Their French mansion was occupied by the Nazis. Betty said the Nazis shot and ate the couple's beloved St. Bernard dogs. They "made a mess of the chateau," she said.

According to newspaper accounts from the time, Betty was without word from her sister for three years, unsure if she was alive.

When the baron died in 1946, Roz Elle married his cousin Eduard Empain. She would remain the Baroness Empain.

Roz Elle had a second child, a daughter Diane, with her second husband. But according to Betty, she wasn't the baron's daughter. "She's fathered by a fellow who worked with the horses on the estate," she said. Diane, in turn, Betty claimed, would have an illegitimate child that their Aunt Lorraine raised back in Columbus, Ohio.

Roz Elle's son, Wado—one of the world's ten richest men—was kidnapped in Paris in 1978 at the age of forty-one and held for ransom for sixty-three days. He was kept in chains to a bed, hooded and treated "with the utmost savagery," she said. He was forced to stand bent over, and his little pinky was cut off and mailed to the family. According to Betty, Wado was never the same after that.

Betty had a final story about her sister. I have repeated it here as best as I can. It is a mystery that might never be solved.

From her apartment in Los Angeles, Betty would speak every Sunday to Roz Elle in France. Roz Elle, in her late eighties, became ill and her daughter Diane and son Wado placed her in a nursing home outside of Paris. According to Betty, Roz Elle didn't want to go. One day, Betty received a call from the family. Betty was told Roz Elle had placed a table on top of another table under a window and jumped out, killing herself. Betty was devastated. This wasn't the sister she knew. Roz Elle was petite, Betty's size, and frail and sick. How could she stack a table on top of another one and then climb on top? She asked Roz Elle's children to explain, but there was no explanation forthcoming.

At first, Roz Elle's children kept in contact. But that soon changed. Betty says Roz Elle had always promised to take care of Betty, monetarily. In fact, she had regularly been helping her out. But Betty never received further monies or communication from Roz Elle's children. For years, the sisters had made plans to move Betty to France to live with Roz Elle. And now her sister was gone and Betty was truly alone.

Betty wrote a poem honoring her sister:

Until you get back, I'll turn out the starish night,
reserve such light, just for the sight of you . . .
Until you get back, I'll turn off the dew each dawn
No flowers are born until they're worn by you
I'll miss you. I'll miss you. Must you go?

CHAPTER TWENTY-EIGHT

You Gotta Have a Gimmick

"A gimmick was a snake or a bird or something."
—Betty Rowland

"Breast size."
—Alexandra, on her own gimmick

"Each girl stamped [her] trademark on her act. Each girl had a little bit of something different," said Dixie Evans. "Each girl wanted to be known for something no one else was doing."

Stripping was more than disrobing for many. It was an opportunity to add humor and artistry to their time on stage. For some, it was an act, an event, a story.

Though she never worked with her, Joan Arline praised Gypsy's mastery of the tease. "She was wonderful at it," Joan said. One of Gypsy's gimmicks was "she would take her things off and dress a girl."

On stage, Gypsy in an evening gown would introduce a chorus of scantily dressed strippers. She would then begin to drape and dress them with long swatches of fabric while she stripped down to a corset. This was her "reverse strip." Gypsy herself never took off much, but what she took off seemed to take forever. She challenged and controlled her audience.

"I take offense at that," Betty Rowland said when I asked what her gimmick had been. "You don't have to have a gimmick. Not everyone had a gimmick. Not Margie Hart." If anything, she "kept going" and that was her gimmick, she said.

As far back as burlesque began, girls were coming up with their "brand," some way of performing that fans would associate with them. Say "Lydia Thompson" and one thought "tights." Mention Billy Watson's Beef Trust, in the 1870s, and one thought of the girls who weighed an average two hundred pounds.

Possibly the woman who started the whole gimmick business wasn't Gypsy, but a Midwestern stripper named Carrie Finnell. Carrie Lee Finnell was born in 1893 in Covington, Kentucky. She was one of six children. She started there in burlesque at fourteen, and though we would consider her to be "hefty" by today's standards, she stripped well into her fifties—weighing an impressive three hundred pounds all the while. She would began on the Columbia Wheel. By 1916, Finnell was in a Ziegfeld chorus line. By the 1920s, she was firmly settled in burlesque.

In the early days, her act was a fifty-two-week strip. She would go on stage and take off one item of clothing a week. Unbelievably, this entertained the audience that returned glove by glove, week by week. She was a huge hit and became a star. She worked for Minsky in the 1920s. She worked for Mike Todd and performed at the 1939 World's Fair.

Carrie did something that was integral to burlesque. She brought humor to the strip. She twirled tassels and, though not beautiful—not even remotely sexy—she packed houses for close to twenty years. Though her girth grew and her looks diminished, this didn't stop her popularity. Her pectoral muscles were billed as "educated muscles." They could march in time to music. She could make her breasts move north, south, east, and west, clockwise and counterclockwise. Her act was billed as the "Most Unusual Act in Show Business." When asked about her breasts, she said, "I make mine work for me."

In a 1936 advertisement, she was billed as the "the highest-paid burly star" (although many would make that same claim). Sometimes she was billed as "The Remote Control Girl," because her boobs seemed to function independently without help from the rest of her body.

"She could make her breasts jump out of her gown. And jump back in again," said Renny von Muchow.

She was the "grandmother of stripteasers," confirmed Rachel Shteir.

Described as a "fat, jolly woman," she died of a heart attack at the age of seventy-six in Fayetteville, Ohio, in 1963, mere days before JFK was assassinated—and two weeks after her husband also died of a heart attack.

Throughout burlesque's history, tassel twirling was a popular gimmick. Tassels were stuck on breasts and bottoms. Some had buckshot loaded into the ends to weigh them.

Some strippers carried fishing poles with candy attached and would fish out to the audience. In burlesque, there was plenty of audience participation.

Maria Bradley remembered, "We'd have baskets with country clothes . . . powder puffs like peaches and pass them out to the audience. . . . There was a number called 'Powder My Back.' All the chorus girls, we'd all go down into the audience, and like, powder people, you know . . . (singing) 'Powder my back every morning.' And we'd all be out there with our powder puffs. And I stopped short because there was my next-door neighbor, cheating on his wife. And like, he was lost for words. And I was lost for words. So I just powdered the next guy."

Candy Cotton would have a candy box and candy tree on stage. She would take pieces of wrapped candy and ask the audience, "Do you want a piece of candy?" and then toss it to them.

Some performers rode bikes onstage or played instruments.

One performer tap danced while taking her clothes off.

Peaches was a stripper who could make her muscles quiver up and down her body, which was much harder than it might sound. Muscle work was difficult, Dixie Evans said. "I always say if you think the strippers don't have any brains, [well] they have a lot of brains to keep those muscles going."

Peaches let Lily Ann Rose catch her wardrobe and watch her number. "She was so beautiful and so clever and really the queen of shake. No one was allowed to watch her because she said, 'They will steal my act.' She trusted *this* girl. And I still remember her singing to the audience as she teased in her lovely costumes: *If I can't sell it, I'll sit on it, I ain't givin' nothin' away.* Then Peaches would begin to shake from her shoulders down to her thighs," Lily said.

"JFK had a crush on Peaches," said David Kruh. "He was head over heels for her. His family had other plans for JFK."

As a chorus girl, Lily Ann Rose would ride the subway to the Casino Theatre. One of her dearest memories was sharing the ride with the headliner Peaches Queen of Shake. "There I was, this teenage wannabe burlesque star working the chorus of the Casino Theatre, and befriended and coached by burlesque's biggest and most beautiful star. Peaches, who was dressed as tailored as a schoolteacher, went unrecognized as just another passenger and we talked and bonded each day on our trip to our respective homes between shows."

Mitzi Doree, the Cuban Bombshell, was known for her shimmy and shake.

Some did comedic strips, like Pat Flannery, who was awkward and funny and wore a sailor outfit. Lily White (there was an inordinate amount of Lilys and Lilis in the profession) "lampooned" herself. Lisa Bell stripped out of a two-piece long john.

Princess Lahoma was billed as an exotic "Indian" dancer with a white teepee.

There were many American Indian dancers with full headdresses and veil dancers. Della Carroll did a dance of the pearls, with her wrists, head, waist, and bosom draped in strings of long pearls.

Alexandra's gimmick was stripping to "The Flight of the Bumble Bee." She would rotate muscles with bows on certain parts of body in black light. "I was classic," she said. "I wasn't wild. But I wasn't conservative either. And I had a bang-up ending. Unwrapping the ribbons."

Betty Rowland recalled one stripper in a baby doll outfit singing to "She Must Have Been a Beautiful Baby."

Alexandra the Great "48"

Some strippers talked to the audience, like Gypsy. They'd make fun of the audiences. That was their gimmick.

Mimi Reed, though never a stripper (she was a novelty dancer) would "pick a guy from audience and put a cancan skirt on him." He would try and follow her as she danced.

Lili St. Cyr was known for her bubble baths—onstage. "In those days, they didn't have bubble machines. And she'd hired one of the chorus girls to lay down in back of the bathtub and blow the bubbles," said Dardy Minsky.

"She would get out and get dressed again," recounted Kelly DiNardo, author of *Gilded Lili*. "And all of this was to get around laws that said you couldn't leave the stage with anything less than what you started with."

There would be much appropriating of each other's acts—if one wanted to see Lili St. Cyr's bathtub act and she wasn't playing Cincinnati, audiences could see a Pepper Powell at their local theatre or any of the other half a dozen imitators scrub-a-dub-dubbing.

Betty Rowland admitted to going to other burlesque shows to check out the competition. "We all did," she said. And others watched to see what "The Red Headed Ball of Fire" was doing.

White Fury said, "I stood in the wings and watched every show."

"I didn't consider myself competition for anyone," said Kitty West.

Harold Minsky had an idea for a gimmick for Rita Grable. "You did have to have a gimmick," she said. "He had a humungous champagne glass made all out of wood." The front of it would open and stairs would come down. "It was really beautiful. I was in the glass. So when the curtain opened, you just saw this big glass and music playing, ah, 'You Go To My Head,' or whatever, I forgot." The stairs opened up and she stood up in a "beautiful orange beaded gown and orange fox stole." She would then walk down the stairs. She was billed as the Girl in the Champagne Glass.

Modern-day stripper Dita Von Teese has revitalized the champagne glass act, done many times in the past, both in glass and wood. Lili St. Cyr did it too, but Grable was one of the first.

There were girls with birds. Rosita Royce had her white doves that fluttered around her, barely concealing her nudity. Yvette Dare performed with parrots that were trained to pluck the clothes off her body.

Dardy developed a young girl with an act with a parrot. The stripper would oil herself and then the bird would climb down from a prop tree set on the stage. The stripper was so slippery from the oil that occasionally the bird would slip off. The stripper put meat in her G-string and the bird dived towards it. "She's laying there doing leg work. The parrot's coming down the tree, over to the drum, beak on rope and pulled self-straight for her rhinestones on G-string. Wings all out. It was something."

Strippers were also identified by their monikers. There was Evelyn West and her Million-Dollar Chest (a respectable size thirty nine and a half inches). Walter Winchell dubbed Margie Hart "The Poor Man's Garbo." Lynne O'Neill was the "Garter Girl," and Joan Arline the "Sexquire Girl."

Besides birds, girls worked with monkeys, snakes, even a bear.

Sequin recalled a stripper who worked with a horse. "It would be in the alley. She'd ride the horse around the stage doing tricks on it, leaning off its side. She called herself Lady Godiva. The horse was trained to do his business in a bucket."

There was "Sally and her Monkey," recalled Sequin. Sally would chain it to the radiator in the dressing room so it would stay warm. "That carries an unpleasant stench," Sequin remembered.

Starting out, Blaze Starr admitted, "I first saw Gypsy and I thought, *Well you gotta have a gimmick, something people remember ya by.* Everything had been used."

She thought "animals." She got an ocelot and dyed it black. "I didn't have sense enough to know; it got sick and died. It wasn't big enough."

So next she bought a Samoa leopard. "Got it through an animal company in New York who found it from a zoo. . . . [Again] I didn't have sense. You can't ever train a cat, couldn't travel with them. I wasn't scared of them. They were babies. It swallowed a rubber ball and died. Then I got a puma, a mountain lion they're called. Big and dangerous. Had it declawed. Died during surgery."

Her bad luck with cats continued, but she hadn't given up yet. "I paid $1,100 for a baby black panther. I'd get it raw steak, just warmed."

Blaze Starr worked with many cats on stage until it got too dangerous

Blaze and her panther were in a hotel in New York and Blaze went out shopping, leaving the panther inside—something she was used to doing. Although she'd leave it in the cage when the maid came, "[The maid] didn't come in and clean. She'd give me clean sheets." While Blaze was shopping, "it got in the shower, turned on the hot water. I come back, the cops and firemen are there. It had flooded a wing of the hotel. No one could go in the room, it was screaming. Weighed one hundred pounds." Blaze went in the room. "It jumped on my back and laid its head on my shoulder, and scratched my brow. I thought it was going for my jugular vein. I knew then. This . . . is scary. I sold it back for five hundred dollars."

A statuesque blonde, still in her seventies, Joan Arline also performed with animals—two Russian wolfhounds. They were a part of her act for many years.

"They made me a lot of money. They lay on a pink fur rug on the floor on command." She bought them when they were three and a half months old and it took her eight months to train them. Their names were Anna and Alisha; she named them after famous ballerinas. They laid there and watched Joan strip . . . and also watched the audience.

Joan Arline performed with two Russian wolfhounds

One night in Syracuse, New York, "a very inebriated customer was whistling," Joan related. Joan was on an elevated floor, and the man was 10 to 12 feet from her. "I was on a pink chaise lounge. . . . [The drunk] threw a steak bone out on the floor. And he was whistling, 'Aye! Aye!'"

Joan continued, "I cut the band. I was looking for the maître d'. He was off somewhere. . . . I went to the mic and I said, 'Sir, at least there are two dogs in the house that know their place. Obviously, you've noticed that they are very beautiful females. But give up! They're not in heat!'" The audience applauded. And she continued with her act while the maître d' ushered out the jokester.

Joan's Russian wolfhounds were highly strung. Once, her six-month-old daughter was playing with them at home and Joan heard a growl. "I bent down quickly to pick my daughter up," she said, but she wasn't quick enough and the dog nipped her daughter's face. "I had my husband take them that night," she said. The dogs were put down.

In addition to stripping with snakes, Zorita was known for her half-woman, half-man costume. Her snake dance, she said, was the consummation of the wedding of the snake.

Sherry Britton used her costumes as gimmicks. She peeled off long chiffon evening gowns to the strains of Tchaikovsky.

Helen Bingler "had an act herself where she bent over backwards on a chair and would drink water," remembered her daughter, Helen Imbrugia.

Others became names because of who they resembled. There was a Jane Russell lookalike. Ann Perri was the Parisian Jane Russell. Harold Minsky named Dixie Evans the Marilyn Monroe of Burlesque (though it caused Dixie some legal troubles). She was sued by the screen goddess.

The Marilyn Monroe of Burlesque – Dixie Evans

"I got a letter. They said I'm using her name without permission. . . . We answered three threatening letters," she said. One day a car pulled up to her agent's office. It was someone from the newspapers who told Dixie they were on her side.

One night Dixie saw Marilyn on the television being taken on a stretcher going to the hospital. "My heart sunk. I sent her a telegram. I don't know what I said. Two weeks later, 'MY DEAR DEAR DIXIE EVANS OF MY MANY FRIENDS AND ACQUAINTANCES THROUGHOUT THE ENTIRE WORLD, YOUR TELEGRAM WAS OF THE GREATEST COMFORT TO ME AT THIS TIME, MARILYN MONROE MILLER.'"

Some women's "gimmicks" were their physicality. Lois De Fee stood six feet four inches, or nearly that, and was billed as the "Amazon" when she was discovered by Harold Minsky. He lured her away from her "bouncer" job at Leon & Eddies nightclub on "Stripty Street," 52nd in New York. (Stripper Sherry Britton worked Leon & Eddies, and Lili St. Cyr headlined for years down the street at Club Samoa.)

In the early 1950s, Ricki Covette was another "Amazon" strip, billed as "the world's tallest strip." Her number had a couch. It was a "sexy type of number that everyone tried to copy." She too was billed as the world's tallest exotic performer. "I had the stamina to carry all the props," she admitted.

Ricki, like so many, "wanted to get away from [her] home and everything." She was raised in Alberta, Canada, by normal-sized parents and was determined to get out. "I'm gonna do something when I graduate," she swore.

She started on a carnival doing Gypsy's show, then went to Chicago for Harold Minsky. Dave Cohen, a big burlesque agent at the time, took her on. She told him, "I refuse to take my clothes off," until he mentioned the salary. She became a headliner.

As a publicity stunt, Lois De Fee wed a three-foot tall midget. Both Lois and Ricki were working 42nd Street. Ricki recalled that Lois "came marching in—in all of her glory—looked up at me and turned around and walked out. I was taller."

Ricki was somewhat masculine looking. When Christine Jorgensen, formerly George Jorgensen, got her sex change, she said, "[everyone] thought I was a sex change. Even the agent who knew me told club owners that. It got so that I couldn't handle it anymore." She quit burlesque.

"Bust size was very big in those days. Everything revolved around that," said Alexandra the Great "48." "It was rare. I came along at an opportune time. Rose [La Rose] took advantage of my measurements."

Sunny Dare had blue hair, Kitty West green—after all, she was supposed to be emerging from under the sea in her oyster shell after one hundred years submerged.

There were a plethora of cat and jungle girl acts.

Tee Tee Red did handstands. "I'd wrap my legs around my neck, if you can imagine that." (I didn't have to. I saw the pictures.)

Some sang.

Tee Tee Red doing yoga onstage

Faith Bacon used fans, but before that she danced with a fake swan. (The dancer's arm was the swan, and her hand the head. It is by all accounts a very sensual dance.) Lili St. Cyr stole her swan act and someone else stole it from her, and on and on. Today we see, in the neo-burlesque movement, the result of years of well-crafted acts.

Props were integral to many of the women's acts. Lili St. Cyr was known not only for her bathtub, but elaborate sets with vanities, mirrors, and hat racks. She variously performed as Cinderella, a matador, a Salome, a bride, a suicide, Cleopatra, and Dorian Gray.

Sequin was the girl in the red velvet swing. Maria Bradley said, "I was in awe. I was catching her wardrobe so I could watch her. She was a beautiful girl." The hammock had silver fringe and she'd screw it into the stage floor. She had a palm tree made and she'd swing in the hammock, singing "I've Got an Island in the Pacific."

She explained her gimmick: "You start with a lovely opening number, then slower, then finally blues, because it was slow and sensuous, and you were down to your bare necessities, lights brought down. Fast, medium, and slow."

Sequin's approach was unusual. Most ended their set with a fast song, leaving the audience stirred.

Others turned their time onstage into scenes, or playlets. Dixie Evans decided to do a clever story about what a girl has to go through to get a job in Hollywood. She performed as if she was auditioning in a producer's office. She made a velvet couch and set up a camera and a producer's chair. She would stroll on the stage, say a little patter about getting a job in the movies. She feigned being chased around the room. Then she'd run to the producer's chair and do an act. Eventually she'd end up on the couch, kicking her legs in the air.

When I met White Fury, she was still wearing her platinum hair and false eyelashes, as she had in the 1960s. Her gimmick was lighting her tassels on fire. "I had gas. A little can of gas and I had long, long tassels and I would dunk 'em into the gas and then light them and turn around. When they came up, I put my head back like this and they came up about this far and went *poof*, you know, and burned the whole front of my hair. I didn't stop, no. I just put those out."

Another time, her gimmick was painting herself to a song.

The comedians, too, had their trademark gags, costumes, or way of talking and walking. Pinky Lee had his tiny bowler hat and his lisp. W. C. Fields pretended to be drunk and hate children. Bert Lahr had a rubbery face and mugged. Ed Wynn wore hats and was called the Perfect Fool. Will Rogers did a trick rope act. Jimmy Durante had that schnoz and that raspy voice. Buster Keaton was deadpan. Sliding Billy Watson made an entrance by sliding center stage. Mike Sachs, before and after he went blind, would move one eye back and forth.

Whatever the gimmick, Betty Rowland believed that "it's a question of being yourself. Sell yourself or your gimmick. Don't overanalyze it."

CHAPTER TWENTY-NINE
The Swinging G-String

"At the end of your act, you back up and the lights dim, and the curtains close,
and you reach down and you unhook and let the G-string fall."
—April March

"She'd show things that she wasn't supposed to show."
—Dardy Minsky

Zorita—a gold-digging bisexual who danced with snakes

Just as the invention of the striptease was the lifesaver for burlesque in the 1920s, flashing would lead to its demise.

In burlesque there were fast acts and slow acts, strips to jazz music and strips to Dixie music. And then there were flash acts.

"I didn't even know what the hell they were talking about. 'Flash,' what?" Maria Bradley said. "Pulling your G-string aside. It would be so instantaneous. I don't know if anyone saw it anyway. That's why burlesque got a bad reputation—but in a fun way."

Author David Kruh related a story of how the girls would paste Brillo pads on the front of their G-strings just before the blackout. The audience "thought they got a flash of something. There is a certain innocence to it. It was about sex, seeing something you weren't supposed to see, but in fact you weren't seeing it. It was theatre of the mind."

Or was it?

Alexandra talked about her mentor Rose La Rose, who was notorious for flashing, and it was not a Brillo pad she flashed. "When I first saw her, you weren't allowed to flash. She had this little gimmick, she wore a 'flapper' and certain ways she moved would announce her presence, to say the least. I was dumbfounded. I had never seen anything like that. It wasn't supposed to be done at all. But Rose was famous for doing things she wasn't supposed to do. I just never forgot that. I wasn't prepared to see the Countess in all her loveliness. I was shocked . . . and I'm sure the police would have been, too."

"Of course, Rose went with the chief of police," Dixie Evans reminded me, so she didn't have to worry on that account.

"I didn't like it on the road because you had to flash. We considered ourselves dancers and performers," said Lady Midnight.

"Rose put me on the flash circuit," said Alexandra. "That means you show a little hair, which I shaved into a heart, which I put a bow on top of. And everybody got a present every night."

"Certain girls . . . as much as they'd tell them not to do it, they'd pack the house." Dixie Evans cited Blaze Fury and the resulting chaos as an example. "Front of house screaming, phone backstage is ringing, but she's packing the house. Certain ones . . . that's just the way it was."

Those I heard accused of flashing included Betty Rowland, Irma the Body, and Margie Hart.

It was dangerous and ultimately led to the closing of the burlesque theatres by LaGuardia. "Strippers got into flashing. Nobody wanted them to do it on a show. Just before the blackout, they would drop something for an instant. I remember my father was dead set against it. They felt it wasn't necessary. They were afraid they'd get busted," said Harry Lloyd.

CHAPTER THIRTY

Stage Door Johnnies

"I had a lot of roses."

—Joan Arline

"I felt like a star. All these people waiting for me."

—Maria Bradley

With the invasion of the British Blondes on American soil came the Stage Door Johnnies. According to author Bernard Sobel, they arrived "in such force in the alley behind the theatre, the police were called in." Maybe it had to do with all that blonde hair, though in later years, red hair would dominate (Tempest, Blaze, Georgia, Ann Corio, Betty Rowland, Tee Tee Red). Maybe redheads eventually dominated the field because they were presumed to be "fiery . . . highly sexed creatures."

"Hell, I got so many roses, I used to bring the roses home to my mother," remembered Maria Bradley.

"We had a big field to pick from," Vicki O'Day agreed.

"I had a waist like this, hair down to here and 'bunnies' out to here," said Carmela.

Besides love notes, flowers, bottles of champagne, and, of course, dates, there were the gifts.

Alexandra the Great said, "Someone anonymous had sent me the pair of earrings with a black stone and diamonds around it and it was for pierced ears and I didn't have pierced ears. So one of the girls said, 'That's one of the most beautiful pair of earrings I've ever seen.' And I gave them to her. And I found out later they were black opals, *real* black opals. I looked more carefully the next time someone sent something back."

Maria Bradley remembered receiving envelopes backstage. "And it would be money." With a note: "We placed a bet for you today, we're the boys in Box B."

"Everyone had groupies," said Rita Grable. "I had a gentleman that was in the pie business. A very big company. Everywhere I opened, I'd get three or four pies, humungous." Rita would go on to marry Sinatra contemporary singer Jerry Vale.

"We had fans that would do things for us—buy us cigarettes, clothes, jewelry, and things," said Vicki O'Day. One of her husbands would go to Trader Vics and have big boxes of food made up and the doormen would deliver it. "We'd all dive in."

"An admirer from the Hudson Theatre after sixty-something years, to this day, he calls every birthday, every Christmas," said Maria Bradley. "It was fulfilling."

Stage Door Johnnies would send "a big birthday cake and all the little glasses to have a glass of champagne for the chorus girls."

Alexandra the Great said, "We would [even] have dinner on aircraft carriers. All that was just a matter of fact. Very exciting times." April March, billed "the First Lady of Burlesque" because of her resemblance to Jackie Kennedy, saw her fair share of Stage Door Johnnies. There were "many, many, many." And yet, "they came and they went," she said. One of her more remarkable suitors was King Saud of Saudi Arabia.

April was working a place in West Palm Beach when two of King Saud's sons came into the club. Two "out of his hundreds of sons," joked April. She and Blaze Starr were performing. "They didn't like Blaze. They invited me to their table." The next day the princes sent a car for April to have lunch. "I'm figuring that would be good publicity." The next night, the king's people got in touch with April. He wanted to meet her. A fellow from the State Department in the meantime contacted April and gave her a letter. He instructed her to slip it secretly to the king. "The government was trying to get something to the king. So they used me as a go-between." April then met the king. "I took Sy, a press agent," she said. After April gave the king the letter, "he went storming out the door. I had no idea to this day what was in that letter." But the fellow that brought her to the king was named Abraham and he "was later beheaded." Meanwhile, April said she realized, "I can't use this publicity. I did all this for nothing."

Maria Bradley recalled that "so many people [were] waiting for us at the stage door. We'd make so many promiscuous dates, that we used to ask if we could go out of the front of the theatre. Or we'd put on a mask, and make our way through the crowd. Once, this guy out there dressed so nice, I was impressed with him. I talked to him, then he said he was an undertaker."

Maria loved her years in burlesque. She started out being a chorus girl. She said those were the "most wonderful days of my life. We had so much fun." She used to get one day off every two weeks. Maria would ask if she could work that day, too. She was told she wouldn't be paid, but she didn't mind. And even though she got into stripping, it was the chorus she loved the most. "Those old days at the Hudson burlesque are especially soft in my heart," she said.

She had known her dear friend Joan Torino since they were twelve. They began dancing in the chorus together when they were sixteen, pretending to be eighteen. "I loved those days," she said.

Their choreographer came up with the idea of a twin strip. Maria asked a Stage Door Johnny, a textile manufacturer, for help with the matching costumes. "I said to him, 'We need material for gowns.' He got us fabric, ice blue from his warehouse. He had costumes made. Joan was tall and had red hair. I made all the changes. We started to rehearse to 'Hold that Tiger' (Georgia Sothern's signature piece). We did that for maybe six to eight weeks. They wanted us to go on the road. I had another Stage Door Johnny get me a trunk. I was ready. . . . Then Joan said, 'I can't go, Mo, I don't want to leave my grandmother,' so that was the end of the Toni twins." But it wasn't the end of Maria's career in burlesque.

Maria also had admirers of the same sex. The "gay girls followed me, even though in burlesque they weren't allowed. . . . They fired me because the gay girls were sitting in the front row," she said.

One of Candy Cotton's Stage Door Johnnies was a wrestler who would call on her mother. Another was a policeman she met backstage who sent her daughter a doll.

Joe DiMaggio drove April March around Washington, D.C., all the while drinking Dom Perignon champagne.

"The Secret Service used to come into the club I worked in and they always wanted to impress the girls," said Alexandra the Great. "That's how I saw the White House. I never went on a tour. I got to see the Thomas Jefferson bedroom—on my feet."

I found among Sherry Britton's papers the following, which she might have written: "Did you know the girls had them in categories? There were Drugstore Johnnies—those who could be counted on to buy a girl the cosmetics she needed. There were Dinner Johnnies, Nightclub Johnnies, and even, honestly, G-string Johnnies. You see, G-Strings were all handmade, elaborately beaded, and cost a small fortune. Of course, for many girls it was a game of 'How much can I get from him before he gets too much from me?'"

Sherry had her share of gifts, including the use of a Cadillac from an admirer that she drove around New York at 4 in the morning looking for—and finding—men.

The women had wonderful adventures outside of work. "It was a great life." And there was no shame in having the men court the girls, Alexandra the Great maintains. "I thought I was very professional. I conducted myself that way. I was treated that way. I think a lot of people have the wrong idea of what it was like."

Lily Ann Rose was a teen when she shared a car with a young JFK.

"One of the girls said that must be Jack Kennedy. He was a handsome young man who came to the burlesque show. Sent a car for me, but when he found out I was only fourteen years old, he stopped the car and sent me home."

Down in New Orleans, Jack came into the club, Blaze recalled. "My boss goes, 'You gotta meet this guy, this is one of the Kennedy boys, and blah blah blah.' Well I wasn't interested. He didn't appeal to me—just a young guy with a bunch of bushy hair and it looked red under the lights. So I let him buy me a fifty, sixty dollar bottle of champagne and I had a few drinks of it and I moved on."

However, the two would run into each other again. It was at the Crossroads in Maryland. He was not yet married. Blaze was single, too. "Then I got married. I took off for six months," she said. When she returned to work at the Crossroads, Kennedy and his crew showed up. He told her he had gotten married and she said she had done the same. He said, "Now we can go out." By the following year, Blaze had dated Kennedy a couple times.

Blaze was working in New Orleans. "I'd met Governor Earl Long, working Sho Bar. Earl was there that night, he had a table. A big club, with a big balcony—everything filled up. People standing at the door. JFK and Jackie came in. I thought, *This can't be. Now this cannot be.* By then I was a Jackie fan. I come out—they were at Earl's table. Earl stood up. Earl told me to be nice to him, 'He's gonna be your next president.' JFK shook my hand as if I'd never seen him before. He said, 'Ms. Starr, you were very good tonight.'" She replied, "I've been told I'm the very best."

Twenty minutes later, Jackie left her husband at the club. "I ain't telling you about the rest of the night," Blaze said.

Tempest Storm also crossed paths with—and dated—Kennedy. "His entourage marched in there one night, 'Would you like to go out with Kennedy?' So I dated him," she said. "I had never said anything about it. I was on a television show in Michigan. The interview was going great, and he said, 'I understand you slept with President Kennedy.' And I said, 'You certainly got my attention.' I said, 'Would you repeat that?' I was stalling for an answer. I says, 'He's not here to defend himself.' But [the interviewer] said, 'Well, what did he talk about in the bedroom?' I said, 'It certainly wasn't politics.'"

Of Stage Door Johnnies, Dixie Evans said, "Usually you sluff them off....You don't know who they are. In the nightclubs you don't go out with the customer. You want that guy to keep coming back." The only way for the men to see the girls again was to buy another ticket, pay for another drink. As Dixie explained, "This club separates the men from the boys. They are paying for your conversation." One time a gentleman from Wall Street told Dixie he was bringing four business associates over. But he warned Dixie, "Don't hustle them. Get four girls. Be real nice." Dixie handpicked the girls for the table and afterward the man from Wall Street gave her money to split with them.

Dixie wondered at all the business cards she used to get. "I had shoe boxes of presidents of corporations.... Now I'm dropping down to vice presidents and secretaries."

Depending on the man, the publicity from dating a Stage Door Johnny could be good for the stripper; it could boost her marketability. Lili St. Cyr was always in the papers for who she dated, divorced, and dallied with. Some girls were hoping to find their prince charming among the Johnnies. It seldom occurred.

Working the Club Samoa, Beverly Anderson recalled a night that her stripper friend Lorraine Cooper, "a cut above most strippers," was backstage with all the other girls preparing for the show. "She was blonde and beautiful and had a white leather makeup case," which impressed Beverly. "'Well, ladies,' Lorraine announced one night, 'my boyfriend is coming tonight to take me away from all this.' She claimed he was going to take her to the French Riviera. The fantasy sounded too good to be true. The other strippers thought she was a wacko. But sure enough, there in the front row was the Aly Kahn, recently divorced or separated from Rita Hayworth. And he did take Lorraine away and she never returned to that club."

The nightclubs were dark refuges for many celebrities. Gary Cooper and Frank Sinatra were frequent customers at Club Samoa on 52nd Street in New York. Stripper Pat Flannery told me how Johnny Carson frequently attended her shows, drinking quietly and politely at a club she worked in Los Angeles. Apparently he was taking everything in, as he would perform familiar burlesque routines on his show. Johnny's sidekick Ed McMahon was a former carnival barker and pitchman.

"A lot of guys, if you worked in the theatres, they would like to wait on the back entrance in hopes that you would come out," said Carmela. "And sometimes I would just stay in, because I was afraid. There were some towns where you had to be afraid. Detroit, I was scared to death. I had a horrible fear in Detroit."

Kitty West had a reason to be afraid of Stage Door Johnnies and other men who were on the prowl at the clubs. "Two men grabbed me. I don't know what they wanted. I started screaming because it scared me half to death. I had green hair and they knew who I was, but finally some stranger rescued me from that," she recalled.

Beverly Anderson said the Stage Door Johnnies were "tacky. I didn't do much with them. I tried to avoid that. I had to lock my door once. Some people were trying to get in. I realized what I was doing was certainly provocative and would lead to something I would be uncomfortable with."

Some of the fan mail from the men was awkward, pleading, or downright bizarre.

To Betty Rowland, a man wrote:

"I am a nudist yachtsman and have been thinking of getting a group of women together—to make a Nude Travel Film—that will take a three-year around-the-world trip. . . . Of course being a nudist I would require all aboard ship to be nude while underway . . ."

Sherry Britton received an even more disturbing letter written in 1940, which she kept for more than sixty years:

"Had the pleasure of watching you perform . . . you had stripped completely in the rear with just a little in front of your lovely box . . . you again came out and bared your body to the waist much to the delight of all and I don't see how the man singer could resist squeezing and kissing your lovely gorgeous red nippled breasts . . . I know I would just love to kiss your lovely shapely bare ass and your lovely box and lovely breasts and svelte navel . . . it's too bad the comedians . . . have to fart with their mouths."

One of the more flamboyant of the Johnnies was Louisiana's Governor Earl Long.

Like Blaze, Tee Tee Red met Governor Earl Long when she was working New Orleans. "Blaze and I were in competition with him. They called him 'the crazy governor,' she said." He would drive down the street in his limousine, throwing hundred bills out the window. He also regularly passed out food to the poor. "He didn't care what people said. He was a lot of fun. He'd throw his money around. He could do whatever he wanted. He could buy the club out if he wanted to. He'd order champagne for everybody," Tee Tee said.

The forty-fifth Governor of Louisiana was colorful, charismatic, and a compelling speaker. Because of his erratic behavior—he blatantly flaunted his many dalliances with strippers—his wife Blanche had him committed to a state hospital. (Hell hath no fury like a wife publicly humiliated.) However, there was no law that said he couldn't run the state from a mental hospital. And so he did. There has been speculation Long was either bipolar or suffering from dementia. He endured strokes and heart attacks that contributed to his declining mental health. He was irascible and unkempt, erratic in speech. In 1959 he famously said on the floor of the State Legislature: "I'm not nuts. If I'm nuts, I've been nuts all my life. Thank ya, and God bless ya."

Governor Long was a regular at the Sho Bar. He would see Blaze until he died in 1960 of a heart attack. Blaze refused money he had left for her in his will.

Another Stage Door Johnny that didn't turn out so well for Blaze was a young man whose father was wealthy and influential. He was "a big politician" and he "tried to buy me off to *not* date his son. That was a downer," she said. Blaze told him, "You don't have to buy me. I'm not looking to marry your son." The father sent his son on a trip around the world to get him away from Blaze. The son called her, but it was too late. "I never loved him after that cause he was a wimp. I got on my knees and prayed, 'Let me get over this man without too much heartache.'"

According to Blaze, the son "ended up marrying a prostitute. The father never knew his wife was a call girl."

Club owner Nils T. Granlund described the girls in that business to be "subjected to more temptation in a day than most other women encounter in a lifetime." How the women dealt with it was revealing.

"You would be surprised how small this country is and you could meet people all over," Carmela told me. "I didn't ever want anyone to go to my kids and say 'Hey, your mom's a hooker.'"

So, though the temptations were great, most enjoyed the attention and gifts and remained true to themselves. Their careers and reputations were too important to jeopardize.

CHAPTER THIRTY-ONE

Money

"Hunger is a good motivation."
—Beverly Anderson
"Wherever you're working and making money, you're happy.
—Dixie Evans

"I became a stripper because you got paid more," said Candy Cotton. One time at the theatre where she was working, a stripper didn't show up and she was hustled onstage as the replacement. She earned more stripping than as a talking woman. "You got paid five dollars more a week. It seemed worth it to me. As I was in black light, it didn't bother me as much because I really and truly believed you couldn't see me. Then I learned you really could." She shrugged. "By then, the nerves went away."

Beverly Anderson "made good money but always owed money. Not a good way to make a living."

"Every six weeks you had to do a strip and you got the magnificent sum of $1.50," added Lorraine Lee.

"I learned a lot about how to survive off my salary," Sequin said. In the beginning, she earned $150 a week. Every time she went around the circuit, she got another gown and made another $100 dollars. Eventually her salary rose to $750. Considering the average rent was $85 a month in 1954, and the average income $3,960, Sequin, like a lot of the ladies, was doing very well. "If you filled the house, they realized you deserved that raise."

Dixie Evans added, "We did have money in those days."

"There was a 60/40 cut" between the comic and the straight man, Chris Costello explained. "The straight man usually got 60 percent." Some partners, like Lou Abbott and Bud Costello, would split it 50/50.

"My father never made money, in burlesque, theatre, or movies," noted Alan Alda.

Besides getting by and paying bills, some strippers made a great living, like Ann Corio. Mike Iannucci explained, "Every year her salary would go up." When theatre owners balked at her demands, she bargained. "I'll come in and work on a percentage," she said. One manager had offered her $3,000 a week but with the percentage, "she ended up making $12,000 for that week." She was popular enough to know the theatre would be filled. "She was a shrewd businesswoman," Mike acknowledged.

For many, it was a living—a very good living. Very few girls, such as Lili St. Cyr, Sally Rand, and Gypsy Rose Lee, earned thousands a week. Sally Rand made $6,000 a week during the 1933 World's Fair. It was riches they wouldn't otherwise have seen as a secretary or clerk, yet many remained in debt or lived paycheck to paycheck.

Everything they needed to improve their acts cost money. Tee Tee Red's wardrobe cost her thousands of dollars. "My wardrobe was very expensive" she remembers. Besides beaded gowns, there were sequined G-strings and pasties, capes, furs, panels, shoes, gloves, purses, hats, and props.

April March's salary "went up to $200 when [she] went to Houston. That was big money at the time," she said. However, she didn't keep it all. In addition to paying for transportation, hotels, and seamstresses, she had to pay 10 percent commission to her agent and costumes. "[The money] went. I can't even sew a button on. Cost me a lot of money on wardrobe," she said.

Joni Taylor noted, "When you were a chorus girl . . . you made forty dollars a week. That was a lot of money. At sixteen, I already had three children. I was supporting them. I had to make enough money to feed my family." No one could say it was an easy paycheck. As a chorus girl, her stage call was a half hour before the show, where the feature just had to be in her spot a half hour before she went on. The chorus girls opened the show. Joni earned an additional ten dollars a month extra to catch the wardrobe of the strippers.

Backstage waiting to perform

Joni would eventually become the captain of the chorus, the one in charge of the dancers. She worked it out, giving each woman an opportunity to make more money than her normal salary, by rotating which girl worked with the comics, which girls caught wardrobes, etc. "Talking women were paid ten dollars extra. I alternated everyone so they could make money. We worked from 11 to 5, dinner break, back by 7, show started 7:30, done by 11," she said. It was a long day of dancing and entertaining.

"Chorus girl[s] in 1953 made seventy-five dollars a week." That was for three shows a night, three numbers a show, seven nights a week, which "broke down to a dollar a dance." They cleared sixty-three dollars a week in burlesque.

During the Depression, "there was no affordable entertainment for working-class people," recalled Dixie Evans. Tickets were cheap; attendance was high.

The price of a ticket varied from 10 cents during the thirties to $4.50 (a "big ticket") in 1960, when Leroy Griffith had a New York theatre. Tempest and Tee Tee Red packed the theatres to the brims. Leroy had Billy Rose's old Diamond Horseshoe club, which seated four hundred and was located downstairs in the Paramount Hotel in Times Square. Despite the steep price, audiences lined up for the three shows a day.

Tempest was earning $2,500 a week at that point.

When Al Baker Jr. ran a theatre, he had Blaze Starr on the marquee and she was earning $2,000 a week. Blaze managed to invest and hang on to her money after she got out. "I'd saved. Mr. Goodman was Jewish and he always explained to me, 'You must save some now for later years, because when you get old and uh, wrinkled and sick and ugly, no man's gonna want you then. There won't be anybody bringing you goodies.'"

Keeping up appearances was important. Girls wore furs, rode in fancy cars, and carried all the accoutrements of being stars. Lili St. Cyr spent thousands dragging expensive bathtubs and beds and other ornate props (mostly real antiques) across the country. When the theatres began to change and stagehands and owners didn't seem to give a damn, it became impossible for her to set up her show herself. She pared down and relied on her Dance of the Seven Veils. It was easier for the now-fifty-year-old stripper to travel with scarves and not wait for anyone else's help backstage—because there was no help.

In 1961, when Ann Corio and her husband Mike Iannucci revived interest in burlesque with the production of their show *This Was Burlesque*, they introduced the same corny sketches to a new generation. "The show became an instant hit," said Mike Iannucci. It opened in New York. "Nine reviews. We had seven fantastic; one wishy-washy review, *New York Times* looked down their nose at it. When I tried to raise money—everyone said you'll be closed down—you have to do it to conform with his [LaGuardia though long dead] restrictions. Two days after we opened, I turned down half a million dollars. People who wanted to invest. It ran five years in New York, toured for twenty-six years. For thirty-one years, the show ran all over the country in major theatres; we gained that respectability. We made a lot of money and kept people happy," he said. Some of the comedians they hired were Morey Amsterdam and Frank Fontaine and even "comics that hadn't been in burlesque; [Ann] taught them to punch a line in."

Strippers generally deserved the high salaries they received. They were generating large sums of money for the producers. However, shows themselves were expensive to produce. By the '50s, casts were trimmed to cut costs. *Uncensored Magazine* complained that this led to less talented performers and the quality of the shows diminished.

Clubs were different than the theatres. They sold alcohol, which brought a whole other aspect—mostly unwelcomed—to the strippers' jobs.

CHAPTER THIRTY-TWO

Mixing

"I would tell them, 'I'm not a bar girl.'"

—Carmela

"Your salary depended on who liked you the most."

—Vicki O'Day

In the theatres, "you were away from the audience. They couldn't touch you or get at you. You didn't have to mix or drink," explained Sequin.

Unlike theatres, the clubs demanded the girls not only dance, but mix with the audience.

Kelly DiNardo said, "A really big part of their job was to mingle with the crowd, to encourage champagne sales and all the girls generally got a kickback on what they sold and what they convinced people to buy."

Mixing with the audience

"Champagne in those days was expensive, $25 to $100 a bottle," recalled Kitty West.

"If you made money for the house, you'd get a raise next time," added Blaze Starr. Clearly the girls had an incentive to sell.

Stripper Vicki O'Day would collect the stir sticks from drinks and turn them in at end of the night. In Boston, her salary was five hundred dollars a week, but the drink minimum in the club was steep. If you didn't turn in enough sticks, "they took it from your salary." Towards the end of her career, she complained there were "so many girls working clubs [it was] almost impossible to make a living." She was over thirty and the new girls coming in were sixteen and eighteen. She had to be clever. "I'd see some fellow across the bar and I'd say, 'If you sit with me, I won't charge you more than one champagne and that will keep the other girls away and you can enjoy your drink.' And so they usually bought me a drink. So I was quite successful at the drinking game."

In Miami, Tee Tee Red had to "mingle" with the customers. "It wasn't easy. It was something that was part of the deal. You had to make your quota. . . . You had to sell a certain amount of champagne to equalize the salary you got."

In one club, a customer asked Dixie, "When you're pouring the champagne, do you spill a drop?'" She responded, "No. I don't." "Well spill it," she was instructed.

"I don't drink," Carmela said. "They'd fix artificial drinks. I drank a lot of orange juice all night. Most places I didn't have to do that."

There were girls that were hired to interact with the audience. They were referred to disparagingly as B girls.

"It is a girl who gets paid nightly. She'll come in dressed beautifully, sitting at the bar or walking around, and a gentleman would be alone and she'll ask him if he wants company. And he'll buy her drinks. Say a drink is $3.00, she'll get $1.50 at the end of the night. Called 'hostesses,' but they're really not," explained Kitty West.

Lili St. Cyr, according to her sister Dardy, made more on champagne sales at Club Samoa than her already generous salary. If a man wanted to have a word or drink with Miss St. Cyr, it was suggested by her maid, Sadie, that the gentleman order a bottle of expensive champagne. Once purchased, Miss St. Cyr would wander through the tables. Several bottles would "accidently" be knocked on the floor (and quickly reordered). Lili split the sales with the owner and from her cut split that with her maid, who worked with her both onstage and off.

Tempest took issue with a club owner wanting her to mix. She told him, "'In my contract, it says I don't do that.' They kept bugging me," she said. She picked up her wardrobe and left. She wanted to keep the mystery by separating herself from the audience.

B girls "had to sit with customers and drink and spit drink back into the glasses. It was horrible. It was unbelievable the things that would happen. Girls would go out with men for money. Men looked at a woman in this profession and never saw beyond the body."

Besides sitting with the customer, enticing him to buy bottles of champagne, there were other ways the clubs made money. "I'd feel bad," Dixie Evans admitted. Many times, she'd be sitting with a sailor or another customer and the cigarette girl would come along. "Would you like to buy an orchid for the lady?" she'd ask. If the customer paid, she would offer to put it in the ice box and "a half hour later, she'd be reselling the same flower to some other sucker."

During WWII, the fellas would crowd into the clubs first thing—"as soon as they got their pay," said Dixie Evans, who did her share of mixing. "A very bad idea."

One time, a man at a bar told her that ship announcements often warned the sailors to "stay away from Dixie Evans." "That's how famous I was. They were trying to warn the service men. . . . [The clubs] had to generate the money. You treat that customer right and if that man sees you're playing in some club, you build up a fan [base]. The nightclubs did a lot of PR. If they see your name on the marquee and they're in town, they'll come to the club."

Mingling did not go on in the theatres. "In theatres, you're getting paid for a show. . . . You're getting paid for a performance," Dixie said.

Despite the different hardships of working in the theatres (long hours) and clubs (mixing and drinking), it still "allowed some women to transform their circumstance in ways they wouldn't have been able to otherwise. Allowed some financial stability," noted Rachel Shteir. It was a way to see the country and sometimes other parts of the world.

Girls also made tips in the clubs. "Made a lot," Vicki O'Day remembered.

Delta Dawn was a stripper who was horribly disfigured by a scar running down her face. "She had to work in black light. Drank booze all the time," Dixie recalled. She advised Dixie on how to avoid turning her tips over to the club owners: "Stick fifty dollars in your cold cream jar to hide money." In New York, Dixie and the other dancers would roll up the money and put it between their breasts. But at the end of the night, all the strippers would be "crawling around the floor, looking for money, 'cause it flew all over" when they got undressed, she said.

CHAPTER THIRTY-THREE

Interlude Before Evening

The word *interlude* is defined as "a short, dramatic piece of a light or farcical nature." *Farce* being the defining characteristic of burlesque.

She was the beautiful blonde who rose to fame by taking off her clothes. At one time, she was the highest-paid stripteaser in America. He was the highest-paid attorney in America. Hers was a body men lusted over. His was a brilliant mind that defended Hollywood's brightest and most scandalous, from Charlie Chaplin and Earl Flynn to the oft-married platinum goddesses Lana Turner and Zsa Zsa Gabor. He was a gentleman that was soft-spoken and polite, with a sterling reputation as hardworking and ethical. She got her start in seedy, smoke-filled nightclubs and burlesque theatres where the men hid their desires under the newspapers that covered their laps.

They were an odd couple: The Body and The Brains. She was thirty-two. He was thirty years her senior. They were as American as apple pie and baseball. Both rose from humble backgrounds to the top of their professions: the lawyer and the ecdysiast.

She had been born Marie Van Schaack, but took the name Lili St. Cyr like a boudoir-fueled wet-dream fantasy and rode it to the top of a B career that still garners legions of fans and imitators today, some fifty years after she tossed her jewel-encrusted G-string for the last time.

He had been born Harold Lee Giesler, but found Jerry suited him better. He was as smart and tenacious as he was homely. He would go to any lengths to win his clients' cases.

They both loved beautiful, well-made clothes. He dressed elegantly in double-breasted suits and wore flamboyant colored ties. She wore diaphanous designer gowns. She was the cold blonde dancing under a violet spot light. She had cornered the market on Elizabeth Taylor-esque tabloid headlines (men, divorces, suicides) before Taylor. They both appreciated the finer things in life, which they could now afford.

Lili would have six marriages, six divorces, and three documented suicide attempts. She would spend her fortune and end her days out of the public eye, largely forgotten by an industry that had died out, a recluse who wouldn't even open her door to delivery men.

Her trial generated columns of press across the country, and Hollywood followed eagerly, thirsty to see the outcome of the scandalous stripper accused of corrupting the morals of the public. She hated the hypocrisy. "If one has morals, they can't be taken away by me or anyone else."

Some thought, because of her profession, she wasn't very smart—just a dumb broad who took off her clothes. Yet the "dumb blonde" was smart enough to know who should be the first person she should call after being arrested for indecent exposure at the popular nightclub Ciro's. Lili hired the most successful attorney in Los Angeles, perhaps in all the country.

BEGINNINGS

Lili was born June 3, 1917, in Minnesota, Minneapolis, to twenty-year-old Idella Peaseau. Upon learning of his wife's pregnancy, Lili's father Edward promptly fled the scene.

Lili was raised by her maternal grandparents Benjamin and Alice Klarquist, who, though strict and nondemonstrative, loved the beautiful girl. The Klarquists moved to Pasadena, California. At fifteen, Lily married for the first time.

Cordy Milne, an international motorcycle racer and celebrity four years her senior, gave Lili her first taste of screaming crowds and fame. They married in England in front of a huge crowd of his fans. The marriage lasted only a few months, but it left Lili with a taste of fame. Having her face and name in the papers was exciting. She was someone.

By the time she was twenty-three in 1940, Lili was drifting. The lifestyle she sought had eluded her. Her career as a showgirl started accidentally enough. Her two younger half-sisters, Barbara and fifteen-year-old Dardy, were auditioning for a spot at the Florentine Gardens on Hollywood Boulevard. Lili, who was sitting off to the side supervising her sisters, was noticed. Dardy was rejected for being too young, but would soon go on to her own burlesque career as a stripper. Barbara and Lili were promptly hired. Lili was earning $27.50 a week as a showgirl.

She married husband number two, a waiter at the Florentine Garden, in a quickie ceremony in Tiajuana.

Realizing she'd have to reveal more than long legs to make headlines and more money, Lili worked her way into the burlesque circuit, becoming the Girl of the Hour at the Music Box in San Francisco. Every hour she came out with one less item of clothing until she was nude except for her G-string.

Lili appeared at the Hollywood in San Diego, where she hooked fishing wire to her G-string and, at the last second of her act, it would go sailing off before the lights dimmed. Husband number two quickly disappeared.

Lili worked hard and conquered the night clubs of New York, landing in the papers as much for her act as for the various men who escorted her. She had shed a couple husbands by the time she'd become a headliner and conquered Montreal's burlesque scene.

MONTREAL'S SWEETHEART

In 1944, Montreal was a beautiful city teeming with nightclubs. Canada's largest and richest city, it was teeming with corruption, vice, and a sprawling entertainment community. The French-speaking city gave Lili a lifelong love of things French. She decorated her home with French regency furniture. Giesler, too, had French regency decor in his home.

At twenty-six, Lili stepped on to the stage at the Gaiety Theatre in Montreal. She proved to be an original performer. She dressed as an expectant bride and as an "Indian maiden," in full headdress. She packed the club and Montreal fell in love with the elegant stripper who changed the face of burlesque. She would hold a deep love of the city for the rest of her life. The feeling was mutual. She would return over and over again, playing to standing-room-only crowds of devoted men and making thousands of dollars.

Husband number three was just around the corner. He was Paul Valentine. Born Valia Valentinoff, he danced as Val Valentine and Paul Valentine. For a while, the married couple worked together (he choreographed some shows), but they divorced after a few short years.

Lili preferred quiet dinner parties at home with her friends instead of nightclubs. She was a very good cook and loved to read books. She didn't bother keeping up with current news, shunning the radio and, later, television, preferring silence. She would spend time in a multitude of dressing rooms either reading or sewing before she went onstage.

She didn't have many friends. Cast members said Lili rarely spoke with them; she wasn't rude, she just stayed in her dressing room, never mingling. She once said her "dressing room was [her] home."

Lili knew her beauty, like all things, had an expiration date. She knew she owed her career to her looks and those were mercurial at the end of the day. She told a fan she believed a woman should "go Garboesque" and disappear at her height to be remembered as she was. She was afraid of growing old.

In 1951, she was thirty-two and already on a fourth marriage that was shaky.

1951

In Montreal she was denounced by the Catholic clergy—a Canadian Jesuit Priest, Marie-Joseph d'Anjou, tried to have her thrown out of Montreal for that oft-repeated indictment leveled at burlesque artists: "offending public morals." Perhaps d'Anjou's morals were the ones that had been strained. He wouldn't be the first man to fall under her spell. Lili bravely sat through her Canadian trial, which was conducted entirely in French, a language she didn't understand. In the end, she was found not guilty.

Back in Los Angeles, just a few short months later, Lili was arrested once again in a case that would fill the papers and grip the nation. Many readers had no idea exactly what a stripper did on the stage; everyone wanted to hear the salacious tidbits.

The defendant was fearful of doing jail time and having her career ruined. But in fact the trial sent her career rocketing into the stratosphere.

GET ME GIESLER

Henry, aka Jerry, Giesler was born in 1886. By the time he met Lili, he had already successfully defended Charlie Chaplin against charges of violating the Mann Act, when the actor purportedly transported and paid for twenty-two-year-old actress Joan Berry to travel across state lines to have sex with him.

He reportedly earned upwards of $100,000 for his brilliant defense of the Little Tramp, who had a penchant for underage leading ladies. Giesler won the case. Never an elitist, Giesler refused to charge a caller for talking to him on the phone and had an open-door policy, available night and day for anyone. He was more interested in defending the rights of clients that were persecuted, not just prosecuted.

In 1943, Giesler fought against Errol Flynn's already tainted womanizer reputation after two nubile young cuties accused the actor of statutory rape. Giesler won. The married Robert Mitchum hired Giesler after he was set up and arrested for smoking marijuana with a young starlet in 1948. On Giesler's advice, Mitchum did sixty days of public service, and his career didn't suffer. Mitchum's long-suffering wife, Dorothy (this author's neighbor), publicly forgave him his trespasses.

Giesler had been practicing law since 1910. First, he was a lowly clerk for famed defense attorney Earl Rogers, after whom Earl Stanley Gardner patterned the fictional Perry Mason. Giesler made his name while Rogers was defending Clarence Darrow, who was accused of bribing a jury. Henry, as Jerry was known then, was asked to research a point of law. When he turned in a hefty thirty-something page report, his boss was impressed. When Darrow was acquitted, Giesler was promoted.

The diminutive, unattractive boy from Ohio with a squeaky voice was often ill as a child. As a teen, he left his family and moved to California, where he took night classes studying law at USC while he worked during the day at whatever job he could find. He went on to make his mark practicing law in Hollywood for more than fifty years, becoming as well-known as his infamous clients.

People would demand, "Get me Giesler!" after 1957 brought the acquittal of screen goddess Lana Turner's daughter Cheryl, who was accused of plunging a ten-inch knife into the hairy stomach of her mother's grease-ball mobster lover, Johnny Stompanato, in the bedroom of Lana's all-white Beverly Hills boudoir. This occurred after a particularly nasty argument the fourteen-year-old overheard, having crept to her mother's door while the argument escalated. Much of the gossip that circulated about the case involved a story in which Lana was the real killer.

Giesler (who had his name in the phone book under both Giesler and Geisler, in case anyone spelled it wrong) was available for each and every call that came into his Broadway and Fifth office in downtown Los Angeles. Clients didn't have to be as famous as the Hollywood elite that generated the headlines. It was a lucrative, demanding practice and his second wife tolerated his late-night preparations for his cases in which he stayed up poring over stacks of documents. Giesler had a reputation for his meticulous preparatory work. He interviewed witnesses oftentimes even before the police.

Once hired by Lili after her arrest, Giesler became ever-present in the stripper's life, trailing after her. He could be seen in photos hovering protectively close by. With Giesler, nothing was left to chance. It was the image he wanted to perpetuate, deference to her statuesque beauty. He referred to her as an "artist." He spent innumerable hours at Lili's house, preparing her for court. He became her number one protector.

At the time of her arrest, Lili St. Cyr had been taking it off for nearly a decade. She spent hours, days, and thousands of dollars preparing acts that involved elaborate sets and ornate costumes, many that she sewed herself. She was a perfectionist, not merely a stripper. An *artist*, Giesler would emphasize again and again in front of the jury and to the ever-vigilant press. He wanted the papers on her side and wasn't afraid to feed them stories. Her profession was misunderstood, marginalized. Lili wasn't doing anything against the law, nor was she doing anything that could be deemed indecent. "Artists" shouldn't be judged by the same standards as others, he argued. Giesler was prepared to show her performance was "art" and asked the court to select a jury that was "capable of judging such things on their artistic merit." He also proposed to the court that Lili perform her act for the jury at a private show at Ciro's. The judge rejected such an offer.

THE ACT

Lili, starting out as a chorus girl, was clever and determined that she wasn't going to toil in the ranks of struggling dancers. And she made it, reportedly earning $200,000 a year at her height. She said about stripping, "I'm flattered by the attention."

Throughout the years, Lili's acts grew complicated and expensive. In Vegas, she stripped from a metal cage that traversed across the room with her perched on a swing just above the audience's reaching hands as she dropped her skimpy panties. Those doing the reaching included both First Lady Eleanor Roosevelt and Ronald Reagan.

Lily even named her scenarios. In "Suicide," she entered the stage semi-dressed in panties and bra. In front of a mirror, she would contemplate her image, run a brush through her short blonde curls, sometimes tossing off her rhinestone jewelry, other times keeping them on as a maid prepared a bath in the ornate and translucent tub center stage. Next, the lithe dancer submerged herself in the tub, running a sponge up her leg, which was jack-knifed into the air for the audience to see. Next, the maid, usually her real and loyal Sadie, would hold a large thick towel between Lili and the audience as Lili emerged, wrapping herself in the folds of the white towel, twirling, giving audiences tantalizing glimpses of a perfect shape, still mostly clothed in net panties and pasties.

Other scenarios were "Cinderella," "Geisha," and "The Picture of Dorian Gray," based on the Oscar Wilde novel. She was, as she told Mike Wallace on his television show, always paying for things (including ex-husbands) and spared no expense for her act, her wardrobe, or her jewels. There would be variations of her bathtub show "Wedding Night," wherein she prepared and bathed as an expectant bride. It was her bathtub act that became her signature piece that would land her in hot water in Hollywood.

CIRO'S

Ciro's was the Sunset Strip's swankiest spot in the late 1940s and '50s. With its red ceiling and matching red banquettes, it's where the kings and queens of Hollywood ensconced themselves with cold martinis and where bad behavior reigned in a clubby, members-only-type atmosphere—not the least of which was Paulette Goddard's giving "favors" under the tables.

Across the street, its competitor, the Brazilian-themed Macambo, fought for top spot with the movie stars, studio heads, and gossip columnists who kept the clubs' names in front of the public. Macambo's decor was courtesy of excessive, whimsical-themed decorator Tony Duquette. Its wallpaper was black and white striped, and cages filled with live parrots and squawking birds lined the walls.

Ciro's imported stellar acts, such as Edith Piaf, Sinatra, Marlene Dietrich, and Mae West. Martin and Lewis became stars at the club. So loyal and grateful were the pair that when they were grossing $100,000 a week around the country, they came back and performed at their old rate of $7,000. Bugsy Siegel had a ringside table. Every night it was see and be seen.

Herman Hover was the short, plump bachelor owner and promoter of Ciro's. He hosted parties for the stars, whom he considered his friends, at his home and evening at his club. Later he would be arrested for the attempted murder of his brother-in-law, whom he tried to choke to death on the streets of Beverly Hills.

Hover had gotten his start with Earl Carroll, the Broadway musical producer known for his barely dressed showgirls. He had earned the nickname the "troubadour of the nude."

Hover would do anything to steal customers from the competition across the street. Ciro's shows were huge, theatrical extravagances, taken from Hover's vaudevillian past. Sonja Henie road an elephant on stage and the acrobatic team the Corsoni Brothers performed. At that point, Hover had never booked a stripper before he met Lili. Surely Lili would pack 'em in. He saw Lili's act in New York and wanted that special brand of glamour and aloofness that she projected onstage in his club. Her reputation in a brash world of strippers was strictly high-class. She wasn't low-brow and bawdy like Rose La Rose, who flashed her pubic hair.

Ciro's had never seen the likes of Lili, with her haughty, Nordic looks, almond-shaped green eyes, high cheekbones, full lips, and a dancer's long, tight body. Her looks were exaggerated in a Sophia Loren kind of way. Her dark eyebrows were drawn into high arcs above her real ones. She was the epitome of the 1950s aesthetic of sophisticated and polished looks, not a hair out of place. Like fashion models Suzy Parker and Dovima, she was the era's aesthetic ideal, slimmer than the sex symbols of decades past. By 1951, she had obtained a shellacked perfection. She was impenetrable, swaddled in fur, cloaked in perfume, and tossing jewels as if they were paste. She was the elusive dame who took it off for strangers.

Lili would reveal her body, but not her soul.

For Lili's debut, Hover spent thousands of dollars expanding Ciro's stage and constructing a set that included a solid silver bathtub for the fair stripper. Nothing was too good for his loyal patrons. Nothing was too good for Lili. Hover was planning the publicity he needed to shove it to those across the street.

Opening nights would always make Lili nervous. She suffered from terrible stage fright, claiming she couldn't stand people to look at her. She was as uncomfortable walking into a cocktail party with all her clothes on, as she was used to being on the stage shedding it for a large crowd.

At Ciro's, she performed to sold-out crowds. The biggest stars, including the LA mayor and a few sheriffs, jammed the club. Lili wowed 'em. She was a hit.

THE ARREST

October 19, 1951. Ciro's was crowded with the usual movie stars—Ronald Reagan, Ava Gardner, Mickey Rooney (whose father Joey Yule was an old burlesque comedian)—who ordered up drinks, waved to studio heads, nuzzled their dates. The regulars were in attendance. They'd come to see Lili's return engagement of her "Interlude for Evening."

Though sold out, the audience in the supper club was more sedate than what Lili was used to in the burly houses where, starting out, she was billed variously as Lili Finova, Lili Fehnova, Lili LaRue, and Lili LaBang. Maybe the movie stars had to act as if they'd seen it all before. Maybe they thought she was nothing more than a spectacular body.

Hover was determined to give his competitors a pain in their cash registers. He was not above calling the police and/or reporters himself when fights broke out among guests, which happened far too frequently. Any publicity helped his club. According to his niece, Sheila Weller, who wrote the book *Dancing at Ciro's*, Hover like all the nightclub owners on the Strip had a special relationship with the LA sheriff's department. Nothing went on in the clubs that the sheriff didn't know about. Insider tips were as prevalent then as they are today. If there were arrests going down, Hover would know. If something ended up in the paper, it was because he wanted it there.

Over steak tartar and escargot, the smell of smoke wafting above patrons' heads, Lili began her act. She laughed, she seduced. One leg smoothly shot into the air. She leaned her head back, smiled. A square diamond necklace framed her neck like a yoke. Champagne corks continued to pop, ice tinkled in drinks, silverware clashed. Busboys in maroon jackets scurried by.

Somewhere Lili had to have become aware of a change in the house—a different sound, a scuffle perhaps. Raised voices. Urgent whispers. Attention was drawn from the stage and, subsequently, her. Something was going on in the house.

Three officers of the law descended upon her. She was under arrest.

In her dressing room, the woman officer confiscated Lili's net panties and rhinestone-encrusted net bra as evidence.

Hover was arrested, too. There was a big splash the next day in all the papers.

Lili was nervous. She'd just been arrested in Montreal and didn't relish the idea of spending time in jail again. There was only so much a performer could endure before she could be labeled off-limits. Lili couldn't afford to be out of work. If she was "trouble" or targeted, perhaps her weekly fee would suffer in addition to her nerves. She had no other skills, no other way to make a living.

TRIAL

December 4th. Lili arrived in court in a dark suit, wrapped in mink for the jury of ten women and two men, carefully assembled from a pool Giesler chose that might appreciate or at least understand Lili's "artistic performance." Giesler had spent careful hours advising his client what to wear. Lili looked like the proverbial million bucks, not like a low-rent peeler. She sat demurely and immaculately groomed, listening to the two arresting police officers describe her act to the jury, detailing her "voluptuous figure," which was now primly out of sight.

Giesler had already used his famous bumbling act to put the jury at ease, fumbling for words, soft-spoken. He was known to appear so ill-equipped that jurors would feel sorry for his clients before testimony even began. It was all an act. He addressed jurors and witnesses with the same quiet respect. His homely looks and lack of flash earned him trust.

Giesler approached the testifying officer, and politely asked the officer to explain what he was doing at the show that featured a well-known stripper. "Eating dinner," the officer replied, as if it was perfectly normal for a sergeant to dine at Ciro's on a cop's salary.

Giesler made a point of asking if Lili's performance at all "excited" the officer. The officer denied that it did. He just continued eating his dinner through it.

"Did you applaud the act?" Giesler softly asked.

"I did," the officer acknowledged.

One can imagine Lili suppressing a smile. It was a good day in court for Jerry and Lili.

December 5th. Lili's act at Ciro's had lasted all of fourteen minutes. The second arresting officer took a good twenty-five minutes to describe it, in detail. The officer testified that Lili "bumped and grinded"—two things Lili had a reputation for *not* doing. The third arresting officer, a female, would testify Lili had worn a bra and G-string, but claimed "there wasn't much you couldn't see." This was the art of burlesque, making them think they saw more than was ever revealed. A good burlesque act was an illusion.

Giesler turned to the jury. He presented his claim that the officers went to Ciro's with the intention of arresting Lili, no matter what her act, in reality, was. Someone had decided before she stepped one painted toenail into her bathtub that her act was going to be indecent. The stripper was framed, Giesler intimated.

Next on the stand was nightclub owner Hover, who, with Giesler's insistence, demonstrated to the eager jury exactly what a "bump" was. Hover told the jury Lili did not perform a "bump" or a "grind" at Ciro's. There were titters of laughter in the court as the fat little nightclub owner attempted an offending move for the jury and reporters.

December 7th. The jury awaited the testimony of the star defendant Lili St Cyr. Fully clothed, Lili slowly and calmly went through the motions of her act; stepping in and out of an imaginary tub, twirling, pirouetting across the courtroom, her courteous attorney playing the role of her attentive stage maid.

With a flourish, Giesler produced the sixty-two-inch-wide, thick towel that Lili wrapped herself in as she emerged from the "tub" like she did every night of her performance. As the "maid," he stood in front of the jury/audience to shield Lili. Sixty-two inches was an awfully big prop and covered up much of the stripper. How much of Lili could really be seen? The jury got it.

The presentation of the case was over. It was time for ten women and two men to decide Lili's future.

After only eighty minutes, the jury was ready with their answer.

While she wrung a lace hanky in her hands, the jury pronounced Lili innocent of lewd and indecent exposure charges.

Lili burst into a relieved smile and shook each and every hand of the jury, declaring it was a victory for strippers and burlesque artists everywhere. "I'm really relieved," she said. "It's a wonderful and a real victory."

She threw her arms around Giesler and smiled for the cameras, holding Exhibit "A" and "B," her rhinestone-encrusted panties and bra. She was radiant. Jerry himself looked extremely satisfied.

The fame Lili acquired from the trial sent her career (and subsequently her earnings) skyrocketing; this brought endless engagements and travel.

Jerry's fame was forever cemented by Lili's touch of glamour. He would be so pleased with the ensuing publicity that followed, he never bothered to bill Lili. Lili and Jerry's shared triumph in court legitimized Lili's career and sprinkled Jerry with stardust. He was a few years away from another blonde damsel in distress, Marilyn Monroe, who it was claimed saw many of Lili's performances so that she could pattern herself after the burlesque queen. Marilyn would turn to the saggy-chinned attorney in tears after her very public divorce from Joe DiMaggio. He would stand patiently beside the teary-eyed blonde like he had for Lili.

Giesler was the ultimate small-time boy with the Midwestern work ethic, determined to make good in the world. And he did. His career went on for almost a half century.

Lili retired from the stage and public life in her early fifties.

The highest-paid stripteaser had no steady income in her last decades. She grew old and bent, suffered from arthritis or osteoporosis, living with her countless cats in an apartment across from Paramount Studios in Hollywood.

At the time of Lili's death, she had become a mere footnote to burlesque, dying in obscurity as she had lived for her last several decades. But for a time, there was no one as famous as Lili St. Cyr.

CHAPTER THIRTY-FOUR
Men Who Made Us Great

"Early burlesque was a family entertainment. That's hard to
believe, but it was."

—Alan Alda

"There were never any newcomers. There was never anyone
new coming into the business."

—Val Valentine

Burlesque shows didn't run themselves. Besides the Minsky brothers, there were many impresarios responsible for the beautiful burlesque shows both in the theatre and clubs.

Legendary producer Billy Rose was diminutive in stature only. So short was Billy, he would supposedly book the seat in front of him when he went to the theatre so his view wouldn't be obstructed.

He was an excellent lyricist. "Me and My Shadow" is one of his most famous compositions. Rose had his fingers in all things burlesque, from producing carnival shows to running nightclubs in the '20s.

He opened Casa Mañana in Fort Worth, Texas. It was an outdoor theatre with a huge revolving stage and a moat. The theatre's "curtain" was a fountain of water spraying up from a circular moat. It was part of the Texas Centennial of 1936. Gypsy Rose Lee gave him "The Evolution of the Striptease" act. The whole revue was so big, with dancers and specialty acts, that more than two hundred local seamstresses were hired. Sally Rand performed her fan dance.

Rose married burly comedian Fanny Brice. During the 1939 World's Fair in New York, Rose presented "Aquacade," a show with bikini-clad girls that reportedly earned him a million dollars. He opened the Diamond Horseshoe Club (later taken over by Leroy Griffith). One columnist wrote about the scads of beauties in the place. "He put a PhD on burlesque—PhD, that means pretty hot dames."

Showman Mike Todd produced burlesque-type shows cleverly using the women and men of burlesque in legit Broadway shows to get around LaGuardia's ban on burlesque. Still, the censors gave him problems, making Lilly Christine tone down her act, along with others.

Todd produced *Star and Garter,* a musical, with girlfriend Gypsy Rose Lee. He also produced the popular *Peep Show.* Apparently things weren't moving fast enough for Gypsy, who married another to make Todd jealous. Later the showman would marry movie star Elizabeth Taylor and die in a plane crash in 1958.

Lili St. Cyr and her sister Barbara began stripping with N.T.G. at LA's Florentine Gardens in the 1930s. Nils Thor Granlund (the girls that worked for him called him "Granny") was born in Sweden in 1889. He would later be much loved by his showgirls. His nightclub and eatery on Hollywood Boulevard was packed with celebrities and servicemen during WWII, making him a top grosser. He introduced Eddie Cantor to radio along with Al Jolson; he helped Joan Crawford, and Jean Harlow and Ruby Keeler (both in burlesque) become stars.

Granny claimed to name Barbara for two of his society friends, Barbara Hutton and Adelaide Moffett. Lili's younger half-sister became Barbara Moffett before becoming an actress under contract with RKO.

Granny helped finance his friend Earl Carroll's *Vanities* show on Broadway.

He died on April 21, 1957, in an automobile accident, trying to stage a comeback in Las Vegas. He was responsible for discovering actress Yvonne De Carlo (*The Munsters*), who claimed his body and made the funeral arrangements, burying him at Forest Lawn Hollywood Hills near a bridle path he rode on when it was open land.

Earl Carroll opened theatres in New York and Los Angeles. Over the entrance, he installed a sign that read, "Through these portals pass the most beautiful girls in the world." Dardy Minsky got her start there.

Carroll hired a young Herman Hover to be his general manager at The Earl Carroll theatre. In his spare time, Hover studied law. He would go on to be the owner of Ciro's nightclub in Hollywood.

Carroll died in a fiery plane crash in Pennsylvania with his girlfriend Beryl Wallace. (Dardy would understudy Beryl, who was heavier and shorter, squeezing herself into the costumes until Carroll finally took pity on her and ordered wardrobe for her tall, lanky figure). It was Beryl's twenty-foot-high neon profile that adorned the Earl Carroll theatre in Los Angeles. Today a copy can be seen at Universal CityWalk at Universal City.

CHAPTER THIRTY-FIVE

The Exotic Others

"They had the most beautiful acts in burlesque. They had dog acts and acrobats."
—Lily Ann Rose

"A man was the best stripper I ever saw."
—Vicki O'Day

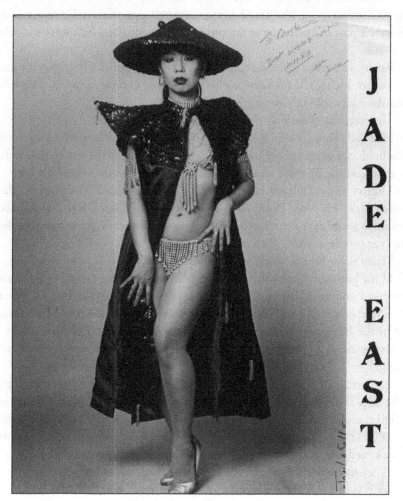

An exotic "Other"

Burlesque, like vaudeville, hosted a variety of novelty acts between the strips and the comics. There were jugglers, celebrity boxers, dog acts, acrobats, ventriloquists, Spanish dancers, singers. . . . Oftentimes, the wackier the better.

"Harmonica acts went over nice," said Renny von Muchow.

"Some acts were goofy and some amateurish," which contributes to our view of it being "innocent today," explained Rachel Shteir.

The Hollywood Theatre had a novelty hypnotist, The Great Alante. "He was a hairdresser and cabdriver and hypnotist all in one," Dee Ann Johnston recalled. "Dad rented him a tux; he didn't have one."

When Renny von Muchow and Rudy met in high school, they used to challenge each other to see who could do the most pull-ups off streetlights. As novelty acts were a part of burlesque at the time, they became hand balancers and joined the circuit.

Renny wanted to make sure, like the girls with gimmicks, that they set themselves apart. He said, "Let's keep our bodies looking as close as twins." This would make their act visibly more impressive, he thought.

They were as close as any two brothers.

Like Sally Rand, Mimi Reed was a "specialty dancer" who performed in night clubs holding a giant rubber ball that she used to walk to the gas station to have the attendant fill. She was strong and lithe and would remain so all her life.

Theatre owner Bob Johnston had a big heart and would "hire everyone down on their luck." He hired boxer Archie Moore, another San Diego guy, to "talk to the audience and sign autographs." Jack Johnson, another boxer, worked for them. "He kept people working for a couple weeks."

"They never fired anyone," said Betty Rowland.

Many burlesque comedians, such as Milton Berle and even Johnny Carson, performed in drag on the stage, and later in television. Drag performers were not only a part of circus life ("Clowns had drag acts," said Janet Davis.) but clearly a part of the burlesque world. Drag performances were "integral throughout . . . vaudeville, circus or burlesque. . . . A great number of performers were explicitly in drag."

The female impersonators performed in burlesque very early on, at least prior to the '20s. The men tucked their penises into their G-strings. It wasn't until after WWII that there were specific theatres geared toward gay and lesbian crowds.

In 1932, the Old Howard had a show "Facts & Figures," in which two male actors kissed and groped each other. The censors were outraged.

"They had special shows for the female impersonators. I worked with Venus. And he was so beautiful. *He* was the star of the show," said Lily Ann Rose.

Transgender burlesque show

"This woman looked like June Allyson. Did spectacular things with his/her body," said Vicki O'Day. "I'd never seen anybody so good. At the end of his act, he pulled off his wig and he was Asian."

Dee Ann Johnston had her own experience with a female impersonator at the Hollywood. "He was a paratrooper; he still looked like a paratrooper even when he was supposed to be a woman. Her name was Tamara something and she sold her book and she did a strip. So there were . . . yeah, there were novelty acts."

"Christine Jorgensen was a young man who went to World War II." The private with the underdeveloped privates, Jorgensen started taking hormones and had one of the first sex change operations in Scandinavia, which was "very shocking in those days," said Steven Weinstein. Though he wasn't the first, he was the first to go public after the operation.

She got into burlesque as a novelty strip act. It was by all accounts a "beautiful act," said Rita Grable. "I worked with her at the Tick Tock in St. Louis. She was wonderful. She looked like a girl. She sang, talked, and took off her gown. She was dressed like me, with pasties, etc." Rita listed her qualities, besides being brave: "sweet, calm, very feminine." They worked together, hung out, and went to dinner together. "People looked at her like she was a freak. She had a hard time. People would recognize her on the street, and point and say things. People are cruel sometimes."

The world easily lumped together strippers and transsexuals, equating them with sideshow freaks. Daisy and Violet Hilton started as "freak" performers in carnival sideshows and rose to incredible fame on the vaudeville circuit. Siamese twins, they were connected near the base of their spine. When it became unseemly to pay money to see "freaks" on display and vaudeville died, the Hilton Sisters descended from the heights of sold-out crowds, in beautiful theatres to land reluctantly in a smoke-filled nightclub with leering men who preferred to see Evelyn West and her Million-Dollar Chest. From my research, I was unable to determine how far down they stripped, but presumably not all the way. They were sensitive about showing where they were connected at the back by "a ribbon of flesh," according to Dean Jensen. Unfortunately, they were hooted off the stage.

In their youth, in the '20s and '30s, the twins had a "winning act" as little girls who played musical instruments, dancing and singing. They were one of the top -grossing acts of vaudeville. They were the stars on the same bill with Bob Hope (a virtual unknown when he started dancing with the sisters), Burns and Allen, and Sophie Tucker. Everyone in America knew the conjoined twins with the ringlets in their hair and large, outsized bows on their heads.

Siamese twins Daisy and Violet Hilton, briefly and miserably in burlesque

From their abusive and Dickensian childhood on display in sideshows, they went on to huge fame. Vaudeville died and the sisters aged; they took what they could, working, among other places, at The Hollywood Theatre in San Diego, where "they stayed drunk the entire time," Dee Ann recalled her father saying. Stripper Val Valentine remembered the sisters' fights in the dressing room next to her.

"Vaudeville didn't exist in the '40s and these people still needed a job, and I guess maybe they were a draw. They were always in the Palace Bar on the bar stool. They died of the influenza in 1969," Dee Ann said.

April March worked with the Strong Brothers, who were midgets. "They were the comics on one of the shows in Washington, D.C. They were English," she said. One of the brothers asked her if she would be embarrassed to go to dinner with him. She said she would love to go. They went to Trader Vic's and April said her date asked for a booster seat.

In burlesque, there were also the "exotic others," who were usually Asian and African American.

In the 1920s and '30s, there was a cabaret club at the Hotel Douglas in San Diego, which claimed to be the "Harlem of the West." The club featured the Creole Cuties Chorus, a group of beautiful black girls. And though not advertised as a "burlesque" club, the Creole Palace had a plethora of similarly clad beauties. The club was black-owned and thrived for more than thirty years, with big-name entertainers such as Bessie Smith and Billie Holiday.

While burlesque shows were strictly segregated, the Creole Palace had a mixed audience, perhaps getting away with it because the girls didn't disrobe. According to Jaye Furlonger, who wrote about the history of San Diego burlesque, there was a "strict racial segregation of the national burlesque industry."

In 1925, the "world's only all-colored musical burlesque" show called *7-11* toured the country.

There had been women of color performing onstage since as early as 1890 in musicals such as *The Creole Show*, but it wasn't burlesque. That was a minstrel-type show. Burlesque incorporated the three-part act of a minstrel show. (Minstrel shows were a popular form of entertainment for the middle-class and made fun of not only stereotypical blacks, but also country-bumpkin types.)

There were black performers in vaudeville, like Ada (sometimes Aida) Overton. She appeared in vaudeville and was considered to be one of the best dancers in her day (she died at thirty-four).

In the 1940s and 1950s, there was an African American strip circuit. "It didn't last for very long," said Rachel Shteir. "Those women never could achieve any level of economic success the way a Gypsy Rose Lee could."

Sadly, so much of this history either wasn't chronicled at the time, or has been lost. Today we know so little about these performers. *Jet Magazine* in the mid-1950s did highlight African American women, but their press was far less than their white contemporaries.

In the 1950s, there was mention of an Elizabeth "China Doll" Dickerson, who covered her costume in balloons. The men seated close popped them until she was nude—or nearly so.

Jean Idelle was one of the only black fan dancers. According to the magazine, so "torrid" was her act, she was forced to lock her dressing room to prevent the Stage Door Johnnies from busting in.

Billed as the "Sepia Sally Rand," Idelle supposedly was the first performer to integrate with the white dancers. She performed at Minsky's Rialto Theatre in Chicago. Retiring after having children, she was called back at age eighty-two to lift her fans again for the Burlesque Hall of Fame weekend.

Vida de Soir was advertised as the "Red Hot Sex Queen."

Besides Idelle, these women couldn't work in first-rate clubs. Latter-day strippers entering the business in the '60s such as Toni Elling, achieved more recognition, though they worked in a very different burlesque. By the '60s it was mainly a strip show.

There were also the "Oriental" performers, the most famous being Noel Toy, who was known as the "Chinese Sally Rand" and performed at the Forbidden City, a San Francisco nightclub, in the 1930s with her fan-and-bubble act. Forbidden City was the first and only Chinese nightclub at the time. Noel's fame would outgrow the place and she would move on to bigger and better fare: Leon & Eddies, the Stork Club in New York, and Lou Walter's Latin Quarter. Here, she said, "old ladies would come and [they] loved me." She showed her breasts and wore a fringed panty.

In an interview she gave when she was eighty-two, the trim and still gorgeous Toy showed the only thing raunchy about her was her laugh. She explained she started as a nude model at Treasure Island at the San Francisco World's Fair of 1939. The owner of the Forbidden City enticed her to work for him. His club was "dying on the vine," according to her, but business picked up when the nude fan dancer hit the floor. She was the only Chinese nude model at the time.

She went on to play minor roles in film and television, and died of a stroke at age eighty-four.

CHAPTER THIRTY-SIX

Pasties and More

"They had crepe-paper costumes on, crepe-paper bras and crepe-paper skirts.
She said, 'I'm not wearing those costumes.'"

—Dee Ann Johnston

"You don't have to take everything off to be beautiful."

—Kitty West

Wild costumes on stage at Earl Carroll's in Hollywood

But what you did take off had to be beautiful. Wardrobe was important and a vital investment.

"I became Vicki O'Day in layers," said the stripper.

Half the fun of stripping was the many pieces one put on prior to taking them off. Costumes were gorgeous, elaborate, sturdy, beaded, heavy, silky—some designer, some sewn by the strippers themselves. The fabrics shone, rippled and floated. They were fantasy outfits that helped create the illusion of the different characters the women pretended to be.

Chorus girls were given their wardrobe, Maria Bradley explained. Strippers had to pay for their own. Many, including Blaze Starr, spent time in the dressing room, sewing. "I sewed my first gown by hand. And that's why I have the most beautiful gowns," she said.

"Blaze was very crafty," Rita Grable verified. "She would make all of her costumes by hand."

Gown sewn by Blaze Starr (in author's collection) made by hand

Lili St. Cyr made some of her own costumes, even after she was a star. They were expertly sewn and have held up some sixty to seventy years later.

Lily Ann Rose recalled sitting backstage, "smoking and sewing" with all the girls in the dressing room. "Beads and sequins were needed to make the costumes shine and stand out on the opening parade numbers. Most of the girls could not afford a two- or three-hundred-dollar costume while making twenty-five or thirty-five dollars a week. So we all just beaded our own. After all, we had hours sitting backstage just talking or waiting."

Dardy added, "Between shows you have nothing to do. Backstage everyone is cutting and sewing. On Sundays, on Halsted Street in Chicago, carts would come with bolts of fabric and girls would go there and buy fabric."

Carmela made a lot of her own costumes. She used "plastic beads instead of crystal because crystal cuts the thread," she said.

Sequin's boyfriend Ted, who got her into burlesque, "had a stripper friend and she taught Sequin how to make G-strings and net bras." She bought a sewing machine and Ted designed the clothing. But her first time out, she had to work with what she had. "The only gown that I really had to work on was my high school prom dress. Of course the zipper got stuck. And one of the customers had to reach up and help me unstick the zipper," she said.

"The one I started out with was an old dress from being a maid of honor," said Taffy O'Neil. Her husband helped her modify it.

Girls starting out who didn't have costumes had to keep that fact a secret. "You don't let the boss know you don't have wardrobe," Dixie Evans said. "Just fake it in the theatre, 'Oh, my trunk's lost.'" Dixie borrowed her outfit from a San Francisco girl. ("San Francisco girls—wonderful," she claimed.)

In the 1870s, the Rentz-Santley Burlesque Company displayed women in one-piece leotards and tights as they sang. Their star, Mabel Santz, was arrested for indecent exposure in 1879 when she lifted her skirts and showed, *gasp*, an ankle.

By the turn of the century, bare midriffs were on display.

"Back then, you couldn't see flesh. You didn't see it until 1962 or '64," said Dixie.

In 1926, Josephine Baker was doing her banana act in Paris at the Folies Bergère wearing nothing but rubber bananas around her waist. She flashed more than Rose La Rose would be accused of doing thirty years in the future.

Those naughty French cancan girls were rumored to be pantyless when they high-kicked above the audiences' heads in musical halls, though this has been disputed, as "drawers" weren't the method of underwear at the time.

For a profession that involved taking off clothes, it sure meant a full trunk of costumes. Packed into those trunks were bras, net panties, G-strings, sheer gowns, panels, sequins, leotards, feathers, headbands, stockings, shoes, garters, nylon hose and mesh, and opera hose, which were longer and reached to the top of the thigh, right below the buttock. Longer by at least three or four inches, opera hose gave a seriously uninterrupted look to the stripper's leg. Then there were tassels, baubles, tiaras, crowns, capes, hats, gloves, jewelry, props, and makeup. Not to mention the animals and their carriers.

Getting one's wardrobe to the next town was always an ordeal. There never seemed to be enough time.

"You came off the stage," Joan Arline said, "of the last show. The wardrobe would be hung and the trunk taken by railway express in the afternoon. So you kept [the] garment you wore, which you wore all week." She would collect her music from the musicians "because the trunk wasn't delivered till next day at 3, 3:30, but you've already done the 1 o'clock show."

Sequin added, "Everything had its place. I was organized. Robes to wear afterwards to get off stage and upstairs. A lot of wardrobe." She traveled with six gowns.

Lady Midnight made her own costumes and bought more elaborate ones from Gussie Gross. "I had beautiful wardrobe to go on the road. It was very exciting. Every week, you'd change a gown. If you did two numbers, you had two different gowns. I did different numbers—did a Batman number, wore a bat cape. Street number like a cancan girl. I didn't like doing the same old thing all the time. I wanted to entertain. I always came up with something different. I didn't want to bore them. And I didn't want to be bored."

Gowns had to be made well to last on the road. "It was an expensive game," Dixie Evans said. Furs were de rigueur, as were expensive cars, perfume, and all the trappings of success. A successful stripper was expected to "walk in with expensive perfume. It's a matter of prestige. I couldn't afford to do all those things they used to tell me," Dixie Evans said.

There were dozens of costumers who made incredible outfits for the strippers. There was Gussie Gross, who was married to a policeman; Bill White made costumes in New Orleans; BB Hughes was known on the West Coast. She made Taffy O'Neil's net pants and bras.

Ann Corio "went for a regular person's wardrobe," Mike Iannucci said. Her preferred costumer for many years was Stella Wilner. Later, Ann and Mike got into a high-fashion business and had Ann's gowns made in Italy. He "sold one of her beaded dresses for $31,000."

Kitty West wore "French bikini-type bottoms, and a full bra. Richard Simmons's father used to make some of my wardrobe. His mother was a singer, in the French quarter."

Val Valentine recalled that "there was a costumer that made gorgeous wardrobe." His name was Tony Midnight.

"I had been a performer myself with the Jewel Box Review. That was a huge show of female impersonators. And I was working on my own clothes. I made the stuff to last. Really, like put together with an iron. It took a beating," said Tony Midnight.

Of the rare people allowed backstage were vendors who sold the girls G-strings and bras and jewelry. There was a man in Manhattan named Paul, and he sold to all the biggies in the '50s: Peaches, Irma the Body, Sally Rand, Lili St. Cyr, Gypsy. He was said to have eight hundred items in his tiny store.

Suzie Cream Cheese was another designer. She made a lot of the costumes for Minsky in Las Vegas.

The more creative strippers used their wardrobes to carve out ways to be recognized. Sherry Britton wore small, sparkly crowns (which I now have and treasure beyond all measure). Betty Rowland had skirts made with a snap up the side (by Gussie) and bandeau tops. Gypsy stripped by pulling out straight pins and tossing them into the audience. Lili St Cyr was known for spending thousands on designer gowns and jewelry.

"When they were headliners, you couldn't wear the same color gown," Carmela explained.

Ann Corio loved the color pink. She would come on stage in a pink gown, wide-brimmed pink hat, and a pink robe. She "closed the show with her strip number 'A Pretty Girl is Like a Melody,'" said Mike Iannucci. "She would strip down to a pink cape and pink leotard with sequins in strategic places." She would open the cape and then close it. "'Oh, I can't take that off, I'll catch cold.' And *boom*, the lights would come down."

In *This Was Burlesque*, Ann Corio had twelve to fifteen gowns. White Fury said, "For every costume, I had a costume maker in Philadelphia. He would make up the show, make backgrounds and suitcases for each thing and gowns and music. I had a jungle house and leopard behind me. An Oriental one with a Chinese dragon behind me and on my dress. It was very pretty."

Joan Arline wanted to be different than the standard stripper. "I never wore a breakaway gown. I wore a zipper and teased with one, zip it down and bring it up, drum beat is edgy and pushing. Gown comes off, corselet twenty-two hooks and eyelets. I worked every one. That was the art of burlesque. It was the art. I hate it when people make fun of it," she said.

"I used pins and glue so it was easy to get out of," recalls Joni Taylor.

It wasn't just what you took off, but how.

Betty Rowland said, "Mistakes can be the best thing that happens." She tried to make it look accidental when her clothes came off. She never stopped dancing once her act started.

"I wore big headdresses and feathers. You pull a feather and pass it by your mouth very innocently. All a tease," said Joan Arline.

Some tricked out their wardrobe. Sally Keith weighted her tassels, as did others. Some did it with bird seed. As she aged, Sally Rand would wear a chiffon dress with fish weights to hold the dress down when she was moving. "Half way through the dance, she'd go by close to the curtains, [and a]person would reach in and pull dress and she could walk away." Her son often helped with this. "I did it for a while—the dress remover," he said. His best friend from high school occasionally played the part, too.

"We never threw our wardrobe; we paid a lot of money for it. We handed it. You paraded to the side and handed it to a chorus girl, whom you paid. Who made an extra five dollars a week," Joan Arline explained. "I had fur and I wanted special attention paid. I paid her extra. Every gown at the waist had two tabs to hang so catcher could fold it over on a hanger and clothes tree with these hangers coming through the curtain."

Some clubs and theatres had personal maids backstage. Tee Tee Red had "Gertie" in New Orleans, who wore a white uniform. "Gertie would help backstage, catch the girls' wardrobe and hang it up. Everyone paid her salary. She was our helper."

Lili St. Cyr's maid would place a sheet on a table backstage so her clothes didn't get dirty after she handed them off.

Sally Rand asserted her costume was "talcum powder."

Sometimes there might be wardrobe malfunctions. Candy Cotton said, "One time my pastie flew off and hit a guy in the eye." Lili St. Cyr would water down the glue on hers, as they often hurt when she took them off at the end of the night.

"In those years in burly, you had to wear pasties. You had to wear G-strings, and panels, a lot of stuff. And you could just remove so much. You could not show the nipples. Now some of the girls . . . they would make believe one fell off . . . like Janet Jackson with a [costume] failure."

Despairing over current strippers' lack of wardrobe, Rita Grable remembered: "The girls wore beautiful costumes and furs when I worked."

So many of the women gave or threw away their costumes when they retired. The costumes held little value when they quit the business. Margie Hart gave hers away to a drag queen. Taffy O'Neil gave hers to another exotic dancer who in turn sold them to a cross-dresser.

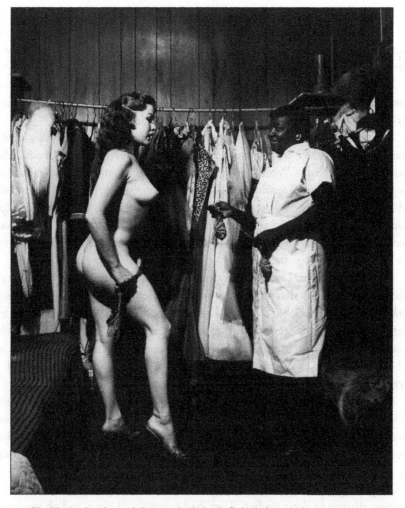

Tee Tee Red with maid Gertie, who helped all the girls with their costumes

Jennie Lee was a tassel twirler with the moniker "The Bazoom Girl." The sailors used to say she was "built like a brick shit house," said her friend Dixie Evans. Net bras, noted some of the women, were surprisingly supportive of big bosoms. Jennie was a force to be reckoned with at five feet nine inches and a very healthy 42-28-40. The Kansas City native did a Mae West number and was said to be very smart. She collected "everything," long before the current thirst for vintage costumes, which could be quite elaborate, distinctive, and expensive with delicate, yet durable material, very often studded with rhinestones and beads. Jennie had a bar in San Pedro called the Sassy Lassy where many ex-strippers used to congregate, often leaving their stuff behind. Jennie kept it all and eventually showed it in a tiny storefront next to the bar. When she moved to a former goat farm out in the Mojave Desert, she took her growing collection of burlesque memorabilia, always intending to open a museum.

She lived in a trailer and with the help of her husband turned her moldering memorabilia into a museum of sorts. Some down-on-their-luck strippers lived there for a time. Both Tempest and Dixie moved out there for years.

Dixie Evans took care of Jennie as she grew sick. Jennie eventually died of breast cancer in 1989, at age sixty-one. When Jennie's husband Charlie died, Dixie inherited "Exotic World," which she turned into a nonprofit organization. She put together annual reunions and stripping contests, trying to draw attention and donations to the aging population of burlesque strippers who needed help in their old age. Dixie wanted an organization for exotic dancers, past and present. "Because we don't have anything. We're excluded from everything. They want to be a part of something," she said.

It was due to Jennie Lee, then to Dixie's efforts (and amazing recall on the entire history of burlesque) that the resurgence of burlesque with the neo-burlesque scene emerged in the 1990s. A whole generation of young women took an avid interest in the exotic dancers of the past and patterned new acts based on old, classic strips. It is a scene that has grown around the world, even in cultures that had no burlesque history. (When our film premiered in the Dublin Film Festival, we were astounded by the amount of burlesque troops performing in Ireland.)

Neo-burlesque no longer "fills a need" like the burlesque houses did during the war and the Depression. It's no longer a ritual and is certainly not the only place to see nudity. The circuit is long over. There are no theatres that have shows three times a day, six days a week, forty weeks a year. It's different. True burlesque was of its time.

Surprisingly, not once during any of my interviews did any of the former strippers disparage their bodies. They had come in all sizes and shapes, some flat-chested, others big-hipped, some bordered on fat. They never worried about weight or their breast size or flab. Some of the dancers had bodies in their youth that were sheer perfection, but not many. They knew they were a hot commodity just the way they were.

Cries of "Take it off!" validated their beauty and their "power" such as it was—maybe just to entice for minutes—over the men in the audience. They were magnificent. Variety in looks and shapes and style was admired.

Kitty West said, "I was a sixteen-year-old girl with a gorgeous body and I didn't know I had a gorgeous body. I didn't know I was good lookin'. I knew nothing."

CHAPTER THIRTY-SEVEN

The Burly Beat

"It is the musician's fault if you don't go over."

—Dixie Evans

"Musicians were always trying to hit on you, but that was par for the course."

—Joan Arline

"The blues and the jazz are what the stripteasers used. The St. Louis Blues and the jazz that came from that Deep South; that's original, American music. And that's what the burlesque entertainers used," Dixie Evans said.

Like their gimmicks and their costumes, the headliners were proprietary about their music. "You couldn't use any music that was even similar to theirs," Carmela said.

Burlesque had its unique rhythm with bongos and drums. Each stripper had her favorite songs. "A Pretty Girl is Like a Melody" was the anthem for dozens of strippers, including Ann Corio and Betty Rowland.

Vicki O'Day loved "Green Onions."

"Everyone liked 'Night Train,'" said Dixie Evans. Parts of "Night Train" were composed as early as 1940 by Duke Ellington and Johnny Hodges. "Strippers would fight over 'Night Train,'" she said.

Georgia Sothern was identified with the frenetic "Hold that Tiger."

"Georgia Sothern had vitality—she'd throw her hair around. Set the place on fire. She was great," musician John Perilli exclaimed.

John Perilli, a handsome older gentleman in a sports coat with a thick New Jersey accent, said, "Having to work as a musician in burlesque, they were looked down upon. It was probably one of the least [prestigious] endeavors you could possibly get into musically." He had received a panicked call from a conductor at The Empire in New Jersey. "He had a problem with the drummer and he said if he didn't get a drummer, he was gonna lose his job. So I said to him, 'I don't know anything from strippers; I never played strippers before,'" he said.

John had been to a burlesque show before, a Minsky show in Chicago, and he thought the drummer was fantastic. "I was twenty-one. To see these chicks start stripping, it was quite an experience. The comics blew my head off. They were marvelous."

Perilli helped his friend out and found himself in the pit of The Empire, having a rocky start with the feature, Dixie Evans. "She was a great dancer but she was rough on drummers, right. And she gave me a terrible time. Finally we got together, became friends, and worked it out."

"They had problems with me," Dixie Evans repeated. "And the only reason I found that out? I look and it says, 'To the drummer: God help you if you can catch this girl's act.' Every place that played, they'd pencil little notes in about me. I thought, *My God, I didn't know they thought that bad about me.*"

Understandably, it was difficult getting used to a different band every week.

"The show opens Friday, so you've got to struggle through the weekend. But by Wednesday you're moving with the band, then it's time to go," Dixie recalled.

Taffy O'Neil said, "Most bands were wonderful." Her manager told her to "never complain to the band about the music. 'It can only get worse.' You learn to work with all that," she said.

During rehearsal, neophyte John Perilli asked the manger, "Do I play the chart or the chicks?" The manager told him to play the chart.

From deep in the pit, the drummer especially had to see the stripper to match her bumps, which was not always possible. This often led to conflicts between dancer and musician.

"If the musicians thought the stripper was going to the front of the house and complaining," Dixie Evans said, "they would and could intentionally screw up the girl's numbers."

The girls traditionally did three numbers, or "trailers." The music changed with each song. "They'd bring in their own charts. They were pros," remembers Dee Ann Johnston.

Maria Bradley would start "out very demure. 'I'm the Girl with the Natural Curl' and 'I'm the Girl with the Toni' and bump." The next song would be a "little bit wilder. Then the end would be very wild. Leave 'em that way."

Dancing in French-speaking Canada, Tee Tee Red handed the musicians her music, who couldn't read the cues she had written in English. "It didn't turn out OK."

Joan Arline said, "All the drummers didn't like Tempest Storm because she couldn't keep time."

"Oh God, she'd screech and scream at the band," remembered Dixie Evans.

Joan continued, "And [Tempest would] be so mad 'cause they didn't catch her bumps. Well, she would never bump, I mean it was at random." Tempest did have a unique style of dancing, throwing her head back and forth and bending her knees deeply. It wasn't elegant; it was raw and exciting and blatantly sexual. She wasn't the slow, sensuous Lili St. Cyr. She was a new generation of '50s strippers who laid it all out there. She was raucous, even awkward, but the audience loved it and that style made her and Blaze Starr famous. Blaze and Tempest bumped, grinded, and worked with the curtains, which the audience loved.

Lillian Hunt trained Tempest and Blaze Starr to "walk in tempo to the drums." This felt a little too "set" for Sequin; it wasn't to her taste. She admired Lili St. Cyr, who appeared to wander and drift across the stage. In watching some of Lili's acts that have survived on film, in some she doesn't even dance much. Hers is pantomime, stretching, acting. She doesn't immerse herself in wild music, she'd not be overtaken. She's in charge of her audience and of her own emotion. She didn't let herself get carried away by the beat. Everything was carefully choreographed, whereas Tempest seems caught up in the savage.

"Lili St. Cyr, the most fascinating chick that I met," said John Perilli. "She did a number that wasn't percussive. She did a thing on Salome and the Seven Veils. She came rolling down the staircase, one step at a time, doing her thing. She got together with me in dressing room, explained what she was gonna do. Subtle playing. That was the best art form of burlesque I ever experienced. The rest of the chicks were straight-ahead percussive. Loud and as busy as you could play."

Rose La Rose came out in a long dress and the song "Who Will Kiss My Oo-la-la?" to which she frequently slapped her "ooh la la" fanny. When she turned around, the back of her dress was cut in the shape of a heart. "With a bunch of snaps," recalled Dixie Evans.

Alexandra said she could never understand how she got out of all of them.

Steven Weinstein said, "Exotic dancers were working at a craft, at a trade." The girls in his father's Colony Club in Dallas were "educated" and "beautiful," he said. They "would come out to a live band, in custom-made costumes." It soon "digressed into a bump and grind; in the beginning it wasn't—but music had an exotic nature, with a certain beat a woman could dance to it and take off clothing," he said.

In its heyday, burlesque productions had full orchestras.

The music was improvised. The strippers had their own arrangements, which they paid for, but their routine wasn't marked. "Drummers had to become imaginative. While working with strippers, they had to constantly be cognizant of what was going on musically," said John Perilli.

Lili St. Cyr often traveled with her own violinist—at her expense.

"Amber Halliday carried her own bongo player—fantastic," said Terry Mixon.

Kitty West traveled with her own drummer.

"One time, I was doing Marilyn," Dixie Evans remembers, "to *Shake, Rattle, and Roll* on my finale. *Shake Marilyn Monroe.*" The stage hands started motioning her to get off the stage, but she was receiving encores. Dixie remained longer onstage than normal. The owner told her, "You just cost me a lot of money." He explained that if musicians played beyond their agreed upon time they were paid time and a half. If six minutes, it's time and a half. "When they give you a signal to cut, you'd better cut. Front of house, they run the show. They can drop the screen on you [that showed the films between live shows]. you'd better get out of the way. You learn respect for working people. And how to conduct yourself with other people."

Steven Weinstein's dad owned the Colony Club in Dallas. "[In] 1949 or 1950, the business was changing. The trend of music went from the big-band era of a Glen Miller sound to more of the Elvis, with one individual singer and a small combo."

Abe Weinstein was looking for a new concept for his club. "He'd heard of burlesque clubs in California with exotic dancers." Abe went to California to learn what the clubs there were doing. And he returned to Dallas with a new format. It was a "high-class joint with beautifully dressed couples."

As musicians were slowly expunged from clubs and theatres, many girls complained that dancing to records was "shoddy," said Betty Rowland. She missed the orchestra and the "spontaneity" that it brought. With a "record, it's the same every time," she said.

Kitty West complained they had to start dancing to juke boxes or tapes when the musicians were cut from shows. "That was not for me. So important to dance with a band. I couldn't imagine myself dancing to video."

In the 1950s, "burlesque was fading down enough that rather than a live band, we had taped music, which was a little nice in a way because it was so dependable. You know . . . the tape didn't drink," Taffy O'Neil said slyly.

CHAPTER THIRTY-EIGHT

The Mob

"In Cincinnati, there was a great mob influence . . . but I will not name names."
—Kitty West

"Gangsters didn't bother you. You're making money for them."
—Dixie Evans

Clearly the Mafia had their fingers in the burlesque pie from at least the 1920s. Author Rachel Shteir believed that in the later years of burlesque in the nightclubs, strippers had to give a cut of their salaries to the mob.

Nils T. Granlund, entrepreneur and radio host in the early twentieth century, claimed that with Prohibition, the mafia infiltrating the night life was a "setup made to order for mobsters. . . . It took money to set up and run clubs."

"Most of the clubs were run by Mafia," confirmed Lily Ann Rose, "and if one of the bosses said they didn't want you, then you were blackballed."

Sally Rand was working a club in Chicago, teasing the crowd with her ostrich fans. One night, her son told me, rival club owner and renowned mobster Al Capone came up to her and told her, "I have bought your contract. You're done here as of tonight. You'll be at my club the following night."

A smart woman, Sally quickly agreed. "OK, sounds like a deal," she said. She finished her work for the night, packed up everything and high-tailed it to New York, later telling her son, Sean, she figured "there was a whole different gang world in New York. Capone won't go on New York territory." She figured she'd be safe there. And she was.

Sally was not only quick witted, but quick thinking. She claimed to have known many girlfriends who would "overhear something and disappear in the East River" of Chicago. She was also good friends with burlesque comedian and former singer Joe E. Lewis, who barely survived his own run-in with some Capone-associated gangsters.

Joe E. Lewis was a honey-throated singer performing at the Green Mill Gardens in the Windy City. One night, some thugs knocked on his door and slit his throat. Such a reputation did Joe E. have for being a prankster that when the maid came in and found him lying there bloody, she thought it was an elaborate joke. It would take Joe E. nearly two years to recover his voice, as part of his tongue was cut off. It was a miracle he lived.

His crime? He had refused to renew his contract at the Green Mill, a club owned by one of Capone's men.

Capone liked Joe E. and felt bad—he hadn't ordered the assault—enough to give Joe E. ten thousand dollars and help him in any way he could.

Lewis left the singing stage and became a comedian in burlesque. He would work for years in Vegas, often sharing the bill with Lili St. Cyr at the El Rancho. He was great friends with Frank Sinatra.

"If you were in show business and you worked in a night club, the club was owned by a member of the fraternity. It was rough and it was tough. Four of my employers. . . . were killed."

Lily Ann Rose said, "People can say what they want about the Mafia. But the Mafia kept things in line, like strippers and dancers. You weren't allowed to go out with the customers. You weren't allowed to prostitute yourself."

"If they ever found you went out with a customer, you'd be fired the next day. They're not gonna operate a club for you to get Johns," agreed Dixie Evans.

Vicky O'Day said, "As long as you did what they wanted and kept your mouth shut and you didn't see anything, they didn't bother you."

"You didn't get in trouble," Alexandra the Great said, "unless you looked for trouble."

Beverly Anderson found the mobsters "fascinating." Beverly was working a club in Atlanta that was owned by a gangster. Beverly, along with the other performers, had to pretend "we didn't know he was the owner of the nightclub."

One time in New York, a gangster who was going with a red-headed stripper was killed at the Park Sheraton. For years, a New York Cabaret ID Card was required of performers. "At the time, dancers had police cards in order to work. It listed the women by height, hair color, etc. and was on file with the mayor's office," Beverly explained. The gangster killed at the Park Sheraton was going with a red-headed stripper. So the FBI looked up redheads' police cards and "came and interviewed me. . . . I thought it was exciting," remembers Beverly. The Gambino Family mobster was Albert Anastasia and it was October 25, 1957, when he was killed in the hotel's barber shop.

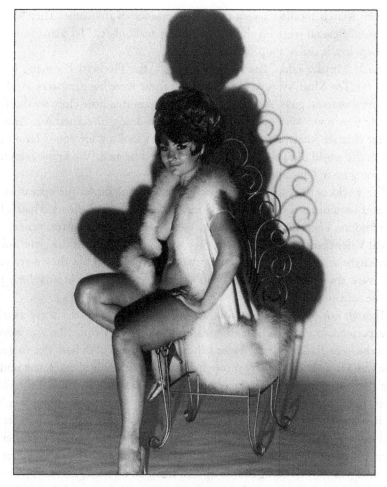

Stripper Vicki O'Day

A side note about police cards: it was said Rose La Rose was partially responsible for abolishing this offensive practice. The cards were akin to prostitutes registering with the police in Europe. Rose, ever the fighter, took it on.

Kitty West recalled the mob in New Orleans, but wanted to keep their identities to herself. "I won't call their names," she said. They respected her and she respected them. "They didn't bother me. They thought that I was the greatest thing ever. They packed the house for me. They left me alone," she said. She felt safe in their presence. "I had a security guard when I went to get something. Wherever I went, I was safe."

April March recalled a very real mob presence in the clubs. They were "all gentlemen." Several were on the Minsky show in Yonkers. "I'd play gin rummy with them in the coffee shop," she said.

Dardy Minsky said, "The mob in Chicago, the Fischetti Brothers, I mean big, on the Ten Most Wanted list, you know, these were big gangsters. And they were just *wonderful* guys. And one night we were in this little club; we didn't tell anybody where we were going or what we were doing or something. And this mobster that we knew came in said, 'So-and-so's looking for you.' Harold said, 'How in the world did you know I was here?' And he said, 'We know everything that's going on in Chicago.'"

The world between the Mafia, the police, and the burlesque operators was close and sometimes the worlds overlapped. N.T.G. claimed the mob had "a high code of honor. I was never gypped or given a bad deal by a gangster owner."

Val Valentine agreed. "Actually, they were very nice to all the girls, anyone you thought was connected, a wise guy or whatever. Oh no, they were great. They were always kinda around. You know, they were like atmosphere people," she said.

Though not directly related to her work, Vicki O'Day had a "scary as all get out" experience from a man she met working in the burly club. She was working where the "nice Italian" family owned the club. And the club had "ties to gangs." There was a hot car gang going through Texas and Arizona. Vicki "knew nothing about this" until one night a man asked her out for a date. He asked if they could stop by his house before going out to a restaurant. When they walked in "they were hauling what was left of someone . . . throwing him in the car. . . . There was blood all over. . . and it was a white carpet, white walls and there was splattering," she said. "I didn't realize the human body could have so much blood. What had happened was the one being beaten up had snitched on them, and they were taking care of him, which was kinda fun—for them—and the man doing the beating sort of lost it, I think. We ended up huddled in the bedroom, a bunch of us, with the door barricaded with this man going wild."

As urban sprawl increased and once middle-class neighborhoods fell derelict, many of the burlesque houses were located in the middle of increasingly unsafe neighborhoods. The nightclubs, run mostly by the Mafia, often created dangerous situations the performers were unwittingly caught up in—perhaps seeing something, or hearing something, they shouldn't.

GUNPLAY IN THE STRIP JOINT screamed the headlines from *True Detective Magazine*.

"It wasn't my fault," April March demurred. The night she performed resulted in two deaths in the club.

On stage at Leon & Eddies nightclub

April was headlining at the Place Pigalle in Miami Beach in September. A Korean, Kun-Wha Yoo, was drinking with two other pals, according to the magazine. April and another exotic, Sharon Sutton, the "Upside Down Girl," drank champagne at the trio's table.

"The Korean and his buddy kept ordering all kinds of bottles of champagne. They presented him with the bill and I guess he didn't like what the bill said," April said. "He ran out of the club."

The bill was seventy-four dollars. Yoo returned to his nearby hotel room, loaded a .38 gun, and then returned to the club.

"I did my performance, got dressed," April said. She was having a cup of coffee, sitting in a white dress at the table.

Yoo returned. He shot Tony D'Arcy, the club's baritone singer, outside. Dead. Next, Yoo shot the doorman Dave Goodman, who tried preventing Yoo from reentering the club. Goodman was shot twice in the legs.

"All of a sudden everybody started screaming and in came this Korean. And I hear, 'bam bam.' It sounded like a car backfiring and here I was under the spotlight. I couldn't move. I guess he was gonna kill me and he was looking right at me. He was like right there. He's shooting up the place," she said. Her friend Sharon was "drunk. She didn't pay any attention to the Korean with the guns.

I screamed. I remember he turned around, looked right at me, aimed the gun. I guess I blacked out. Sharon came over and got in front.... She caught the bullets instead of me."

The bongo player took a large bongo drum and knocked Yoo out. "I guess I went into shock because when I awoke I was at an agent's apartment and everybody tried keeping the newspapers and everything away from me.... So here anyway *True Detective Magazine* called me 'a femme fatale.' It wasn't my fault at all."

These situations didn't happen all the time, but more than one stripper had memories similar to April March's. Sheila Rae recalled a different gun battle in the club where she worked. "Guy came in and shot his wife during the show. She was onstage." Why did he shoot her? "She was playing around," Sheila said. Another time a woman shot her ex-convict of a husband in the club.

In 1954, at the New Follies in Los Angeles, ardent fan Roger Whittier died onstage clutching Loretta Miller's photos after being shot by police. He had burst into the club, gun in hand, vowing to get the red-headed stripper lots of publicity.

By the nature of who they associated with and where they performed, danger often was a very real threat for the dancers.

"I worked in Pueblo, Colorado," Vicki recalled, "and something was going on there at night." She had a hotel room next to the club that had no lock on the door. "I moved furniture in front of door. All night long I could hear trucks outside. I knew if I looked out that curtain, I was dead."

Her agent's secretary called her with advice. "You've got to get out of there. Tell them you're a witness in a car wreck and you have to be back up in Denver." She tried to use this excuse, but the owner of the club became angry. Vicki's agent then sent protection.

A "four-foot-tall cowboy. I thought *he's* gonna protect me?" She then went back to the club to retrieve her wardrobe, but half of it was gone. She went storming to the thug behind the bar and demanded her clothes. "He went back and brought a gun, pointed it right at my nose. 'Get what you got and get the f— out of here.' So I got the f— out of there with my little two-foot-tall cowboy and went to Denver."

But the threat wasn't over. The owner of the new club told her two men wanted to buy her a drink one night. One was silent; one was good looking. The attractive one said, "I heard you worked in Pueblo."

Vicki played dumb—or smart. "Pueblo? Where's that."

This went on for several nights. Vicki continued to act clueless. The last night, the guy said, "'You're OK, Vicki. We'll leave you alone.' To this day, I don't know what the heck was going on. Pueblo is where government printing is done. Anyway ... I hope he doesn't see this."

CHAPTER THIRTY-NINE

Texas Justice

"Dallas in the '50s at Abe's colony club, they remember Candy Barr."
—Steven Weinstein

"I was taken, done, and that was it."
—Candy Barr (*Oui Magazine*)

While most strippers were arrested at least once in their career, police made an example out of Candy Barr.

"Candy Barr blew the top off of burlesque," Steven Weinstein said. His father Abe nurtured her career as a star stripper at his Colony Club in Dallas. Candy Barr looked like your average 1950s girl next door: petite, sweet, and voluptuous with dyed blonde hair. She was born with the decidedly unglamorous name of

Juanita Slusher in Texas. Her childhood was far from the elegant surroundings she would work in at the height of her career.

Born poor with four siblings in the tiny town of Edna, Texas (the town boasts only a 3.9-square-mile radius, mostly farmland and oak trees), her mother died when she was nine. Juanita was sexually abused when she was a young teen. She ran away from home at thirteen to Dallas, where she fell in with a crowd that forced her into prostitution, keeping her a virtual prisoner.

The young teen did whatever she had to in order to survive. The talk was she worked as a maid in a hotel by day and a prostitute at the very same place at night. She was forced into selling her body to eat and have a place to sleep. She was a kid without family, with no protection. Candy would vary her stories, playing loose with the truth and the painful memories, but it was not an easy time for her.

Married briefly at fourteen, she worked as a cocktail waitress. At sixteen, she said, she was drugged and forced to participate in a hardcore porno film called *Smart Alec* in 1951. It was graphic and seedy, involving a traveling salesman, a hotel room, and a threesome with another girl. Candy would later say because she had only seven cents in her purse at the time, she did the film. She was a kid who was broke and hungry. The shame would haunt her and stay with her forever. *Smart Alec* would become the first hugely popular stag film widely circulated and made Candy well known for her enthusiastic performance and her lush young body, measuring 38-24-35.

As a teenager, Candy met Jack Ruby through his sister. It was said he was infatuated with her. Their paths would cross again years later.

Candy's ascent in burlesque was rapid, though sadly, her decline even more so. She began her transformation by dyeing her dark hair platinum. She was flamboyant and outspoken, with a pneumatic body men went crazy for.

She worked for Abe Weinstein at his Colony Club, becoming something of a protégé and friend of the club owner. She became a popular headliner with the new name of Candy Barr because of her sweet tooth and love of candy bars. She wore a cowboy hat, boots, and six-shooter holster.

With "ties to local gangsters and Mickey Cohen," according to Steven Weinstein, Candy was caught with marijuana and sent to jail. Abe got her out. She then shot her second husband (who survived) in self-defense. Again she was lucky and got off.

But Dallas law had it in for the buxom, green-eyed temptress. She had a seedy reputation with law enforcement, who became obsessed with bringing down the popular stripper. There were unproven rumors of the many pornos she continued to star in, though they were untrue. Dallas believed it and went after her.

According to the 1986 *Texas Monthly*, the cops kept a constant surveillance on her apartment and tapped her phone. Eventually busted by a room full of cops, the five-foot-three-inch stripper (who was clearly dangerous) was caught with a small amount of marijuana in her apartment (supposedly belonging to another stripper). Candy's sweet luck had finally soured. She was sentenced to fifteen years in Huntsville State Penitentiary in 1957, although she filed an appeal. Her real crime was she was a woman who took her clothes off.

While the case dragged on, her fame grew and she continued to perform at the Sho Bar in New Orleans, Las Vegas, and Los Angeles. Mickey Cohen met her around then, fell in love, tried to protect her, and lavished her with gifts and cash. She famously slugged him in the mouth. As her appeal was about to be denied, Cohen decided to spirit her off to Mexico. For the trip, they disguised her by having her hair dyed by hairdresser Jack Sahakian, whom she promptly fell in love with. The two ended up getting married in 1959.

Finally, her appeals ran out and she was hauled off to prison, leaving a small daughter behind.

Steven Weinstein remembers accompanying his parents for a visit with Candy Barr in the pen for two hours every other Sunday. "I had to be at that time eight or nine years old. Why in the world they would take a kid?" She made art in prison that she would give to his parents. She would also begin to write poetry.

She was sprung after three years and went back to dancing. Abe rehired her. But "she was very difficult to get along with. Dad stopped putting up with her stuff."

Following a friend, she moved to Brownwood, Texas. Purportedly, Jack Ruby helped her out, if giving her two purebred dogs could be called "helping out." He thought she could breed them.

She posed nude when she was fifty years old for *Oui Magazine*, gradually fading into obscurity. She died at age seventy, in 2006, no longer the headline-making star. Steven Weinstein recalled, "She didn't age well . . ."

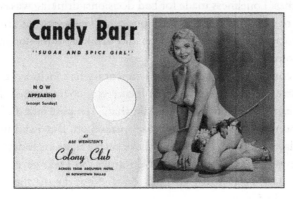

Candy Barr

CHAPTER FORTY

... And a Grind

"A gyration of the hips, clockwise or anti-clockwise, and is slightly faster than the hula-hula hip movement. It ends up with a bump."
—*Uncensored Magazine*

"To bear down on harshly; crush."
—*Webster's New World Dictionary*

In 1954, according to a Miami newspaper, stripper Pat "Amber" Halliday petitioned the court to release her from a particularly onerous contract with her manager. Her contract called for a 50/50 split, but she told the judge she rarely saw even half of the five hundred dollars she earned weekly. Amber claimed to be a reluctant stripteaser, wanting only to be a housewife. The manager also beat her. The judged released Halliday from her contract, saying she'd "sold herself down the river." As late as 1959, the supposedly reluctant stripper was still fully in the business of shedding her clothes.

There were many downsides to the business of burlesque, including divorce, loneliness, drinking, rough conditions on the road, mixing with the men in clubs. Travel kept the girls away from husbands, and kids grew up resenting mothers away for long stretches. Loneliness made for bad decisions; drinking was convenient. In every sense of the word, working in burlesque could be a torturous grind. For some.

"A career carousing around at night and drinking does not mix. And you make your choice," said Tempest.

Tempest complained that a prior documentary had included a comment by former seamstress Gussie Gross which incorrectly characterized Tempest as a fat boozer. "I can't understand why she did that," Tempest told me. "No, I didn't weigh 170 pounds. I didn't have my nose worked on. But I did use a quart of scotch every day. I sat in it! That's why I have such a tight ass today!"

"I don't smoke. I don't drink. I don't do drugs. So I was never introduced to that aspect. In fact, I never saw anybody do it. Now, doesn't mean they didn't," said Alexandra the Great.

Sheila Rae was a former blonde, voluptuous stripper whom I spoke with at the reunion. She no longer looked anything like her blonde, curvaceous glossy photos. She sat quietly in her wheelchair, obviously ill (she had cancer of the bone and hip, possibly breast), one arm painfully swollen, with short, curly, thinning hair, wearing no makeup like a modest overweight grandmother. She may have looked that way, but she certainly didn't act it. She was salty and fun with a great sense of humor and a scrapbook full of memories.

"I got loaded one night and I walked—I was so drunk—the stage was way up high. The bartender caught me, or I would have broke my neck. I watched myself with the drinking after that."

Dixie Evans said, "We had big signs everywhere, 'no alcohol no alcohol,' but... they'd slip it into their pocketbooks and this one girl, I remember, she said, 'Look, when you buy a pocketbook you always have to just take a bottle and make sure... it's big enough to put a bottle in.'"

"We used to get these little 7-Up bottles filled with gin, and that would get us through the midnight show," said Maria Bradley.

Owners discouraged performers from leaving the theatre between shows. Betty Rowland said, "They didn't want you to go out, because if you went out to a restaurant or go out maybe for a little cocktail or something, you might not come back for the midnight show."

Lorraine Lee recalled a time in Cleveland after the performers went to dinner and returned for another show. Lorraine was onstage with her husband, Dick, and they were doing a scene. "We were out for a seven-minute bit—for forty-five minutes," she said. They were ad-libbing, waiting for the next stripper to come on.

"Some guy in the audience had a cough," Lorraine noticed. To eat up time, Lorraine said, "Wait a minute, I'll get you cough drops." She went back to her dressing room and got some lozenges. Finally Lorraine found out that "the feature was drunk and they were walking her around, trying to sober her up." One time, a clearly tipsy Maria Bradley stumbled onstage and the stage manager came back and asked her what the problem was. Maria blamed it on her shoes.

"Mom dragged someone off the stage one night," recalled Dee Ann Johnston. The dancer was clearly drunk. "They didn't put up with that."

Alan Alda related how many of the comics would be drunk and get into fights. Rags Ragland got in a bar fight, protecting a dancer, and got hit over the head with a bottle, then went back and did the show.

The bar next to the Follies in Los Angeles saw a lot of Gus Schilling, a top banana who would drink their between shows.

Gaby Olah was just one of many strippers who developed a dependency on alcohol. Gaby danced under the name Terry Mixon. Her father was a dancer and her mother and stepfather were both aerialists in the circus. Gaby was born in 1927.

By 1943, her parents had settled in Boston. Gaby and her mother, whose stage name was Madeline Mixon, went to the Old Howard to look for work as dancers. Her mother was by then forty-five or forty-six. Gaby had seen shows at the Old Howard where there was "nothing offensive. Girls had more on than at the beach today." Her mother procured them both jobs, saying they were the Mixon *sisters*. They worked with Lily Ann Rose's mother, Margie LaMont, and Georgia Sothern. Eventually they told management they were mother and daughter. The mother lied and said Gaby was fifteen, even though she was eighteen. Terry remembered working with Rose La Rose, who was "nice to work with." Rose "held the audience in palm of her hand."

The old burlesque training was tough and the performers more so. Gaby contracted polio and was in the hospital in isolation. When she got out, she returned to the Old Howard. "I was dragging my right foot badly," she said.

The stage manager told her, "You're going back in the line."

She responded, "You're crazy; I can't dance."

The manager repeated, "I'll put you in the back of the line." He set up a dressing room right offstage so she wouldn't have to use the stairs.

"After a week he had me go up and back down the stairs." He had learned it would strengthen her leg. And it did. "You can't tell today, only if I get very tired," she said of her weak leg.

In 1948, Gaby had a child and was growing tired of four shows a day's worth of stripping and chorus girls. Once the baby was born, her husband asked her to stop working.

"I had a drinking problem," Terry said. She was trying to quit, but had "no control of it. I blamed burlesque, because of traveling, without my mom or anyone on the road, no husband," she said. She was lonely. "And where do you go at 11:30 at night when you don't know anyone?"

Well, as we have learned, there is always a convenient bar next to the burlesque theatre.

"I didn't know it was a disease. . . . [I had] bad drinking times," she said. Comedians Mike Sachs and Irving Benson would pour her on and off trains. However, "I could do a scene—even in a blackout."

She joined a circus and became "a drunken aerialist."

She had an epiphany about her drinking at a show in Toledo. "I climbed up rope thirty feet in the air. . . . I felt if I let go, I could fly. I realized I was insane and drinking had gotten to me."

She decided to do something. She went to rehab and AA and detoxed in 1965 or '66. After one relapse, she had her last drink in 1971. Sober, she married again. Together the couple raised seven kids. She realized with that responsibility, she couldn't "afford to drink."

One of the children was a "retarded boy," she said. She grew comfortable with his disability as it meant she'd never have to be alone. Her marriage had started out as a "business deal." He needed a mother for his children and she needed a father for hers. Eventually, she "fell in love with that man, [even though it was] selfish reasons why I married him."

Surprisingly, even with the number of performers who liked to drink, there were few accidents on stage. Still, smart performers would check the stage, especially in an unfamiliar theatre, before going on. If they had time.

"[Stages] are all different," Tee Tee Red explained. There would always be "something wrong with them" somewhere. She tried making a habit of checking out the stage prior to her shows. It wasn't always possible. One night, she caught the heel of shoe in a hole as she was doing a spin. She was thrown up in the air and "landed between the whiskey bottles. It was a stage with a runway and it ballooned in the middle and I flew out upside down, bottles along the stage. Didn't get scratched up. Bruises. Back up on stage and started all over again; the show must go on. Audience laughing, they thought it part of act."

On another stage with no time prior to the show, Tee Tee Red (who performed acrobatics) was doing walkovers. The stage had a slant, which she didn't notice until the momentum of the raked stage caused her to go over the stage and into the audience. She managed to land on her feet, hopped back up onstage, and continued dancing.

Sequin was all too familiar with accidents on stage. "I had a big giant hammock that screwed into the stage floor and I would swing on it, actually swing on it. And it was kind of a nice thing. One time it broke. It just collapsed right down on the floor. I didn't fall too far, but my dignity was ruffled a bit."

One time in Canada, Betty Rowland was working and a there was a substitute man who came in to take care of the theatre floor with linseed oil. She "fell three times. Went from one powder box to another." The management thought she "couldn't dance because she spent her time on the floor, falling."

"One time as a chorus girl, I was on a swing," Joan Arline recalled. "I slid off and landed in the audience. Had to get up, brush myself off. So embarrassing." There were also accidents of a more serious nature. Once in Montreal, a fire escape, or an inner staircase, collapsed and killed several audience members during a packed Lili St. Cyr show. Supposedly, the owners, not wanting to disturb their star, kept the news from her and she didn't find out about it until much later.

In Philadelphia, Sequin set off the smoke alarms. She had black powder and a pan and her boyfriend wanted a flash before she came on. She would dance around a fire. "He must have used too much black powder" because during the Ravel music, "it got very smoky," she said. The fire department was called.

Whether on or offstage, the girls faced problems in the real world just like everyone else. Sally Rand, for example, was robbed in her dressing room in 1957. Since the strippers were typically paid in cash, the robber was able to get away with quite a bit.

There were also occasionally issues with the audience members. Most audiences were respectful, but every now and then an odd incident occurred.

Joan Arline said she was once performing and at "ringside was a drunk woman, whispering louder and louder things like 'whore' and 'slut.' People around her were 'shhhing.' I stopped my act and said, 'You know, Madame, it's women like you that make men go with me.' She left."

Joan, like many of the strippers, could take care of herself. Her act, her time under the violet spotlight, was precious and she didn't want anything ruining it.

Customers could and did get too close. One customer bit Sally Rand on her *derriere*. Sally screamed and the man ran out. Years later, he came up to her and told her he had done it. She swore he broke the skin.

"I consider this an act of God: I was complaining about getting out of the business," began Alexandra the Great. "Someone threw a bomb in this club. Thank God it was not a big one, but I was not having a good night before this happened. I went to Dallas and decided to change careers. The business had changed and I was no longer comfortable."

If it wasn't the customers that were raunchy, it may have been the venues. When Robert Alda was working the People's Theatre in the Bowery, both the theatre and the surrounding neighborhood were run down, with rats running freely backstage. Alda shook his head and told *Uncensored Magazine* that "the best booking I get is in a joint like this."

Sherry Britton felt the same way about the People's Theatre, where tickets were only ten cents. "[This is] the home port of the city's alcoholics. The soggy peepers staggered into my view."

Jack Ruby's Carousel Club had a reputation of being low rent, as well. And the pudgy man himself was known to have a nasty temper: violent and vitriolic. Sally Rand once worked for Ruby at one of his clubs and said, "He wasn't a nice guy." She thought he shot Oswald because he was "selfish and had nothing to lose, as he was terminally sick," her son recalled.

Ruby's club had a two-dollar cover charge, and the club was square, with dark red carpeting and black plastic booths. The stage was said to be no bigger than a boxing ring. Ruby's "dancers," it was rumored, were often hookers.

Jack Ruby's reputation as a "bad guy" with a bad temper drew a harder kind of stripper. The Carousel Club was "not a high-class place." Girls didn't like to admit they had worked there after Kennedy was shot, according to Steven Weinstein.

Ruby was jealous of Abe Weinstein and his classy joint up the street, the Colony Club. "Jack was trying to take my father's entertainers away from him. Enticing them to come work for him. It was not a couples' place. Jack Ruby loved the policemen, anything that had to do with police department. . . . He let [the policemen] know they could come in for free, and drink for free."

Kennedy was shot on a Friday afternoon. Jack Ruby went to the newspapers and placed an ad stating the Carousel Club would be closed. It "made Ruby look good. My father was a business man. It's Friday. It's the weekend. It's the night-club business. My father didn't close. We were all so distressed. Things like this happen. People still want to go out. They want to drink. They want to keep their mind out of it," said Steven Weinstein.

Well, Ruby came into the Colony "before midnight," Weinstein said. "He confronts my dad, 'you so-and-so,' cussing him out. 'You lousy no good . . . how could you be open? Our president's dead!'"

By this time, the club's bouncer, Tex, a hulking six-foot-seven-inch big guy "notices Ruby coming in, hears the argument. Abe is explaining why he's open and Ruby takes a swing. Tex stands there between and takes it in the chest. Grabs Ruby in an arm lock and moves him out of the club."

As burlesque moved into the 1940s and '50s, some seedier clubs sprung up hoping to earn some of the burlesque dollars. In some places like Calumet City, outside Chicago, where the strip clubs were rough, the girls bordered on prostitution. The clubs were difficult and grungy, and only those down on their luck worked there.

According to an article in *Billboard* in 1952, the AGVA lost jurisdiction in Cal City after a strike and things got worse for the girls. One performer claimed she had to "hustle drinks."

"I was protected from some of the harder drinking, some of the bad spirit between some of [the strippers]. Some were rough with one another. [That includes] physical violence," said Alan Alda.

"'Easy?' It wasn't easy being a stripper." Vicki O'Day said.

Accidents weren't the only challenges strippers occasionally faced onstage. The competition between strippers often led to trouble, too. Alexandra recalled one amateur night where the local girl was getting such a big hand that Alexandra, who was set to go on next, couldn't go. "I was annoyed. They just wouldn't stop clapping for her. I was supposed to come out. . . . Ego got the best of me and I told them to turn the spotlight on. I had a white robe [that was] transparent. I took everything off [except that] and I walked on stage."

The spotlight hit her in all her nudity. "And I stood there for a second. There was dead silence. Because I didn't have anything on." She walked the runway and "they went crazy. They grabbed my robe," she said. And Alexandra was pulled into the crowd.

CHAPTER FORTY-ONE

The Show Must Go On

"From the front you'd never know how old she was. Body still good.
Still good breasts. She took good care of herself."
—Al Baker Jr. on a seventy-something
Tempest Storm still stripping

"When it's time to go on, you go on."
—Alexandra the Great "48"

On the road and in the theatres, the hours were long. Week after week, month on end, performers worked, sacrificing time spent with children and families to put on a show. They were entertainers at heart and nothing kept them from getting up to perform.

If someone was flaky, and Betty Rowland said not many were, "they fell by the wayside."

I found the performers' spirits to truly be indomitable despite personal and professional setbacks. "So American, the will to keep going, despite the adversity," noted Shteir.

"How did you know about that?" Dixie Evans asked me. "I don't talk about that." The pain in Dixie's eyes even so many years later was heart-wrenching. Had anyone before me brought up the subject of the baby she gave up for adoption in 1926?

"Me? It was me that had a daughter up for adoption? Well, no, what happened was I'd signed the adoption papers in the hospital and, uh, then I quick called my girlfriend and I said, 'I'm not going through with this' and I got out of the bed and we're running down the hall and we get in the car and the police are after us. Yeah. Oh yeah. The daughter was adopted by the State Senator of Nevada. Someone from the sherriff's office came. They said, 'Don't you ever put your foot in the State of Nevada. . . . we'll frame you and put you in jail and everything. And don't ever come back.' Yeah. That scared me. I didn't play Nevada for a long time. I told a girl up there in Reno to find out her address where she lives. I was just gonna ring the doorbell and say 'Avon Lady,' you know, but my girlfriend went and talked to [my daughter], and she said, 'No, she didn't want me, so I don't want her.'"

Dixie, as strong as she was on the outside, was still clearly wounded by this decision. "I would have felt the same way as her. I didn't resent her. I'm proud she married well and all of that," she said.

"Gave me a good excuse to drink a bottle of scotch that night. . . . For years every Wednesday and Sunday, I'd wake up and pillow would be wet, tears would start and couldn't stop. You grow up, or become callous, or accept the fact," she said.

Dixie would marry boxer Harry Bridle. "Fifth-ranking contender for middle-weight championship for the world." They were married only briefly. She never had any other children.

**

Lou Costello and his wife Anne had three children, including Lou Jr., who was almost a year old when tragedy struck. Chris Costello, Lou's daughter, explained that Lou "had asked my mother to keep the baby up that night to see if he would be able to recognize his voice on the air. And my mother went out to get something for the baby's first birthday and there were people there in the home. He was put out in his playpen."

"It was an Indian summer day and he managed to loosen a slat from the play-pen, go through and then out through a courtyard into the pool. By the time my mother found him, it was too late. So they brought my father home.

"He said, 'I'm going back to do the show.'

"His sister Marie said, 'Lou, how? How can you go back?'

"'Because I promised that baby that he would hear my voice tonight and wherever God has taken my son, I want him to know he can still hear me.'"

Chris continued. "He loved children. . . . He related to children. He was relating to himself."

Lou Costello went on to perform that night, although he never would get over the loss of his son. He had a bracelet made with the baby's name on it that he always wore. It was camouflaged in his films. "He never ever took it off," Chris said. "The light went out in him."

Lou was the perfect example of a strong trend throughout the industry: Performers performed no matter what.

Beautiful, tall blonde Taffy O'Neil was no stranger to this idea. She was married and working in Los Angeles when she forced herself to focus on her career instead of the pain surrounding her.

"My son also got polio the year that I went to work, just before the vaccine. He was in the hospital for a year and I would get home at 2:30–3:00 in the morning and get up early and take him to Santa Monica from Torrance for his treatments," she said.

Taffy was reserved, blonde, blue-eyed, a nice self-effacing lady who could have been anyone's still pretty grandmother, certainly not someone who took off her clothes. Her figure when she danced had been incredible.

She would go in the pool with him. He wore a leg brace and learned to walk again. She would "nap when he could. It was a tough time, especially tough on him. Three surgeries."

Alexandra the Great also learned to perform under pressure and heartache.

"I was getting ready to perform and the owner told me I had a phone call. And they never do that," said Alexandra the Great. "It was Rose. There were rumors that she was not feeling well. And she told me the rumors weren't true. We talked forty-five minutes. She told me how much she cared about me and I asked to come to see her and she said she wanted to gain some weight.... And when I got back to Hawaii, I heard that she died. So ... sad. I wasn't ready for that."

Alexandra regretted not being able to say goodbye to her friend. "I wish I would have gone to Toledo when she told me not to. I was so upset when I heard the news, I divorced my husband. Because he said, 'Come back or I'm leaving.' I had to come back before I was ready. I would have gone to Toledo."

Dancers also learned to work through illnesses and injuries.

"You couldn't say, 'I'm sick.' You go to work no matter what," Dixie Evans said. During one of her first shows, she just so happened to get her period. "What am I gonna do? I've got to wear a big Kotex." One of the dancers gave her a tampon. She wasn't sure how to use it. "I shoved the whole cardboard up there. It hurt real bad."

"It's work," Dardy Minsky simply said. "There is nothing glamorous about show business. The perks are: You are up at 9:30 after going to bed at 3 o'clock, doing your makeup and hair to go into a cold dirty theatre. Traveling. You never know where the hell you are."

Alda said burlesque was a "training ground" and he "was proud of it." But "it was tough," he said.

Still, the strippers and comedians always rose to the occasion. Come rain or shine, they were up on that stage giving it their all.

CHAPTER FORTY-TWO

Gossip

"She tried to, um, commit suicide three times.
She got involved with someone and he was involved with some drugs.
And, I think, got Lili involved."

—Kelly DiNardo

"I heard she had her bush in rollers or something.
Did you hear that? In curlers?"

—Dixie Evans

There was a lot of conjecture about what went on with these women who took their clothes off for a living, which lead to petty gossip and malicious lies—or truths.

"We were considered second-class," said Vicki O'Day. Besides being considered prostitutes by the general public it was also assumed the burlesquers had no real talent.

"A lot of the chorus girls came into burlesque having been hookers or still were hookers or went back to that," said Alan Alda.

In my interviews, there was one name that evoked a passionate response: Rose La Rose. Whether it was gossip or a firsthand account, they had a lot to say about Rose.

"Oh, she was raunchy," said Lily Ann Rose. "Really raunchy."

"Oh, you don't dare bring up her name," Dixie Evans warned me.

Rose La Rose was known as the bad girl of Burlesque because of her gay abandon on the stage. Born in New York's Little Italy in 1919 as Rosina DePella, she was fourteen and working as a ticket taker for Minsky. According to Joan Arline, Rose was selling tickets in the booth when another stripper fell ill and Rose was pushed on stage. "She was very good," Joan said.

When she performed, "nobody got to see her," recalled Dixie Evans.

From the start, Rose liked to push the limits. She was dark-haired, heart-shaped, not busty, but beautiful and appealing. "She walked pigeon-toed," Dixie

Evans said. "But that's kinda cute." Rose would travel the circuit with her Mama Jennie. They "fought like cats and dogs," according to Terry Mixon. But if Mama Jennie wasn't on the road, Rose would call her every night.

Author Collyer called Rose a "savage undresser." It would take a full, unheard-of thirty minutes for her to finish her strip. Most stripped in less than fifteen minutes. Rose loved the spotlight and the screaming. She was small—five feet four inches—and she did a strip in reverse. "The act had her begin with no more covering than a newspaper. She folded it until it got smaller and smaller. Only then did she get into her gown."

Rose taunted her audience. "I like to hear the audience gasping," she once said.

Her popularity was undeniable. "Rose was always the biggest seller. People would wait around the block to see her. She was a magnificent performer and she had a dynamic personality. And I thought she was very funny," said Alexandra the Great "48".

"I saw Rose at sixteen with a friend in St. Louis at the Opera House. All I remember is the curtain opened and she looked lovely. She walked back and forth. She turned around and now I understand why her name was 'Bare Assy.' She was."

There was the mixed feeling that because of performers like Rose, who tested the limits of nudity, burlesque developed a bad reputation. But there were those that admired her fiery, rebellious ways, too.

"Rose was known for doing things she wasn't supposed to. She was a character. Very mischievous. She loved to laugh and get on you. She'd chase you around the theatre calling you all kinds of names."

Rose told club owner Leroy Griffith that a young Sammy Davis Jr. (three or four at the time), working the circuit with his dad and uncle as a tap dancer, would stand in the wings and watch (presumably Rose stripping). One day she went into his dressing room and nailed his dance shoes to the floor as payback.

Rose was a smart businesswoman and knew how to get a raise, as she related to Alexandra. "She was playing the Grand and she went downstairs to check the house. There was a line around the block. She didn't think her salary matched that line. She said she became very ill over that and had a problem getting out of bed. And wasn't able to get out of bed until they increased her revenue. Rose always taught me to check the house out. She'd call when I was in different cities. 'How's the house?' She negotiated my salary. I learned from her when to get sick or when to be well," Alexandra said.

Rose eventually had her own theatre, the Town Hall in Cleveland.

Rose La Rose

Friday nights, the college boys came to the show. One night Alexandra convinced Rose to join her and some college boys after the show at a party. It got so wild the two had to sneak out a bathroom window.

"There were stories of her on safari in Africa, [that] she killed a bear. She was a big, big name," according to Dixie.

"She used to like taking off her clothes," said Alan Alda. As a neophyte actor of sixteen, he performed in the play *White Cargo* with Rose. She would come onstage with a towel. "Backstage she'd be walking around chastely holding a silk cloth over her chest, you know, while she's waiting to go on, and every once in a while she'd drop it for the stagehands. She just couldn't get enough of showing herself off. So it must have been an illness she had," Alda mused. "Perhaps she had a form of 'naked-osis.'"

One former exotic told me how Rose would throw wild parties with her "flunky Tommy," who would eventually take over the Town Hall. Tommy was big—six feet five inches—and "dumb as an ox." At parties, she would "have him perform. He had a twelve-inch thing. He was the star of the show at Rose's parties."

Rose La Rose died of cancer at the very young age of fifty-nine in July 1972.

Industry gossip didn't stop with Rose's death, however. There was always plenty to go around.

Bud Abbott had epilepsy, for example. "He had it under control," but would instruct Lou if "he started to tense up, to punch him as hard as possible in the gut." And of course Lou would do it. "It would [look] like he was angry," which contributed to the rumors that the two didn't like each other, though Chris Costello insists there was no lasting rift. Bud was scared of his epilepsy and would start drinking to control it.

Alexandra said, "I met my share of people in Washington, D.C., including Gerald Ford, [who] was carried out of that club stoned."

There was another famous stripper whose name got a strong reaction during my interviews.

Margie Hart—the one that got burlesque banned from New York

"Margie Hart? Oh boy, you don't dare mention her name much. She's the one that closed New York. It was rumored that on New Year's Eve in New York at this theatre, Margie was gonna take it all off," said Dixie Evans.

"The reason LaGuardia was so vehement about shutting down striptease was because Margie Hart flashed her pubic hair or she wore a G-string with fake pubic hair on it and flashed that," said Shteir.

After Margie reportedly flashing her pubic hair, Dixie Evans remembers, "the police came in and closed the theatre down and I think they took [Margie] to jail and they all got booked." This was not exactly an infrequent occurrence, as we have learned.

Many believed that Margie alone was responsible for the ban on burlesque in New York. It wasn't just the flashing that was the problem, however; it was also the "competition." Broadway owners didn't want burlesque biting into their apple and they were looking for an excuse to close it. Of course, it just moved across the bay to New Jersey.

Sherry Britton vehemently expressed her belief that it was Margie's fault that burlesque was kicked out of New York. Sherry claimed Margie was the first to go without her G-string.

I interviewed Margie's elegant sister, Kathleen, and Margie's daughter, Morgan.

"We called her Maggie," Kathleen said, sitting in her mansion in West Palm Beach—an old Spanish home built in the 1920s on the water, with a large portrait of her former husband hanging behind her on the wall of her current husband's home.

Margaret Bridget "Margie" Cox came from a family of nine siblings. "Our family ran from a nun to a priest to a lady of burlesque." Kathleen was the youngest: "Age is something you never talk about in my family. It's on no one's tombstone. We don't do that." Maggie was somewhere in the middle. Her father was a minor executive with the Singer Sewing Company. They were an Irish Catholic family.

Maggie ran away at sixteen or seventeen to join a show in Chicago. Her father found her and dragged her back. Then, a few months later, Maggie did it again. "They let her," Kathleen Ross said. Their parents were shocked but got used to it. "Girls wear less at the beach today," she said.

Maggie changed her last name to Hart, which was her mother's maiden name. She was red-headed, five feet seven inches, and slender, with a cute upturned nose, surgically modified.

Maggie had beautiful costumes, net bras, pasties, fringy G-strings, beaded and feathered. "Made by the best." She started in the chorus, but "they plucked her out to make her a star." She was so gorgeous. And she was a big name in bur-lesque in the 1930s and '40s. She was in it for "maybe ten years."

Kathleen remembered standing backstage of her much older (by at least six-teen years) sister, catching her wardrobe. She commented there were "nice girls in burlesque" and Lili St. Cyr was "one of the nicest and prettiest."

Morton Minsky contends Margie copied Rose's act and carried a bible under her arm on stage, playing up her All-American appeal. He claims, "She always had us worried" because of the amount she showed.

Collier's magazine claimed Margie worked a mere four minutes in a ninety-minute production. Lili St. Cyr would say she worked thirty-eight minutes a day out of four shows.

"To be a feature, you had to work ten minutes," Joan Arline explained.

Margie was the first stripper to hire a press agent and invested her earnings in real estate. She had a two-floor, swanky apartment on 25 Central Park West with French antiques, and Kathleen recalled parties with the Marx Brothers and Red Buttons in attendance.

A professional, she had "zipper rehearsals" beause she was so fearful of hav-ing her disrobing snagged, said Morton Minsky. She seldom drank and didn't run around to nightclubs.

She was married several times. One husband was a comedy writer and her press agent, Seaman Block Jacobs; another had a gambling club; one "strange man who didn't last long"; and finally the "love of her life," John Ferarro, a Los Angeles councilman. "She worshiped him." They lived in a Bel Air home and entertained often.

She had a stroke in her seventies and her last few years were bad. But her spirit was strong. "You couldn't get her down," Kathleen remembers. Maggie died in 2000.

CHAPTER FORTY-THREE
Women Who Changed Burlesque

"You weren't allowed to pose with nude boobs. I wish you could."
—Blaze Starr

"Somehow this wild redhead and the running up and
down and the boobs and bumping and grinding—
somehow, it changed the course of stardom."
—Dixie Evans

Tempest Storm

TEMPEST STORM

Born Annie Blanche Banks in 1928 in rural Georgia, Tempest Storm had a typical hardscrabble childhood during the Great Depression. "I picked cotton, chopped cotton. And I said, 'Oh my God, I've got to get out of this poor environment that I'm in,'" she said.

Back-breaking work was the least of Annie's worries. "I was pulled up into the hills by five guys and raped one by one when I was fourteen." An uncle also tried to rape her. She left home early, marrying a man for twenty-four hours (it was later annulled) to get out of the house. Her stepfather was "a mean man," but her husband scared her worse and she returned home.

Determined to leave Georgia behind her, the fifteen-year-old married husband number two, a salesman, after knowing him a week. He brought her to California. The marriage lasted six months. "I was brave enough to go with him," she said. Tempest got herself a job as a car hop. After work, she'd go out for coffee with the other girls until sometimes four in the morning. One night, "I got home at 4:30 a.m. and he had come home unexpected and accused me with going with all kinds of men. I knew he had a gun. He said, 'I'm gonna kill you.' So he threw me down on the bed and he's trying to put his fist down my throat. I kicked him off me and started to run out the door, he picked up the gun and I heard it click. That was the last time I ever saw him," she said.

When I met Tempest in 2006, she was living in an immaculate, but small, apartment in Las Vegas in a terrible part of town. (When we drove up to her building, the gang members in the parking lot had what looked to be a hot stereo, freshly ripped, with wires asunder.)

Tempest had just gotten out of the hospital and was rail thin. Dixie told me she was anorexic. Tempest herself admitted she would only eat diet food. She was tall with a regal bearing. She sat ramrod straight and her thick red mane of hair flowed over her shoulders. Her makeup was flawless, her skin glowing.

Despite her starvation diet, she took pride in the fact that she took care of herself. She was warm and funny and forthright, even though her reputation had always been that of a difficult diva.

"I wanted to make something of myself," she explained. Her work ethic contributed to her reputation of being temperamental, she said. She cared deeply about her performance and her appearance.

The 1950s were ready to shed the Lili St. Cyrs with their demure, ladylike scenes, and embrace Elvis Presley and rock 'n' roll and the new breed of burlesque woman who embodied the changes happening in the country.

"When Tempest came along, it changed the course of stardom. A different style. Wild," said Dixie Evans. Tempest drove a red Cadillac convertible swathed in mink.

Her mentor, former stripper, teacher, and Follies Theatre director Lillian Hunt, gave Annie Blanche Banks her new name.

One day, Lillian declared, "We have to change your name."

"What do you have in mind?" She said, "What about Sunny Day?"

Annie replied, "I really don't feel like a Sunny Day. Gimme another one."
Lillian tried again. "How 'bout Tempest Storm?"

"I'll take it!" And that was that.

Tempest was one of the only strippers who legally changed her name to her moniker. She said she half regretted it. "I can't go anywhere," she said.

Though she co-wrote her autobiography with a former reporter, Tempest felt it didn't do her justice and wasn't entirely accurate.

Tempest was known for her "million-dollar chest," the way she tossed her long red hair on stage as she bent forward and back, knees spread, thighs strong. Her moves were often bombastic, full-throttle sex—she convulsed, she crouched, she bent, she twisted. Her act was often accompanied by simulated thunder and rain. Her measurements were rumored to be anywhere from 41DD to 48DD. Tempest herself says she is a modest 40.

"I remember paying Tempest in those days $1,800 a week, and $1,800 a week in those days was good money. She completely sold out the house and it was like, 1,400 seats," remembered Leroy Griffith.

"I just got $10,000 in San Francisco last year," Tempest said. Unfortunately, she later fell and broke her hip in Las Vegas performing on stage in 2010, truly ending her days on the stage. She possibly ties Ann Corio for the stripper who worked the longest.

Tempest said she never felt a stigma being in burlesque. She was one of the rare few who felt this way.

"You have such nudity in motion pictures; we looked like angels. I never approved of complete nudity. That took away from burlesque. It was entertaining, sensuous, sexy numbers that you did. You left something to the imagination. Now out there they want to see your tonsils. . . . I'm not judging. Everybody to their own thing."

Tempest had affairs and marriages, a personal life as turbulent as her name. She would have good publicity and troubles with the government. Like Lili St. Cyr, who was busted for not paying taxes, Tempest and her third husband, singer Herb Jeffries, were indicted on four counts of failing to file tax returns.

With Jeffries, she had a daughter, Patricia. Her daughter, whom she was reluctant to talk about, lives in Indiana and is a nurse. "She has a girl, twenty. My little granddaughter. She has autism. Tragedy. She's smart as a whip."

She was more willing to talk about her romantic life and her relationship with her parents. "I really don't know what I've been looking for in men. I think I was looking for the father that I never had. [My parents] separated before I was born. And she never had any photos of him. My brother says, 'Oh! Here's a picture of your real father.' Well, I went crazy. I walked over and said, 'Mother who is this?' She said, 'I don't know.' I said, 'You better tell me who it is. Is that my father?' 'I don't know!' I said, 'Well, I'll ask you one more time, is that my father? If you don't tell me the truth, you won't have to wait to die because I'm gonna take this pillow and smother you to death.'"

More recently, Tempest lived with a man for ten years, and when they broke up, he sold all her clothes. "Another [ex] was under the care of a psychiatrist. He was in the hospital and died," she said. His family didn't tell her.

"My choice of men has been rotten. The last one was no better. He turned around and did the same thing. Left me with nothing. We lived like millionaires in Newport Beach," she said.

A true legend, a true lady, someone who made a difference in her life, pulled herself up from horrible circumstances and was proud of what she did.

"I'm so classy, they don't know what the hell to do with me."

**

BLAZE STARR

Like Tempest Storm, Blaze was gang raped as a teenager.

The stripper's fortunes would rise and fall over a long career. Immortalized in the film *Blaze* starring Paul Newman, she has a winning attitude, a sense of humor, and strong sense of self-worth. "I look after me. Cuz I'm number one," she explained unapologetically. Blaze, too, had red hair, not quite the florescent color of Tempest's, but a dark auburn.

Born in 1932 as Fannie Belle Fleming in the coal-mining territory of West Virginia, her father died of black lung, leaving her mama with nearly a dozen children to support.

"In West Virginia," she explained, "there is a lot of spousal abuse. We'd walk through the hills two miles to get to school and kids would have their tales of 'Daddy beat mommy and he blacked both eyes, broke her ribs.'" The men would get drunk, then cry and ask for forgiveness. It taught her a valuable lesson. "I never wanted to be in a position to have someone support me. I would make my way," she said.

She explained, "Everyone was poor in those years. It was a luxury to own a cow. There were no doctors in the area; people rode horses and wagons." Her mother was a schoolteacher in a one-room school, and "every eighteen months a baby would come." Blaze had eleven siblings, one died at six months. She helped raise the others.

"I used to sing alto in church every Sunday. I was very close with my mom. She told me whatever I do, do it the very best and don't let anything stop you," she said.

Blaze quickly grew into a mature-looking teen. She was proud of her 38DDs. She sang me a song that she had written about them.

"I was working in a donut shop in Washington, D.C., and this man came in. He asked me do I sing. And I told him, 'Yeah, I sing and yodel.' Which I did. You know, I do. He said, 'Well, I need a girl for my show.' And he took me over to see his show that night. And I played some songs and sang."

Dixie Evans remembered, "He said, 'Oh, come on, you've got to go out and take something off.' And she says 'no.' So she's standing there and he said, 'Blaze, Blaze will you, will you take off something?' 'No. No.' 'Will you take it off for America?' And she said yes, and she took off her bra and the servicemen hollered."

"I wanted to be a movie star at first," Blaze said. She watched Marilyn Monroe films. Stardom of another kind was in store for the newly christened Blaze. She would become associated with the Two O'Clock Club in Baltimore. The club was located on a section known as The Block, crowded with other burlesque clubs, such as the Kit Kat, Gaiety, and the Pussycat Club (where according to author Diane Giordmaina in *Sinatra and the Moll*, Blaze bought interest in the club for an ex-boyfriend). The Two O'Clock was managed by Solly Goodman, who became Blaze's manager.

She worked the theatre during the daytime and the Two O'Clock at night. "I was sixteen. Nothing but energy. I loved every minute of it. I loved the audience going wild. I loved making my new shiny gowns. It's great if you can do something you like and earn a living."

Blaze apparently gave them something to scream about. One news article claimed she dropped her sequin G-string down to her knees and was hauled into court and fined fifty dollars.

She worked hard to be top at her profession. "She didn't like sharing the billing with me. She wanted to be the one and only Blaze," April March said.

Not only did Blaze make most of her gowns, handy with needle and thread, she was a girl who knew her tools. During her act, she "used candles on a little table. I lit them as soon as I started taking my clothes off. I would blow it out with my mouth, but it looked like my boob was doing it. I thought, *This is good. I need some fire*."

She got her own tools and cut a foot out of the back of the couch. She wanted it to appear as if her dancing made the couch catch on fire. With the help of some stage hands, she got an empty can of peaches, got a heating "thing from [an] electrical place," and rigged it with "some safety pins" to her couch, she said. She would plug it in and during her act, "smoke would come up. Soon as I smelled it, I'd have to turn it off. Sometimes [I'd] forget; [we] would have real fire. This is great, everyone's going wild, because it's unexpected. I'd done all I could do up there, wiggling around."

About men, she was sage: "Most of 'em cheat. It don't mean a thing." One husband confessed to sleeping around. He told her, "'Yes, I did. It didn't mean no more than taking a good shit.' He confessed, so we divorced. A much-married husband. He died at fifty-two from lung cancer," she said.

Her most famous affair was a long-term relationship with the wild Governor Earl Long.

Then the day came for her to quit burlesque. "I had a small heart problem. I didn't want to die on the stage practically naked. I wound up going to a hospital and they did five bypasses. And ah, doctor told me I couldn't work anymore for a couple years."

She went rock hunting and made jewelry by hand that she sold in a mall. "I went to North Carolina and hunted for rubies and emeralds. Learned to cut 'em," she said.

Blaze sold her club in 1975, traveled a bit, worked a couple gigs, and had a good income from savvy investments she had made over the years.

Blaze with Paul Newman briefly brought her back into the limelight. Since then, she remains mostly unseen, living in the hills where she was born, surrounded by family. She had a brother who was mentally and physically handicapped that she took care of after their mother died. She was happy

Blaze and Paul Newman on the set of the movie *Blaze*

watching her favorite TV show *MacGyver* and reading. "I haven't been able to do that for years," she said.

GYPSY

The most common name associated with burlesque is that of the mythical character Gypsy Rose Lee, a larger-than-life invention. She wrote her memoir playing fast and loose with the truth to be remembered as she wanted to be remembered. And the myth has stuck.

Still, her story is fascinating. Gypsy is remembered for changing burlesque, for bringing it to society, for showing the world strippers could be smart, could "talk," and could remove a little clothing, too. Her name still blazes above marquees across the country, years after her death, memorialized in the musical *Gypsy*. While it is largely forgotten or overlooked, the play is officially billed as *Gypsy: A Musical Fable*. And with good reason.

Gypsy was born in 1911, to a mother who often lied about her age. Mama Rose Hovick was an overbearing mother who made Gypsy give up her birth name of "Ellen June" to her prettier sister born two years later. The beloved June and the renamed Rose Louise toured vaudeville, where June easily outshone her darker, awkward sister. June was quickly making gobs of money, but life with Mama wasn't easy, and at thirteen she ran away. It was left to Rose Louise to make mama proud and bring home the bacon.

Mimi Reed worked with Gypsy at Minsky's on 42nd Street. "She was there starting, and her mother was the one that made her big. She wouldn't let her associate with anyone unless they could further her career."

Rose found that she could excel in burlesque by playing up the "tease" in the strip, using humor and her intelligence to make her act unique. She had found her calling. Now she would be calling the shots with Mama Rose.

She was rail thin, unlike the voluptuous strippers she employed in her act. She had bearing and grace and command of her audience and smoked heavily. When asked about Gypsy, who competed for crowds at the same time as his beloved Ann Corio, Mike Iannucci laughed and said, "She's gone now so she can't come after me," before saying, "She wasn't attractive, but she was a talker." She had a witty banter with the audience as she peeled garter, hat, gloves.

She elevated the striptease with her sophisticated repartee. She tried Hollywood, where she would shoot several pictures under the name Louise Hovick because of her striptease reputation. She did not excel at the movies and returned to burlesque.

"Gypsy was really the only one who went from burlesque into a Broadway show, and was successful," said Betty Rowland. "She could talk and that was something the rest of us didn't do."

She was the Queen of the Strippers. She was the one who garnered riches and sophisticates as fans, and the one who hobnobbed with Carson McCullers, Christopher Isherwood, and artist Max Ernst. At the pinnacle of her career in burlesque, she was referred to as "The Gyp" by her many and varied friends.

She was the stripper who made good with a gimmick. In her biography, her friend, producer Leonard Spigelgass, wrote, "Gypsy Rose Lee had no major talents. And I'm quoting her." That didn't mean she didn't have the brains and the drive to parlay taking off her clothes in crappy theatres across America into a television talk show, several books, plays, and a memoir that would be turned into a perennial Broadway musical.

She worked with boyfriend and producer Mike Todd on *Streets of Paris* and *Star and Garter* on Broadway, which many other burlesque acts joined. According to Collyer, Todd didn't have many nice things to say about his former love. When Gypsy and her Chihuahua passed him one day, he was overheard saying, "There goes the two greatest no-talent queens in the show business."

Married three times, Gypsy had a son, Erik, with director Otto Preminger, but refused to tell Erik his father's identity until he was in his twenties, claiming it wasn't any of his business who she slept with. She traveled with Erik, who she kept in the shadow of her legend, and had him help her with her act.

Oftentimes billed as "America's Leading Literary Figure," Gypsy made $100,000 with her Royal American Beauties on the circus tour. She did a reverse strip, dressing the lovely ladies. It was 1949 and she was thirty-eight years old.

The show was enormously successful. She claimed to love traveling in her own trailer and working eight to fifteen shows a day for a magnificent sum of $10,000 a week. Occasionally she would toss her fishing pole over her shoulder and go out and catch dinner.

Gypsy lived in a grand twenty-six room townhome on the Upper East Side (East 63rd—it still stands today) in Manhattan and had an elaborately decorated home in Beverly Hills.

There was another side to Gypsy—one that those behind the scenes were privy to.

"She was an impossible woman," Dardy Minsky said.

Gypsy was on the stage in New Orleans doing her number when Erik's nurse came to Harold Minsky and told him "the boy had swallowed a pin." Without hesitating, Harold threw the boy in a cab and off they went to a local hospital. Fortunately the pin hadn't gone very far down his throat and it was removed. The boy was fine and they returned to the theatre. "And when Gypsy heard that [Harold] didn't stop [her number] to go get her off stage . . . she was so furious, she walked out of the theatre. And never came back."

"She was very ungrateful," Dardy said. "She had no talent. She couldn't sing, she couldn't dance. She had a very bad body. She was smart as a whip. Physically—nothing going for her."

"Ann was way above her as far as earning money and as far as pleasing the people. Gypsy had a way about her," Mike admitted. "She made a heck of a living."

Gypsy's winning act was "silly, playful, and corny," Rachel Shteir explained. But it was also a glamorous one. "She dressed up and then withheld from them, leaving them wanting more than they saw or could ever have seen. Gypsy used a line Ann Corio teased with to close her act. "I can't take that off, I'd catch cold," she'd say. Lili St. Cyr would also use a version of this parting line before dancing off stage, leaving the crowds hollering.

In 1962, Janet Sovey was a former Property Mistress of the North Shore Music Theatre in Massachusetts. The company was producing the play *Mame*. Gypsy Rose Lee sailed into town to star in the title role. "We eagerly awaited the arrival of Gypsy Rose Lee. The first day of rehearsal, this woman shlogs onto the lot, terrible saggy old housedress with clearly no underwear. Somebody said, 'That's Gypsy Rose Lee,'" Janet said.

Erik would often speak of how his mother wore old, stained clothes, spilled with either coffee or tea and cigarette ash, when she traveled.

Morton Minsky recalls her downing glasses of brandy.

"Once the pressure was on in rehearsal, her whole attitude changed greatly and I think she was panicked," Janet remembered. "She would refer to herself in the third person. She always talked about herself as 'Gypsy.' She had that strange overbite. And she'd talk about 'Oh Gypsy didn't mean that.' And every other word was 'Jesus Christ God all fucking mighty.' It seemed to have been important to her to appear very legitimate even though she'd been a big burlesque star. It was my impression that most nights she was drinking. One of the actors in the cast kinda looked out for her and it was sad."

Did her name bring people to the theatre? "The name did bring people. I don't know if they were thrilled when they saw her. She wasn't up to the material," Janet said. "Backstage during the fast changes, Gypsy would say loud enough for audience to hear, 'Jesus Christ, don't look at Gypsy. Gypsy's naked.' Then everyone would turn around to see what the commotion was instead of watching the scene."

It was a shame that as big of a star as Gypsy was, she was unable to peel off the stigma of burlesque. Perhaps she still felt herself in the shadow of her sister Baby Jane, never able to live up to Mama Rose's impossible standards, no matter how much success she achieved.

Gypsy died of lung cancer in 1970. The world of popular burlesque owes much to her for the barriers she broke, the society she forced to embrace her, for her having lived a truly original life. Gypsy enjoyed her fame and the luxury it brought and she will forever be remembered fondly as "The Gyp."

CHAPTER FORTY-FOUR
A Leap of Faith

"Try to get yourself arrested as much as possible."
—Faith Bacon on how to get publicity

"I would like to come to Harvard."
—Faith Bacon (*The Harvard Crimson*)

The original fan dancer Faith Bacon

Faith Bacon was heralded as "the world's most beautiful" woman. She claimed to be the originator of the fan dance. A contemporary and rival of the world-famous Sally Rand, Bacon danced at the 1933 Chicago's Century of Progress at the same time as Sally.

While Rand garnered all the headlines, Bacon, a former Earl Carroll Vanities dancer, went on to enjoy her own decade of outrageous success, which then sputtered to an end all too soon.

Faith was an inspiration for dozens of dancers, including Lili St. Cyr, who saw her dance at the Orpheum Theatre in Los Angeles. Lili would create a "Bird of Paradise" act based on a bird act Faith had performed. Faith also danced à l'après-midi d'un faune (Prelude to the Afternoon of a Fawn). Lili would borrow that, also.

Faith was a sensation and earned great sums, performing to standing-room-only crowds. As she aged, the work dried up and she became addicted to drugs. She resorted to performing in low-class dives as the work became increasingly hard to come by. By all accounts, she was a troubled woman.

On the night of September 26,1956, Faith, a gorgeous blonde dancer of extraordinary talents, threw herself out of the window of the Alan Hotel in Chicago as her horrified roommate—some say lover—looked on. She died at Grant Hospital of a fractured skull and perforated lungs. It was not an easy end to a life that hadn't been lived easily.

She was born Faith Yvonne Bacon in Los Angeles on July 19, 1909, to Frank and Charmione Bacon. Charmione, or "Cherie" as she called herself, was a frustrated dancer who, at seventeen, gave birth to a pretty little daughter that she saw as her last grasp at fame. Little is known about Faith's mother except that she was exceptionally pushy when it came to signing Faith up for dance lessons and pushing her into a career that she had hoped for herself.

Soon divorcing Frank, Cherie took on managing Faith's career in the theatres, posing as her sister. An acquaintance of Faith's claimed Cherie kept Faith on sleeping pills and would seduce Faith's wealthy suitors. Faith, according to this acquaintance, indulged in numerous affairs with women as well as men. Cherie held onto Faith's salary, doling out just what she needed and no more.

Faith would grow into a pert, blond Clara Bow-lookalike with fragile, doe eyes and heart-shaped lips and a lithe body. She got herself a job as a chorus girl in "Earl Carroll's Vanities of 1930." Earl Carroll was a producer and director of lavish musicals starring beautiful nudes. Faith quickly found herself arrested, however, for lewd and indecent behavior. Instead of posing nude and being still, which was legal, it had been Faith's idea to be motionless when nude, but to move when she was covered by large ostrich feathers. It got them all arrested. Hauled into court with the other lovelies from the show, Faith proclaimed her act to be art. She showed up in court wearing a fur and cloche hat.

An early Earl Carroll program billed Faith as the "creator of the fan dance." This predates Sally Rand's fan dance at the 1933 Chicago World's Fair.

Throughout the 1930s Faith worked high-class joints at Chicago's Colosimo's Club, the Empire, and the Haymarket. She also worked in New York and the Florentine Gardens in Los Angeles (again for Earl Carroll), always billing herself as the "originator of the fan dance." She did her "Bird of Paradise" dance and was once on a bill with a trained seal. After her initial arrest, her lovely picture continued to grace newspapers.

In 1933, a car struck her, breaking her ribs. In 1934, she would again be arrested at the Hawaiian Gardens for an indecent performance of "Girly Show" and rushed to the hospital for an appendectomy.

Sometime in the late 1930s, she met a wealthy businessman, Ed Hanley, when she was dancing in Tucson, Arizona. Faith was in the company of her "sister" Cherie. Cherie wanted the handsome Ed for herself. But Ed was taken with Faith. (Later Ed would refuse to believe Cherie was his girlfriend's mother when confronted with the truth.) Eventually Cherie departed for places unknown. She would marry a refrigerator salesman and die in Denver. It appears she had little, if any, contact with Faith in subsequent years. She certainly wasn't there when Faith, near the end of her life, returned to her hometown in Pennsylvania for help.

T. E. Hanley was born in Bradford, Pennsylvania, in 1893 to a wealthy family. A bit of an eccentric, he amassed a huge collection of art. He had a socialite wife who divorced him and he would eventually marry Tullah Innes, a Hungarian exotic dancer whose paths crossed with Faith's often, first in San Francisco in a vaudeville theatre. Tullah describes Faith as timid and shy. According to Tullah, Faith was a lesbian out of necessity, as her mother kept her from the men. However, Faith did have a long affair with Hanley that must have been deep and intense enough for him to feel obligated to help her in her final days.

By 1935, newspapers boasted she was earning as much as five hundred dollars a week, but in 1936, Faith fell through a glass-topped, specially made drum during her "Bird of Paradise" dance. She suffered severe cuts on her legs and was taken to the hospital for twenty-six stitches in both legs. She attempted to sue the club for $100,000 and eventually received a mere $5,000. She claimed to have a long recovery. Faith was hurting, and not just physically.

It made Faith furious that Sally Rand continued to be billed as the originator of the Fan Dance. She was getting all the attention while stealing Faith's creation. There is much evidence on Faith's behalf, but Sally Rand had become synonymous with fan dancing. Faith's title had been stolen. And this, perhaps more than anything, led to Faith's downfall.

In 1938, Faith filed a suit against Sally Rand for $375,000, claiming when she did the fan dance in 1930, she allowed Sally to hold her ostrich fans backstage. And the turncoat stole the act. Faith claimed Sally's imitation dance hurt her reputation as an artist. Faith would lose this suit and further tarnish her reputation.

In 1939, she was once again arrested. This time for wearing a skimpy white bathing suit, or leotard, and walking a doe on a rhinestone leash down Park Avenue as an advertisement for her World's Fair appearance. Newspapers called her "publicity hungry."

One reviewer said she "parades through a moth-eaten fan dance that has lost its punch long ago." Faith was spiraling.

A despondent Faith increasingly relied on barbiturates and had frequent affairs with women. She became obsessed with her looks as she saw herself aging. She tried to keep her age a secret, often claiming to be ten years younger than her actual age. She took whatever work she could in increasingly sleazy clubs, carnivals, and even Tijuana nightclubs. Club owners became reluctant to book her because she was unreliable and often out of it, either from drugs or drink.

In 1948, a fragile Faith checked herself into a sanitarium for rest after a "humiliating" tour on a carnival. She told reporters that the owner of the carnival wanted to push her out of the dance troupe and threw tacks across the stage before she danced.

The next ten years were no better.

In 1952, she claimed to have teamed up with singer Jimmy Farrell to market a line of beauty products. (Sometimes billed as "the new Danny Thomas," he was a minor star in the 1930s. Farrell was most remembered for singing with the Johnny Green Orchestra.) Also in 1952, she visited her then- married millionaire beau Ed Hanley at his home in Bradford, Pennsylvania. The walls in his home were hung with Picassos, Cezannes, Goyas, and on and on. Ed was married to Tullah, a wild woman who said "sex is my hobby." Tullah would write a scandalous biography about her varied and prolific sex life.

Faith arrived at the Hanleys' via bus. Tullah gave her some clothes, remembering that Faith couldn't even cover her last hotel bill. Faith told them she'd just been sprung from a hospital stay of several months due to a nervous breakdown. She was very thin, slept late, and she was still "gobbling" pills. Ed and Faith probably resumed their affair behind the watchful eye of Tullah. Later, Tullah found ardent love letters from Faith in her husband's desk. After ten days, the couple shipped the drugged Faith back to Buffalo where she had another gig.

Faith's bad luck continued along with her drug problem. She was seen in the winter snow wearing sandals. Work was ever harder to come by.

In 1954, Faith borrowed money and opened a ballet school in Hammond, Indiana. She was found unconscious on the dance floor after taking too many sleeping pills.

Somewhere along the way, she married Sanford Hunt Dickinson, a musical consultant, but they spent years estranged and at her funeral, he was nowhere to be found. Three weeks prior to her death, she returned to Erie looking for a job or solace from whatever family remained there. Perhaps she stopped in Bradford and saw Ed Hanley.

Returning to Chicago, Faith sought work, anywhere, but no one wanted her. She walked to the *Daily News* for a little empathy. The reporter chronicled that Faith was so down on her luck, she had nothing left but her name. And it was a name no one cared about.

Faith and a new roommate—or lesbian lover, according to Tullah—forty-year-old grocery clerk Ruth Bishop shared a dingy room sans bathroom at the Alan Hotel.

On the day of Faith's suicide, Ruth would later tell police the two had been arguing for close to six hours about whether Faith should return to Erie. Ruth claimed Faith received an allowance from her family and would have to return if she wanted more money. That was probably pure fiction, as her family never came forward after her death. The only money she likely received was from Ed Hanley. Faith was all alone and surely felt it.

As Ruth followed the former "World's Most Beautiful Girl" around the room, the platinum blonde suddenly flung herself through the window. Ruth reached for her, but felt Faith's dress tear and her friend went sailing down. To Ruth's horror, the former fan dancer fell for two and a half stories, landing on the roof of a saloon.

It is most certainly true that Faith was the original fan dancer. Author and burlesque expert Sobel mentions Faith covering her nakedness with a fan as early as 1931. Her nudity had been elegant, her dance artistic. But that wasn't enough and she fell to petty grievances and lawsuits, ruining her reputation even as she sought to regain it.

When neither family nor husband came forward, the AGVA claimed Faith's broken body. She was buried in Wunder's Cemetery in Chicago. Ruth Bishop ordered a wood box for five dollars, but the subsequent bill was returned as "address unknown." Ruth had vanished without paying for Faith's final resting place. The indignities never stopped.

Faith Bacon's grave remained without a marker until 1958, when Ed Hanley, after being informed by Faith's former secretary Margie that his lover had killed herself, paid fifty dollars for a simple marker. Faith's tender-hearted lover also paid for seasonal flowers to be place on her grave for the next ten years and for the perpetual care of her final destination. But when Hanley died in 1969, the flowers stopped. He left a note for the cemetery, saying he was a "good friend of Faith's" and indeed he was. He was, perhaps, her only one.

CHAPTER FORTY-FIVE
Bye-Bye Burlesque

"How tough it must have been to have an industry die out on you like that."
—Walt Collins

"A lot of friends didn't make it once they got out."
—Renny von Muchow

On stage

With owners demanding it and audiences expecting it, strippers began to flash more than they had in previous years.

"Girls were beginning to get raunchy and get props to use . . . like poles. They'd back up to poles and rub up and down, or swing on the pole. I don't think that's sexy," said Kitty West. "They would wear less and less. They wouldn't come out in a gorgeous gown and disrobe gracefully. They started coming out with nothing hardly and ending with less. The further it went, I just gave it up. I didn't want any part of that."

There became more of a "divide between high-class striptease and really grungy, kinda going towards what we think of now as modern porn," explained Rachel Shteir. There was no middle ground. "It was no longer connected to vaudeville. It was dead."

More and more dancers decided to hang up their rhinestone G-strings and get out.

Tee Tee Red said, "I was forty-nine and I was dancing in a go-go place. By then, nightclubs were all gone. The first place I worked, in Miami, none of the girls had wardrobe, didn't know how to wear wardrobe, didn't know how to take it off." Because the size of the stages had shrunk in clubs, there were no longer big production numbers or long lines of chorus girls. Tee Tee couldn't wear big gowns. "I went up in a negligee. I says, 'Well I'm turning fifty; it's time for me to retire.'"

Burlesque was no longer what it had been when it started with the British Blondes. The tease was dropped, the humor whittled down to a few tired old comedians just trying to get by in the clubs.

In New York and other large cities, strippers were hired for retirement parties and conventions. "Every hour, on the hour you can work," said Dixie Evans. "They rent a hall at [the] Waldorf" and hired strippers. Mara Gaye, Sherry Britton, they all worked them.

Sherry Britton working at a private party

The new breed of stripper was more nasty than naughty. By the tail end of the 1950s, burlesque was no longer.

Our habits had changed, too. For many boys, what had been a rite of passage, sneaking into theatres to experience their first glimpse of naked flesh, was quickly replaced with X-rated films and gentlemen's strip clubs, where there was little to take off. It was full-throttle nudity.

Playboy Magazine, founded in 1953, became widely available, and that became many young men's first experience with naked women—not the burlesque theatre.

Even the appearance of the bikini had an impact on strippers, or more accurately, their audience. There was no need to pay to see a dancer in panties when one could see less on a beach.

Making its debut in 1946, the bikini was invented by a French engineer, Louis Réard and was modeled for the first time by a nude dancer from the Casino de Paris. In a few years, the bikini was commonplace, allowing women to showcase more of their bodies than ever before and making burlesque moot.

Then in 1948, there was this little invention called television that kept Americans at home for the first time. Television was a boon for the burlesque comedians, giving their old routines new life in front of thousands.

When Milton Berle's show first aired in 1948, there were only 500,000 sets in America. More than half of American households owned a television in 1954. A decade later, those little boxes with the "wiggly lines" were in 90 percent of households.

With a surplus of money after WWII, American families purchased even more televisions. It was on everyone's must-have list. Sales skyrocketed. Television took a huge bite out of the burlesque show.

"You couldn't withstand television," Dixie Evans lamented.

Berle's show was a huge hit. So influential was Uncle Miltie that it was said the nation stopped on Tuesday evenings when his show aired. This wasn't good for the theatre or nightclub business.

"People stayed at home," Dixie Evans recalled sadly. "And looked at these little wiggly lines." The theatres tried to lure the paying customers in with promises of air conditioning. "Big signs outside the theatre said 'air conditioning,'" recalled Dixie. Oftentimes the strippers would show up and demand to know why "air conditioning" was on the banners and not their names. "But it didn't work. People stayed home. Television put burlesque out of business."

Dixie and the other girls would watch TV in the Chinese restaurants between shows. One time a comic told her, "Don't you know that's gonna put you out of business?"

While the comedians fared OK, the strippers had a choice to either remove more or call it quits. Their skills as strippers didn't translate into any other viable form of entertainment. The exotics weren't actresses.

"Strippers really don't have any talent. They have a nice body and that's about it," quipped Dardy Minsky. "And will travel."

I found the performers I interviewed to be resilient. They survived the burlesque stigma throughout the years, only to have the industry fade away with nowhere else in show business for them to work.

"The audience changed," Betty Rowland remarked. There would be maybe five or six people in a show. The "presentation [was] not there. Neither was the audience." They weren't showing up.

"The unions closed a lot of the theatres because they couldn't keep up with the salaries," said Val Valentine.

In the beginning of burlesque, "stripping hadn't been the big thing. But it got to be that way because of competition," explained Betty Rowland. One club or theatre would have three strippers, the club across the street would have four, even if they were "less talented." It became quantity over quality.

"It was the girls that were the stars. It should have been the comics," said Joan Arline.

"There was no Stinky and Shorty," Al Baker, Jr. lamented, referencing two popular comics. "These guys just aren't around."

"The comedians lost their power and it was a strip show," Mike Iannucci told me. He complained of the strippers of the 1950s and '60s being the "anything goes era." They were all flashing. "She had a way, no matter what she wore, she would be nude by the time the thing was over. Blaze Starr, that's what killed burlesque originally. She was a latter-day stripper. When you give someone an inch, they take your arm; that's how some of the strippers were."

Younger dancers were competition for the stars who'd been around for decades. "I was hearing about age—*how old are you?* would be the first question," remembers Tee Tee Red.

"I wanted to go out while I was on top," Kitty West said. "I didn't want to say, 'Well, gee look at that old woman up here dancing.' I didn't want that."

Boston was Vicki O'Day's last strip. "I wanted to quit before people made fun of me. It was so rough and so awful and I was an alcoholic. I was just going downhill and that was my swan song. They loved me because I brought in a lot of booze. But I was falling apart." Eventually Vicki got sober on her own "without a program. There is a strength there."

Marilyn Monroe died in June of 1962, killing Dixie's career as the Marilyn Monroe of Burlesque. "I fell to pieces," she said. Her husband told her, "'Dixie,

Marilyn's dead.' I leaped up and hit him. 'I hate you. I hate you.' I went to the couch and popped a can of beer. Three solid days that TV rolled. I didn't know what to do," she said. She told her husband she was going to send flowers. She was friends with Walter Cronkite, so she called the newscaster. He found out where Dixie could send the flowers. "A white heart with a red rose in the center. Flowers got there. I cried and cried. I didn't cry for my lost career. I cried because Marilyn was gone forever."

Dixie was booked in a club in Canada. She "got all made up" as Marilyn and walked into the club. A "woman screamed and dropped her drink. I had to do the act anyway. After that booking, I fell apart."

In 1968, the City Council in Toledo banned burlesque. Rose La Rose was forced to close The Esquire, losing thousands of dollars of weekly income and displacing many.

Alexandra the Great worked until she was forty-eight. "I lost a lot of interest when Rose died. Rose guided and directed me. In those days, you needed an act, you need costuming, you needed professional photographs, and in some ways you needed a sponsor. You couldn't just walk in off the street. Rose taught me the things I needed to know to be a feature," she said. And so much had changed. "It was the end of burlesque. When it finally did change, it had no appeal to me anymore."

Candy Cotton regretted that "it couldn't have lasted longer. It was a very close knit group of people and . . . you always felt welcomed. I never felt alone and I always liked that."

Chorus girls backstage

Alexandra said, "I miss the music and costumes. You have to know when it's time to leave. And I think I left at the right time."

"I thought I was gonna stay beautiful forever. I didn't think I was ever gonna grow old. When you're in your twenties, you know, what the heck do you know? You think, 'Oh, this gravy train's gonna run forever,'" remembers April March.

By the 1960s, a "burlesque" show was stripped of chorus girls minus the production numbers, divested of novelty acts, and missing live musicians. The emcees were gone, song and dance acts banished, and specialty dancers were dropped.

"Striptease didn't really survive in the '60s because of porn, but also because of the women's movement," said Rachel Shteir.

After the bikini, *Playboy Magazine*, and television came the pornography—which put the final nail in the striptease coffin.

Blaze Starr remembers, "You were on the stage during your act and it was a huge club. And over all the way across the building on the wall was hardcore porn."

"Porno came in and hurt burlesque. A lot of girls didn't know what to do, where to go. Burlesque was in a gray area," said Dixie Evans. "A lot had no place to go. They'd get a job at Walmart and cry, 'It's all over.'" Most missed the crowds and the applause. They were unprepared for "normal" life. The glamour and glitz was gone.

Val Valentine said, "I miss my gypsy life. I'm restless and can't seem to focus on where I'm at now; it's boring."

There was adrenaline that went along with the performing and traveling despite how difficult it might be.

Sherry Britton thought other strippers "glorified it. Their important moment of fame, where thank goodness I had gone on. I was the only one that ever spoke against burlesque."

April March said to herself, "I think I'm gonna get out of nightclubs." She felt the theatres were "safer" than the clubs. "Nightclubs had turned. Girls had to drink, sit with people, and this and that. The misconception was not-talented people. And prostitutes."

Dee Ann Johnston noticed that "years ago [the girls were] experienced. Towards the end, if you're walking and breathing, you're in."

As more burlesque theatres closed, short films of the women's performances began to travel in lieu of the large casts, taking the place of live performances often in tents in carnivals. These cheap-to-make films replaced a burlesque show, the producers thinking, "We'll get into film" and film 'em and take those around," said Betty Rowland.

Of these early "stag films," most of the performers didn't even know where they were shown. They just filmed a couple, made a few dollars (unless you were Lili St. Cyr, who made $5,000 for the day's work). "These films, along with postcards, were sold in the 1930s as 16mm home projection movies, or were projected in the back rooms of adult bookstores. In the 1940s, production of such under-three-minute films increased to be shown on panorama visual jukeboxes in a continuous loop of four to eight short-short strip acts," said Rachel Shteir.

In the early '50s, nudie-cutie burlesque films were shown between live acts, eventually supplanting the performers by the late '50s. The films were shown individually or in groups on a looped reel in adult magazine shops and movie houses and carnival tents, or sold as 8mm and 16mm films for stag parties and home viewing.

Lili St. Cyr would perform two routines in the 1960s for Robert Altman on the short-lived Scopitone, the precursor to MTV and music videos. The Scopitone was a jukebox video.

Why didn't the women, as beautiful as any movie star, get snapped up by Hollywood? Dixie Evans explained that when the studios put up the money and asked who was the star and were then told it was a burlesque performer, "studios assumed they had a bad reputation." They were good enough for B pictures, but "major films? No."

Tee Tee Red complained, "Go-go killed burlesque. Girls were coming out with nothing and dancing like monkeys on a pole."

Rita Grable relates. "It started to deteriorate when I left burlesque. In the late '50s, by the '60s over, started to get sleazy. It wasn't like it was."

"It starting getting more difficult . . . I didn't want to work anymore." Terry Mixon said the strippers were "working too strong for me. A lot of girls quit—Lotus Dubois quit. They were getting raunchy—cutting out comics."

"What happens to great athletes after their heyday?" asked Dardy Minsky. "Most of the girls married and had a couple kids. There is a life after show business."

"What do you do when you can't do that last handstand?" asked Renny von Muchow. "Our careers in show business ended when flesh acts were not in demand anymore."

"I was at this place in Canada called The Queen's Hotel and I couldn't kick my leg over my head," recalls White Fury. "And I thought it was time to leave."

Lady Midnight went to work in a factory as she was "very good on lathes and machinery and things like that. I liked doing that a lot."

Walt Collins said, "Dad left the business to provide a home and a normal life for me."

Lee Stuart said, "I went to work for the *Houston Chronicle*."

After Candy Cotton retired, she went to school and learned electronics. "I worked as a waitress, took the kids, and moved to California. I worked in aerospace electronics."

Renny said, "I worked in the morgue and I took pictures of anything they needed."

Joan Arline became "an elder in the church. And I taught dancing at the church. One night I did a number to *The Lady is a Tramp*," she said. Joan retained her showgirl figure, and showed me her long legs that were still shapely despite having had a chunk removed due to cancer.

Kitty West wanted another child. She worked until she was thirty, but claimed it was hard to quit because she was so famous. "People would fly in to see me. I wanted to be a mother." She eventually became the director of sales for Hilton Hotels and gave burlesque lessons on the side.

Joni Taylor thought, "It's time for me to stay home and be a mother."

Vicki O'Day became a chef and sold perfume in a department store, tended bar, and held odd jobs.

Lorraine Lee and Dick Richards carried on. "We didn't exactly quit—we went into the dinner theatres, which was like a burlesque revue."

Renny found a kind of reverse snobbery among some of his performer friends. "A lot of friends didn't make it once they got out. I'm a photographer at the VA hospital. They asked, 'What kind of money can you make?' I'm making eighty-seven dollars a week.' You're kidding? Man I'll never get out of show business. I wouldn't stoop to work for eighty-seven dollars.'" Renny would explain: "I'm building something."

Lili St. Cyr had a hard time adjusting to aging and the attention her beauty had garnered being out of the spotlight. She became a recluse for the last twenty years of her life. For years, she sold three 8x20 photos of herself for ten dollars to fans who wrote her at her home address.

Dixie became involved in helping some of the old dancers. Kitty West called Dixie Evans crying. She survived Hurricane Katrina in 2005. Two years later, as she was sitting in her FEMA trailer that had finally arrived, she told Dixie it was so small, her feet were in the bathtub when she sat on the toilet. "She lost everything. And she has cancer," Dixie said. Dixie felt Kitty was close to ending her own life. Dixie organized some old guys at a bar that remembered Evangeline the Oyster. "I wrote to a girl who has a bar, get all those old guys around the bar and have them chip in five dollars. Write the girl, she's about ready to commit suicide." Kitty told Dixie, "'I can't take it anymore, I have nothing. I'm wiped out.' Little by little money pours in. Original organization was a way to form and help these women."

After Jennie Lee died, Dixie soldiered on, writing all the legends to please contribute to the museum in Helendale, which was a "nightmare" for Dixie to organize. Dixie invited Lili St. Cyr, Betty Rowland, and Sherry Britton to a strip contest. None of them showed up.

Over the years, a slow dribble of fans helped keep some of the old burlesque ladies alive by sending the odd bit of money and attention.

During the 1990s, there began a neo-burlesque movement across both America and Europe. At many of these shows, seminars, and conventions, the "legendary ladies" sold their photos and conducted seminars and classes, occasionally performing.

Kitty was strong when I met her. Her beloved son was building her a bigger trailer where her dream house had once stood. The eye of Katrina had traveled right through her neighborhood. She said there were people and dead animals up the trees after the storm passed. The place still looked a mess. There were no street signs and many businesses were still boarded up.

Alexandra the Great said, "It was a wonderful business. It was very good to me. I met some wonderful people and I saw some wonderful places."

Kitty West – Evangeline the Oyster Girl wiped out
after Hurricane Katrina with the very pregnant author

"It was the only kind of happy time I had," said Dixie Evans. "It was great. Yeah."

Maria Bradley remembered, "They were truly, truly, truly the happiest days of my life."

Rita Grable agreed. "I've never been ashamed of what I've done. Never. All my friends know it."

"It was a great life. I have no complaints," said Alexandra the Great. "I thought I was very professional. I conducted myself that way. I was treated that way. I think a lot of people have the wrong idea of what it was like. I'm not shy about saying I've been in the business. It was very good to me. I miss it as it was. But everything changes."

"I don't think any of us thought about how cute we were," said Vicki O'Day, "until you're older and look back."

"I used to get roses every night. That's all gone, too. That was the good days. That was the fun days. They're all gone now," said Tee Tee Red.

Even Beverly Anderson had to admit it was a "great experience, taught me a lot."

Candy Cotton claimed, "It was a true art form."

"Yeah, I'm still shaking my booties and the beat goes on," joked Tempest Storm.

"I think when you look at women of that era they led amazing lives. They did the absolutely best they could under the situation and they did even better than that. You know they learned to survive," said Kelly DiNardo.

And they survived with grace and humor.

Before surgery for possible breast cancer, Sally Rand's son Sean related, Sally knew she would be knocked out when she went into surgery so she got a yellow notepad, wrote a note, and taped it to her chest with the gown on top. When the doctors went in to operate and they pulled Sally's gown off, they doubled over laughing. She had written, "If you need to remove one, put the other in the center so at least I'll be a novelty."

Dixie fondly recalled the best lesson she ever learned. Brand new to the business, she made the mistake of saying to one girl, "'I'm only breaking in an act. I'm not in burlesque.' She yanked me out in the alley. 'Listen bitch, don't ever say that in a burlesque show. You *better* make it big, because if you ever come crawling back here, we're like the Mormons, we'll shun you.'" Dixie then realized that the other performer was right. "Be proud of where you are and what you're doing. It was an industry. A huge industry."

"Now that we're talking about it being gone, it makes me sad," said Maria Bradley.

CHAPTER FORTY-SIX

Blackout

"...fabulous, wonderful world you'll never create again."
—Chris Costello

"Too long these burlesque girls have been held down on the
low rung of the entertainment ladder, but no more....
They have a right to climb the ladder to the top."
—Dixie Evans

Original burlesque was performed with a wink and a nod. It was a tease. It was raucous, simple humor. It was accessible, upfront, sometimes brazen, always provocative. It was *stripped* of pretension. It never tried to be anything more than good entertainment for the common man.

In the dark theatres, the women of burlesque seemed attainable, representative of the American Dream—success, happiness, and a woman to call their own.

"Immigrants came to America with nothing in common, not language, religious culture, except lack of women," jokes Geoffrey Gorer in *Hot Strip Tease*.

The burly show died after degenerating into the strip clubs we know today, where nothing is removed, or left to the imagination. The tease vanished fifty years ago. No one goes to a strip club today to see an elaborate production. Patrons are there for the nudity, not for entertainment. There are no big-name strippers left. That kind of fame was last afforded famed topless stripper Carol Doda, known for her enormous silicone breasts in the 1970s.

There is no longer a place where novelty entertainers can make a steady living performing their quirky acts. No comedians can work forty-plus weeks a year, three shows a day, five on weekends, to *full* houses. Burlesque has been replaced.

We forget the comics were venerated by audiences or that dancers were worshiped and glorified as much as any Hollywood movie star. Theirs was not an image projected on a screen. They were in the flesh mere feet away with the sweat visible on their brow, with the sound of their beads rattling in the air. They were sexy, spicy, and tantalizing. They were tangible and visceral in every sense. It was "entertainment with the glamour and the nude," said Dixie Evans.

It was uniquely American, if only because we invented the striptease.

During its day, burlesque pushed the envelope of what one could hear and see. But tastes changed, the audience grew sophisticated and jaded and restless— always demanding new, faster, more.

Those burlesque days of old are gone and most of the people have passed. But they left so much for us to appreciate.

Burlesque is everywhere. "I see burlesque in TV commercials," observed Dixie Evans.

Indeed, television and film carry on the tradition. It could easily be argued the humor of Monty Python and *Saturday Night Live* owes everything to the burlesque skits of the past, passed on from those like Johnny Carson on *The Tonight Show* to the next generation. Films like *The Hangover* and *Bridesmaids* borrow from burlesque.

Reality television is burlesque, whether it is intended to be or not. The "housewives" are burlesque. Lady Gaga is pure burlesque, backed up by pure talent. As are Katy Perry, Madonna, Bette Midler, and RuPaul. Rappers are burlesque with their lyrics and their big diamonds and their baggy pants.

Mae West, though never in burlesque, made a career burlesquing sex in her plays —plays that got her arrested and charged with "corrupting the morals of youth."

Classical striptease in its golden age had an impact on American culture, fashion, advertising, music, and every form of entertainment. It was so-called low culture that spilled over into the mainstream because of its vitality and messiness. Burlesque influenced and fascinated many artists such as Reginald Marsh, who frequented the burlesque houses from the 1920s through the '40s, painting beautiful depictions of strippers in their glory (I'm the proud owner of one). He called burlesque "a part of American life."

The burlesque performers worked and lived under a veil of illegitimacy, the bastard children of entertainment. Their ability to rise above it was admirably and profoundly American. Their struggles, perseverance, and eventual triumph are ours.

"With strippers and dancers, we have as a society, kind of, this mixed view of them. On the one hand, they're desirable and titillating. And on the other hand, they're going against the status quo," said Kelly DiNardo. "And we sort of have this reproachful disdain for them."

"They were put down, partly in response to how society viewed them. It's just the way the life evolved. They spent a lot of time in bars," said Alan Alda.

Burlesque was a mixed bag of talents. Like anything else, some were professional and supremely talented, others were there to get by and could have cared less about burlesque.

But the whole industry suffered the indignity of *not counting*, though it generated untold amounts of money. They weren't important. The performers had no talent. They were in burlesque because they couldn't make it anywhere else. They were sexual deviants.

"There were a few bad apples, a few prostitutes in the bunch. But very few. Probably fewer than there were secretary prostitutes. I worked with two girls who were virgins. One was desperately trying to lose her virginity," remembers Vicki O'Day.

"Things that give an audience pleasure are always at the bottom rung. Even though it takes skill, because there was an erotic element to burlesque, the comics, straight men and talking women, all were downgraded by society. 'Cause [they were] involved in something that gave pleasure," said Alan Alda.

"It wasn't a dirty business, but it wasn't totally innocent either. It was an intensified mix of many different kinds of human activity in a special little caldron that the rest of the world didn't get to see except over the footlights."

The performers gave of themselves and most were satisfied with their lot.

"House singers weren't hoping one day to be big recording stars," Maria Bradley claimed. "Almost everyone in burlesque, it was a world of its own. I don't even think it entered anyone's mind to go further ... they were in their own little world."

To see it from the inside let Alda see it in a more "human way." He didn't know there was a world outside of burlesque. "I actually thought that we were the privileged people and civilians were to be pitied because they didn't know how to make people laugh. They had to come watch us to laugh. The burlesque company could make each other laugh all night long on the train. They didn't need to pay anybody to make them laugh."

We can finally, appropriately honor and remember the thousands of men and women—only a small portion that have been highlighted here that made burlesque such an integral, if often marginalized, part of American history.

As Alan Alda remembers, "They were not just hardworking, but artists, some of them."

**

Finally, as a testament to the strippers' influence one need only read the letters sent to them during the wars by American troops overseas. The men in uniform wrote the strippers, pouring their hearts out and asking for photos:

"The picture sure is grand and it helped to give us the inspiration to carry on the best we knew how. . . . don't let anyone tell you you didn't do your part in this war, because you did and you have one gang who appreciates it. Thanks sincerely the Radio Gang."

1942: "All the boys here in camp have someone that they hold as their, you might say, 'dream girl,' and so I made you mine, do you mind very much."

1945 from the South Pacific: "Saw your picture . . . we were in pretty rough water at the time and believe me when I saw that picture of you the old sea calmed right down for me."

"Our organization was recently attached to another outfit in Calcutta, India. They had a picture of you pinned to the wall in the Transportation Dept. We feel that the efficiency and morale of the organization will be greatly improved if you send us a print."

France, 1944: "Since I saw your beautiful picture . . . I have been so upset that I almost failed to dodge an 88. (Incidentally 88's is a type of artillery weapon used by the Jerries.) I only hope you can read this letter as am wrighting [sic] by candle light, while listening to 88's sing a weird sinister tune."

The last G-string has been dropped, the last drum roll struck, the applause fades. The burlesque house is dark.

Goodnight.

Burlesque: a big gaudy show

305

A Burly Timeline

1866 The Black Crook performs to sold-out audiences

1869 The British Blondes invade the shores of America

1890 Chorus girls added to the end of shows

1893 Hoochie coochie dancers, Little Egypt performs at Columbian Exposition in Chicago

1899 Watson's Beef Trust—the fat girls rule the stage

1900 Inception of the Columbia Wheel and Empire Circuit

1905–06 The wheel split into eastern and western circuits

1910 Stock burlesque invented

1917 Abe Minsky introduces the runway to his theatre; Mae Dix removed a collar and cuffs

1920s Striptease emphasized in shows

1925 Raid at Minsky's

1931 Burlesque goes to Broadway

1933 Chicago World's Fair introduces fan dancing with Sally Rand and Faith Bacon

1937 LaGuardia bans burlesque in New York City

1939 The worst of the Depression is over

1941 With WWII there is a surge in attendance at the burlesque houses as soldiers line up

1946 The bikini is invented

1948 The Milton Berle television show airs

1953 The Old Howard closed because of Rose La Rose flashing

1969 Denmark legalizes pornography

1972 *Deep Throat* hits theatres

Burly in the Sky

Since May of 2006 in Las Vegas, we've lost many of our friends. As Lee Stuart emailed me, they've "passed on to the big Burlesque stage, wherever it may be."

Carmela Rickman
Beverly Anderson
Lee Stuart
Tony Midnight
Mimi Reed
Sheila Rae
Terry Mixon
Sherry Britton
Mike Iannucci
Sunny Dare
Al Baker, Jr.
Joan Arline
Nat Bodian
Harry Lloyd
Helen Imbrugia
Dixie Evans

Acknowledgments

I have an abundance of thank yous due. I am truly grateful for all those that took the journey with me behind and in front of the camera. Your support and belief has been tremendous. Sheri Hellard for taking this journey with me, plane rides, early hours and all! I couldn't have done it without you by my side, holding that camera for some of the wackiest adventures I think we'll ever have.

My friend Donnalee Austen, the best producer in the world. Dianna Miranda-Buck, always an inspiration and a "can-do" kind of friend. Toni Bentley, a beautiful, brave author and a fountain of information and support and great stories. Michelle Bega, all our plotting and planning over lunches at e. baldi always pays off. You are my champion.

First Run Pictures for getting the film out to audiences. Jackie Levine for your fearless support and many phone calls to the "powers that be." The Card Sharks: you keep me laughing and inspire me. Pat Carroll, thank you for your constant nuggets of information of little-known facts you dig up—a much bigger thank you is coming for the next book.

Melaine Britton, Sherry's memories and things are my touchstones; thank you for entrusting them to me. Thank you to Val Valentine in particular and April March, and others who kept me supplied with stories, pictures, and scrapbooks. Betty Rowland for trusting your sisters' stories with me. For a little bit of a thing, you are a powerhouse. Thank you Lillian Kiernan Brown and your daughter Katherine Kiernan Fries. Lily, your courage and enthusiasm and support of me is tremendous.

Dorothy Colman, a fan of burlesque and these women, connected me to many and shared stories I wouldn't have otherwise heard. Danny Passman and the gang at Gang, Tyre, Ramer & Brown—you've done a lot to see this in print. My editor Jennifer McCartney—you got it—your enthusiasm and belief in the burly folks is astounding. Thank you Oleg and Christina at Skyhorse Publishing for doing everything and all to get this to the broad audience these "broads" deserve.

Morgan McDonald, who tries to keep me organized—a herculean task. Thank you to the ImageMovers family—Derek, Will, Monique, Matt, Jack, and Steve, and in memorium, Sharon Felder. To Zane, Rhys, and Zsa Zsa, I owe you an apology for hours and days spent elsewhere. And not least, by any means, *grazie mille* to my love, my husband Bob, who is an inspiration and always says "do it." I couldn't without you.

Notes

INTRODUCTION

"this travesty originated what was to be called legitimate burlesque." Pg 12 of Bernard Sobel's *Burleycue, A Pictorial History Of Burlesque*

"people in that era . . ." Dixie Evans interview with author

CHAPTER 1

"audiences – it was always full." Mimi Reed interview with author

"they were there to have fun." Maria Bradley interview with author

"everyone thought we were preoccupied. . ." Val Valentine interview with author

"were no big American stars" Rachel Shteir interview with author and rest of chapter

"legitimized" August 1954 *Uncensored Magazine*

"variety act with a little more spice." Renny von Muchow interview with author

"burlesque was essentially a vaudeville . . ." Nat Bodian interview with author

"its actually who you are . . ." Dixie Evans interview with author and rest of chapter

"I just knew I was gonna be a famous movie star" Lady Midnight interview author – and the rest of her quotes in chapter

"it was a job" Lorraine Lee interview with author- and the rest of her quotes in chapter

"we didn't have books" Blaze Starr interview with author

"wicked stepmother" Helen Imbrugia interview with author

"because I worked in black light" Candy Cotton interview with author

"it was a time where people couldn't get work . . ." Alan Alda interview with author. And rest of chapter

"minks, sables . . ." Tempest Storm interview with author

"it was called the poor man's" Mike Iannucci interview with author – and rest of chapter

"No. Because everyone was working in it." Betty Rowland interview with author.

"there was a time when you could fill an opera" interview with Alexandra the great 48 with author

"if there was a chorus line, they usually did a nice build up" Joni Taylor interview with author

"I was part of that" Sherry Britton interview with author

"it wasn't considered a great art form" John Perilli interview with author

"I don't think people know where to put strippers . . ." Kelly DiNardo interview with author.

CHAPTER 2

"My mother found out . . ." Joni Taylor interview with author

"I'm not gonna do too long . . ." Sunny Dare speaking at the Las Vegas reunion 2006.

"many of us were not too catty" Vicki O'Day interview with author.

"broke into show business" Lorraine Lee at the Vegas reunion

"My stepmother said. . ." Lady Midnight at the Vegas reunion

"I started in a chorus line" Candy Cotton at the Vegas reunion

"I was born on the carnival" Sunny Dare at the Vegas reunion

"I started in the carnival" Daphne Lake at the Vegas reunion

"We rehearsed between shows" Joni Taylor at the Vegas reunion.

CHAPTER 3

"I was embarrassed" Beverly Anderson Traube interview with author – and rest of chapter

CHAPTER 4

"Even my husband" Joan Arline interview with author

"My mother always wished . . ." Candy Cotton interview with author

"Mother thought it was beautiful" Kitty West interview with author.

"strip all the way" April March interview with author

"How am I gonna tell him what I'm doing?" Rita Grable interview with author.

"but they never saw it either" Sequin interview with author

"You knew about the stigma" Dixie Evans interview with author and rest of chapter

"didn't all come from bad" Val Valentine interview with author

CHAPTER 5

"I threw up" Terry Mixon interview with author

"You want to try a strip" Betty Rowland interview with author

"willful removing of one's clothes" Sobel, Burleycue:

"forgetting to don her body" *Vaudeville Encyclopedia* page 304

Billy ordered the "accident" Morton Minsky book page 34

"Mademoiselle Fifi was the one" Rachel Shteir interview with author and all her other quotes in chapter

Demanding their girls "accidentally" HM Alexander's Strip tease

"four times" Aug *Uncensored Magazine*

"disaster" Beverly Anderson interview with author

"would you like to go into burlesque" Rita Grable interview with author

"The first time I stripped" Lady Midnight interview with author

"From being a chorus girl I went" Candy Cotton interview with author

"You're going on" Terry Mixon interview with author

"I was afraid I'd fall off the stage" Alexandra the great 48 interview with author

"terrififed" Dixie Evans interview with author

"joined the Sally Rand" Sunny Dare interview with author

"my first act, the women" Vicki O'Day interview with author

"In those days we didn't" Kitty West interview with author

"weren't really actresses" Rachel Shteir interview with author

CHAPTER 6

"I didn't bump and grind" Joni Taylor interview with author

"It was an amazing" Prof. Janet Davis interview with author

"The circus created the midway" James Taylor interview with author OR James Taylor in *Bound by Flesh*

"market itself as" Prof Janet Davis of the University of Texas at Austin, interview with author

"people on the margins" Professor Janet Davis interview with author

"I really did. I went with a" Dixie Evans interview with author

"I went to the girls show" Daphne Lake interview with author

"carnival life" Candy Cotton interview with author

CHAPTER 7

"She was nude" Prof Janet Davis interview with author and all the other quotes in this chapter

"train them for support" Jewish Women's Archive (online) article entitled "Clara de Hirsch Home for Working Girls" by Reena Sigman Friedman

"sound American" Prof Janet Davis interview with author

"douche bag" Prof Janet Davis interview with author

"Sometimes hands . . ." Prof Janet Davis interview with author

"ethnic" "jewish" Prof Janet Davis interview with author

"ruddy" Prof Janet Davis

"all over the garden" *New York Times* April 22, 1915

"it shouldn't matter" Prof Janet Davis interview

"all together" Prof Janet interview

"You have a square neck" Prof Janet interview

"once the neck gets use" Prof Janet interview with author

"terrified" "fascinated" Prof Janet interview

"when signaled" Prof Janet Davis interview

CHAPTER 8

"The Minsky's at best" Rachel Shteir interview with author

"The climate of that community" Morton Minsky

"exotic dancing venus" *Charleston Gazette*, Tuesday Dec 30, 1975

"I can still move every part" *Charleston Gazette*, Tues. Dec 30, 1975

"Theatres at that time were going broke" Betty Rowland interview with author

"grinding" – "requisite bumps" "old days" "hootch number" Sobel, a pictorial history of burlesque

"filler in for the strip numbers" Sobel, a pictorial history of burlesque

"an immigrant thing to being . . ." Rachel Shteir interview with author

"it wasn't what you took off" Dixie Evans interview with author

"he made over a million" Dardy Minsky interview with author

"Find these sweet little girls" Dardy Minsky interview with author

"He had clubs all over the country" Dardy Minsky interview with author

"quaint" Dardy Minsky interview with author

"everyone in Vegas in the '50s" Dardy Minsky interview with author

"wonderful man" Rita Grable interview with author

"Sir" "I do thirteen" April March interview with author

"a lot of work" Betty Rowland interview with author

"would have Dardy" Beverly Anderson interview with author

"Harold would stand" Dardy Minsky interview with author

"we ran into three people" Dardy Minsky interview with author

"made the sisters" Dixie Evans interview with author

"if we had a few more Harold Minsky's" Dardy Minsky interview with author

CHAPTER 9

"They didn't think highly" Maria Bradley interview with author

"Women would strip" Renny von Muchow interview with author

"vaudeville became burlesque" Nat Bodian interview with author

"theatres could be the grungiest." Rachel Shteir interview with author

"A lot of people were of the opinion that you were a hooker." Carmela Rickman, interview with author

"a Frigidare or a car" Betty Rowland interview with author

"its completely vanished" Rachel Shteir interview with author

"slow, medium and ending fast" Sequin interview with author

"pulled out of chorus and made" Joan Arline interview with author and all other quotes from this section

"One time one of my pasties flew off" Candy Cotton interview with author

"They got tape on the inside" Tee Tee Red interview with author

"I wanted to be on the stage" Joni Taylor interview with author and the rest of her quotes in this section

"weren't gonna leave" Dixie Evans interview with author

"And its because of her" Kitty West interview with author and the rest of her quotes in this section

"the world's loveliest feminine form" Girl Show, Al Stencil

"as all young girls did." April March interview with author and the rest of her quotes in this section

"April was class" Alexandra the Great interview with author

"I thought the money sounded" Taffy O'Neil interview with author and the rest of her quotes in this section

"there was no such thing" La Savona interview with author

"her real name was Ada" Tee Tee Red interview with author and the rest of her quotes in this section

"Memories, Love Zorita" Note in author's collection

"I had some fun times with Zorita" April March interview with author

"Zorita came through" Terry Mixon interview with author

"most all came from" Dixie Evans interview with author

CHAPTER 10

"The comics were the main" Joan Arline interview with author – and the rest of her quotes from this section

"you could see the sweat" Alan Alda interview with author and the rest of his quotes

"Too bad about Molly . . . (through) make you an exception?" Aug. *Uncensored Magazine*

"best school for the comedians" pg 204 *Burleycue*, by Sobel

"burlesque people are different" Chris Costello interview with author

"Top banana" Mike Iannucci interview with author

"bring on the girls" Harry Lloyd interview with author and all his here

"comics would rehearse" H.M. Alexander, Strip Tease

Harry Lloyd interview with author and all his quotes here.

"They all had a different style" Lee Stuart interview with author

"They took old comedy skits" Alan Alda interview with author

"Jess Mack was a straight man" Harry Lloyd interview with author

"burlesque Was just a way to pay" Morton Minsky pg 128

"Johnny Carson did" Rita Grable interview with author

"He loved the burlesque" Mike Iannucci interview with author

"People would laugh" Dixie Evans interview with author

"Straight: Hello there bud" Harry Lloyd interview with author

"the humor was great" Renny von Muchow interview with author

"professional dumb guy" Jack O'Brian Prescott Evening News Sept 9, 1946

"I still credit everything" Aug . *Uncensored Magazine*

"He started as a dramatic actor" Lady Midnight interview with author

"stock comedians" Dee Ann Johnston interview with author

"the comics in burlesque were mean" Beverly Anderson interview with author

CHAPTER 11

"they usually sang" Ann Corio's book *This was Burlesque*

"it was my kind of trash" Lee Stuart interview with author (and rest of quotes in chapter

"the role of the straight man" Alan Alda interview with author and rest of quotes in chapter

"he never got credit" Chris Costello interview with author

"had a whiskey tenor" Mike Iannucci interview with author

CHAPTER 12

"I lived in a cocoon" Alan Alda interview with author and rest of quotes in chapter

CHAPTER 13

"By change he happened" Chris Costello interview with author and all rest in this chapter

CHAPTER 14

"Chorus girls" Taffy O'Neil interview with author

"Backstage was always" Alexandra the great interview with author

"Shows had to go fast" Betty Rowland interview with author

"I remember once" Lily Ann Rose email to author in 2013.

"Sammy Price" Joan Arline interview with author.

"There was a smell in the" Alan Alda interview with author

"we all decided" Joni Taylor interview with author

"They will fight backstage" Dixie Evans interview with author

"they'd put itchin' powder" Tempest Storm interview with author

"You met wonderful people" Sequin interview with author

"greatest feuds" Morton Minsky's *Minsky's Burlesque* pg 154

"all girls between shows" Dixie Evans interview with author

"between shows we'd go" Lady midnight interview with author

"One time after too many drinks" Maria Bradley interview with author

"I'd stay in my dressing room" Candy Cotton interview with author

"I stayed in the dressing room" April March interview with author

"Many times backstage" Sean Rand interview with author

CHAPTER 15

"Use of bed" Boston License and Censor Bureua

"Never let your nipple show" Maria Bradley interview with author

"some towns were a little bit" Beverly Anderson interview with author

"In Boston, the watch" Lily Ann Rose interview with author

"Boston was the strictest" Sequin interview with author

"The vice squad" Dixie Evans interview with author

Buffalo," Taffy O'Neil interview with author

"In Dallas" April March interview with author

"We had a lot of laws" White Fury interview with author

"Detroit" Joan Arline interview with author

"If you touched a curtain" Lorraine Lee interview with author

"I had to get off the stage" April March interview with author

"It was to get" Betty Rowland interview with author

CHAPTER 16

"A sharp hip" Aug. *Uncensored Magazine*

"A bump" – newspaper 1951 during trial of Lili St. Cyr

"Bumps into the curtain" Alan Alda interview with author

"I'd come out booming" Vicki O'Day interview with author

"Make love to her audience" Aug. *Uncensored Magazine*

"She didn't believe" Kitty West interview with author

"Lillian Hunt" Dixie Evans interview with author

CHAPTER 17

"I was put in" April March interview with author

"I was met" Vicki O'Day interview with author

"Harold used to" Dardy Minsky interview with author

"an hour or two" Leroy Griffith interview with author

"I was routinely arrested" Dixie evans interview with author

"I went to jail" Kitty West interview with author

"at Walgreens" Alexandra the great interview with author

"Clubs would call" Betty Rowland interview with author

"When it was mop time" Betty Rowland papers in author's collection

"absolutely misery" Betty Rowland papers in author's collection.

"refused to give her time" Betty Rowland papers in author's collection.

"technical advisoer" betty Rowland papers in author's collection

"believing you will profit" Papers from Sherry Britton's scrap books in author's collection

"politicians were trying" Blaze Starr interview with author

"They arrest the whole place" La Savona interview with author

"Sometimes they just liked" Ricki Covette interview with author.

"And I kept that" Lily Ann Rose interview with author

"downright naughty" *Uncensored Magazine*

"too far" *Uncensored Magazine*

CHAPTER 18

"people in that era" Dixie Evans interview with author

"The fact that the strippers" Mike Iannucci interview with author

"power to license" 1937 *Time Magazine*

"Everyone ran to their agents" Betty Rowland interview with author

"be came the base" Nat Bodian interview with author

CHAPTER 19

"you make" Dixie Evans interview with author

"the biggest majority" April March interview with author

"But always owed" Beverly Anderson interview with author

"I learned" Sequin interview with author

"Good salary" Terry Mixon interview with author

"The chorus girls would have" Betty Rowland interview with author

"AGVA didn't" Maria Bradley interview with author

"for anything" Joni Taylor interview with author

"IF you were a good" Val Valentine interview with author

"Comics in them" Al Baker, Jr. interview with author

"The burlesque houses" Renny von Muchow interview with author

"every six weeks" Lorraine Lee interview with author

"I was never stood" Sequin interview with author

"I signed on for thirty-" Lee Stuart interview with author

"We got in trouble" Tee Tee Red interview with author

"walking in late" Carole Nelson interview with author

"I always had to make money to pay" Mike Wallace interview with Lili St. Cyr *Behind the Burly Q* film

"half a million dollars" Susan Weiss interview with author

"She coached" Alexandra the great interview with author

"I knew there would be a day" Vicki O'Day interview with author

"Experienced" Dee Ann Johnston interview with author

"Few crossed" Rachel Shteir interview with author

"the house singer or the juvenile" *Uncensored Magazine*

CHAPTER 20

"I married" Joan Arline interview with author and rest of chapter

"My family" La Savona interview with author

"Gee anyone can do" Kay Hanna interview with author

"and I'd getup and I'd sing" Sequin interview with author

"married life didn't" Val Valentine interview with author

"my man's gonna" Blaze Starr interview with author

"I married the man" Sean Rand interview with author

"usually you had" Al Baker, Jr. interview with author

"I saw a pair" Lorraine Lee interview with author

"Jimmy Matthews" lady Midnight interview with author

Vicki/Alexandra/April/Kitty – interview s with author

"couldn't handle" Tee Tee Red interview with author

"My last" Tempest storm interview with author

"One night she accused" Alan Alda inte with author

"took me" Barry Siegfried interview with author

"When you start" White Fury interview with author

"she walked across" Candy Cotton interview with author

"mother's bookie" Carmela interview with author

"all my boyfriends" Cyrse Sciandra

"babysit" Dixie Evans interview with author

"I wanted a model train" Harry Lloyd interview with author

"Bud and Lou" Al Baker Jr. interview with author

Chapter 21

"What kind" Maria Bradley interview with author

"I couldn't sing" Dixie Evans interview with author

"warbling" Billboard 1944. And "lovely"

"Betty Grable" Mimi Reed interview with author

"Mimi and Thareen were" Stewart Edward Allen interview with author

"they had a contest" Renny von Muchow interview with author and rest of chapter

CHAPTER 22

"My whole thing" Al Baker interview with auth

"I faked" Sequin interview with auth

"trunk full of" Lily Ann Rose correspondence with author

"the year of the big flood" Al Baker Jr. Interview with author and all the rest of chapter

"in those days" Leroy Griffith interview with author

"we keep the door" Tee Tee Red interview with author and the rest of chapter

"I wanted to be just" Lily Ann Rose interview with author and the rest of this chapter

"very nervous." Sequin interview v with author and rest of chapter

CHAPTER 23

"New Orlean as" Kitty West interview with author

"in theatres" Alexandra the interview with author

"Agent would book" Sequin interview with author

"I was booked two" Dixie Evans interview with author

"come in at noon" Betty Rowland interview with author

"Burlesque" Mike Iannucci interview with author

"scramble" White Fur interview with author

"I traveled to" Joan Arline interview with author

"On tour was pretty" Kitty west interview with author

"walking down" Alan Alda interview with author

"You traveled with" Al Baker Jr interview with author

"The burlesque" Carmela interview with author

"one time" Beverly Anderson interview with auth

"Christmas we had to work" Maria Bradley interview with author

"The performers" Dee Ann Johnston interview with author

"We carried" Lorraine Lee interview with author

"it was an adventure" Vicki O'Day iner with author

"the travel and ours" Harry Lloyd interview with author

"they had big, beautiful" Mimi Reed interview with author

CHAPTER 24

"out front" Dixie Evans interview with author and rest of chapter

"Candy butchers" Val Valentine interview with author and rest of chapter

"The candy butchers paid" Dardy Minsky interview with author and rest of chapter

"The burlesque theatres" Nat Bodian interview with author and rest of chapter

"either bought the candy" *Popular Mechanics* Aug. 1927

"There was an artistry" Rita Grable interview with author

CHAPTER 25

"Theatre work" Alexandra the Great interview with author and rest of chapter

"You just keep" Taffy O'Neil interview with author and rest of chapter

"I liked theatres" Lady Midnight interview with author

"You get stage fright" Dixie Evans interview with author and rest of chapter

"I always had" April March interview with author

"the Minskys of LA" Betty Rowland interview with author

"You can't graduate" Mike Iannucci interview with author and rest of chapter

"Minsky theatres were especially nice" Dixie Evans

"seedy" Woodward Avenue by Rober t Genat

"Roses's was the most fun" Alexandra the Great interview with author and rest of chapter

"Sketchy" Dee Ann Johnston interview with author and rest of chapter

"You're late" Dee Ann Johnston interview with author

"Eating pork and beans" Dee Ann Johnston interview with author

"the bigger the theatre" Dixie Evans interview with author

"small stage" Dee Ann Johnston interview with author

"these girls were performers" Dee Ann Johnston interview with author

"Stars of the Hollywood" Dee Ann Johnston interview with author

"was a San Diego guy" Dee Ann Johnston interview with author

"They didn't do completes" Dee Ann Johnston interview with author

"doing more than they" Dee Ann Johnston interview with author

"brothel" Vicki O'Day interview with author and rest of chapter

"stage" "cutting board" Sheila Rae interview with author

"New Orleans was fantastic" Kitty West interview with author

"New Orleans had jazz" Tee Tee Red interview with author

"quaint" Dardy Minsky interview with author

"all ex-hoodlums" Dardy Minsky interview with author

"no union stamp" Dixie Evans interview with author

"stage hands had a strong" Sequin interview with author

"most of us who were" Lady Midnight letter to author

"we didn't know at the time" Betty Rowland interview with author

"you didn't have an audience" Taffy O'Neil interview with author

"standing behind the curtain" Lady Midnight interview with author

"We'll get into film" Betty Rowland interview with author

"you know I'd rather" Dee Ann Johnston interview with author

CHAPTER 26

"A woman's greatest asset" Ann Corio

"I confess that I am a brazen" Sally Rand

"two went down" Mike Iannucci interview with author and the rest of chapter

"busy making a living" "always mama's" Mike Iannucci interview with author

"As long as they looka" Mike Iannucci interview with author

"she was competing with Gypsy" Mike Iannucci interview with author

"deserting her and discoloring her eye" Walter Winchell column

"released" "escaped" Mike Iannucci interview with author

"special occasions" Mike Iannucci interview with author

"he treated her just" Mike Iannucci interview with author

"this shouldn't be" Carole Nelson interview with author

"it had generated" Mike Iannucci interview with author

"we emphasized comedy" Mike Iannucci interview with author

"she'd listen to" Carole Nelson interview with author

"They had almost no work" Mike Iannucci interview with author

" a little chubby girl" Mike Iannucci interview with author

"was the daughter" Carole Nelson interview with author

"clean" Mike Iannucci interview with author

"Could do almost anything" Mike Iannucci interview with author

"great sense of humor" Carole Nelson interview with author

"Bozo was the pet" Mike Iannucci interview with author

"Miss Corio, who looks" *New York Times* June 24, 1982

"She didn't have to do any more" Mike Iannucci interview with author

"fading from us" Carole Nelson interview with author

"The last day I saw" Carole Nelson interview with author

"awful" "bad guy" Sam Shad interview with author

"I'm pushing seventy-six" Mike Iannucci interview with author

NOTES

"She was a little different" Dixie Evans interview with author and rest of chapter

"one of the big things" Sean Rand interview with author and rest of chapter

"I thought a girl who went on the stage" Studs Terkel *Hard Times* page 170

"I can get a horse" Sean Rand interview with author

"girlfriend called" Sean Rand interview with author

"disintegrate" Sean Rand interview with author

"it was easy to track her" Sean Rand interview with author

"wad of money" Sean Rand interview with author

"relentless tried to find" Sean Rand interview with author

"guts for her time" Sean Rand interview with author

"bubble dance" "Hill billy" Mike Iannucci interview with author

"you never saw anything" Mike Iannucci interview with author

"the doctors didn't think" Sean Rand interview with author

"everyone from the show" Sean Rand interview with author

"I have something to reveal" Sean Rand interview with author

"bought fans from Sally" Alexandra the Great interview with author

"Those were the fans" Sean Rand interview with author

"Georgia had something" Maria Bradley interview with author

"she couldn't even spell" Dixie Evans interview with author

"she wasn't a dancer" Rita Grable interview with author

"you could steal" Beverly Anderson interview with author

"she was dynamic" Rita Grable

"breadliners" *Salt Lake Tribune* 1942

"Sally keith" Lily Ann Rose interview with autho and rest of chapter

"she was just" David Kruh interview with author

"very observant" Susan Weiss interview with author and rest of chapter

"the act was unique" David Kruh interview with author

"That I know" Susan Weiss interview with author

"she was robbed" Lily Ann Rose interview with author

"well respected" Dixie Evans interview with author

"the queen of the small claims court" Sherry Britton interview with author

"death's door" Sherry Britton interview with author

"despised" Sherry Britton interview with author

"cavorting with different" Sherry Britton interview with author

"performed oral sex" Sherry Britton interview with author

"young handsome husband" Sherry Britton interview with author

CHAPTER 27

"I said" Betty Rowland interview with author and rest of chapter

"we'll go home next week" Betty Rowland interview with author

"drab theatrical hotel" Bernard, Susan *Blondes, Brunettes and Redheads*, page 235

"beauty was startling" Bernard, Susan *Blondes, Brunettes and Redheads* page 234

"The Three D's" "dishes" Betty Rowland interview with author

"didn't do too well" Betty Rowland interview with author

"we on the west coast" Vicki O'Day interview with author

"Black satin and pearls" Burke, Carolyn *Lee Miller*, by, page 152

"quite elegant" Kathleen Ross interview with author

"Until you get back" poem by Betty Rowland recited in the film *Behind the Burly Q*

CHAPTER 28

"A gimmick" Betty Rowland interview with author

"breast size" Alexandra the great interview with author

"each girl" Dixie Evans interview with author

"she was wonderful" Joan Arline interview with author

"I take offense at that" Betty Rowland interview with author

"educated muscles" *Cabaret Magazine* 1957

NOTES

"I make mine work for me" *Cabaret Magazine* 1957

"she could make" Renny von Muchow interview with author

"grandmother of" Rachel Shteir interview with author

"we'd have baskets" Maria Bradley interview with author

"do you want a piece of" Candy Cotton interview with author

"I always say" Dixie Evans interview with author

"She was so beautiful" email from Lily Ann Rose to author

"JFK had a crush" David Kruh interview with author

"There I was" that paragraph – email from Lily Ann Rose to author

"I was classic" Alexandra the great interview with author

"pick a guy" Mimi Reed interview with author

"in those days, they didn't" Dardy Minsky interview with author

"she would get out" Kelly DiNardo interview with authoror

"we all did" Betty Rowland interview

"I stood in the wings" White Fury interview with author

"I didn't consider myself" Kitty West interview with author

"you did have to have" Rita Grable interview with author

"she's laying there" Dardy Minsky interview with author

"it would be in the alley" Sequin interview with author

"I first saw Gypsy" Blaze Starr interview with author

"they made me a lot of money" Joan Arline interview with author

"a very inebriated" Joan Arline interview with author

"had an act" Helen Imbrugia interview with author

"I got a letter" Dixie Evans interview with author

"sexy type of number" Ricki Covette interview with author and rest of chapter

"came marching in" Ricki Covette interview with author

"breast size was big" Alexandra the Great interview with author

"I'd wrap" Tee Tee Red interview with author

"I was in awe" Maria Bradley interview with author

"you start with a" Sequin interview with author

"I had gas" White Fury interview with author

CHAPTER 29

"At the end of your act" April March interview with author

"She's show things" Dardy Minsky interview with author

"I didn't even know" Maria Bradley interview with author

"thought they got a flash" David Kruh interview with author

"When I first saw" Alexandra the Great interview with author

"of course Rose" Dixie Evans interview with author

"Rose put me on the flash" Alexandra the Great interview with author

"certain girls" Dixie Evans interview with author

"strippers got into flashing" Harry Lloyd interview with author

CHAPTER 30

"I had a lot of roses" Joan Arline interview with author

"I felt like a star" Maria Bradley interview with author

"fiery . . ." Roach, Marion *The Roots of Desire* 2006.

"Hell, I got" Maria Bradley interview with author

"We had a big" Vicki O'Day interview with author

"I had a waist" Carmela interview with author

"Someone had sent" Alexandra the Great interview with author

"everyone had groupies" Rita Grable interview with author

"big birthday cake" Maria Bradley interview with author

"many, many," April March interview with author

"Did you know" Sherry Britton's papers in author's collection

"it was a great life" Alexandra the Great interview with author

"one of the girls" Lily Ann Rose interview with author

"my boss" Blaze Starr interview with author

"Now we can go out" Blaze Starr interview with author

"his entourage" Tempest Storm interview with author

"usually you sluff them off" Dixie Evans interview with author

"a cut above" Beverly Anderson interview with author

"A lot of guys" Carmela interview with author

"two men grabbed me" Kitty West interview with author

"I am a nudist" letter from Betty Rowland's papers in author's collection.

"Had the pleasure" Sherry Britton's papers in author's collection

"Blaze and I" Tee Tee Red interview with author

"I'm not nuts" Governor Earl Long 1959, Radio

"big politician" Blaze Starr interview with author

"subjected to more temptation" Bernard, Susan *Blondes, Brunettes and Redheads*

"you would be surprised" Carmela interview with author

CHAPTER 31

"hunger is a" Beverly Anderson interview with author

"Where you're working" Dixie Evans interview with author

"I became a stripper" Candy Cotton interview with author

"made good money" Beverly Anderson interview with author

"every six weeks" Lorraine Lee interview with author

"I learned a lot about" Sequin interview with author

"we did have money in those days" Dixie Evans interview with author

"There was a 60" Chris Costello interview with author

"My father never made money" Alan Alda interview with author

"Every year" Mike Iannucci interview with author

"I'll come in and work" Mike Iannucci interview with author

"My wardrobe" Tee Tee Red interview with author

"went up to" April March interview with author

"when you were a chorus" Joni Taylor interview with author

"chorus girl in" Maria Bradley interview with author

"there was no" Dixie Evans interview with author

"big ticket" Dixie Evans interview with author

"I'd saved" Blaze Starr interview with author

"The show became an instant" Mike Iannucci interview with author

CHAPTER 32

"I would tell" Carmela interview with author

"Your salary" Vicki O'Day interview with author

"you were away" Sequin interview with author

"A really big part" Kelly DiNardo interview with author

"Champagne in those" Kitty West interview with author

"if you made money" Blaze Starr interview with author

"mingle" Tee Tee Red interview with author

"When you're pouring" Dixie Evans interview with author.

"I don't drink" Carmela interview with author

"it is a girl" Kitty West interview with author

"accidentally" Dardy Minsky interview with author

"In my contract" Tempest Storm interview with author

"had to sit with" Tempest Storm interview with author

"I'd feel bad" Dixie Evans interview with author

"allowed some women" Rachel Shteir interview with author

"made a lot" Vicki O'Day interview with author

"She had to work in" Dixie Evans interview with author

"If one has morals," Lili St. Cyr speaking to Mike Wallace in the film *Behind the Burly Q*

"go Garboesque" Ben Bethia interview with author

CHAPTER 34

"early burlesque" Alan Alda interview with author

"There were never" Val Valentine interview with author

CHAPTER 35

"They had" Lily Ann Rose interview with author

"Harmonica" Renny von Muchow interview with author

"Some acts were goofy" Rachel Shteir interview with author

"he was a hairdresser" Dee Ann Johnston interview with author

"lets keep our bodies" Renny von Muchow interview with author

"hire everyone" Dee Ann Johnston interview with author

"he kept people working" Dee Ann Johnston interview with author

"they never" Betty Rowland interview with author

"Clows had drag" ADD PROFESSOR Janet Davis interview with author

"integral" Prof Janet Davis interview with author

"They had special" Lily Ann Rose interview with author

"This woman looked" Vicki O'Day interview with author

"He was a paratrooper" Dee Ann Johnston interview

"Christine Jorgensen" Steve Weinstein interview with author

"beautiful act" Rita Grable interview with author

"A ribbon of flesh" Dean Jensen interview with author in film *Bound by Flesh*

"winning act" interview with Amy Fulkerson with author in film *Bound by Flesh*

"they stayed drunk" Dee Ann Johnston interview with author

"They were the comics" April March interview with author

"exotic other" Rachel Shteir interview with author

"strict racial segregation" *San Diego's Bygone Burlesque: The Famous Hollywood Theatre* by Jaye Furlonger

"It didn't last very" Rachel Shteir interview with author

"torrid" Feb. 1953 *Jet Magazine*

CHAPTER 36

"They had crepe" Dee Ann Johnston interview with author

"You don't" Kitty West interview with author

"I became Vicki" Vicki O'Day interview with author

"I sewed my first" Blaze Starr interview with author

"Blaze was very crafty" Rita Grable interview with author

"smoking and sewing" Lily Ann Rose email to author

"Between shows" Dardy Minsky interview with author

"plastic beads" Carmela interview with author

"had a stripper" Sequin interview with author

"The one I started out with" Taffy O'Neil interview with author

"You don't let the boss" Dixie Evans interview with author

"back then you couldn't see flesh" Rachel Shteir interview vie with author

"you came off the stage" Joan Arline interview with author

"everything had its place" Sequin in interview with author

"I had beautiful wardrobe" Lady Midnight interview with author

"it was an expensive game" Dixie Evans interview

"went for a regular" Mike Innucci interview with author

"French bikini" Kitty West interview with author

"there was a costumer" Val Valentine interview with author

"I had been" Tony Midnight interview with author

"When they were" Carmela interview with author

"closed the show" Mike Iannucci interview with author

"she would strip down" Carole Nelson interview with author

"Oh I can't take that off" Mike Iannucci interview with author

"for every costume" White Fury interview with author

"I never wore" Joan Arline interview with author

"I used pins" Joni Taylor interview with author

"Mistakes" Betty Rowland interview with author

"I wore big" Joan Arline interview with author

"Half way through the" Sean Rand interview with author

"We never threw" Joan Arline interview with author

"Gerty would help" Tee Tee Red interview with author

"One time my pastie" Candy Cotton interview with author

"In those years" Rita Grable interview with author

"The girls" Rita Grable

"built like a brick" Dixie Evans interview with author

"everything" Dixie Evans interview with author

"Because we didn't have" Dixie Evans interview with author

"I was 16" Kitty West interview with author

CHAPTER 37

"It is the" Dixie Evans interview with author

"Musicians" Joan Arline interview with author

"The blues" Dixie Evans interview with author

"You couldn't use" Carmela interview with author

"Everyone" Dixie Evans interview with author

"Georgia Sothern had" John Perilli interview with author

"Having to work" John Perilli interview with author

"They had problems with me" Dixe Evans interview with author

"Most bands" Taffy O'Neil interview with author

"They'd bring in their" Dee Ann Johnston interview

"It didn't turn out" Tee Tee Red interview with author

"All the drummers" Joan Arline interview with author

"Oh God" Dixie Evans interview with author

"walk in tempo" Sequin interview with author

"Exotic dancers" Steven Weinstein interview with author

"Amber Halliday" Terry Mixon interview with author

"1949 or 1950" Steven Weinste interview with author

"He'd heard of" Steven Weinste interview with author

"Shoddy" Betty Rowland interview with author

"That was not for me" Kitty West interview with author

"burlesque was fading" Taffy O'Neil interview with author

CHAPTER 38

"In Cinncinati" Kitty West interview with author

"Gangsters" Dixie Evans interview with author

"setup" Bernard, Susan *Blondes, Brunettes and Redheads*

"Most of the clubs" Lily Ann Rose interview with author

"I have bought" Sean Rand interview with author

"okay sounds like a deal" Sean Rand interview with author

"People can say" Lily Ann Rose interview with author

"if they ever found" Dixie Evans interview with author

"As long" Vicki O'Day interview interview with author

"You didn't" Alexandra the Great interview interview with author

"fascinating" Beverly Anderson interview with author

"at the time, dancers" Beverly Anderson interview with author

"I wont call their names" Kitty West interview with author

"all gentlemen" April March interview with author

"The mob in Chicago" Dardy Minsky interview with author

"high code of honor" Bernard, Susan *Blondes, Brunettes and Redheads*

"Actually they were" Val Valentine interview with author

"scary" Vicki O'Day interview with author

"it wasn't my fault" April March interview with author

"Guy came in" Sheila Rae interview with author

"I worked in Pueblo" Vicki O'Day interview and rest of chapter

CHAPTER 39

"dallas in the '50s" Steven Weinstein interview with author

"I was taken" Candy Barr in *Oui Magazine* 1976

"Candy Barr blew" Steven Weinstein interview and rest of chapter

"she was very difficult" Steven Weinstein interview

CHAPTER 40

"A gyration" *Uncensored Magazine* Aug. 1954

"To bear down" www.Merriam-Webster.com

"sold herself" 1954 Miami newspaper

"a career" Tempest Storm interview with author

"I don't smoke. I don't drink." Alexandra the Great interview with author

"I got loaded" Sheila Rae interview with author

"We had big signs" Dixie Evans interview with author

"We used to get" Maria Bradley interview with author

"They didn't want" Betty Rowland interview with author

"We were out" Lorraine Lee interview with author

"Look at these shoes" Maria Bradley

"Mom dragged" Dee Ann Johnston

"nothing offensive" Terry Mixon interview with author

"nice to work with" "held audience" Terry Mixon interview with author

"are all different" Tee Tee Red interview with author

"I had a big giant" Sequin interview with author

"fell three times" Betty Rowland interview with author

"One time as a chorus" Joan Arline interview with author

"he must" Sequin interview with author

"ringside" Joan Arline interview with author

"I consider this an act of God" Alexandra the Great interview with author

"the bet booking I get" *Uncensored Magazine*

"This is the home port" Sherry Britton interview with author

"He wasn't nice" Sean Rand interview with author

"not a high class place." Steven Weinstein interview

"hustle drinks" *Billboard* 1952

"I was protected" Alan Alda interview with author

"easy" Vicki O'Day interview with author

"I was annoyed" Alexandra the Great interview with author

CHAPTER 41

"From the front" Al Baker Jr. interview with author

"When its time" Alexandra the Great interview with author

"They fell" Betty Rowland interview with author

"So American" Rachel Shteir interview with author

"how did you know that" Dixie Evans interview with author

"Fifth-ranking" Dixie Evans interview with author

"had asked" Chris Costello interview with author

"My son" Taffy O'Neil interview with author

"nap when he could." Taffy O'Neil interview with author

"I was getting ready" Alexandra the great interview with author and rest of section

"You couldn't say" Dixie Evans interview with author

"Its work" Dardy Minsky interview with author

"training ground" Alan Alda interview with author

CHAPTER 42

"She tried to" Kelly DiNardo interview with author

"I heard she had her" Dixie Evans interview with author

"we were considered" Vicki O'Day interview with author

"A lot of the chorus" Alan Alda interview with author

"Oh she was" Lily Ann Rose interview with author

"Oh you don't dare" Dixie Evans interview with author

"fought like" Terry Mixon interview with author

"savage undresser" Collyer, Martin. *Burlesque: The Baubles . . . Bangles . . . Babes.* New York: Lancer, 1964. Print. page 46.

"The act" Collyer, Martin. *Burlesque: The Baubles . . . Bangles . . . Babes.* New York: Lancer, 1964. Print. page 49

"I like to hear" Collyer, Martin. *Burlesque: The Baubles . . . Bangles . . . Babes.* New York: Lancer, 1964. Print. page 50

"rose was always" Alexandra the Great interview with author through "all kinds of names"

"She was playing the Grand" Alexandra the Great interview with author

"there were stories" Dixie Evans interview with author

"She used to like" Alan Alda interview with author

"flunky Tommy" April March interview with author

"dumb as an ox" April March interview with author

"have him perform" April March interview with author

"He had it under control" Chris Costello interview with author

"I met my share" Alexandra the Great interview with author

"Margie Hart" Dixie Evans interview with author

"the reason LaGuardia" Rachel Shteir interview with author

"the police came" Dixie Evans interview with author

"We called her Maggie" Kathleen Ross interview with author

"Made by the best" Kathleen Ross interview with author

"they plucked" Kathleen Ross interview with author

"maybe ten years" Kathleen Ross interview with author

"nice girls" Kathleen Ross interview with author

"she always had us worried" *Minsky's Burlesque* page 153

"To be a feature" Joan Arline interview with author

"zipper rehearsals" *Minsky's Burlesque* page 248

"strange man" "love of her life" "she worshiped him" Kathleen Ross interview with author

CHAPTER 43

"You weren't allowed" Blaze Starr interview with author

"somehow this wild" Dixie Evans interview with author

"I picked cotton" Tempest Storm interview with author

"When Tempest came along" Dixie Evans interview with author

"We have to change your name" Tempest Storm interview

"I remember paying" Leroy Griffith interview with author

"I look after me" Blaze Starr interview with author

"He said" Dixie Evans interview with author

"She didn't like sharing" April March interview with author

"She was there starting" Mimi Reed interview with author

"She's gone now" Mike Iannucci interview with author

"Gypsy was really" Betty Rowland interview with author

"Gypsy Rose Lee" Spigelgass, Leonard. *Gypsy: Memoirs of America's Most Celebrated Stripper*

"There goes" Collyer, Martin. *Burlesque: The Baubles . . . Bangles . . . Babes.* New York: Lancer, 1964. Print. page 52

"She was an impossible" Dardy Minsky interview with author

"the boy had swallowed a pin" Dardy Minsky interview with author

"Ann was way above her" Mike Iannnucci interview with author "silly, playful" Rachel Shteir interview with author

"We eagerly awaited" Janet Sovey interview with author

CHAPTER 44

"I would like to" *The Harvard Crimson*, Feb. 25, 1939

"sex is my hobby" Hanley, Tullah. *Love of Art*

"Gobbling" Hanley, Tullah. *Love of Art* pg 211

CHAPTER 45

"How tough" Walt Collins interview with author

"A lot of friends" Renny von Muchow

"Girls were beginning" Kitty Wst interview with author

"divide between" Rachel Shteir interview with author

"I was forty nine" Tee Tee Red interview with author

"every hour" Dixie Evans

"wiggly lines" Dixie Evans interview with author

"Strippers really don't have" Dardy Minsky interview

"the audience changed" Betty Rowland interview with author

"the unions closed" Val Valentine interview with author

"It was the girls" Joan Arline interview with author

"There was no Stinky" Al Baker Jr. Interview

"The comedians lost their" Mike Iannucci interview with author

"I was hearing about age" Tee Tee Red interview with author

"I wanted to go out" Kitty West interview with author

"I wanted to quit" Vicki O'Day interview with author

"I fell to pieces" Dixie Evans interview with author

"I lost a lot of interview est" Alexandra the Great interview with author

"it couldn't have lasted" Candy Cotton interview with author

"I thought I was gonna stay" April March interview with author

"Striptease" Rachel Shteir interview with author

"You were on stage" Blaze Starr interview with author

"porno came in" Dixie Evans interview with author

"I miss my" Val Valentine interview with author

"glorified it" Sherry Britton interview with author

"I think I'm gonna" April March interview with author

"years ago" Dee Ann Johnston interview with author

"These films, along" Rachel Shteir interview with author

"studios assumed" Dixie Evans interview with author

"Go-go killed burlesque" Tee Tee Red interview with author

"it started to deteriorate" Rita Grable interview with author

"It started getting" Terry Mixon interview with author

"What happens" Dardy Minsky interview with author

"What do you do" Renny von Muchow interview with author

"I was at this" White Fury interview with author

"very good with" Lady Midnight interview with author

"Dad left the" Walt Collins interview with author

"I went to work" Lee Stuart interview with author

"I worked as a waitress" Candy Cotton interview with author

"I worked in the" Renny von Muchow interview with author

"an elder" Joan Arline interview with author

"people would fly" Kitty West interview with author

"its time for me" Joni Taylor interview with author

"We didn't exactly" Lorraine Lee interview with author

"A lot of friends" Renny von Muchow interview with author

"She lost everything" Dixie Evans interview with author

"nightmare" Dixie Evans interview with author

"it was a wonderful" Alexandra the Great interview with author

"It was the only kind of" Dixie Evans interview with author

"They were truly" Maria Bradley interview with author

"I've never been" Rita Grable interview with author

"It was a great life" Alexandra interview with author

"I don't think" Vicki O'Day interview with author

"I used to get" Tee Tee Red interview with author

"great experience" Beverly Anderson interview with author

"It was a true" Candy Cotton interview with author

"yeah, I'm still" Tempest Storm interview with author

"I think when you" Kelly DiNardo interview with author

"If you need to remove one" Sean Rand interview with author

"I'm only breaking" Dixie Eveans interview with author

"Now that we're" Maria Bradley interview with author

CHAPTER 46

"fabulous" Chris Costello interview with author

"Too long" Dixie Evans interview with author

"entertainment with" Dixie Evans interview with author

"I see burlesque" Dixie Evans interview with author

"with strippers" Kelly DiNardo interview with author

"They were put" Alan Alda interview with author

"There were a few" Vicki O'Day interview with author

"Things that give" Aland Alda interview with author

"it wasn't a dirty business" Alan Alda interview with author

"House singers" Maria Bradley interview with author

"human way" Alan Alda interview with author

Letters on page 305 to Sherry Britton now in author's collection

Bibliography

Alexander, H. M. *Strip Tease, the Vanished Art of Burlesque.* New York: Knight, 1938. Print.

Allen, Robert Clyde. *Horrible Prettiness: Burlesque and American Culture.* Chapel Hill: University of North Carolina, 1991. Print.

Brown, Lillian Kiernan. *Banned in Boston: Memoirs of a Stripper an Autobiography.* N.p.: n.p., n.d. Print.

Burke, Carolyn. *Lee Miller: A Life.* New York: Knopf, 2005. Print.

Cohn, Art. *The Joker Is Wild; the Story of Joe E. Lewis.* New York: Random House, 1955. Print.

Collyer, Martin. *Burlesque: The Baubles . . . Bangles . . . Babes.* New York: Lancer, 1964. Print.

Corio, Ann, and Joseph DiMona. *This Was Burlesque.* New York: Madison Square, 1968. Print.

Costello, Chris, and Raymond Strait. *Lou's on First: A Biography.* New York: St. Martin's, 1981. Print.

Davis, Janet, ed. *Circus Queen & Tinker Bell.* Urbana: University of Illinois, 2008. Print.

DiNardo, Kelly. *Gilded Lili: Lili St. Cyr and the Striptease Mystique.* New York: Back Stage, 2007. Print.

Frankel, Noralee. *Stripping Gypsy: The Life of Gypsy Rose Lee.* Oxford: Oxford UP, 2009. Print.

Friedmann, Josh Alan. *Tales of Times Square.* Portland: Feral House, 1986. Print.

Genat, Robert. *Woodward Avenue: Cruising the Legendary Strip.* North Branch, MN: CarTech, 2010. Print.

Giesler, Jerry, and Pete Martin. *Hollywood Lawyer: The Jerry Giesler Story.* New York: Perma, 1962. Print.

Giesler, Jerry, and Pete Martin. *The Jerry Giesler Story.* New York: Simon and Schuster, 1960. Print.

Gorer, Geoffrey. *Hot Strip Tease and Other Notes on American Culture.* London: Cresset, 1937. Print.

Granlund, N. T., Sid Felder, and Ralph Hancock. *Blondes, Brunettes, and Bullets.* New York: D. McKay, 1957. Print.

Hanley, Tullah. *Love of Art & Art of Love.* San Francisco: Piper, 1975. Print.

Havoc, June. *Early Havoc.* New York: Simon and Schuster, 1959. Print.

Havoc, June. *More Havoc.* New York: Harper & Row, 1980. Print.

Jorgensen, Christine. *Christine Jorgensen: Personal Autobiography*. New York: P.S. Eriksson, 1967. Print.

Knox, Holly. *Sally Rand, from Film to Fans*. Bend, OR: Maverick Publications, 1988. Print.

Kruh, David. *Scollay Square*. Charleston, SC: Arcadia Pub., 2004. Print.

Minsky, Morton, and Milt Machlin. *Minsky's Burlesque*. NY: Arbor House, 1986. Print.

Mizejewski, Linda. *Ziegfeld Girl: Image and Icon in Culture and Cinema*. Durham, NC: Duke UP, 1999. Print.

Murray, Ken. *The Body Merchant: The Story of Earl Carroll*. Pasadena, CA: W. Ritchie, 1976. Print.

Peretti, Burton W. *Nightclub City: Politics and Amusement in Manhattan*. Philadelphia, PA: University of Pennsylvania, 2011. Print.

Preminger, Erik Lee. *Gypsy & Me: At Home and on the Road with Gypsy Rose Lee*. Boston: Little, Brown, 1984. Print.

Preminger, Erik Lee. *My G-String Mother: At Home and Backstage with Gypsy Rose Lee*. Berkeley, CA: Frog, 2004. Print.

Rich, Lucille. *No Hells or Damns Allowed*. N.p.: Self, 2001. Print.

Roach, Smith Marion. *The Roots of Desire: The Myth, Meaning, and Sexual Power of Red Hair*. New York: Bloomsbury, 2005. Print.

Rose Lee, Gypsy. *Gypsy: Memoirs of America's Most Celebrated Stripper*. Berkeley: Frog, 1957. Print.

Rothe, Len. *The Bare Truth—Stars of Burlesque of the '40s and '50s*. Atglen, PA: Schiffer Pub., 1998. Print.

Rothe, Len. *The Queens of Burlesque: Vintage Photographs of the 1940s and 1950s*. Atglen, PA: Schiffer Pub., 1997. Print.

Rothman, Hal, and Mike Davis. *The Grit beneath the Glitter: Tales from the Real Las Vegas*. Berkeley: University of California, 2002. Print.

Sante, Luc. *Low Life: Lures and Snares of Old New York*. New York: Vintage, 1992. Print.

Schwarz, Ted, and Mardi Rustam. *Candy Barr: The Small-Town Texas Runaway Who Became a Darling of the Mob and the Queen of Las Vegas Burlesque*. Lanham: Taylor Trade Pub., 2008. Print.

Shteir, Rachel. *Gypsy: The Art of the Tease*. New Haven [Conn.: Yale UP, 2009. Print.

Shteir, Rachel. *Striptease: The Untold History of the Girlie Show*. New York: Oxford UP, 2004. Print.

"Sinatra and The Moll - Diane Giordmaina : IUniverse." *Sinatra and The Moll - Diane Giordmaina : IUniverse*. N.p., n.d. Web. 08 Feb. 2013.

Slide, Anthony. *The Encyclopedia of Vaudeville*. Westport: Greenwood, 1994. Print.

Sobel, Bernard. *Burley-Cue*. New York: Farrar & Rinehart, 1931. Print.

Sobel, Bernard. *A Pictorial History of Burlesque*. New York: Putnam, 1956. Print.

Starr, Blaze, and Huey Perry. *Blaze Starr: My Life as Told to Huey Perry*. New York: Pocket, 1989. Print.

Stencell, A. W. *Girl Show: Into the Canvas World of Bump and Grind*. Toronto: ECW, 1999. Print.

Storm, Tempest, and Bill Boyd. *Tempest Storm: The Lady Is a Vamp*. Atlanta, GA: Peachtree, 1987. Print.

Sullivan, Steve. *Va Va Voom!: Bombshells, Pin-Ups, Sexpots and Glamour Girls*. Los Angeles: General Pub. Group, 1995. Print.

Terkel, Studs. *Hard Times: An Oral History of the Great Depression*. New York: Pantheon, 1970. Print.

Weller, Sheila. *Dancing at Ciro's: A Family's Love, Loss, and Scandal on the Sunset Strip*. New York: St. Martin's, 2003. Print.

Zeidman, Irving. *The American Burlesque Show*. New York: Hawthorn, 1967. Print.

Index

INDEX

INDEX

Reader's Guide Questions

The author states a lot of strippers got into burlesque because they had little choice, either because of economics or family situations. Can you identify with their plight?

Most strippers said they loved their time in burlesque but simply forgot it when they got out. Do you think most chose not to talk about it because of the stigma that continued? Why would they feel like talking about it now, fifty years later?

Burlesque died out for a variety of reasons in the late 1950s. What are some of the current popular entertainments today that might suffer that same fate due to advancing technology? And how do we preserve past culture?